Harvard Educational Review

VOLUME 78   NUMBER 1   2008

The *Harvard Educational Review* is a journal of opinion and
research in the field of education. Articles are selected, edited,
and published by an editorial board of graduate students at
Harvard University. The editorial policy does not reflect an
official position of the Faculty of Education or any other
Harvard faculty.

Editorial and Business Office
Harvard Graduate School
   of Education   TEL: 617-495-3432
8 Story Street, 1st Floor   Within USA: 1-800-513-0763
Cambridge, MA 02138–3752   FAX: 617-496-3584
Email: hepg@harvard.edu
Website: www.harvardeducationalreview.org
HER Online Subscribers website: http://www.edreview.org

Douglas Clayton, *Director*
Laura Clos, *Manuscripts*
Wendy Rosko, *Subscriptions*
Jeffrey C. Perkins, *Marketing Manager*
Dody Riggs, *Production Manager*

The *Harvard Educational Review* (ISSN 0017–8055) is published
four times a year, in Spring (March), Summer (June), Fall
(September), and Winter (December) by the Harvard Graduate
School of Education, Harvard University. Editorial and Business
Office: Harvard Graduate School of Education, 8 Story Street,
1st Floor, Cambridge, MA 02138-3752. Periodicals postage is
paid at Cambridge, MA 02138-3752, and additional mailing
offices. Postmaster: Send address changes to Harvard Educational Review, Harvard Graduate School of Education, 8 Story
Street, 1st Floor, Cambridge, MA 02138-3752. Subscribers are
asked to send the mailing label from their most recent copy
when requesting a change of address.

Subscription information: *U.S.:* individuals, 1 year, $59.00, 2 years, $99.00; institutions, 1 year, $167.00, 2 years, $287.00; students (in a degree program), 1 year, $29.00. *Canada:* individuals, 1 year, $83.74, 2 years, $138.03; institutions, 1 year, $204.00, 2 years, $358.00. *All other international:* individuals, 1 year, $99.00, 2 years, $159.00; institutions, 1 year, $215.00, 2 years, $371.00. *Canada includes 5% GST* (#129-795-027). Foreign subscriptions must be prepaid in U.S. dollars; checks must be drawn on a U.S. bank. Correspondence should be addressed to: *Harvard Educational Review,* Harvard Graduate School of Education, 8 Story Street, 1st Floor, Cambridge, MA 02138-3752. Phone: 1-800-513-0763; 617-495-3432. Single and back issue copies: $15.00. Special issues and symposia are priced individually.

Microform is available from University Microfilms, Inc., 300 N. Zeeb Rd., Ann Arbor, MI 48106; telephone 1-800-521-0600.

The *Harvard Educational Review* accepts contributions from teachers, practitioners, policymakers, scholars, and researchers in education and related fields, as well as from informed observers. In addition to discussions and reviews of research and theory, *HER* welcomes articles that reflect on teaching and practice in educational settings in the United States and abroad. Authors can elect to indicate whether they are submitting their manuscript as an article, a Voices Inside Schools article, an essay review, or a book review. **Guidelines for Authors are located at the back of the issue.**

Indexed in the *Educational Index* and *Book Review Index.* Appropriate articles abstracted in *Academic Abstracts, America: History and Life, Current Index to Journals in Education, Educational Administration Human Resources, Family Resources Database, Historical Abstracts, Psychological Abstracts, Research into Higher Education, Social Science Source, Social Work Research and Abstracts, Sociological Abstracts, Sociology of Education Abstracts, United States Political Science Documents,* and *Urban Affairs Abstracts.* Printed by The Sheridan Press, Hanover, PA 17331. Typography by Sheila Walsh, Somerville, MA 02143.

Harvard Educational Review

VOLUME 78   NUMBER 1   2008

Introduction: Why Adolescent Literacy Matters Now

> As I see it today, the ability to read awoke in me some long dormant craving
> to be mentally alive.
>
> —Malcolm X

As editors of the *Harvard Educational Review*, a journal that is read by a broad range of education researchers, policymakers, and practitioners, we aim to address topics that are timely and have central importance to the field. In deciding to devote a Special Issue of the journal to the topic of adolescent literacy, we thought carefully about the role of literacy within the broader enterprise of education, and we asked ourselves two main questions: First, why literacy? And second, why adolescent literacy in particular?

Our answer to the first question was straightforward: If knowledge is power, then literacy is the key to the kingdom. For centuries, the ability to read and write has given power to those who possessed it, although access to book learning — indeed, to books themselves — was often limited to a privileged minority (Vincent, 2000). Today, by contrast, we inhabit a digital age in which written texts are more widely and democratically available than ever before. A prerequisite for access, however, is still the ability to comprehend and appraise those texts. Individuals who lack strong skills for finding, understanding, and evaluating written information cannot easily arm themselves with that information or use it to advance the causes they value. And because a free society depends on an informed and autonomous citizenry, the loss is not theirs alone. As we confront some of the great questions of our time — about war and diplomacy, immigration and citizenship, health care and human rights, and fair access to education and employment — literacy liberates us from dependence on received wisdom and allows us to find and weigh the evidence ourselves. Simply put, literacy is a cornerstone of our freedom.

Given the importance of literacy to a free society, it is no surprise that among the "three Rs" of formal schooling — reading, 'riting, and 'rithmetic — the first two emphasize literacy. In the United States, preparing students to read and write fluently has long been a central responsibility of the public schools (Rav-

Harvard Educational Review   Vol. 78   No. 1   Spring 2008

itch, 2000), and the emphasis that No Child Left Behind places on students' reading performance has only increased the centrality of literacy instruction. Moreover, schools have historically organized their curricula around academic disciplines (Sizer, 2004), which rely heavily on texts to store and communicate knowledge. The consequence is that reading and writing proficiency are critical determinants of students' overall success in school. In truth, sophisticated reading and writing skills may vary among disciplines: Gleaning insight from a mathematical treatise is different, after all, from analyzing Borges. But insofar as literacy involves interpreting, evaluating, and making use of the information in texts, advancing students' literacy skills lies close to the heart of the educational enterprise.

We also see literacy as timely and essential as it relates to our second question, "why adolescent literacy in particular?" Research tells us that around grade four, students make the critical transition between "learning to read and reading to learn" (Chall, 2000, p. 99). It is this transition that makes adolescent literacy instruction distinctive — and distinctly challenging. The kind of literacy that safeguards self-determination is not simply about decoding words on a page or recounting the chronology of a story — skills that are necessarily emphasized as students first learn to read. Rather, it is about engaging with complex ideas and information through interaction with written documents. Using texts as vehicles for learning, critiquing, and extrapolating from extant knowledge is the domain of the postprimary and especially the secondary grades, and that domain is not restricted to language arts classrooms. Understanding texts, weighing their merits, and utilizing the information they offer are skills that adolescents draw on throughout the academically fragmented school day. However, the *kinds* of reading and writing they perform throughout the day vary considerably. Therefore, a central challenge of adolescent literacy instruction lies in recognizing that effective literacy skills differ among disciplines and in helping students develop the range of skills that facilitate success in many contexts.

A second distinctive challenge of adolescent literacy instruction lies in attending to adolescents' developmental needs as they mature from children into young adults. To engage adolescents, literacy instruction must capture their minds and speak to the questions they have about the world as they contemplate their place within it. It must allow them to interact with intellectually challenging content even as it sharpens their ability to derive meaning from texts. Pedagogy and content that adhere too closely to what works with young children are not likely to hold the attention of curious young adults, nor will they prepare those young adults for the rigors of a postsecondary education, where disciplinary knowledge and critical, independent thinking are prized.

The bad news in the United States today is that far too many students leave secondary schools without the advanced literacy skills they need to succeed in higher education or to flourish in a knowledge-based economy (Biancarosa & Snow, 2006). The good news is that creative researchers are pursuing ways to change the status quo. In recent years, scholars and policymakers have devoted increasing attention to the urgency of adolescents' literacy needs and to the distinctive challenges posed by those needs. Our goal in assembling this *Harvard Educational Review* Special Issue is to share some of their latest efforts — quantitative and qualitative, large-scale and small — with a wide range of education stakeholders.

The contributors to this Special Issue bring many lenses to the topic and offer multiple views on what it will take to help adolescents who struggle with academic reading and writing. Vicki Jacobs opens the issue with "Adolescent Literacy: Putting the Crisis in Context," which describes how the current adolescent literacy "crisis" emerged and how the United States has responded thus far. As she recounts trends in reading instruction from the eighteenth century to the present, Jacobs argues that the United States has long harbored concerns about older students' reading skills. The difference today, she explains, lies in the framing of the problem, the pedagogies teachers use, and the nation's general expectations for young people's literacy achievement.

The subsequent three articles examine the difficulty of teaching literacy in secondary schools and the reasons content-area teachers may balk when asked to teach reading explicitly. In "Teaching Disciplinary Literacy to Adolescents: Rethinking Content-Area Literacy," Timothy and Cynthia Shanahan open with a contemporary overview of adolescent literacy achievement in the United States. They go on to describe a qualitative study they undertook with a group of mathematicians, chemists, and historians to identify how reading approaches differ among the disciplines, and to devise reading strategies that, if taught explicitly, might help students internalize the core principles of each discipline.

In "Redefining Content-Area Literacy Teacher Education: Finding My Voice through Collaboration," Roni Jo Draper also describes collaborating with content-area experts — in this case, teacher educators in mathematics, music, and theater — and explains how this collaboration changed her view on the role literacy instruction should play in content-area classrooms. Draper calls for a broad definition of literacy that reflects disciplinary mastery, and she argues that content-area literacy instruction should support rather than supplement disciplinary learning.

In the next article, "Cognitive Strategies for Adolescents: What We Know about the Promise, What We Don't Know about the Potential," Mark Conley describes the trend toward teaching students to adopt the "cognitive strategies," or thought processes, of proficient readers, such as summarizing, predicting, and inferring as one reads. Arguing that these strategies are often taught in ways that oversimplify the intellectual demands of disciplinary and workplace thinking, Conley calls for more research on advanced cognitive processes and on ways to help educators teach cognitive strategies more purposefully.

The next four articles call attention to the multiple, nested contexts within which literacy instruction for adolescents is carried out, including social groups, neighborhoods, schools, and states. These articles remind us that efforts to support adolescent readers and writers must consider the milieus in which the work is undertaken. The first two articles suggest that effective literacy instruction must attend to adolescents' developmental needs by understanding the contexts in which they live and the purposes reading and writing serve in their lives. Specifically, in "The Complex World of Adolescent Literacy: Myths, Motivations, and Mysteries," Elizabeth Birr Moje, Melanie Overby, Nicole Tysvaer, and Karen Morris present results from a large-scale, mixed-methods study exploring the in-school and outside-school literacy activities undertaken by adolescents in a midwestern, mostly Latino community. Using survey and interview data, Moje and her colleagues counter the myth that adolescents do not read outside of school. They also describe ways teens use reading and writing to participate in social networks or to enhance their social capital through learning.

In "Toward a More Anatomically Complete Model of Literacy Instruction: A Focus on African American Male Adolescents and Texts," Alfred Tatum argues that schools' narrow focus on strategies for reading, to the exclusion of culturally attuned rationales, results in their failure to address the literacy needs of many African American male adolescents, particularly those living in high-poverty communities. Tatum offers an "anatomically complete" framework that considers the theoretical (head), instructional (body), and professional development (legs) components of effective literacy instruction. He then presents a case study demonstrating how relevant texts can give African American adolescent males new lenses through which to interpret their lives and the world.

Further exploring the nested contexts in which literacy instruction occurs, the next two articles address the need for school-level and state-level policies that support effective literacy teaching for adolescents. In "Implementing a Structured Reading Program in an Afterschool Setting: Problems and Potential Solutions," Ardice Hartry, Robert Fitzgerald, and Kristie Porter describe their multisite randomized trial designed to study the effects of a technologically intensive reading program, READ 180, in an afterschool context. They focus on results from their implementation study, which show that effective program implementation depends largely on school-level administrative decisions about issues such as staffing, classroom assignments, preparation time, snack-time scheduling, and technology support and maintenance.

In the next article, "State Literacy Plans: Incorporating Adolescent Literacy," Catherine Snow, Twakia Martin, and Ilene Berman describe two literacy institutes offered for state education policymakers at the Harvard Graduate School of Education in 2000 and 2001. The authors review literacy policies that were developed by four participating states and then call on the research community to support state policymakers in promoting effective literacy instruction beyond grade three.

We also present an essay review of three recent publications on adolescent writing instruction. In "Beyond *Writing Next*: A Discussion of Writing Research and Instructional Uncertainty," David Coker and William Lewis review *Writing Next*, a meta-analysis of quantitative writing-instruction research, as well as two other publications by *Writing Next* authors Steve Graham and Delores Perin. Coker and Lewis recommend *Writing Next* for its clarity and rigor but consider whether a schism between two writing-research traditions — one based in composition studies and the other in educational psychology — may prevent the report from informing the work of as many teachers and teacher educators as it might otherwise reach.

The issue concludes with two editors' reviews of recently published books and reports on adolescent literacy. In the first of the reviews, Sabina Rak Neugebauer examines two recent reports on the literacy-acquisition needs of English-language learners (ELLs). She commends the reports' recommendations for better tracking and support of ELLs but argues that the reports' rhetoric should place the burden more explicitly on the education system, rather than on the students themselves. Finally, in a review of two recent adolescent literacy books for school leaders, Jacy Ippolito demonstrates how the volumes complement each other and together fill a gap in the literature currently available to administrators, teachers, and literacy coaches who seek better ways to support struggling adolescent readers.

We are delighted to bring you the work of these authors. We hope you find their ideas as encouraging as we do in working toward a day when all students leave secondary school able to engage deeply with the written word.

JACY IPPOLITO
JENNIFER L. STEELE
JENNIFER F. SAMSON
Special Issue Editors

References

Biancarosa, G., & Snow, C. E. (2006). *Reading next — A vision for action and research in middle and high school literacy: A report to Carnegie Corporation of New York* (2nd ed.). Washington, DC: Alliance for Excellent Education.

Chall, J. S. (2000). *The academic achievement challenge: What really works in the classroom?* New York: Guilford Press.

Haley, A., & Malcolm X. (1964). *The autobiography of Malcolm X: As told to Alex Haley.* New York: Ballantine.

Ravitch, D. (2000). *Left back: A century of battles over school reform.* New York: Touchstone.

Sizer, T. R. (2004). *Horace's compromise: The dilemma of the American high school.* New York: Mariner Books.

Vincent, D. (2000). *The rise of mass literacy: Reading and writing in modern Europe.* Cambridge, England: Blackwell.

Acknowledgments

Assembling an *HER* Special Issue is a team effort, and there are a few people to whom we owe special gratitude. First, we wish to thank the Carnegie Corporation of New York, and Carnegie program officer Andrés Henríquez in particular, for providing guidance and financial support for the dissemination of this Special Issue. We would also like to thank Catherine Snow for her support and encouragement. In addition, Douglas Clayton and Jeffrey Perkins of the Harvard Education Publishing Group, our parent organization, have worked diligently to ensure that this issue reached a broad audience of researchers and practitioners. We are grateful to Laura Clos for shepherding manuscripts through the review process, and we thank Dody Riggs for ensuring that every article was subjected to timely and rigorous copy editing. Finally, we thank the authors who accepted our invitation to contribute to this Special Issue, for it is their dedication to adolescent learners that moves the field forward, improving our understanding of how to serve those students well.

Adolescent Literacy: Putting the Crisis in Context

VICKI A. JACOBS
Harvard Graduate School of Education

In this article, Vicki Jacobs argues that as the nation strives to improve the literacy achievement of U.S. adolescents, educators must reframe the current "crisis" as a critical point on a continuum of historical efforts to address the particular challenges of postprimary-grade reading. Specifically, Jacobs examines the definition of adolescent literacy in the context of reading stages, which explain the contiguous and continuous relationship between primary-grade and later reading. She also discusses how historical relationships between skill and process instruction and between reading specialists and content-area faculty have contributed to the issues we face at this particular point on the continuum. Jacobs concludes by highlighting the opportunities ahead for researchers, policymakers, and practitioners who are positioned to respond to the adolescent literacy crisis and improve adolescent literacy achievement.

The Crisis

National concern about the reading proficiency of U.S. adolescents has increased in intensity over the past twenty years to the point of alarm and has been cast most recently in the language of crisis. This recent concern is most likely rooted in data provided in two national reports released in the 1980s. *A Nation at Risk* (National Commission on Excellence in Education, 1983) reported dismal statistics about adolescents' reading abilities, noting, for example, that "about 13 percent of all 17-year-olds in the United States [could] be considered functionally illiterate" and that "functional illiteracy among minority youth may run as high as 40 percent" (p. 11). The report argued that "average achievement of high school students on most standardized tests [was] now lower than 26 years ago when *Sputnik* was launched" (p. 11). Most distressing was these adolescents' lack of "higher-order" intellectual skills: "Nearly 40 percent cannot draw inferences from written material; only one-fifth can write a persuasive essay; and only one-third can solve a mathematics problem requiring several steps" (p. 11). The 1984 *Report Card*

Harvard Educational Review   Vol. 78   No. 1   Spring 2008

from the National Assessment of Educational Progress (NAEP, 1985) implicitly confirmed the National Commission's contentions when it indicated that gains in reading for thirteen- and seventeen-year-olds had either flat-lined or increased insignificantly since 1971.

Such data raised concern about the ability of the nation's youth to participate productively in a workforce that was facing an increasingly complex world economy. While the labor market had long required high levels of mathematical, verbal, and technological literacy (National Governors Association Center for Best Practices, 2005), such literacies were no longer sufficient as the need for more-sophisticated problem-solving and communication skills grew (Levy & Murnane, 2004; see also Murnane & Levy, 1996).

Subsequent NAEP results have done little to assuage national concern about the promise of the current generation of adolescents to meet academic and workforce challenges. NAEP results from 2002 indicated that roughly 25 percent of eighth- and twelfth-grade students read below basic levels (Alliance for Excellent Education, 2005a, p. 1), and that more than six million adolescents have been "left behind" academically and will be similarly disadvantaged when they enter the U.S. labor market (p. 2). Results reported in the NAEP's 2007 *Report Card* indicate that there has not been any "significant change in the percentage of [eighth-grade] students at or above the *Proficient* level" when compared to the 1992 and 2005 data (Lee, Grigg, & Donahue, 2007, p. 3). Furthermore, the 2007 NAEP scores revealed that while "White, Black, and Hispanic students all scored higher in 2007 than in the first assessment 15 years ago at . . . [grade] 8," the achievement gap between minority and White students "at this grade level [had] not narrowed" (Lee et al., 2007, p. 3; also see the NAEP's Trial Urban District Assessment, Lutkus, Grigg, & Donahue, 2007). In fact, the NAEP data from 2007 are hauntingly reminiscent of scores from more than twenty years ago, with literacy achievement scores for adolescents remaining static (NAEP, 1985).

The Response

Despite the sense of urgency generated by such reports, an organized response to the apparent crisis in adolescent reading did not gain momentum until the mid- to late 1990s. This delay was due in part to the nation's ongoing commitment to addressing early reading difficulties and developing effective primary-grade reading instruction and materials. However, as national reports such as the National Reading Council's *Preventing Reading Difficulties in Young Children* (Snow, Burns, & Griffin, 1998) and the National Reading Panel's *Teaching Children to Read* (2000) recommended courses of action for addressing primary-grade reading, and as federal funding for programs such as Reading First under the No Child Left Behind Act of 2001 (U.S. Department of Education, 2001) provided support for implementing those recommendations, the time had finally come to turn full attention to older readers.

In 1999, the International Reading Association (IRA) issued a position statement on adolescent literacy (Moore, Bean, Birdyshaw, & Rycik, 1999) in which it described the short shrift that the reading skills of older students had long suffered:

> No one gives adolescent literacy much press. It is certainly not a hot topic in educational policy or a priority in schools. In the United States, most Title I budgets are allocated for early intervention — little [is] left over for the struggling adolescent reader. Even if all children [do] learn to read by Grade 3, the literacy needs of the adolescent reader [are] far different from those of primary-grade children. (p. 1)

The IRA's position statement outlined seven principles to promote adolescents' literacy growth.[1] Not the least of these was a sweeping mandate to provide adolescents with "homes, communities, and a nation that will support their efforts to achieve advanced levels of literacy and provide the support necessary for them to succeed" (Moore et al., 1999, p. 9).

On the heels of the IRA's position statement, a series of reports and position papers responded to the call for action (see Table 1). Notable among these reports were the RAND Corporation's *Reading for Understanding* (Snow, 2002), which proposed a research agenda to address the "pressing problem" of comprehension,[2] and *Reading Next: A Vision for Action and Research in Middle and High School Literacy* (Biancarosa & Snow, 2004), which outlined fifteen elements of effective adolescent literacy programs and literacy achievement.[3] These two landmark reports were followed by others that outlined criteria for effective literacy programs (Alliance for Excellent Education, 2004b) and for the preparation of reading practitioners (International Reading Association, 2000a, 2000b, 2004, 2006). The National Council of Teachers of English issued a call to action (2004), as well as briefs on principles of adolescent literacy reform (2006b) and policy (2007).

The U.S. government followed suit in 2004 by authorizing the Striving Readers Program (Office of Elementary and Secondary Education, 2006), a $200 million effort to target struggling readers in low-income middle schools and high schools.[4] In 2005, several policy pieces emerged, including the RAND Corporation report, *Achieving State and National Literacy Goals* (McCombs, Kirby, Barney, Darilek, & Magee, 2005); *A Governor's Guide to Adolescent Literacy* from the National Governors Association Center for Best Practices; and the National Association of Secondary School Principals guide for "creating a culture of literacy" for middle and high school principals.[5] In 2007, the National Endowment for the Arts followed up its 2004 report, *Reading at Risk*, with *To Read or Not to Read: A Question of National Consequence.* Thus, adolescent literacy, which had not even appeared on the IRA's "What's Hot" list until 2001, had been elevated to "very hot" by 2006 (Cassidy, Garrett, & Barrera, 2006).

Even while we continue to define principles for adolescent literacy reform (National Council of Teachers of English, 2006a, 2006b, 2007) and the prac-

TABLE 1   *Sample Responses to the Adolescent Literacy Crisis*

1997:   IRA's Reading Initiative established

1998:   Vacca's "Let's Not Marginalize Adolescent Literacy"

1999:   IRA / Moore, Bean, Birdyshaw, & Rycik's *Adolescent Literacy: A Position Statement for the Commission on Adolescent Literacy of the International Reading Association*

2000a: IRA's *Excellent Reading Teachers: A Position Statement on Adolescent Literacy*

2000b: IRA'S *Teaching All Children to Read: The Roles of the Reading Specialist*

2002:   RAND / Snow's *Reading for Understanding: Toward a Research and Development Program in Reading Comprehension*

2004a: The Alliance for Excellent Education's *Reading for the 21st Century: Adolescent Literacy Teaching and Learning Strategies*

2004b: The Alliance for Excellent Education's *How to Know a Good Adolescent Literacy Program When You See One: Quality Criteria to Consider*

2004:   Carnegie Corporation / Biancarosa & Snow's *Reading Next: A Vision for Action and Research in Middle and High School Literacy*

2004:   NCTE's *Guidelines: A Call to Action. What We Know about Adolescent Literacy and Ways to Support Teachers in Meeting Students' Needs*

2004:   NEA's *Reading at Risk*

2004:   Striving Readers funded

2005a: Alliance for Excellent Education's *Adolescent Literacy: Opening the Doors to Success*

2005b: Alliance for Excellent Education's *Adolescent Literacy Policy Update*

2005:   Carnegie Corporation / RAND / McCombs, Kirby, Barney, Darilek, & Magee's *Achieving State and National Literacy Goals: A Long Uphill Road.*

2005:   National Governors Association Center for Best Practices' *A Governor's Guide to Adolescent Literacy*

2005:   National Association of Secondary School Principals' *Creating a Culture of Literacy: A Guide for Middle and High School Principals*

2005:   Snow, Griffin, & Burns's *Knowledge to Support the Teaching of Reading: Preparing Teachers for a Changing World*

2006:   NAEP / NASBE Study Group on Middle and High School Literacy's *Reading at Risk: The State Response to the Crisis in Adolescent Literacy.*

2006a: NCTE's *Position Paper on the Role of English Teachers in Educating English Language Learners*

2006b: NCTE's *Principles of Adolescent Literacy Reform: A Policy Brief*

2007:   Alliance for Excellent Education / Heller & Greenleaf's *Literacy Instruction in the Content Areas: Getting to the Core of Middle and High School Improvement*

2007:   NCTE's *Adolescent Literacy: A Policy Research Brief*

2007:   NEA's *To Read or Not to Read: A Question of National Consequence*

tices that will support adolescents' literacy development most effectively, this area appears still to be in crisis (NAEP, 2006). The use of the language of crisis has successfully brought the needs of adolescent readers to the fore politically, theoretically, and practically. However, while addressing the urgency that the notion of crisis implies, we may have lost sight of the fact that concern about the reading achievement of older students is far from new and that its history has been well documented (see Anders & Guzzetti, 1996; Robinson, 1977; Ruddell, 1997; Smith, 1965). By situating the current crisis as a particular point on a historical continuum of attention paid to the dilemma of adolescent students' reading, we might understand better how and why adolescent literacy has arrived at this point and how we should proceed.

The purpose of this article, then, is to examine historical trends concerning two issues that are at the core of understanding the adolescent literacy crisis: (1) the definition of adolescent reading, and (2) trends in reading instruction for older students.[6] By examining these two issues from a historical perspective, we can identify recurrent tensions and questions that we must address today if we are to move beyond the immediacy of the crisis and meet the needs of all adolescents well into the future.

Adolescent Reading: Definitions of and Purposes for Older Children's Reading

Before we consider how to address the current problem of adolescent literacy, we need to understand what we mean by "adolescent" reading — its demands, the skills required to meet those demands, and how those skills differ from those required by reading at an earlier age. This section examines adolescent literacy in the context of the stages of reading development in an effort to understand more clearly what criteria we might use when choosing instructional practices that will best address the current reading crisis.

There has long been agreement that "the needs of the adolescent reader are far different from those of primary children" (Moore et al., 1999, p. 1). In 1917, E. L. Thorndike (cited in Hunnicutt & Iverson, 1958, p. 195), a noted American psychologist at the turn of the twentieth century, made a clear distinction between the skill necessary "to read" and the reasoning ability necessary to comprehend, noting that comprehension required the mind to "select, repress, soften, emphasize, correlate, and organize all under the influence of the right mental set or purpose or demand" (pp. 139–140).

Decades later, R. L. Thorndike (1973–1974), E. L. Thorndike's son, identified age thirteen, or the onset of adolescence, as the time when "reading is no longer — to any substantial degree — a decoding problem. . . . It is a thinking problem" (p. 144), a "reasoning process rather than a set of distinct and specialized skills" (p. 135). His research challenged teachers to incorporate "better and more inventive teaching — not solely to read, but also to think, because as we improve the understanding with which a child reads, we may concurrently improve the effectiveness with which he processes a wide range of information important in his development" (p. 146).

To access information and meaning from reading as described by the Thorndikes, children must develop proficiency in a broad range of skills over time. The course of developing these skills has been described in staged models of reading, which draw heavily from developmental theories about the stages of cognitive development (e.g., Inhelder & Piaget, 1958; Piaget, 1970; Perry, 1970). Chall's (1983) reading stages distinguished primary-grade reading from later reading as the difference between *learning to read* and *using reading to learn*. A close examination of the demands of reading and the skills required at each stage clarifies the distinctions between earlier reading and the kind of reading required of adolescents.

Stage 0: Getting Ready to Read

The earliest stage of reading is actually a prereading or "reading readiness" stage that takes place before children enter school and begin formal reading instruction. The degree to which children are "ready to read" when they enter school depends to a great extent on their exposure to and opportunities to participate in literacy-rich environments and activities during this time (Chall & Jacobs, 1996; Chall, Jacobs, & Baldwin, 1990; Snow, Barnes, Chandler, Goodman, & Hemphill, 1991).

Before they enter school, children become acquainted with letters, words, and books and how they are used. They learn about the roles that reading and writing can play in daily life as they observe others reading a variety of printed texts (e.g., newspapers, books, magazines, and e-mail) and writing for varied purposes (e.g., writing e-mail, making grocery lists, noting appointments on a calendar). When given materials and opportunity, children often play at reading and writing; for example, reciting their favorite stories as they turn pages of a book, singing the alphabet, calling out the names of familiar signs, and trying to print their names or write stories using modified spelling systems such as "invented spelling" (see Chall, 1983, pp. 13–15, 85; Sulzby, 1986). The praise children receive from their caregivers promotes an intrinsic motivation to read. As they listen to stories that others read to them, they develop an appreciation for reading as an engaging and rewarding experience. Children also begin to build the vocabulary and conceptual knowledge that will inform their later reading through outings, listening to conversations about events outside everyday life, or hearing and then discussing texts that contain language and vocabulary that are more challenging than what they use or hear in everyday conversations (Chall, 1983; Chall & Jacobs, 1996).

Stages 1 and 2: Learning and Practicing Beginning Reading Skills

When children enter school, they require direct instruction to learn a myriad of basic reading skills. They learn alphabetic principles, the order and sounds of the alphabet. They hone their phonemic awareness skills that allow them to "manipulate the [discrete] sounds in spoken syllables and words" (National Reading Panel, 2000, p. 7). They develop an understanding of phonics and of the relation between letters as symbols and sounds as they apply to reading and spelling. They also learn how to "blend or segment the sounds in words" (National Reading Panel, 2000, p. 7) so that they will be able to recognize and decipher words — that is, to decode print accurately.[7]

In addition to direct instruction, children require the opportunity to consolidate and practice their decoding skills in order to achieve fluency — the ability to decode text easily, smoothly, and at a good pace (Chall et al., 1990). The materials children use must be accessible so they can focus on practicing their decoding skills. Therefore, the materials children use are generally graded texts that rely on controlled vocabulary and on content and contexts that are familiar to children's daily lives. Because such texts are not necessarily designed to challenge children's language development, it is critical that young students be exposed to texts from a variety of genres that are more difficult than those they can read independently. Reading aloud and then discussing such texts with children is an important way to extend their knowledge base and familiarize them with the vocabulary and sentence structures that are less common in their everyday language experience (Chall & Jacobs, 1996).

In sum, children in the earliest grades require direct skill instruction, opportunities to practice those skills, and a rich language environment. Historically, the "reading wars" have pitted skill-based reading instruction (typically, but too simply, generalized as phonics instruction) and meaning-based reading instruction (typically, but too simply, generalized as "language enrichment" or "whole language") against each other (Snow & Juel, 2005; see also Chall, 1967; Goodman, 1986). At one point, especially during the 1980s, meaning-based approaches predominated, sometimes at the cost of skill-based instruction (Goodman, Bird, & Goodman, 1991). Recommendations for "balanced" reading instruction in the early years seem to have resolved this conflict (Adams, 1994) by addressing the pressing need that children, especially those who come to school less ready to read than others, have for both skill- and meaning-based instruction (Chall et al., 1990; Snow et al., 1991; see also Delpit, 1988).

— The Importance of Fluency

Children who have acquired decoding and fluency skills by the end of third grade will most likely be prepared to learn how "to acquire knowledge, broaden understandings," and cultivate their "appreciations of the written word" (Harris & Hodges, 1995, p. 213). They will be prepared to learn how to tackle the specialized language and concepts that are representative of particular fields of study and less common to everyday language and experience. Those who have not achieved automaticity and fluency in their reading will be severely limited in their access to the more technical, syntactically complex, and dense reading that is characteristic of content-based reading. Without access to print, they cannot acquire the knowledge that later learning presupposes (Chall, 1983, pp. 20–23, 86–87). Typically, these students begin to fall behind academically, exhibiting what teachers have long observed to be the "fourth-grade slump" (Chall, 1983; Chall & Jacobs, 2003).[8]

It is important to note that while successful transitional-stage readers have achieved automaticity and fluency, children still require direct instruction to learn how to learn from text. "One of the dilemmas facing most adolescents in an academic context . . . is that few effectively [have] learn[ed] how to use reading . . . to explore and construct meaning in the company of authors, other learners, or teachers" (Vacca, 1998, p. 608). In fact, beyond decoding and fluency skill, differences in later grades between better and poorer readers are most apparent in their ability to apply the skills of independent reading (see also Hammill & Bartel, 1995, p. 97; Meltzer, Roditi, Haynes, Biddle, Paster, & Taber, 1996, p. 40; Scala, 2001, pp. 81, 82).

Stage 3: Reading for Learning the New
Beginning around fourth grade and proceeding through the middle grades, children begin to use reading to learn new ideas and gain knowledge from a wide variety of genres and fields of study, generally from a single viewpoint or perspective (Chall, 1983, p. 85). During this transitional stage, students begin to develop a cadre of skills that they will use to grow into independent readers during the high school years and beyond. In short, they learn how to be strategic readers. They learn about the relation between motivation and intellectual curiosity that is required for inquiry-based reading. They use their background knowledge and experience (the "given") to develop a context for their reading and the ability to organize and use that background knowledge to learn most efficiently from text (the "new"). They develop the metacognitive ability to monitor and adjust their reading as needed (Hammill & Bartel, 1995; Langer, 1982; Miholic, 1994; Stahl, 1997). They learn how to apply vocabulary, comprehension, and study skills to determine purposes for reading; make predictions; locate main ideas; question, analyze, and synthesize text; navigate varied text structures; identify and clarify multiple points of view; acknowledge the effect of context on meaning; and draw on background knowledge and previous academic and life experience to construct meaning (Armbruster, Lehr, & Osborne, 2001; Chall et al., 1990; Curtis, 2002; National Reading Panel, 2000).[9] If students are to acquire these advanced reading skills and become critical readers within their disciplines, then teachers need to go beyond assigning merely *what* to read by giving students explicit explanations about the *why* and *how* of their reading.

Stage 4: Reading Multiple Points of View and Stage 5: Constructing and Reconstructing Meaning
When reading at the high school level (stage 4) and beyond (stage 5), students require broad and deep background knowledge and experience (espe-

cially that which comes from previous reading), strategic reading skill, and the metacognitive skill to monitor and correct the course of their reading as necessary. During the high school years, students analyze and synthesize discipline-specific texts while juggling multiple layers of meaning from multiple points of view that often contrast and conflict. In college and beyond (stage 5), readers establish their own academic, professional, and personal purposes for reading, and they read for what is explicit and unsaid in text (Chall, 1983, p. 87). They synthesize, analyze, and make judgments about what they read, often in light of multiple viewpoints, while having to "construct knowledge on a high level of abstraction and generality" (p. 24). They have the skills and self-awareness to be independent readers of multiple disciplines.

The Location of Adolescent Literacy in Stages of Reading

Where, then, in the context of reading stages, does *adolescent* literacy begin, and how might we define it? The National Council of Teachers of English (2006b), in its definition of adolescent literacy, notes that it is

> more than reading and writing. It involves purposeful social and cognitive processes. It helps individuals discover ideas and make meaning. It enables functions such as analysis, synthesis, organization, and evaluation. It fosters the expression of ideas and opinions and extends to understanding how texts are created and how meanings are conveyed by various media, brought together in productive ways. . . . This complex view of literacy builds upon but extends beyond definitions of literacy that focus on features like phonemic awareness and word recognition. (p. 5)

While this definition distinguishes adolescent literacy as being distinct from but related to primary-grade reading, noticeably absent is an indication of when the challenges of adolescent reading begin. We generally have associated the challenges of adolescent literacy with the middle and high school grades into which U.S. schools separate "tweens" (ages ten through twelve) and teenagers (ages thirteen through eighteen), respectively. However, the accepted stages of reading development suggest that the challenges adolescents face begin much earlier, in grades three or four, when the requirements of learning begin to differentiate by content. Simply dichotomizing primary-grade and adolescent reading effectively ignores the critical role that the transitional, intermediate elementary years can and should serve in helping students prepare to meet the demands of adolescent learning.[10]

Acknowledgment that issues of adolescent literacy are pertinent to grades four through twelve is fairly new (e.g., Heller & Greenleaf, 2007; McCombs et al., 2005; National Governors Association Center for Best Practices, 2005), and research is just beginning to reexamine the factors that contribute to the fourth-grade slump evident in assessments and academic achievement. Current efforts would do well to build on earlier theory and research (e.g., Chall,

1983; Chall & Jacobs, 2003) concerning the critical transition between prima-ry-grade and later reading. Indeed, if we think of reading as a series of stages, the adolescent literacy crisis becomes less of a startling phenomenon and more of a challenge particular to a certain point of reading development.

The History of Reading Instruction for Older Readers

As the challenges of reading change across the stages, so must the focus of reading instruction. Historical trends in instruction parallel and clarify the historical definition of and purposes for older children's reading, and they also offer us wisdom and caution as we seek promising practices for adolescent readers. The next section of this article examines historical trends in read-ing instruction for postprimary-grade students in an effort to understand the roots of reading as "literacy," as well as the evolution of current instructional recommendations (see Robinson, 1977; Ruddell, 1997).

Skill Instruction

Tension between skill- and meaning-based approaches and between remedial and developmental approaches has existed throughout the history of reading instruction of older readers, sometimes productive and sometimes not.

The origin of skill instruction in the history of U.S. education — teaching discrete strategies to support children's acquisition of beginning reading skills or the later skills needed for comprehension — can be traced to the eigh-teenth century. As early as the mid-1700s, reading instruction generally con-sisted of students learning letters and consonant-vowel clusters, the spelling and pronunciation of short words, oral reading, and the memorization of sen-tences and sections of text primarily, if not exclusively, from the Bible (Robin-son, 1977, p. 46). Such skill-based instruction persisted through the mid-1800s with the addition of a kind of phonics instruction, which stressed articulation, pronunciation, and the "correction" of dialects. When schools became dif-ferentiated by grade in the mid-1800s, the reading materials children used became differentiated by grade as well (pp. 46, 48). At the same time, there was "some attention [given] . . . to meaning in the upper grades through ques-tions on the content and definitions of words, both of which were specified in the book" (Smith, 1965, cited in Robinson, 1977, p. 48).

The rise of industrialism in the early 1900s led to an increasing emphasis on reading for meaning "to meet the varied needs of society" (Robinson, 1977, p. 50). At the same time, alarm rose during World War I over the fact that few soldiers could read even the simplest directions (see Smith, 1965, p. 158). The response to this problem was to focus secondary reading instruction on the remediation of particular skills such as decoding, fluency, reading speed, vocabulary, comprehension, and study skills (Ruddell, 1997, p. 8). Remedial approaches assumed that successful reading was the mastery of the "progres-sion of [these] distinct and measurable skills" (Anders & Guzzetti, 1996, p. 7) common to the reading of any discipline.

The Responsibility for Skill Instruction

The "intermediate children" who struggled with reading received special instruction in classes that were designed to remedy their skill deficits (Robinson, 1977, pp. 51–52). Because reading instruction took place in these separate "pull-out" programs, regular classroom teachers at the intermediate level and beyond most likely came to understand reading as its own separate content, one that students would learn and practice either in previous grades or through specialized instruction. In short, there was no apparent reason for regular classroom teachers to assume they had any specific responsibility for reading instruction.

Until the late 1960s and early 1970s, the reading specialists who were responsible for reading instruction had few textbooks to guide their teaching (Early, 1977). The skill-based materials that reading specialists used included linguistic readers, which focused on word or spelling patterns and patterns of sentences (Robinson, 1977, p. 55), and workbooks that provided opportunities to practice word identification and sentence-level skills.

In 1965, the U.S. government funded Title I through the Elementary and Secondary Education Act in order to support compensatory reading instruction for students living in poverty (Dole, 2004). Generally, reading specialists provided Title I instruction, continuing the tradition of providing supplementary skill instruction to small groups of children in pull-out conditions, quite separate from the regular classroom (Dole, 2004, pp. 462–63; see also Anders & Guzzetti, 1996, pp. 8–9). Textbooks on the teaching of reading generally offered reading specialists guidance on teaching particular skills, principally those related to vocabulary, comprehension, and studying. Some promoted the development of whole-school reading programs, focusing not only on skill instruction but also on the importance of diagnostics, student and program evaluation, the school as an environment for reading, and cross-staff development.

The Emergence of Process Models of Reading

During the 1970s, at the same time that skill instruction seemed sacrosanct, "there was [also] a decided expansion of developmental reading programs in high schools" (Robinson, 1977, pp. 55–56) that was accompanied by an interest in the meaning-based aspects of reading and its sociological and psychological contexts. Several emergent models of learning and reading processes during the late 1960s and 1970s explained the reading process in psycholinguistic, sociolinguistic, and cognitive terms.

Psycholinguistic models of reading (see Goodman, 1967; Smith, 1971) explained how readers integrate linguistic information (e.g., from phonology, syntax [including text structure]) and semantics (Smith, Otto, & Hansen, 1978, p. 23). These models advanced the notion that reading was a meaning-making activity that required readers to utilize a variety of skills and strategies in a variety of contexts (p. 23). Sociolinguistic models of reading examined "differences in dialect, differences among ethnic groups and information processing skills, differences in cognitive style, and differences arising from affective factors" (Kling, 1971, cited in Smith et al., 1978, p. 23), drawing attention to the multiple demands that varied contexts impose on receptive and expressive language. Cognitive models of reading (see Guthrie, 1977; Spiro, Bruce, & Brewer, 1980) focused on the contribution of a reader's memory, prior knowledge, and interest in comprehension on successful reading (see also Readence, Bean, & Baldwin, 1981). Cognitive models drew from research on the relationship between language processing and the physiology of the brain (e.g., Geschwind, 1962), theories about information processing (Venezky & Calfee, 1970), and more general models of how the mind represents, organizes, and processes information (e.g., "schema theory" as explained by Anderson & Pearson, 1984; see also Rumelhart, 1980, 1984).

As models of learning and comprehension emerged, tension grew between traditional, sequential skill instruction and the more progressive notion that the "reading needs of children [could] best be met through their reasoning *processes* as they carry out their own purposes and solve their own problems" (Robinson, 1977, p. 51, emphasis added). Thus, by the late 1970s, while textbooks still offered guidance on the teaching of discrete skills, they also began to recommend practices to support the development of "high-level reading skills such as critical reading" (p. 55). Textbooks described the reading process, noting how motivation and affect as well as personalization played important roles in comprehension. (Here and elsewhere, refer to Appendix A for references to sample textbooks.) The instructional recommendations they made built on theories about the psychology of reading, the psycholinguistic factors that influence reading, and cognition.

At the same time textbooks and materials moved toward process models of reading comprehension, they began to distinguish later reading as *secondary*. Some textbooks noted the distinction between middle and secondary reading, but the instructional practices they recommended for teaching comprehension or vocabulary skills were largely the same for both levels. Other textbooks focused on instruction exclusively at the high school or middle school level. Whatever grade-level focus these textbooks took, however, in the 1970s none used the words *adolescent* or *literacy* in their titles.

Repositioning the Responsibility for Middle and Secondary Reading Instruction from the Reading Specialist to the Content-Area Teacher

The notion that reading instruction belongs in the content-area classroom has deep historical roots. In the early 1900s, Huey (1908/1968), a pioneer in the psychology of reading, advocated embedding reading instruction in the study of content so that it might "disappear in the study of 'central subjects'" (p. 371). He argued further that "whatever needs to be read in living the natural life of the school is proper subject-matter for 'reading lessons'; that is, reading matter gives opportunity for practice and for wise direction in reading effectively" (p. 371). After Huey, the national Right to Read campaign, whose slogan was "Every teacher a teacher of reading," drew "attention to the reading needs of secondary students" (Early, 1957, cited by Ruddell, 1997, pp. 10, 11) and to how reading skills could be used to support students' learning, particularly of subject-matter content. In the 1970s, the shift from thinking of reading as an accrual of discrete skills to reading as a meaning-based process was accompanied by a shift in the responsibility for secondary reading instruction from the reading specialist to the content-area teacher.

The first textbook to be exclusively dedicated to the teaching of reading in the content areas was published in 1970 (Herber, 1978, p. 1). Those that followed examined how instruction on the skills and processes required by later reading could be adapted to meet the demands of content-area learning, in both general and specific content areas. By the early 1980s at least twenty content-area reading texts had been published (Dupuis, 1984, p. 5), and the assertion that content-area teachers should "take responsibility for teaching the reading and writing strategies essential in their classrooms [was] an old cry" (Berger & Robinson, 1982, p. 5).

While there may have been little debate about whether or not reading had a place in middle and high school education — particularly in content-area classrooms — there was considerable confusion and apprehension among secondary teachers about how and when it should be taught, to whom, and by whom (Early, 1977, p. 189). Based on their historical understanding that reading, as content, was the responsibility of "someone else," content-area teachers responded at best with resistance and at worst with antagonism to mandates calling for them to teach reading. Understandably, they protested that they didn't have the training to be reading teachers or the curricular time to "stop" and teach the "content" of reading in addition to that of their discipline (Jacobs, 1999; Jacobs & Wade, 1981). At the same time, in the midst of the 1980s economic recession, funding for professional development decreased dramatically, the reading specialist's position was frequently the victim of budget cuts, and content-area teachers, by and large, had fewer resources to turn to as their students continued to struggle.

Complicating the challenge of moving reading instruction into the content-area classroom was the fact that little research had examined the effectiveness of various secondary-reading instructional techniques within the context of the regular secondary classroom (Dupuis, 1984, p. v). What research had been done primarily confirmed the fact that "content teachers [knew] less than they need[ed] to about reading in general and the specific aspects of teaching reading within their own subjects" and that content-area teachers continued to feel hopeless or frustrated "in the face of students who could not read their classroom materials" (Dupuis, 1984, p. 1).

The textbooks published through the 1980s on the teaching of reading did little to help teachers understand how they could use reading to support students' achievement of disciplinary goals (see Jacobs, 2002). These textbooks were often organized around a particular theory about reading and learning, such as cognitive theories, linguistic and psycholinguistic theories, and affective/motivational theories. Most of these texts took a "one-size-fits-all" or "holistic" approach to content-area reading (Anders & Guzetti, 1996, p. 9), focusing on diagnostics of students' reading ability and of textual difficulty; skills such as decoding, reading rate, comprehension, vocabulary, and study skills; and processes that were common across content areas.[11] Few texts offered teachers support in thinking about how reading-skill instruction might sustain students' achievement of their particular content-based learning goals, and this contributed to their continuing perception of reading instruction as an add-on (see Jacobs, 2002). However, a growing emphasis on reading as "literacy" in the 1990s would ensure a place for reading instruction in the content-area classroom.

An Emerging Emphasis on Reading as Literacy

The term *literacy* has been defined in U.S. educational history variously as orality, the ability to sign one's name, and the ability to recite and copy (Myers, 1996). In the latter half of the nineteenth century, the definition of literacy expanded to include "efficient communication to others and the decoding of unfamiliar texts" (Hull, 1998, p. 179). Today, educators commonly agree that adolescents come to school with knowledge of multiple discourses or literacies, "including those of ethnic, online, and popular culture communities," which they use for "social and political purposes as they create meaning and participate in shaping their immediate environments" (National Council of Teachers of English, 2007). Within academic study, the sociopolitical nature of literacy requires readers not only to "identify the meaning of texts and create their own personal interpretations, but also gain awareness of how texts may be manipulating their perspectives" (Elkins & Luke, 1999).[12] Thus, literacy has come to include but is not restricted to academic learning (see Alvermann, 2001; Barton, 1994).

Beginning in the 1990s, discussion about content-area reading and reading across the curriculum shifted to discussion about content literacy. Similarly, secondary reading began to be reframed as adolescent literacy. The term *literacy* appeared increasingly in the titles of textbooks, which acknowledged the social and political contexts of reading. Most of these textbooks urged teachers to consider how race, ethnicity, language, socioeconomic status, gender, motivation, and special needs contributed to learning. Teachers were warned that "until we [tap] the multiple literacies in adolescent's lives, we will continue to see adolescents develop a disinterested cognitive view of in-school literacy functions and a more enthusiastic sociocultural view of out-of-school discourse functions" (Bean, Bean, & Bean, 1999, p. 447).

To address the problem of adolescents' lack of interest in school-based academic literacy, textbooks advised teachers to depend less on "text-bound modes of teaching that place adolescents in passive roles" and more on inquiry-based instruction that allowed students to be active learners (Bean et al., 1999, p. 447). Recommendations for instruction included teaching for understanding (Perkins, 2004; Perrone, 2000; Wiggins & McTighe, 1998), which defines learning as an inquiry-based process, and collaborative learning (Bruffee, 1992; Walters, 2000), which builds on constructivist principles of learning as a social activity that is embedded in sociocultural systems (Sparks & Hirsh, 1997, p. 2; Vygotsky, 1962).[13]

Thus, while more-recent textbooks on the teaching of reading still focus on specific reading skills, they do so in the context of the reading process or of "strategic reading"; that is, the intentional and deliberate use of strategies that support comprehension, such as metacognition (Irvin, 1998, pp. 8–9). Some continue to focus on reading and learning in content areas. Other textbooks, drawing from the rich literature on content-area writing and the writing process, have addressed writing as a means to learn, including learning from printed text, as well as a skill in itself. Textbooks have also addressed the teaching of middle and high school students who struggle with reading and the role technology can play in reading, including how technology-based discourse can be construed as a form of literacy.[14]

Finally, while research has long examined the instructional needs that English-language learners (ELLs) might experience in reading, recommendations for supporting the reading development of adolescent ELLs in the content-area classroom (e.g., Ariza, 2006; Chamot & O'Malley, 1994; Echevarria, Vogt, & Short, 2000) and, specifically, in the English language arts classroom (National Council of Teachers of English, 2006a; Short & Fitzsimmons, 2007) have emerged relatively recently.[15] While the "best" ways to support ELLs remain controversial, recommendations for classroom teachers focus to a great extent on vocabulary instruction, the role of background knowledge and experience in learning, and the selection and use of relevant literature to teach reading and writing skills.

Conclusion

This article has examined historical trends in the definition of reading and instructional practices for adolescents in order to understand how we have arrived at this particular point on the historical continuum of the amount of attention being paid to the reading of older children. This brief review suggests that while we are faced with multiple challenges as we address the needs of adolescent readers, we also have the opportunity to apply the wisdom of the past to our future efforts.

First, the demands of adolescent literacy clearly begin much earlier than the middle and secondary school grades traditionally associated with adolescence. We may do better by defining the purposes, skills, and challenges that postprimary-grade reading requires at different points on a developmental continuum. A renewed focus on stages of reading would serve four goals:

1. It would clarify purposes for and the timing of teaching and practicing particular reading skills across grades K–12.
2. It would recognize the need to begin explicitly teaching later reading skills in the intermediate elementary grades immediately after children have achieved fluency.
3. Because the focus of reading stages is on reading development rather than on remediation, stages suggest that the number of adolescents requiring remediation may decrease with timely scaffolding.
4. By considering both reading skills and processes within a reading-stage framework, any argument between the two would become unnecessary and perhaps obsolete.

Second, throughout shifts in adolescents' reading instruction, the question of how to support adolescents who struggle with reading (see Curtis, 2002; Curtis & Longo, 1999) has remained a dilemma that we have the opportunity to address explicitly. Whole-school literacy programs (Alliance for Excellent Education, 2004b; Fisher, 2001; Schoenbach, Greenleaf, Cziko, & Hurwitz, 1999) and afterschool programs (see Hartry, Fitzgerald, & Porter in this issue) have been shown to effectively target the needs of all readers, including those who struggle. In addition, computer-assisted instructional programs have proven to be a powerful tool for teachers of struggling readers (National Reading Panel, 2002) — provided such programs offer students intensive and elaborate feedback on their responses along with opportunities to correct their mistakes and rehearse correct responses. It is also essential that schools provide students with additional research-based instruction and practice in reading (Hall, Hughes, & Filbert, 2000). In other words, computer-assisted instruction enriches but cannot replace the teacher's role.

Who should provide this additional instruction and practice in reading during the school day remains an open question. If the trend persists and we continue to transfer the responsibility for adolescent reading instruction (including for struggling readers) to content-area teachers, we need to understand that these teachers face a daunting task — especially if the ultimate goal is to create excellent classroom reading teachers (International Reading Association, 2000a).[16] At the very least, education leaders and policymakers would do well to follow the Alliance for Excellent Education's (2007) four general principles in encouraging "larger numbers of content[-area] teachers to integrate literacy instruction more fully into their everyday practice" (p. 25):

1. The roles and responsibilities of content-area teachers must be clear and consistent.
2. Every academic discipline should define its own essential literacy skills.
3. All secondary school teachers should receive initial and ongoing professional development in the literacy of their own content areas.
4. Content-area teachers need positive incentives and appropriate tools to provide reading and writing instruction. (pp. 25–29)

The importance of high-quality professional development in advancing both preservice and in-service teachers' expertise in content-based literacy should not be underestimated. At its best, professional development is at the heart of curricular reform, fostering the creation of professional communities in which teachers can "share knowledge and treat each other with respect[,] . . . [engage in collaborative] inquiry and reflection[,] . . . and feel confident and well prepared to meet the demands of teaching" (Holloway, 2003, cited in National Council of Teachers of English, 2006b, p. 10).

Professional development offered to content-area teachers needs to acknowledge the historical reasons for their resistance to the notion that they are "teachers of reading." Content-area teachers are concerned primarily, and rightly so, with students' achievement of content-specific goals. While most preservice and in-service efforts provide teachers with a variety of skill-based strategies for integrating reading into their instruction, they generally do not provide teachers with the means to examine why and how reading strategies can facilitate content-area learning.

At a minimum, content-area teachers deserve the time to reflect on the principles and practices of reading that they already use successfully to support their students' content-area learning. Teachers might define their discipline-based learning goals collectively, and then reflect on what they already do effectively to support their students' achievement of those goals. Teachers might consider how they inform students of learning goals and how they expect students to demonstrate learning. They might examine how they prepare students for learning, activating and organizing relevant background knowledge and experience, introducing new vocabulary and concepts, and helping students anticipate and engage with content. They might share how they guide students through progressively deeper levels of understanding, providing means by which students can integrate the "given" that they bring to text and the "new" that a text provides. They might examine the means they give their students to analyze, synthesize, and test the validity of what they have learned before they have to demonstrate that learning (Jacobs, 2002).

Following such conversations, teachers can begin to understand the symbiotic relationship between reading and learning as meaning-making processes, and how the learning strategies they use to teach their content also serve as a means to hone students' comprehension, vocabulary, and study skills without interrupting content-area learning. They can begin to understand that while they are not teachers of reading, by capitalizing on reading skills and processes they are helping their students become independent learners who are able to comprehend the "world" as well as the "word" of their disciplines (Freire, 1998).

Finally, we need to clarify the responsibilities of reading specialists, literacy coaches, and content-area teachers and how those involved in literacy instruction should work together. In the wake of the shift in content-area teachers' responsibility for literacy instruction, the responsibilities of the reading teacher have shifted as well (International Reading Association, 2000b). While reading specialists have long been responsible for providing struggling readers with supplemental direct services and for providing classroom teachers with consultative services (Robinson & Thomas, 1969), they more recently have been assigned the lead responsibility for literacy "coaching"; that is, giving classroom teachers the professional development they need to learn how to serve the literacy needs of all of their students well (Dole, 2004). Due in part to the urgency of the current crisis, we have been quick to establish guidelines concerning the role and qualifications of the reading coach (International Reading Association 2004; Toll, 2007; Walpole & McKenna, 2004) and standards for middle and high school literacy coaches (International Reading Association, 2006). However, we have done so even while the distinction between the work of the reading specialist and the literacy coach remains unclear and while the training and effectiveness of literacy coaches are being called into question (City, 2007).

History reminds us that while the attention currently being paid to the plight of older students' reading is long overdue, we would do well in the shock of this most recent "awakening" to proceed not out of alarm but, rather, with studied concern that acknowledges and builds on the research and practice of our predecessors. We need to remind ourselves of the interrelationship of theory and practice and how both are influenced by popular, even pendular, trends. In the throes of this current historical crisis, we should remember above all that the ultimate reason for our renewed interest in adolescent literacy is, in fact, the same one that has sparked the interest of numerous generations before us. We have long wanted to provide our children with the best education possible to ensure that they will grow into a critical citizenry and live the most significant lives that they can. By placing literacy at the heart of educational reform, the opportunity to achieve this goal is unprecedented.

Notes

1. The principles included the following:

   1. Adolescents deserve access to a wide variety of reading material that they can and want to read.
   2. Adolescents deserve instruction that builds both the skill and desire to read increasingly complex materials.
   3. Adolescents deserve assessment that shows them their strengths as well as their needs and that guides their teachers to design instruction that will best help them grow as readers.
   4. Adolescents deserve expert teachers who model and provide explicit instruction in reading comprehension and study strategies across the curriculum.
   5. Adolescents deserve reading specialists who assist individual students having difficulty learning how to read.
   6. Adolescents deserve teachers who understand the complexities of individual adolescent readers, respect their differences, and respond to their characteristics.

7. Adolescents deserve homes, communities, and a nation that will support their efforts to achieve advanced levels of literacy and provide the support necessary for them to succeed.

2. The RAND report explains the "pressing problem" of comprehension as "older students' inability to meet the increasing challenges of complex texts, the low comprehension performance of U.S. students as compared to those in other countries, unacceptable gaps in reading performance between children in different demographic groups, scant attention to the training and support of content teachers to promote comprehension in their disciplines, and the implementation of policies and programs without empirical evidence of their success or rigorous evaluation" (Snow, 2002, p. xi).

3. The fifteen recommendations included direct, explicit comprehension instruction; effective instructional principles embedded in content; motivated and self-directed learning; text-based collaborative learning; strategic tutoring; the use of diverse texts; intensive writing instruction; a technology component; ongoing, formative assessment of students' progress; extended time for literacy; long-term and ongoing professional development; interdisciplinary and teamed instruction; school-based leadership; and comprehensive and coordinated, schoolwide literacy programs (Biancarosa & Snow, 2004, pp. 3–5).

4. Striving Readers is "aimed at improving the reading skills of middle school– and high school–aged students who are reading below grade level [in] Title I eligible schools that are at risk of not meeting or are not meeting adequate yearly progress (AYP) requirements under the No Child Left Behind Act, or that have significant percentages or number of students reading below grade level, or both. . . . Striving Reader programs include each of three key components: (1) supplemental literacy interventions targeted to students who are reading significantly below grade level; (2) cross-disciplinary strategies for improving student literacy, which may include professional development for subject matter teachers and use of research-based reading and comprehension strategies in classrooms across subject areas; and (3) a strong experimental evaluation component" (U.S. Department of Education, Office of Communications and Outreach, 2007, p. 155).

5. The National Governors Association Center for Best Practices publication, *A Governor's Guide to Adolescent Literacy* (2005), summarizes the challenges of defining and addressing adolescent literacy and five general strategies that governors and states can use to improve adolescent literacy: (1) Build support for a state focus on adolescent literacy, (2) raise literacy expectations across grades and curricula, (3) encourage and support school and district literacy plans, (4) build educators' capacity to provide adolescent literacy instruction, and (5) measure progress in adolescent literacy at the school, district, and state levels.

6. This article restricts its discussion of adolescent literacy to reading while acknowledging that the domain of literacy is far more complex than reading alone.

7. Phonemic awareness is a strong predictor of later reading achievement as early as kindergarten or first grade and "is frequently confused with phonics instruction, which entails teaching students how to use letter-sound relations to read or spell words. [Phonemic awareness] instruction qualifies as phonics instruction when it involves teaching children to blend or segment the sounds in words using letters" (National Reading Panel, 2000, p. 7).

8. In a study of why some children from low-income families succeed at reading while others do not, Chall, Jacobs, and Baldwin (1990) found that while all of the above-average readers (as defined against national norms) at any of three grade levels (grades 2-3, 4-5, and 6-7) demonstrated accurate and fluent reading, no more than 40 percent of those described as below-average readers at any one grade were able to do so. Furthermore,

at grades 6-7 even the above-average readers, who had had sufficient word-attack skills to do well in the early and later elementary grades began to slip against national norms. Their fluency skills were not enough to allow them to keep pace with the increasing conceptual demands of middle-grade reading.

9. Much has been written on the importance of direct teaching of academic language that is common across disciplines and that is specific to disciplines. See, for example, Allen (2007); Beck, McKeown, and Kucan (2002); McKeown and Curtis (1987); Stahl (1999).

10. For example, the National Council of Teachers of English, in *Principles of Adolescent Literacy Reform* (2006b), refers only to the middle and high school grades.

11. Contrast these with Dupuis (1984), who examined the research on content-area reading in context of specific subject matter. Also see textbooks published in the 1970s, which examined the implementation of reading instruction in specific content.

12. It is worth noting that the IRA's *The Literacy Dictionary: The Vocabulary of Reading and Writing* (Harris & Hodges, 1995) included an extensive definition of "literacy," but only an abbreviated definition of "reading to learn." In fact, the dictionary did not include any terms such as "content-area reading," "secondary reading," or "reading-across-the-curriculum."

13. Constructivism draws heavily upon Freire's (1971) belief that learning is a matter of construction of meaning in socially relevant contexts and from Vygotsky's (1962) notions that "high mental functions have their origins in social activity" (Hausfather, 1996, p. 1) (see also Dixon-Krauss, 1996); and that "direct teaching of concepts is impossible and fruitless" (p. 83). Constructivism argues that the sociocultural contexts of the classroom and the value that the teacher places upon students' contributions to each other's learning have a powerful impact on the way and the extent to which learning takes place and is perceived as relevant by students.

14. The Roe, Stoodt, and Burns series on secondary reading illustrates the trends in emphases from the late 1970s to the present. The 1978 edition, called *Reading Instruction in the Secondary School*, included discussion of reading disabilities, the selection of reading material, assessment, word recognition, concept and vocabulary development, comprehension, study skills, reading in specific content areas, and school reading programs. The 1983 and 1987 editions' titles (*Secondary School Reading Instruction: The Content Areas*) reflected the field's attention to content-area reading. The 1980s texts added discussion of reading as a cognitive process and of issues related to writing. While the title of the 1991 edition did not change, it discussed a wider variety of issues related to literacy, such as the interrelation between reading and writing and the challenges content-area teachers face when using reading with a diverse student population (e.g., challenges posed by students' varied background environments and cultures, languages, and previous education). The 1995 and 1998 editions had the same title, *Secondary School Literacy Instruction: The Content Areas*, which reflected the trend toward reading as literacy. These texts provided added discussion of technology in teaching both reading and writing, of contexts for content-based literacy instruction, and reading assessments for diverse student populations. They also added a focus on thematic teaching. The previous focus on "study skills" moved to "strategic" reading for comprehension, the location and organization of information, and reading-study strategies for textbook use. The 2001 edition, *Secondary School Literacy Instruction*, deepened discussion of technology in literacy learning and addressed the role of multiple literacies in learning. Even while the focus of the Roe, Stoodt, and Burns editions broadened and evolved, each text was organized to address assessment and comprehension, vocabulary, and study skill development.

15. The National Council of Teachers of English (2006a) outlined "the knowledge and skills mainstream teachers need to have in order to develop effective curricula that engage English language learners, develop their academic skills, and help them nego-

tiate their identities as bilingual learners" (p. 1). Guidelines focused on knowledge of students, teaching language, teaching literacy (reading and writing), teaching language and content, selecting materials, and the low-level literacy of immigrant students.

16. The International Reading Association (2000a) notes that "excellent reading teachers understand how literacy develops in children, can assess progress and relate instruction to previous experience, know a variety of ways to teach reading, provide a range of materials and texts for children to read, [and] tailor instruction to individual students. Further, "[to] ensure that children have the excellent reading teachers they deserve, teachers must view themselves as lifelong learners, administrators must be instructional leaders, teacher educators must provide their students with a solid knowledge base and extensive supervised practice, legislators and policymakers must understand the complex roles of the teacher, [and] parents, community members, and teachers must join in providing learners with rich opportunities to explore, practice, and develop literacy." For an extended summary, visit http://www.reading.org/resources/issues/positions_excellent.html

References

Adams, M. J. (1994). *Beginning to read: Thinking and learning about print.* Cambridge, MA: MIT Press.

Allan, K. A., & Miller, M. S. (2000). *Literacy and learning in the content areas: Strategies for middle and secondary school teachers.* Boston: Houghton-Mifflin.

Allen, J. (2007). *Inside Words: Tools for teaching academic vocabulary: Grades 4–12.* Portland, ME: Stenhouse.

Alliance for Excellent Education. (2004a). Reading for the 21st century: Adolescent literacy teaching and learning strategies. *Issue Brief,* January 2004. Retrieved January 11, 2008, from http://www.all4ed.org/publication_material/issue_policy_briefs

Alliance for Excellent Education. (2004b). How to know a good adolescent literacy program when you see one: Quality criteria to consider. *Issue Brief,* May 2004. Retrieved January 11, 2008, from http://www.all4ed.org/publication_material/issue_policy_briefs

Alliance for Excellent Education. (2005a). Adolescent literacy: Opening the doors to success. *Issue Brief,* January 2005. Retrieved January 11, 2008, from http://www.all4ed.org/publication_material/issue_policy_briefs

Alliance for Excellent Education. (2005b). Adolescent literacy policy update. *Issue Brief,* June 2005. Retrieved January 11, 2008, from http://www.all4ed.org/publication_material/issue_policy_briefs

Alliance for Excellent Education. (2007). *Literacy instruction in the content areas: Getting to the core of middle and high school improvement.* Retrieved January 11, 2008, from http://www.all4ed.org/files/LitCon.pdf

Allington, R., & Strange, M. (1980). *Learning through reading in the content areas.* Lexington, MA: D. C. Heath.

Alvermann, D. E. (2001). Reading adolescents' reading identities: Looking back to see ahead. *Journal of Adolescent & Adult Literacy, 44*(8), 676–690.

Alvermann, D. E. & Phelps, S.F. (1998). *Content reading and literacy* (2nd ed.). Boston: Allyn and Bacon.

Anders, P. L., & Guzzetti, B. J. (1996). *Literacy instruction in the content areas.* New York: Harcourt Brace College Publishers.

Anderson, R. C., & Pearson, P. D. (1984). A schema-theoretic view of basic processes in reading comprehension. In P. D. Pearson (Ed.), *Handbook of reading research* (pp. 255–291). New York: Longman.

Ariza, E. N. W. (2006). *Not for ESOL teachers: What every classroom teacher needs to know about the linguistically, culturally, and ethnically diverse student.* Boston: Pearson Education.

Armbruster, B. B., Lehr, F., & Osborne, J. (2001). *Put reading first: The research building blocks for teaching children to read (kindergarten through grade 3).* Washington, DC: The Partnership for Reading.

Aukerman, R. (1972). *Reading in the secondary school classroom.* New York: McGraw-Hill.

Baird, S. (1978). *Strategies in teaching reading: Secondary.* Washington, DC: National Endowment for the Arts.

Barton, D. (1994). *The social basis of literacy. Literacy: An introduction to the ecology of written language.* Cambridge, MA: Blackwell.

Bean, T., Bean, S. K., & Bean, K. F. (1999). Intergenerational conversations and two adolescents' multiple literacies: Implications for redefining content area literacy. *Journal of Adolescent & Adult Literacy, 42*(6), 438–448.

Bean, R., & Wilson, R. (1981). *Effecting change in school reading programs: The resource role.* Newark, DE: International Reading Association.

Beck, I. L., McKeown, M. G., & Kucan, L. (2002). *Bringing words to life: Robust vocabulary instruction.* New York: Guilford Press.

Berger A., & Robinson, H. A. (Eds.). (1982). *Secondary school reading: What research reveals for classroom practice.* Urbana, IL: ERIC Clearinghouse on Reading and Communication Skills, National Institute of Education and National Conference on Research in English.

Biancarosa, G., & Snow, C. E. (2004). *Reading next: A vision for action and research in middle and high school literacy: A report from Carnegie Corporation of New York.* Washington, DC: Alliance for Excellent Education. Retrieved January 11, 2008, from http://www.all4ed.org/publication_material/reports

Billmeyer, R., & Barton, M. L. (1998). *Teaching reading in the content areas — If not me, then who?* (2nd ed.). Aurora, CO: Mid-continent Research for Education and Learning.

Boke, N. (2004). *I'm a reader: Reading to learn: A classroom guide to reading strategy instruction.* Montpelier, VT: Vermont Department of Education.

Brozo, W. G., & Simpson, M. L. (1999). *Readers, teachers, learners: Expanding literacy across the content areas* (3rd ed.). Upper Saddle River, NJ: Prentice Hall.

Bruffee, K. (1992). Collaborative learning and the conversation of mankind. In A. Goodsell, M. Maher, & V. Tinto (Eds.), *Collaborative learning: A sourcebook for higher education, Volume 1* (pp. 23–33). University Park, PA: National Center on Postsecondary Teaching, Learning, and Assessment.

Brunner, J. F., & Campbell, J. J. (1978). *Participating in secondary reading: A practical approach.* Englewood Cliffs, NJ: Prentice Hall.

Burmeister, L. E. (1978). *Reading strategies for middle and secondary school teachers* (2nd ed.). Reading, MA: Addison-Wesley.

Burron, A., & Claybaugh, A. L. (1974). *Using reading to teach subject matter: Fundamentals for content teachers.* Columbus, OH: Charles E. Merrill.

Cassidy, J., Garrett, S. D., & Barrera, I. V. (2006). What's hot in adolescent literacy, 1997–2006. *Journal of Adolescent & Adult Literacy, 50*(1), 30–36.

Chall, J. S. (1967). *Learning to read: The great debate.* New York: McGraw-Hill.

Chall, J. S. (1983). *Stages of reading development.* New York: McGraw-Hill.

Chall, J. S., & Jacobs, V. A. (1996). The reading, writing, and language connection. In J. Shimron (Ed.), *Literacy and education: Essays in memory of Dina Feitelson* (pp. 33–48). Creskill, NJ: Hampton Press.

Chall, J. S., & Jacobs, V. A. (2003). The classic study on poor children's fourth-grade slump. *American Educator, 27*(1), 14–15, 44.

Chall, J. S., Jacobs, V. A., & Baldwin, L. E. (1990). *The reading crisis: Why poor children fall behind.* Cambridge, MA: Harvard University Press.

Chamot, A. U., & O'Malley, J. M. (1994). *The CALLA handbook: Implementing the cognitive academic language learning approach.* Reading, MA: Addison-Wesley.

City, E. A. (2007). Is coaching the best use of resources? *Harvard Education Letter*, September/October, 2007, 8; 6-7.

Conley, M. W. (1995). *Content reading instruction: A communication approach.* New York: McGraw-Hill.

Culp, M. B., & Spann, S. (1979). *Me? Teaching reading? Activities for secondary content area teachers.* Santa Monica, CA: Goodyear Publishing Co.

Cunningham, J. W., Cunningham, P. M., & Arthur, S. V. (1981). *Middle and secondary school reading.* New York: Longman.

Curtis, M.E. (2002, May). Adolescent reading: Trends in recent research and implications for instruction. Paper presented at Practice Models for Adolescent Literacy Success: The Second Workshop on Adolescent Literacy, Baltimore, MD.

Curtis, M. E., & Longo, A. M. (1999). *When adolescents can't read: Methods and materials that work.* Cambridge, MA: Brookline Books.

Daniels, H., & Zemelman, S. (2004). *Subjects matter: Every teacher's guide to content-area reading.* Portsmouth, NH: Heinemann.

Davis, E. D. (1976). *Teaching reading in the secondary school.* Dubuque, IA: Kendall/Hunt.

Dechant, E. (1973). *Reading improvement in the secondary school.* Englewood Cliffs, NJ: Prentice Hall.

Delpit, L. (1988). The silenced dialogue: Power and pedagogy in educating other people's children. *Harvard Educational Review, 58,* 280–298.

Dillner, M., & Olson, J. (1977). *Personalizing reading instruction in middle, junior, and senior high schools.* New York: Macmillan.

Dishner, E. K., Bean, T. W., & Readence, J. E. (1981). *Reading in the content areas: Improving classroom instruction.* Toronto: Kendall/Hunt.

Dixon-Krauss, L. (1996). *Vygotsky in the classroom: Medicated literacy instruction and assessment* (pp. 14–16). White Plains, NY: Longman.

Dole, J.A. (2004). The changing role of the reading specialist in school reform. *The reading teacher, 57*(5), 462–471.

Duffy, G. G. (Ed.). (1974). *Reading in middle school.* Newark, DE: International Reading Association.

Duffy, G. G. (Ed.). (1990). *Reading in the middle school.* Newark, DE: International Reading Association.

Dupuis M. M. (Ed.). (1984). *Reading in the content areas: Research for teachers.* Newark, DE: International Reading Association.

Dupuis, M. M., Lee, J. W., Badiali, B. J., & Askov, E. N. (1989). *Teaching reading and writing in the content areas.* Glenview, IL: Scott, Foresman.

Early, M. J. (1957). What does reading research reveal about successful reading programs? In M. A. Gunn et al. (Eds.). *What we know about high school reading.* Champaign, IL: National Council of Teachers of Reading.

Early, M. (1977). Reading in the secondary school. In J. R. Squire (Ed.), *The teaching of English: The seventy-sixth yearbook of the National Society for the Study of Education, Part I.* Chicago: University of Chicago Press.

Echevarria, J., Vogt, M. E., & Short, D. (2000). *Making content comprehensible for English language learners: The SIOP model.* Boston: Allyn and Bacon.

Elkins, J., & Luke, A., (1999). Redefining adolescent literacies. *Journal of Adolescent & Adult Literacy, 43,* 212–215.

Estes, T., & Vaughan, T. (1978). *Reading and learning in the content classroom.* Boston: Allyn and Bacon.

Fay, L., & Jared, L. A. (1975). *Reading in the content fields: An annotated bibliography.* Newark, DE: International Reading Association.

Fisher, D. (2001). We're moving on up: Creating a schoolwide literacy effort in an urban high school. *Journal of Adolescent & Adult Literacy, 45*(2).

Forgan, H. W., & Mangrum, C. (1976). *Teaching content area reading skills.* Columbus, OH: Charles E. Merrill.

Freire, P. (1971). *Pedagogy of the oppressed.* New York: Herder and Herder.

Freire, P. (1998). First letter: Reading the world/reading the word. In *Teachers as cultural workers: Letters to those who dare teach* (pp. 17–26). Boulder, CO: Westview Press.

Geschwind, N. (1962). The anatomy of acquired disorders of reading. In J. Money (Ed.), *Reading disability.* Baltimore: Johns Hopkins University Press.

Goodman, K. S. (1967). Reading: A psycholinguistic guessing game. *Journal of the Reading Specialist, 6,* 126–135.

Goodman, K. S. (1986). *What's whole in whole language.* Toronto, Canada: Scholastic.

Goodman, K. S., Bird, L. B., & Goodman, Y. M. (1991). *The whole language catalogue.* Santa Rosa, CA: American School Publishers.

Guthrie, J. T. (Ed.). (1977). *Cognition, Curriculum, and Comprehension.* Newark, DE: International Reading Association.

Hafner, L. (1974). *Improving reading in middle and secondary schools.* New York: Macmillan.

Hafner, L. (1977). *Developmental reading in the middle and secondary schools: Foundations, strategies, and skills for teaching.* New York: Macmillan.

Hall, T. E., Hughes, C. A., & Filbert, M. (2000). Computer-assisted instruction in reading for students with learning disabilities: A research synthesis. *Education & Treatment of Children, 23*(2), 173–193.

Hammill, D. D., & Bartel, N. R. (1995). *Teaching students with learning and behavior problems* (6th ed.). Austin, TX: Pro-Ed.

Harker, W. J. (Ed.). (1985). *Classroom strategies for secondary reading.* Newark, DE: International Reading Association.

Harris, T. L., & Cooper, E. (Eds.). (1985). *Reading, thinking, and concept development: Strategies for the classroom.* New York: The College Board.

Harris, T. L., & Hodges, R. E. (Eds.). (1995). *The literacy dictionary: The vocabulary of reading and writing.* Newark, DE: International Reading Association.

Hausfather, S. J. (1996). Vygotsky and schooling: Creating a social context for learning. *Action in Teacher Education, XVIII,* 1–10.

Heller, R., & Greenleaf, C. L. (2007). *Literacy instruction in the content areas: Getting to the core of middle and high school improvement.* Washington, DC: Alliance for Excellent Education. Retrieved January 11, 2008, from http://www.all4ed.org/files/LitCon.pdf

Herber, H. (1978). *Teaching reading in content areas.* Englewood Cliffs, NJ: Prentice Hall.

Hill, W. R. (1979). *Secondary school reading: Process, program, procedure.* Boston: Allyn and Bacon.

Holloway, J. H. (2003). Sustaining experienced teachers. *Educational Leadership, 60*(8), 87–89.

Huey, E. B. (1968). The psychology and pedagogy of reading. Cambridge, MA: MIT Press. (Original work published 1908)

Hull, G. (1998). A conversation with Miles Myers. *Journal of Adolescent & Adult Literacy, 42*(3), 178–183.

Inhelder, B., & Piaget, J. (1958). *The growth of logical thinking from childhood to adolescence.* New York: Basic Books.

International Reading Association. (2000a). Excellent reading teachers: A position statement of the International Reading Association. *Journal of Adolescent & Adult Literacy, 44*(2), 193.

International Reading Association. (2000b). Teaching all children to read: The roles of the reading specialist. *Journal of Adolescent & Adult Literacy, 44*(2), 99.

International Reading Association. (2004). *The role and qualifications of the reading coach in the United States.* Newark, DE: Author.

International Reading Association. (2006). *Standards for middle and high school literacy coaches.* Newark, DE: Author. Retrieved January 11, 2008, from http://www.reading.org/downloads/resources/597coaching_standards.pdf

Irvin, J. L. (1998). *Reading and the middle school student: Strategies to enhance literacy* (2nd ed.). Boston: Allyn and Bacon.

Irvin, J. L., Buehl, D. R., & Klemp, R. M. (2003). *Reading and the high school student: Strategies to enhance literacy* (2nd ed.). Boston: Allyn and Bacon.

Jacobs, V. A. (1999). What secondary teachers can do to teach reading: A three-step strategy for helping students delve deeper into texts. *Harvard Education Letter,* July/August, 4–5.

Jacobs, V. A. (2002). Reading, writing, and understanding. *Educational Leadership, 60*(3), 58–61.

Jacobs, V. A., & Wade, S. (1981). Teaching reading in the content-areas. *Momentum, 12*(4), 8–10.

Kane, S. (2007). *Literacy learning in the content areas* (2nd ed.). Scottsdale, AZ: Holcomb Hathaway.

Kane, R. B., Byrne, M. A., & Hater, M. A. (1974). *Helping children read mathematics.* New York: American Book Company.

Karlin, R. (1977). *Teaching reading in the high school* (3rd ed.). Indianapolis, IN: Bobbs-Merrill.

Karlin, R. (1984). *Improving reading in the content areas.* New York: Harper Collins.

Kling, M. (1971). Quest for synthesis. In F. B. Davis (Ed.), *The literature of research in reading with emphasis on models* (pp. 2–3). New Brunswick, NJ: Rutgers University Graduate School of Education.

Laffey, J. L. (1972). *Reading in the content areas.* Newark, DE: International Reading Association.

Lamberg, W., & Lamb, C. E. (1980). *Reading instruction in the content areas.* Chicago, IL: Rand McNally.

Langer, J. A. (1982). The reading process. In A. Berger & H. A. Robinson (Eds.), *Secondary school reading: What research reveals for classroom practice* (pp. 39-52). Urbana, IL: ERIC Clearinghouse on Reading and Communication Skills.

Lapp, D., Flood, J., & Farnan, N. (1996). *Content area reading and learning: Instructional strategies* (2nd ed.). Boston: Allyn and Bacon.

Lee, J., Grigg, W., & Donahue, P. (2007). *The nation's report card: Reading 2007.* (No. NCES 2007-496). Washington, DC: National Center for Education Statistics; Institute of Education Sciences, U.S. Department of Education.

Lenski, S. D., Wham, M. A., & Johns, J. L. (1999). *Reading & learning strategies for middle & high school students.* Dubuque, IA: Kendall/Hunt.

Levy, F. & Murnane, R. (2004). *The new division of labor: How computers are creating the next job market.* Princeton, NJ: Princeton University Press.

Liebert, B., & Liebert, M. (1979). *A schoolwide secondary reading program: Here's how.* New York: John Wiley & Sons.

Lutkus, A. D., Grigg, W. S., & Donahue, P. L. (2007, November) *The nation's report card: Reading 2007: Trial urban district assessment results at grades 4 and 8.* Washington, DC: National Assessment of Educational Progress. Retrieved January 11, 2008, from http://blog.reading.org/archives/003438.html

Manning, M. M., & Manning, G. L. (1979). *Reading instruction in the middle school.* Washington, DC: National Endowment for the Arts.

Manzo, A. V., & Manzo, U. (1997). *Content area literacy: Interactive teaching for active learning* (2nd ed.). Upper Saddle River, NJ: Prentice Hall.

Manzo, A. V., Manzo, U. C., & Estes, T. H. (1997). *Content area literacy: Interactive teaching for active learning* (2nd ed.). New York: John Wiley & Sons.

Manzo, A. V., Manzo, U. C., & Thomas, M. M. (2005). *Content area literacy: Strategic teaching for strategic learning* (4th ed.). New York: John Wiley & Sons.

McCarthy, M. J., Rasool, J., & Banks, C. (1993). *Reading and learning across the disciplines.* Belmont, CA: Wordsworth.

McCombs, J. S., Kirby, S. N., Barney, H., Darilek, H., & Magee, S. (2005). *Achieving state and national literacy goals, a long uphill road.* Report to the Carnegie Corporation of New York, RAND Corporation Technical Report Series. Santa Monica, CA: RAND Corporation. Retrieved January 11, 2008, from http://www.rand.org/pubs/technical_reports/TR180-1/

McIntyre, V. B. (1977). *Reading strategies and enrichment activities for grades 4–9.* Columbus, OH: Charles E. Merrill.

McKeown, M. C., & Curtis, M. E. (1987). *The nature of vocabulary acquisition.* Hillsdale, NJ: Lawrence Erlbaum.

Meltzer, L. J, Roditi, B. N., Haynes, D. P., Biddle, K. R., Paster, M., & Taber, S. E. (1996). *Strategies for success: Classroom teaching techniques for students with learning problems.* Austin, TX: Pro-Ed.

Miholic, V. (1994). Metacognitive reading awareness inventory. *Journal of Reading, 38*(2), 84–86.

Miller, W. H. (1974). *Teaching reading in the secondary school.* Springfield, IL: Charles C. Thomas.

Moore, D. W., Bean, T. W., Birdyshaw, D., & Rycik, J. A. (1999). *Adolescent literacy: A position statement for the Commission on Adolescent Literacy of the International Reading Association.* Newark, DE: International Reading Association.

Moore, D. W., Moore, S. A., Cunningham, P., & Cunningham, J. W. (1986). *Developing readers and writers in the content areas.* White Plains, NY: Longman.

Moore, D. W., Moore, S. A., Cunningham, P. M., & Cunningham, J. W. (2001). *Developing readers and writers in the content areas K–12* (4th ed.). Boston: Pearson Education.

Moore, D. W., Readence, J. E., & Rickelman, R. J. (1989). *Prereading activities for content area reading and learning.* Newark, DE: International Reading Association.

Morretta, T., & Ambrosini, M. (2000). *Practical approaches for teaching reading and writing in middle school.* Newark, DE: International Reading Association.

Murnane, R., & Levy, F. (1996). *Teaching the new basic skills: Principles for educating children to thrive in a changing economy.* New York: Free Press.

Myers, M. (1996). *Changing our minds: Negotiating English and literacy.* Urbana, IL: National Council of Teachers of English.

National Assessment of Educational Progress. (1985). *The reading report card: Progress toward excellence in our schools: Trends in reading over four national assessments, 1971–1984.* Princeton, NJ: Educational Testing Service.

National Assessment of Educational Progress. (2006). *Reading at risk: The state response to the crisis in adolescent literacy.* A Report of the NASBE Study Group on Middle and High School Literacy (Rev. Ed.). Alexandria, VA: National Association of State Boards of Education. Retrieved January 11, 2008, from http://nasbe.org/adolescent_literacy/files/reading_at_risk_full_report.pdf

National Association of Secondary School Principals. (2005). *Creating a culture of literacy: A guide for middle and high school principals.* Reston, VA: Author.

National Commission on Excellence in Education. (1983). *America at risk: An imperative for educational reform.* Washington, DC: Author. Retrieved January 11, 2008, from http://www.ed.gov/pubs/NatAtRisk/index.html

National Council of Teachers of English Commission on Reading. (2004). *A call to action: What we know about adolescent literacy and ways to support teachers in meeting students' needs*. Urbana, IL: Author. Retrieved January 11, 2008, from http://www.ncte.org/about/over/positions/category/read/118622.htm

National Council of Teachers of English (2006a). *NCTE position paper on the role of English teachers in educating English language learners*. Urbana, IL: Author.

National Council of Teachers of English. (2006b). *NCTE principles of adolescent literacy reform: A policy brief*. Urbana, IL: Author.

National Council of Teachers of English. (2007). *Adolescent literacy: A policy research brief*. Urbana, IL: Author.

National Endowment for the Arts (2004). *Reading at risk: A survey of literary reading in America*. Washington, DC: Author.

National Endowment for the Arts. (2007). *To read or not to read: A question of national consequence*. Washington, D.C.: Author.

National Governors Association Center for Best Practices. (2005). *Reading to achieve: A governor's guide to adolescent literacy*. Washington, DC: Author. Retrieved January 11, 2008, from http://www.nga.org/files/pdf/0510govguideliteracy.pdf

National Reading Panel. (2000). *Report of the national reading panel: Teaching children to read*. Washington, DC: National Institute for Literacy. Retrieved January 11, 2008, from http://www.nichd.nih.gov/publications/pubskey.cfm?from=reading

National Reading Panel. (2002). Computer technology and reading instruction. In *Teaching children to read: Reports of the subgroups* (pp. 6.1–6.14) (NIH Pub. No. 00-4754). Washington, DC: U.S. Department of Health and Human Services. Retrieved January 11, 2008, from http://www.nichd.nih.gov/publications/nrp/upload/report_pdf.pdf

Office of Elementary and Secondary Education, U.S. Department of Education. (2006). *Striving readers program*. (No. CFDA Number: 84.371A). Washington, DC: U.S. Department of Education. Retrieved January 11, 2008, from http://www.ed.gov/programs/strivingreaders/index.html

Olson, A., & Ames, W. (1972). *Teaching reading skills in secondary schools*. Scranton, PA: Intext Educational.

Perkins, D. (2004, September). Knowledge alive. *Educational Leadership 62*(1), 14–18.

Perrone, V. (2000). Chapter 6: Toward a pedagogy of understanding. In *Lessons for new teachers* (pp. 103–119). Boston: McGraw-Hill.

Perry, W. (1970). *Forms of intellectual and ethical development in the college years: A scheme*. New York: Rinehart & Winston.

Piaget, J. (1970). *Structuralism*. New York: Basic Books.

Piercey, D. (1976). *Reading activities in content areas*. Boston: Allyn and Bacon.

Readence, J. E., Bean, T. W., & Baldwin, R. S. (1981). *Content area reading: An integrated approach*. Dubuque, IA: Kendall/Hunt.

Readence, J. E., Bean, T. W., & Baldwin, R. S. (2001). *Content area reading: An integrated approach*. (7th ed.). Dubuque, IA: Kendall/Hunt.

Richardson, J. S., & Morgan, R. F. (1994). *Reading to learn in the content areas*. Belmont, CA: Wadsworth.

Robb, L. (2000). *Teaching reading in the middle school*. New York: Scholastic.

Robinson, A. (1975). *Teaching reading and study strategies: The content areas*. Boston: Allyn and Bacon.

Robinson A., Thomas E. L. (Eds.). (1969). *Fusing reading skills and content*. Newark, DE: International Reading Association.

Robinson, H. A. (1977). Reading instruction and research: In historical perspective. In H. A. Robinson (Ed.), *Reading & writing instruction in the United States: Historical trends* (pp. 44–58). Newark, DE: International Reading Association.

Roe, B., Stoodt, B., & Burns, P. (1978). *Reading instruction in the secondary schools*. Chicago, IL: Rand McNally.

Roe, B., Stoodt, B., & Burns, P. (1983). *Secondary school reading instruction: The content areas* (2nd ed.). Boston: Houghton-Mifflin.

Roe, B., Stoodt, B., & Burns, P. (1987). *Secondary school reading instruction: The content areas* (3rd ed.). Boston: Houghton-Mifflin.

Roe, B., Stoodt, B., & Burns, P. (1991). *Secondary school reading instruction: The content areas* (4th ed.). Boston: Houghton-Mifflin.

Roe, B., Stoodt, B., & Burns, P. (1995). *Secondary school reading instruction: The content areas* (5th ed.). Boston: Houghton-Mifflin.

Roe, B., Stoodt, B., & Burns, P. (1998). *Secondary school literacy instruction: The content areas* (6th ed.). Boston: Houghton-Mifflin.

Roe, B., Stoodt, B., & Burns, P. (2001). *Secondary school literacy instruction: The content areas* (7th ed.). Boston: Houghton-Mifflin.

Ruddell, M. R. (1997). *Teaching content reading and writing* (2nd ed.). Boston: Allyn & Bacon.

Ruddell, M. R. (2005). *Teaching content reading and writing* (4th ed.). Hoboken, NJ: John Wiley & Sons.

Rumelhart, D. E. (1980). Schemata: The building blocks of cognition. In R. J. Spiro, B. C. Bruce, & W. F. Brewer (Eds.), *Theoretical issues in reading comprehension* (pp. 33–58). Hillsdale, NJ: Lawrence Erlbaum.

Rumelhart, D.E. (1984). Schemata and the cognitive system. In R. S. Wyer & T. K. Srull (Eds.), *Handbook of social cognition* (pp. 161–188). Hillsdale, NJ: Lawrence Erlbaum.

Rycik, J. A., & Irvin, J. L. (2005). *Teaching reading in the middle grades: Understanding and supporting literacy development.* Boston: Pearson Education.

Ryder, R. J., & Graves, M. F. (1998). *Reading and learning in content areas* (2nd ed.). Columbus, OH: Merrill/Prentice Hall.

Samuels, S. J., & Pearson, P. D. (1986). *Changing school reading programs: Principles and case studies.* Newark, DE: International Reading Association.

Santeusanio, R. P. (1983). *A practical approach to content area reading.* Reading, MA: Addison-Wesley.

Scala, M. C. (2001). *Working together: Reading and writing in inclusive classrooms.* Newark, DE: International Reading Association.

Schoenbach, R., Greenleaf, C., Cziko, C., & Hurwitz, L. (1999). *Reading for understanding: A Guide to improving reading in middle and high school classrooms.* Urbana, IL: National Council of Teachers of English.

Shepherd, D. L. (1983). *Comprehensive high school reading methods.* Columbus, OH: Charles E. Merrill.

Short, D. J., & Fitzsimmons, S. (2007). *Double the work: Challenges and solutions to acquiring language and academic literacy for adolescent English language learners: Report for the Carnegie Corporation of New York.* Washington, DC: Alliance for Excellent Education. Retrieved January 11, 2008, from http://www.carnegie.org/literacy/pdf/DoubletheWork.pdf

Smith, F. (1971). *Understanding reading: A psycholinguistic analysis of reading and learning to read.* New York: Holt, Rinehart and Winston, Inc.

Smith, N. B. (1965). *American reading instruction* (Rev. ed.). Newark, DE: International Reading Association.

Smith, C., & Elliott, P. (1979). *Reading activities for middle and secondary schools: A handbook for teachers.* New York: Holt, Rinehart and Winston.

Smith, C., Smith, S., & Mikulecky, L. (1978). *Teaching content reading: A book-thinking process.* New York: Holt, Rinehart and Winston.

Smith, R., & Barrett, T. (1983). *Teaching reading in middle grades.* Reading, MA: Addison-Wesley.

Smith, R., Otto, W., & Hansen, L. (1978). *The school reading program.* Boston: Houghton-Mifflin.

Snow, C. E. (2002). *Reading for understanding: Toward a research and development program in reading comprehension.* (Monograph No. MR-1465-OERI). Santa Barbara, CA: RAND Corporation. Retrieved January 11, 2008, from http://www.rand.org/publications/ MR/MR1465/

Snow, C. E., Barnes, W.S., Chandler, J., Goodman, I.F., & Hemphill, L. (1991). *Unfulfilled expectations: Home and school influences on literacy.* Cambridge, MA: Harvard University Press.

Snow, C. E., Burns, M. S., & Griffin, P. (Eds.). (1998). *Preventing reading difficulties in young children: Precursors and fallout.* Washington, DC: National Academy Press. Retrieved January 11, 2008, from http://www.ed.gov/inits/americareads/ReadDiff/read-sum. html

Snow, C., Griffin, P., & Burns, M. S. (Eds.). (2005). *Knowledge to support the teaching of reading: Preparing teachers for a changing world.* San Francisco, CA: Jossey-Bass.

Snow, C. E., & Juel, C. (2005). Teaching children to read: What do we know about how to do it? In M. Snowling & C. Hume (Eds.), *The science of reading: A handbook* (pp. 501– 520). Malden, MA: Blackwell.

Sparks, D., & Hirsh, S. (1997). *A new vision for staff development.* Alexandria, VA: Association for Supervision and Curriculum Development.

Spiro, R. J., Bruce, B. C., & Brewer, W. F. (Eds.). (1980). *Theoretical issues in reading comprehension: Perspectives and cognitive psychology, linguistics, artificial intelligence, and education.* Hillsdale, NJ: Lawrence Erlbaum.

Stahl, S. A. (1997). Teaching children with reading problems to recognize words. In L. R. Putnam (Ed.), *Readings on language and literacy* (pp. 131-154). Cambridge, MA: Brookline Books.

Stahl, S. A. (1999). *Vocabulary development.* Cambridge, MA: Brookline Books.

Standal, T. C., & Betza, R. E. (1990). *Content area reading: Teachers, texts, students.* Englewood Cliffs, NJ: Prentice Hall.

Sulzby, E. (1986). Young children's concepts of oral and written language. In K. Durkin (Ed.), *Language development in the schools years* (pp. 95–116). London, England: Croom-Helm.

Thomas, E. L., & Robinson, H. A. (1982). *Improving reading in every class: A sourcebook for teachers.* Boston: Allyn and Bacon.

Thorndike, E. L. (1917/1958). Reading as reasoning. In C. W. Hunnicutt & W. J. Iverson (Eds.), *Research in the three R's* (pp. 139–141). New York: Harper & Row.

Thorndike, R. L. (1973–1974). Reading as reasoning. *Reading Research Quarterly, 9,* 135–147.

Toll, C. (2007). *Lenses on literacy coaching: Conceptualizations, functions, and outcomes.* Norwood, MA: Christopher-Gordon.

Tonjes, M. J., & Zintz, M. V. (1981). *Teaching reading, thinking, study skills in content classrooms.* Dubuque, IA: William C. Brown.

U. S. Department of Education. (2001). *No child left behind.* Retrieved January 11, 2008, from http://www.ed.gov/policy/elsec/leg/esea02/index.html

U.S. Department of Education, Office of Communications and Outreach. (2007). *Guide to U.S. Department of Education Programs.* Washington, DC. Retrieved January 25, 2008 from http://www.ed.gov/programs/gtep/gtep.pdf

Vacca, R. T. (1981). *Content area reading.* Boston: Little, Brown.

Vacca, R. T. (1998). Let's not marginalize adolescent literacy. *Journal of Adolescent & Adult Literacy, 41*(8), 604–609.

Vacca, R. T., & Vacca, J. A. L. (2005). *Content area reading: Literacy and learning across the curriculum.* Boston: Pearson.

Venezky, R. L., & Calfee, R. L. (1970). The reading competency mode. In H. Singer & R. B. Ruddell (Eds.), *Theoretical models and processes of reading* (pp. 273–291). Newark, DE: International Reading Association.

Vygotsky, L. S. (1962). *Thought and language.* Cambridge, MA: MIT Press.

Walpole, S., & McKenna, M. C. (2004). Providing professional support. *The literacy coach's handbook: A guide to research-based practice.* New York: Guilford Press.

Walters, L. S. (2000). Putting cooperative learning to the test and building a bridge between research and practice. *Harvard Education Letter, 16*(3), 1–6.

Wiggins, G., & McTighe, J. (1998) *Understanding by design.* Alexandria, VA: Association for Supervision and Curriculum Development.

The author would like to acknowledge, gratefully, the support that Jacy Ippolito and Judith Wasserman provided in ensuring the successful completion of this essay.

APPENDIX A   Sample Textbooks on the Teaching of Middle School and Secondary Reading

1960s–1970s

Aspects of Reading Skill and Instruction that Cross Content

Brunner & Campbell, 1978	Karlin, 1977
Burmeister, 1978	Laffey, 1972
Burron & Claybaugh, 1974	Liebert & Liebert, 1979
Culp & Spann, 1979	Olson & Ames, 1972
Dillner & Olson, 1977	Piercey, 1976
Estes & Vaughan, 1978	Robinson, 1975
Fay & Jared, 1975	Smith & Elliott, 1979
Hafner, 1974	Smith, Smith, & Mikulecky, 1978
Herber, 1978	

Teaching Particular Reading Skills (e.g., assessment, comprehension, vocabulary, study skills)

Brunner & Campbell, 1978	Karlin, 1977
Burmeister, 1978	Liebert & Liebert, 1979
Culp & Spann, 1979	Olson & Ames, 1972
Dillner & Olson, 1977	Piercey, 1976
Hafner, 1974	Smith & Elliott, 1979
Herber, 1978	

The Reading Process

Dillner & Olson, 1977	Hill, 1979
Herber, 1978	

Motivation and Affect

Burmeister, 1978	Liebert & Liebert, 1979
Hafner, 1974	Smith & Elliott, 1979

Personalization

Burmeister, 1978	Dillner & Olson, 1977

The Psychology of Reading

Karlin, 1977	Liebert & Liebert, 1979

Psycholinguistics and Reading

Hafner, 1974	Smith, Otto, & Hansen, 1978
Liebert & Liebert, 1979	

Cognition and Reading

Burmeister, 1978

Whole-School Reading Programs

Duffy, 1974	Robinson & Thomas, 1969
Liebert & Liebert, 1979	Smith, Otto, & Hansen, 1978

"Secondary Reading" in the Title of the Textbook

Aukerman, 1972	Dechant, 1973
Baird, 1978	Miller, 1974
Brunner & Campbell, 1978	Olson & Ames, 1972
Burmeister, 1978	Roe, Stoodt, & Burns, 1978
Davis, 1976	

Textbooks with "Middle School" and "Secondary/High School" in Their Titles

Burmeister, 1978	Hafner, 1974 & 1977
Dillner & Olson, 1977	Smith & Elliott, 1979

Middle School Reading Only

Duffy, 1974	McIntyre, 1977
Manning & Manning, 1979	

1960s–1970s (continued)

High School Reading Only
   Karlin, 1977

Textbooks with "Content," "Content Area," or "Subject Matter" in Their Titles
   Burron & Claybaugh, 1974   Herber, 1978
   Culp & Spann, 1979   Laffey, 1972
   Estes & Vaughan, 1978   Piercey, 1976
   Fay & Jared, 1975   Smith, Smith, & Mikulecky, 1978
   Forgan & Mangrum, 1976

Teaching Reading within Particular Content
   Burmeister, 1978   Karlin, 1977
   Dillner & Olson, 1977   Liebert & Liebert, 1979
   Hafner, 1974   Piercey, 1976
   Herber, 1978   Roe, Stoodt, & Burns, 1978
   Kane, Byrne, & Hater, 1974

1980s

Aspects of Reading Skill and Instruction that Cross Content
   Allington & Strange, 1980   Moore, Readence, & Rickelman, 1989
   Dishner, Bean, & Readence, 1981   Readence, Bean, & Baldwin, 1981
   Dupuis, 1984   Roe, Stoodt, & Burns, 1987
   Dupuis, Lee, Badiali, & Askov, 1989   Santeusanio, 1983
   Harker, 1985   Thomas & Robinson, 1982
   Karlin, 1984   Tonjes & Zintz, 1981
   Lamberg & Lamb, 1980   Vacca, 1981
   Moore, Moore, Cunningham, & Cunningham, 1986

Instructional Focus on Cognition Theory
   Allington & Strange, 1980   Harris & Cooper, 1985
   Dupuis, Lee, Badiali, & Askov, 1989   Readence, Bean, & Baldwin, 1981

Instructional Focus on Linguistics and Psycholinguistic Theories
   Allington & Strange, 1980   Readence, Bean, & Baldwin, 1981

Instructional Focus on Theories about the Role of Affect and Motivation in Reading
   Dupuis, Lee, Badiali, & Askov, 1989

Whole-School Reading Programs
   Bean & Wilson, 1981   Samuels & Pearson, 1986

Textbooks with "Middle School" and "Secondary/High School" in Their Titles
   Cunningham, Cunningham, & Arthur, 1981

Textbooks that Focused on Middle School Only
   Smith & Barrett, 1983

Textbooks with "Secondary/High School" in Their Titles
   Berger & Robinson, 1982   Roe, Stoodt, & Burns, 1983 & 1987
   Harker, 1985   Shepherd, 1983

Textbooks with "Content," "Content Area," or "Subject Matter" in Their Titles
   Allington & Strange, 1980   Moore, Moore, Cunningham, & Cunningham, 1986
   Dishner, Bean, & Readence, 1981   Moore, Readence, & Rickelman, 1989
   Dupuis, 1984   Roe, Stoodt, & Burns, 1983 & 1987
   Dupuis, Lee, Badiali, & Askov, 1989   Santeusanio, 1983
   Karlin, 1984   Vacca, 1981
   Lamberg & Lamb, 1980

1990s–2000s

Aspects of Reading Skill and Instruction that Cross Content

Alvermann & Phelps, 1998   Manzo & Manzo, 1997
Brozo & Simpson, 1999   Ryder & Graves, 1998
Irvin, 1998

Reading Process and Strategic Reading

Allan & Miller, 2000   Brozo & Simpson, 1999
Anders & Guzzetti, 1996   Manzo, Manzo, & Thomas, 2005
Boke, 2004   Schoenbach, Greenleaf, Cziko, & Hurwitz, 1999

Whole-School Reading Programs

Allan & Miller, 2000   Kane, 2007
Duffy, 1990   Manzo, Manzo, & Thomas, 2005
Irvin, 1998   Robb, 2000
Irvin, Buehl, & Klemp, 2003

Textbooks with "Middle School" and "Secondary/High School" in Their Titles

Allan & Miller, 2000   Schoenbach, Greenleaf, Cziko, & Hurwitz, 1999
Lenski, Wham, & Johns, 1999

Textbooks that Focused on Middle School Only

Irvin, 1998   Robb, 2000
Morretta & Ambrosini, 2000   Rycik & Irvin, 2005

Textbooks with "Literacy" in Their Titles

Allan & Miller, 2000   Manzo & Manzo, 1997
Alvermann & Phelps, 1998   Manzo, Manzo, & Estes, 1997
Anders & Guzzetti, 1996   Manzo, Manzo, & Thomas, 2005
Brozo & Simpson, 1999   Readence, Bean, & Baldwin, 2001
Irvin, 1998   Roe, Stoodt, & Burns, 1998, 2001
Kane, 2007   Vacca & Vacca, 2005

Textbooks with "Content Area" (or "Across Disciplines") in Their Titles

Billmeyer & Barton, 1998   Moore, Moore, Cunningham, & Cunningham, 2001
Conley, 1995   Readence, Bean, & Baldwin, 2001
Daniels & Zemelman, 2004   Richardson & Morgan, 1994
Irvin, Buehl, & Klemp, 2003   Ruddell, 1997
Lapp, Flood, & Farnan, 1996   Ryder & Graves, 1998
McCarthy, Rasool, & Banks, 1993   Standal & Betza, 1990

Textbooks with both "Content Area" and "Literacy" in Their Titles

Allan & Miller, 2000   Brozo & Simpson, 1999
Alvermann & Phelps, 1998   Kane, 2007
Anders & Guzzetti, 1996   Manzo, Manzo, & Estes, 2001
Billmeyer & Barton, 1998   Vacca & Vacca, 2005

Textbooks that Include Focus on Writing

Alvermann & Phelps, 1998   Manzo & Manzo, 1997
Anders & Guzzetti, 1996   Moore, Moore, Cunningham, & Cunningham, 2001
Brozo & Simpson, 1999   Ruddell, 1997, 2005
Irvin, 1998   Ryder & Graves, 1998

Textbooks that Include Focus on Technology

Brozo & Simpson, 1999   Roe, Stoodt, and Burns, 1998 & 2001
Kane, 2007   Ryder & Graves, 1998
Manzo & Manzo, 1997   Vacca & Vacca, 2005
Readence, Bean, & Baldwin, 2001

Note: This table, while far from complete, includes sample textbooks from different decades with selected foci.

Teaching Disciplinary Literacy to Adolescents: Rethinking Content-Area Literacy

TIMOTHY SHANAHAN
CYNTHIA SHANAHAN
University of Illinois at Chicago

*In this article, Timothy and Cynthia Shanahan argue that "disciplinary literacy" —
advanced literacy instruction embedded within content-area classes such as math, science, and social studies — should be a focus of middle and secondary school settings.
Moving beyond the oft-cited "every teacher a teacher of reading" philosophy that has
historically frustrated secondary content-area teachers, the Shanahans present data
collected during the first two years of a study on disciplinary literacy that reveal how
content experts and secondary content teachers read disciplinary texts, make use of
comprehension strategies, and subsequently teach those strategies to adolescent readers. Preliminary findings suggest that experts from math, chemistry, and history read
their respective texts quite differently; consequently, both the content-area experts and
secondary teachers in this study recommend different comprehension strategies for
work with adolescents. This study not only has implications for which comprehension strategies might best fit particular disciplinary reading tasks, but also suggests
how students may be best prepared for the reading, writing, and thinking required by
advanced disciplinary coursework.*

Reading is commonly viewed as a basic set of skills, widely adaptable and applicable to all kinds of texts and reading situations. Accordingly, in the 1990s,
most states took on the challenge of improving young children's reading skills,
assuming that once the basics of literacy were accomplished, students would
be well equipped for literacy-related tasks later in life (Blair, 1999). The idea
that basic reading skills automatically evolve into more advanced reading skills,
and that these basic skills are highly generalizable and adaptable, is partially
correct: The basic perceptual and decoding skills that are connected with early

Harvard Educational Review   Vol. 78   No. 1   Spring 2008
Copyright © by the President and Fellows of Harvard College

literacy learning (e.g., phonics, phonological awareness, sight vocabulary) are entailed in virtually all reading tasks (Rayner & Pollatsek, 1994).

However, as one moves along the continuum of literacy learning, what is learned becomes less generally useful. Take one very simple example: Children in kindergarten and first grade may learn to read words like *of, is,* and *the.* These words are ubiquitous; they appear not only in primers but in the *New York Times,* U.S. State Department documents, medical books, and so on. As learning progresses, instruction necessarily focuses attention on words in more constrained and specific contexts. For example, it is beneficial to be able to pronounce and interpret words like *paradigm, rhombus, esoteric,* and *reluctant,* but these words have relatively less general applicability (e.g., *rhombus* may only appear in math books, and *esoteric* is rarely included in primary school texts and only shows up occasionally after that).

The Need for Advanced Literacy Instruction

We have spent a century of education beholden to this generalist notion of literacy learning — the idea that if we just provide adequate basic skills, from that point forward kids with adequate background knowledge will be able to read anything successfully. That view once seemed feasible because, following it, schools were able to produce a sufficiently educated population for the nation's economic needs. Although many students did not actually accomplish the highest, most specialized kinds of reading, there were enough to provide all of the chemists, accountants, engineers, and managers needed by the nation's economy. Those who developed more sophisticated reading skills with a minimum of later instructional support moved into jobs that required greater amounts of literacy, and those who did not extend their literacy skills worked in blue-collar jobs. A kind of stasis existed. Literacy was somewhat correlated with income, but there were high-literacy jobs that were low paying (e.g., teaching, secretarial work) and low-literacy ones that provided higher wages (e.g., auto assembly).

During the past generation, the expansion of information-based technology, the internationalization of labor markets, and the changing of workplace demands have increased the importance of literacy as an ingredient of economic and social participation (Carnevale, 1991). Increasingly U.S. jobs — even the shrinking pool of blue-collar jobs — require and depend upon reading. A generation ago, jobs in factories, foundries, and mills commonly required no reading, and many other jobs (e.g., law enforcement, practical nursing, trucking) required reading in limited amounts, but this has changed. The rising correlation between education and income is evidence of the increasing literacy orientation of many workplaces (Arc, Phillips, & McKenzie, 2000; Barton & Jenkins, 1995). Likewise, literacy is now clearly implicated in health maintenance (Berkman, DeWalt, Pignone, Sheridan, Lohr, Lux, et al., 2004), academic success (American College Testing, 2006), avoidance of the criminal justice system (Beck & Harrison, 2001), and social and civic involvement (Kirsch, Jungeblut, & Jenkins, 1993), including voting and keeping informed of public issues (Venezky, Kaestle, & Sum, 1987).

Despite the growing need for literacy, especially higher-level literacy skills, assessment data suggest that adolescents today read no better, and perhaps marginally worse, than a generation ago. According to the most recent National Assessment of Educational Progress (NAEP) (Grigg, Donahue, & Dion, 2007), high school students are scoring lower in reading now than they did in 1992. Fewer high school students are reading at proficient levels, and markedly more are reading at below-basic levels. Reading scores for U.S. eighth graders stayed steady during that period (Perle, Grigg, & Donahue, 2005), but only about 70 percent of students who enter eighth grade in the United States even complete high school (Frost, 2003). According to American College Testing (2006), the proportion of students on track for successful college work actually diminishes as students advance through U.S. schools from eighth through twelfth grade.

The most recent international data are no more reassuring than the national test scores (Kirsch, de Jong, Lafontaine, McQueen, Mendelovits, & Monseur, 2002). The Programme for International Assessment (PISA) is a standardized assessment designed specifically to compare student achievement across international boundaries. This evaluation reveals that American 15-year-olds do not perform as well in reading as their age-matched peers in fourteen other countries: Australia, Austria, Belgium, Canada, Finland, France, Iceland, Ireland, Japan, Korea, New Zealand, Norway, Sweden, and the United Kingdom. The students in most of these countries perform better than U.S. students on all of the various reading scales. Meanwhile, American high school students cannot read at the level necessary to compete in a global economy, and many are likely to have difficulties in taking care of their health needs (Berkman et al., 2004) or participating in civic life (Kirsch et al., 1993; Venezky et al., 1987).

In the 1990s, recognizing that U.S. schools were no longer producing enough highly educated students who could participate in jobs that required reading, various state and federal programs were initiated to improve reading achievement among young children. Within the scope of the standards movement in education, many state governors declared third-grade reading attainment to be the goal, and a plethora of new programs and initiatives emerged, including, at the federal level, the Reading Excellence Act (which, among other things, rewarded states for upgrading their reading preparation standards for primary-grade teachers), Early Reading First, and the now-beleaguered Reading First (U.S. Department of Education, 2007). Publishers responded with new upgraded curricular materials and assessments targeting the reading needs of young children, and early interventions for unsuccessful beginners (such as Reading Recovery) became commonplace in the schools. These extensive (and expensive) efforts have apparently been successful, as national reading scores for young children have climbed since 1992, and growth has been apparent in both NAEP test scores and trend items (Perle et al., 2005; Perle & Moran, 2005). America's nine-year-olds are reading markedly better by all measures than they were fifteen years ago.

However, the idea that early literacy improvement would automatically lead to consequent later growth in literacy has not panned out. Early learning gains, instead of catapulting students toward continued literacy advancement, disappear by the time these students reach eighth grade (Perle et al., 2005). The idea that enhanced early teaching practices will continue to provide literacy advantages without continued enhanced teaching efforts — the so-called "vaccination" conception of teaching (Shanahan & Barr, 1995, p. 982) — does not appear to hold. Apparently, strong early reading skills do not automatically develop into more complex skills that enable students to deal with the specialized and sophisticated reading of literature, science, history, and mathematics (Perle et al., 2005). Most students need explicit teaching of sophisticated genres, specialized language conventions, disciplinary norms of precision and accuracy, and higher-level interpretive processes. Simply put, sound later-reading instruction needs to be built on a solid foundation of sound early-reading instruction if students are going to reach literacy levels that enable them to compete for the most lucrative jobs in the U.S. economy. Sixty-five thousand immigrant workers enter the United States each year in order to make up for the shortfall in availability of managers, engineers, analysts, and other high-education/high-salary positions, and there is continued pressure to increase these numbers (Levy & Murnane, 2004; Mitchell, Carnes, & Mendosa, 2006).

Given these gaps, there is a clear need to expand literacy instruction upward through the grades and to better support the reading of older students. But how can that best be accomplished? One possibility would be to focus mainly on extending basic literacy instruction upward for the lowest-achieving adolescents. However, a consideration of the new demands for literacy (Levy & Murnane, 2004) would suggest that there is a growing need for more sophisticated literacy development, and not just for the lowest achievers. Thus, there is a need to identify what a more advanced literacy curriculum might be and to determine how it could best be implemented. The remainder of this article will describe a Carnegie-funded research project that is identifying sophisticated, high school–appropriate literacy skills and exploring how to implement them within teacher-preparation programs.

A Model of Literacy Progression

The pyramid in Figure 1 illustrates our perspective on how the development of literacy progresses. The base of the pyramid represents the highly generalizable basic skills that are entailed in all or most reading tasks. These skills include basic decoding skills, understanding of various print and literacy conventions (e.g., understanding that text must be meaningful, the primacy of print versus illustrations, directionality, concept of word), recognition of high-frequency words, and some basic fluency routines (e.g., responding appro-

FIGURE 1   *The Increasing Specialization of Literacy Development*

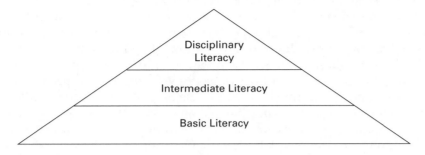

Basic Literacy: Literacy skills such as decoding and knowledge of high-frequency words that underlie virtually all reading tasks.

Intermediate Literacy: Literacy skills common to many tasks, including generic comprehension strategies, common word meanings, and basic fluency.

Disciplinary Literacy: Literacy skills specialized to history, science, mathematics, literature, or other subject matter.

priately to basic punctuation). Students also come to expect certain organizational or structural properties in texts, such as the basic problem-centered formulation of stories or the list structure in simple expository texts, and they come to assume the presence of an author, though their conception of *author* is not particularly rhetorical, intentional, or separate from the reader's own perspective (Shanahan, 1992, 1998). Most children master these kinds of basic reading skills and conventions during the primary grades, and even those slow to develop tend to master all of these skills before high school entry.

As students go beyond these basic aspects of literacy, usually by the upper elementary grades, they begin to add more sophisticated routines and responses to their reading repertoires. These more sophisticated responses are not as widely applicable to different texts and reading situations, but nor are they particularly linked to disciplinary specializations. Students develop the skills that allow them to decode multisyllabic words quickly and easily, and they learn to respond with automaticity to words that do not appear with high frequency in text. They also learn to interpret and respond appropriately to less common forms of punctuation (e.g., split quotes, commas in a series, colons) and to know the meanings of a larger corpus of vocabulary terms, including many words that are not common in oral language (though again, these are not necessarily the highly specialized and technical terminologies of the disciplines).

Various reading comprehension responses and strategies come into play as well. For example, students develop the cognitive endurance to maintain attention to more extended discourse, to monitor their own comprehension, and to use various fix-up procedures if comprehension is not occurring (e.g., rereading, requesting help, looking words up in the dictionary). Students also gain access to more complex forms of text organization (e.g., parallel plots, circular plots, problem-solution, cause-effect), and begin to use author intention as a general tool for critical response (that is, they start to infer author purpose and to consider the implications of the choices that emanate from such a purpose). The majority of American students gain control of these intermediate reading tools by the end of middle school, but it is common to find high school students who still struggle to read texts because they have not mastered those tools.

Finally, during middle school and high school, many students begin to master even more specialized reading routines and language uses, and these particular outcomes, although powerful and valuable, are also more constrained in their applicability to most reading tasks. The constraints on the generalizability of literacy skills for more advanced readers — symbolized here by the narrowing of the pyramid — are imposed by the increasingly disciplinary and technical turn in the nature of literacy tasks. A high school student who can do a reasonably good job of reading a story in an English class might not be able to make much sense of biology or algebra books, and vice versa. Although most students manage to master basic and even intermediate literacy skills, many never gain proficiency with the more advanced skills that would enable them to read challenging texts in science, history, literature, mathematics, or technology (Grigg et al., 2007; Kutner, Greenberg, Jin, Boyle, Hsu, & Dunleavy, 2007).

In literacy development, progressing higher in the pyramid means learning more sophisticated but less generalizable skills and routines. The high-level skills and abilities embedded in these disciplinary or technical uses of literacy are probably not particularly easy to learn, since they are not likely to have many parallels in oral language use, and they have to be applied to difficult texts. (The difficulty of texts may arise from high levels of abstraction, ambiguity, and subtlety, or from content that differs from, or even contradicts, students' life experiences. For example, physics texts might explore conceptions of how objects fall that are inconsistent with how most individuals conceptualize such phenomena.) But something else makes these high-level skills very difficult to learn: They are rarely taught. By the time adolescent students are being challenged by disciplinary texts, literacy instruction often has evaporated altogether or has degenerated into a reiteration of general reading strategies (the general study skills that have usually been the mainstay of "content-area reading") — most likely to benefit only the lowest-functioning students (Bereiter & Bird, 1985). Given the range of student abilities and the difficulty of learning these more sophisticated routines, is it any wonder so many teachers fail to teach these aspects of literacy at all (Alvermann, O'Brien, & Dillon, 1990; Pressley, 2004)?

The pyramid illustrates the increasing specialization of reading skills, but a similar structure could be used to accurately illustrate the declining amount of instructional support and assistance that is usually provided to students as they progress through the grades. Given the common belief that literacy skills are fully developed in the early grades, we would expect less literacy instruction in the upper grades — the vaccination model. However, there are also many institutional barriers that prevent the delivery of effective reading instruction in the middle and high school grades. Table 1 summarizes some of the differences between elementary and secondary school literacy instruction and context, and it reveals a much greater infrastructure of social and material support for reading instruction for younger students than for older ones.

Addressing the Need

Obviously, there are many barriers to successfully addressing the nation's literacy needs among adolescents, perhaps none more important than the preparation of a teaching force capable of delivering the needed instruction. To that end, the Carnegie Corporation recently began funding a network of preservice teacher-education projects. These projects require several teacher-preparation institutions across the country to identify effective practices for teaching adolescent literacy and to develop course curricula that would help prospective teachers integrate literacy instruction into the content domains. These individual projects are quite diverse in their approaches to these issues (for more information on this effort, see www.carnegie.org/literacy/initiative.html). Our Carnegie project has challenged us to rethink the basic curriculum of adolescent literacy instruction, particularly with regard to reading comprehension strategy instruction within the disciplines. Specifically, we spent the first year of our project working with specialists in mathematics, chemistry, and history to identify sophisticated and appropriate reading skills that would better enable students to progress in these subject areas, and then, using that information, we began studying how to help students learn these skills. We spent the second year of the project attempting to implement these new strategies in urban high schools and in our secondary teacher-preparation programs.

One of the requirements of the initiative was to involve members of the arts and sciences in these efforts to rethink our response to adolescent literacy. We accomplished this task by creating teams for each of three disciplines: chemistry, history, and mathematics. The teams included two "disciplinary experts," university professors who were researchers in their discipline; two teacher educators who prepared teachers to teach that discipline in high school; two high school teachers who taught disciplinary content to students at diverse schools in and around Chicago; and two literacy experts (us). This research design reflected our assumption that teachers in the disciplines resist literacy strategy instruction when that instruction is promulgated by individuals who are literacy experts without particular content knowledge (O'Brien, Stuart, & Moje, 1995). Acknowledging the limitations of our disciplinary knowledge, we

TABLE 1   *Institutional and Contextual Differences in Elementary School and Middle/ High School Literacy Instruction*

	Elementary School Literacy	Middle/High School Literacy
Teacher Literacy Preparation	Extensive certification standards often requiring multiple courses in reading (Darling-Hammond, 1999)	Limited certification standards usually not linked to specific grade level or content standards; often no course requirements at all (Barry, 1994)
Student Learning Standards	Grade-specific learning standards for reading in all 50 states (U.S. Department of Education, 2005)	Almost no grade-specific or subject-specific reading standards (American College Testing, 2006)
Federal Support for Reading Instruction	Reading First ($5 billion)	Striving Readers ($30 million)
Screening and Monitoring Assessments for Guiding Instruction	DIBELS, PALS, TPRI, etc.	None
Reading Textbooks and Instructional Materials Aimed at Improving Reading	Extensive numbers of core, supplemental, and intervention programs	Severely limited (though growing) numbers of commercial programs — mainly intervention programs aimed at low-achieving readers (Deshler, Palincsar, Biancarosa, & Nair, 2007)
Organization of Instruction	Mainly self-contained classrooms that permit intensive and extensive literacy instruction Extensive reading supports offered to low-achieving readers, including in-class and pull-out interventions	Departmentalized teaching that limits the possibility of extended literacy instruction Severely limited instructional interventions to support struggling readers
Parent Involvement	Great amount of parent awareness, involvement, and extensive ability to help their children develop literacy	Limited parent awareness of literacy development, limited involvement in helping their children with academic learning

were willing to rethink traditional reading comprehension strategy instruction based on the insights we could draw from these content specialists.

We also entered this study with a particular notion of "disciplinary knowledge." We believe, along with a number of linguists and cognitive scientists (Bazerman, 1998; Fang, 2004; Geisler, 1994; Halliday, 1998; Schleppegrell,

2004), that although the disciplines share certain commonalities in their use of academic language (Snow, 1987), they also engage in unique practices. That is, there are differences in how the disciplines create, disseminate, and evaluate knowledge, and these differences are instantiated in their use of language.

There are at least three views regarding why this is so. One view is that the various disciplines — ostensibly to protect the public from "charlatans" but really to preserve a power base — created professional organizations with standards and distinct ways of expressing themselves (Geisler, 1994). Others reject that view, claiming instead that the differences are a natural outgrowth of differences in the nature or kind of knowledge being created by the disciplines (Schleppegrell, 2004). Still others argue that these differences are more a reflection of the *activities* in which the disciplines find themselves engaged (Bazerman, 1998). These activities include struggles for power, alliances, theoretical shifts, the creation of new forms of knowledge, and so on, which converge in acts of written communication. Together these positions are persuasive that the function of discipline-based texts is both ideational and social. Texts serve to advance knowledge while at the same time serving to maintain a field's hegemony. The end result is that the literacy demands on students are unique, depending on the discipline they are studying.

Since we initially needed to identify the specialized reading skills and demands within the disciplines, we spent the entire first year of the Carnegie project immersed in discovering how each of these disciplines used literacy, employing several procedures to help us work toward that sometimes-elusive goal. We brought each panel together and had the panel members read various documents (e.g., textbooks, articles, web pages) for the purpose of learning how they approached reading and what they saw as the challenges to students. To guide discussions about student difficulties, we provided the teams with a literacy framework that included the dimensions of vocabulary, comprehension, fluency, and writing and asked them to identify the challenges in each dimension that students faced while reading discipline-based texts.

We also asked the disciplinary experts to read and think aloud about their own reading processes. In separate meetings, each of the experts read and thought aloud about a text that we provided (one that could be used by a high school student) and a text they were currently reading in their profession (the mathematicians chose articles, the chemists chose articles and trade magazines, and the historians chose books). We taped and transcribed these think-alouds and took both the protocols and a summary to the disciplinary-group meetings, where we discussed the results. From those think-aloud discussions, we distilled a list of "reading facilitators" that the discipline experts used as they read. We also introduced the concept of *strategy* to the teams, showed them some commonly used "across the content area" strategies that are often taught in reading courses, and asked them for a critique. In addition, we charged the teams with proposing strategies that they thought could help students learn from their texts. These newly proposed strategies were then critiqued by the groups.

The other major goal of the project was to see if we could implement these strategies successfully with high school students and train beginning teachers to teach these strategies to their students. The high school teachers on our panels spent the second year pilot-testing some of these strategies in their class-rooms — those that the groups believed would be most helpful. We observed and videotaped these teachers as they engaged in this teaching, later showing the videotapes to the team for their insights on how the strategies might be strengthened. These teachers also reported back to the disciplinary groups and shared the students' products that emerged from the lessons they taught. We used those pilot tests to identify potentially useful strategies for more rig-orous later study. We also involved students who were enrolled in a teacher-preparation course for middle and high school literacy teaching in observa-tion of these teachers and provided them with information about the project. Now we are revising that course to ensure that the literacy in the disciplines is more accurately and appropriately represented and that the preservice teach-ers learn strategies more specific to the specialized needs of their discipline.

Lessons Learned in the First Year

The first year of the project allowed a specification of how deeply different the disciplines are. Each of the disciplinary experts emphasized a different array of reading processes, suggesting the focused and highly specialized nature of literacy at these levels. For example, during think-alouds, the mathematicians emphasized rereading and close reading as two of their most important strat-egies. One of the mathematicians explained that, unlike other fields, even "function" words were important. "'The' has a very different meaning than 'a,'" he explained. Students often attempt to read mathematics texts for the gist or general idea, but this kind of text cannot be appropriately understood without close reading. Math reading requires a precision of meaning, and each word must be understood specifically in service to that particular meaning. In fact, the other mathematician noted that it sometimes took years of rereading for him to completely understand a particular proof.

The chemists were most interested in the transformation of information from one form to another. That is, when reading prose, they were visualizing, writing down formulas, or, if a diagram or a chart were on the page, going back and forth between the graph and the chart. One chemist explained, "They give you the structure, the structure of the sensor is given, so I was looking at the picture as I was reading and I tried to relate what was in the picture to what they were saying about how mercury binds to one part of the molecule." This explanation, corroborated by the chemists' other comments, helped us understand that in chemistry, different or alternative representations (e.g., pictures, graphs or charts, text, or diagrams) of an idea are essential for a full understanding of the concepts. These various representations are processed recursively as reading progresses.

The historians, on the other hand, emphasized paying attention to the author or source when reading any text. That is, before reading, they would consider who the authors of the texts were and what their biases might be. Their purpose during the reading seemed to be to figure out what story a particular author wanted to tell; in other words, they were keenly aware that they were reading an interpretation of historical events and not "Truth." Note what one historian said when reading a text about Abraham Lincoln: "I saw, oh . . . I don't know him [the author] very well, but he is part of a right-wing group of southern conservatives who is a secessionist. I'm not sure that the best model for thinking about Lincoln as a president is one that comes from a racist. So I have my critical eyes up a little bit, so it's a bit of a stretch to be friendly to, so I wanted to make sure to read it fairly."

In this nuanced example, the historian is revealing that he does not read the text as truth, but rather as an interpretation that has to be judged based on its credibility. He attempts to evaluate its credibility through an examination of the author's biases. Knowing that the author belongs to a right-wing southern secessionist group, the historian understands that any criticism of Abraham Lincoln's role in the Civil War may be fueled by this right-wing stance. However, he also knows that he, as a reader, has his own biases, and that his disregard for right-wing secessionist groups might color his reading to the point that he could miss important insights. The point is that he reads with a view in which both author and reader are fallible and positioned.

We have come to believe that the varied emphases shown in these examples are related to the intellectual values of a discipline and the methods by which scholarship is created in each of the fields. History relies heavily on document analysis (*document* being widely defined to include film, interview protocol, primary, secondary, or tertiary documents, and so on). These documents are collected after an event has occurred, and the selection and analysis of documents take place somewhat simultaneously. Thus, it is possible for a historian to choose and analyze evidence, unwittingly perhaps, that corroborates a previously held perspective. The historians we studied read with that caution in mind. Unfortunately, the nature of historiography (that is, how history is written and presented) is not often the subject of discussion in adolescent history classes. Students believe that they are reading to learn "the facts" and fail to take into account potential bias unless they are explicitly taught to do so (Hynd-Shanahan, Holschuh, & Hubbard, 2005).

Unlike historians, chemists create knowledge through experimentation. The findings of experiments are somewhat dependent upon the quality of the instrumentation, the design, and the statistical analysis. However, these variables are all decided on prior to the actual experiment. The findings are generalizable to other experiments under the same conditions. Although chemists are not uncritical readers, we found that the chemists we studied did have more confidence than historians in the utility of the knowledge that had been created; they believed they could use that knowledge to predict what would happen under similar conditions. What was important to them in reading, consequently, was a full understanding of the way an experiment took place and the processes it uncovered. Gaining that full understanding required them to think about the phenomenon being presented in prose, to visualize it, and to manipulate it in formulas and equations.

The mathematicians we studied were theoretical rather than applied mathematicians. In their field, errorless proofs are by their very nature true, and the purpose of their work is to create these proofs; hence, to create truth. Because proofs must be error free, they are read carefully in order to discover any possible error. Every word matters. Rereading is essential. One mathematician said, "I try to determine whether it [the solution to the problem] is correct. That's the important criteria, and it's by no means assumed. It would be unusual to read a paper like this and not find something incorrect." This mathematician is illustrating the belief that truth (correctness within the confines of a particular problem) is attainable if one can determine an error-free solution. However, errors are easy to make, so vigilance is required.

In summary, the disciplinary experts we studied approached reading in very different ways, consonant with the norms and expectations of their particular disciplines. We left this phase of the study convinced that the nature of the disciplines is something that must be communicated to adolescents, along with the ways in which experts approach the reading of text. Students' text comprehension, we believe, benefits when students learn to approach different texts with different lenses. There is evidence to suggest that this is true. Studies attempting to teach history students to "read like historians" have found that students who are taught to use the approaches that historians use when they read (to evaluate the source and context of the textual information and corroborate it with other texts) learn to think more critically about what they read (Hynd-Shanahan et al., 2005; VanSledright & Kelly, 1998), and to write better essays (De La Paz, 2005), although they do not necessarily end up with more historical information (Nokes, Dole, & Hacker, 2007). Studies of adolescent students' science writing have found writing improvement when teachers show students how to write for different purposes (e.g., to describe, to persuade) and how to use different structures (e.g., research articles, lay explanations, patent applications, lab notes) for scientific writing (Hand & Prain, 2002).

In addition to studying the processes that experts used as they read, we also studied the team members' perceptions of the literacy challenges that students face as they read — and learn to read — disciplinary texts. As stated earlier, we provided the teams with a framework that included four literacy components: vocabulary, comprehension, fluency, and writing. We explained and demonstrated what these components are, requested that the team read various texts used in high schools, and asked for their thoughts about the problems students would have when confronted with such materials. Not only did the three teams approach reading in different ways, they also had unique ideas about the challenges students would face regarding each of the components.

Regarding vocabulary, for example, the mathematicians and chemists alike noted the challenge of words that had both general and specific meanings. However, unlike the chemists, the mathematicians were adamant that the precise mathematical definition needed to be learned — memorized, as it were — in order to obtain true understanding of the mathematical meaning in contrast to its more general meaning. For example, a student must know that *prime* refers to *a positive integer not divisible by another positive integer (without a remainder) except by itself and by 1*. Prime also means *perfect, chief,* or *of the highest grade,* but none of these nonmathematical meanings aids in understanding the mathematical meaning. In contrast, the historians did not even mention words with both general and specific meanings. Rather, they noted that although history did not have as much technical vocabulary as other fields, technical terminology was often co-opted from fields such as political science, economics, and sociology. In addition, the historians noted that the difficulty level of the general vocabulary could be quite high. Terms such as *aggressive* or *adversarial* are difficult, yet their meaning is not necessarily specific to history. They also mentioned that students often had to read and understand words that are not current (e.g., the Gilded Age) or that need to be understood metaphorically (e.g., Black Thursday*)*.

The mathematicians also emphasized that letters and symbols signify specific meanings in some cases but, as variables, change their meaning in others. Being able to read these symbols embedded in both English prose and algebraic equations was considered to be crucial. For instance, when one of the mathematicians was thinking aloud during the reading of a journal article, he explained that one of the first things he did when reading was to memorize the variables that were to be used in the rest of the article. Even though the article began as mostly prose, he would soon be reading only symbols, and he did not want to interrupt his flow of thought by having to return to the definitions. Further complicating the use of symbols, the chemists noted that symbols needed to be understood at both macro and micro levels. For example, each symbol on the atomic chart must be thought of not only in terms of the substance it describes, but also in terms of its atomic makeup. That is, H_2O is not just the symbol for *water* in the same way that *n* is the symbol for *number;* H_2O also specifies that there are two atoms of hydrogen for every atom of oxygen.

Linguists have studied the differences in social science and science texts, and their studies corroborate these findings. A characteristic of academic language, for instance, is *nominalization* — the transformation of a verb to a noun (Halliday & Martin, 1993; Martin, 1993). In science texts, nominalization is used to create technical vocabulary. For example, rather than write "salt dissolved," a scientist might write "salt goes through a process of dissolution." Nominalization serves to move a phenomenon from the particular or specific to the abstract or general. The term *dissolution* can be used to describe the process that occurs with a variety of substances, and it should be learned apart from its association with salt. The meaning of *dissolution* as it is used in chemistry is quite specific and very different from its other meanings, two of which are "indulgence in sensual pleasures; debauchery" and "extinction of life: death" (Pickett, 2000). Although the specificity of technical definitions was mentioned by the chemists with whom we talked, nominalization was not. Nevertheless, the phenomenon does have implications for high school chemistry students. The abstract language that is used in chemistry texts is daunting for many high school students because it makes the subject matter more distant and disconnected from everyday experiences.

In history texts, nominalization and the resulting abstraction do exist, but these occur most frequently with general terms (Schleppegrell, 2004). Note the following hypothetical example to illustrate this point:

> The enlargement of the nation's capacity to produce weapons, the advent of the aeroplane, and the improvement in worldwide communication systems through the telegraph increased the likelihood that the United States would enter the war.

In this example, the events are nominalized as subjects of the sentence and are buried in the clauses. The process, *increased,* is realized as the verb. Even without technical vocabulary, this sentence is difficult. An expert knows after reading the sentence that the United States produced weapons, developed a viable airplane, and utilized the telegraph to communicate with other countries, but that is not the point of the sentence. In addition, the arcane spelling of *aeroplane* may reflect the time period described but it is likely unknown to many students. History texts, then, present challenges to readers that are qualitatively different from those presented by texts in other disciplines.

Science texts have a high degree of lexical density, higher than that of either mathematics or history. *Lexical density* is marked by the number of content words embedded in clauses, by the total number of content words, or through the percentage of content words in relation to the total number of words (Fang, 2004). These content words are technical terms, which must be deeply learned in order to learn the science behind them. For example, biology students must not only know that *digestion* is the assimilation of food in the body, but also understand the process by which digestion occurs.

The differences among the texts of different disciplines result in unique challenges for readers. These text differences, however, are not often within the purview of literacy courses in teacher-preparation institutions, nor are they the subject of discipline-based methods course work; for that matter, they are not usually discussed in the basic content courses teachers take within their discipline. As a result, teachers are not prepared to address the challenges posed by the special demands of texts across the various disciplines. Yet, adolescent students engage in a daily struggle to learn the content of the various disciplines — content that is instantiated in the academic discourse that is an outgrowth of the differences in the disciplines themselves.

Thus, the first year of the study helped us to understand the special literacy demands presented by the different disciplines. The interviews, discussions, analytic tasks, and informal conversations revealed three very different approaches to reading that drew on the ways these disciplines create, communicate, and evaluate knowledge.

Lessons Learned in the Second Year

In the second year of our study, we focused on the creation of discipline-specific strategies. This work was challenging. Every member of each team seemed fully fascinated by the key role of literacy in their own lives and in the lives of high school students learning disciplinary concepts, and they could clearly discuss the unique challenges that students faced as they read texts within their discipline. However, the experts, and in some cases the teacher educators and high school teachers, displayed some reluctance in embracing the idea of strategy instruction. For most the concept was new, and the content-area reading strategies we shared with them may have seemed a little contrived. Thus, our introduction to strategy instruction in the team meetings fell somewhat flat, except in history, where one of the high school teachers was "a strategy nut" (a title given to him by one of the disciplinary experts). This reluctance was revealing to us because it mirrored the disinclination of the preservice students in the high school literacy class.

The chemistry team's reluctance only changed when we introduced our version of structured note-taking or structured summarization, a strategy that we based specifically on their insights about chemistry reading. Using this strategy, students are required to take notes in a chart format. Each section of the chart reflected the information that these chemistry specialists indicated would comprise an essential reading of chemistry texts. That is, because chemistry is about the properties of substances and their reactions, a reader who paid attention to these elements would be engaging in a disciplinary-focused reading. Thus, the chart required students to summarize substances, properties, processes, and interactions. We had illustrated the chart using information from one of the chemistry textbooks the team members had shared with us. One of the chemists who had been somewhat dismissive of teaching traditional content-area reading strategies (such as summarization) in chemistry classes reacted by saying, "Well, if they used this, they would be learning chemistry." He then suggested a modification (the inclusion of a place to summarize atomic expression). Evidently, the difference between this strategy and a strategy like summarization was its subject-matter specificity. This strategy was not just about understanding text; it was also about understanding the essence of chemistry.

This structured-summarization strategy meshed well with concerns the chemists had expressed earlier when they examined high school chemistry textbooks: the need to identify where the chemistry was. That is, although they understood that some of the information in the text was included purely for motivational purposes or to establish context for students, they were concerned that what students were actually supposed to learn about chemistry was obscured and hidden by these devices. One of the chemistry teachers bitterly complained about a text she had to use in which each chapter began with a real-life problem (such as lake pollution) that was then followed by an explanation of the chemistry behind the problem. She complained that the students were not learning the chemistry. Chemistry learning is somewhat hierarchical in nature. The concepts build on each other, and these concepts can then be applied to situations. That is, the principles are taught as abstractions and the particulars are exemplars of the abstractions. This chemistry book, however, perseverated on the particular, providing students with little real opportunity to learn the abstractions that could be used to solve other problems.

Mathematicians revealed a similar concern. They decried the presence of "extraneous" text in mathematics textbooks. As Solomon and O'Neill (1998) explain, mathematicians make fairly clear distinctions between the complementary informal or introductory material in text that includes analogies, examples, motivations, and so on, and the formal structure of definitions, theorems, proofs, and explanations. The panelists were concerned that students would not be able to make those distinctions, and thus that the textbooks are made more difficult rather than easier by the inclusion of such devices.

In the mathematics team meeting, even the mathematics-specific strategies we generated garnered little enthusiasm. However, one of the mathematics teacher educators shared some of their preferred strategies with the group. One was a mathematics-structured note-taking strategy. In this strategy, students would write the mathematics "big idea" that was being studied in the first column. In the next column, they would write the explanation of the big idea, and in the following columns, they would provide an example, show a formula, make a graph or diagram, or otherwise illustrate the big idea. They were to complete this work as they were reading and then use it as a study guide prior to a unit test. The mathematicians wanted to make sure that if a concept was being defined, the precise mathematical definition would be used and the idea would be added to the chart.

In the history meetings, the team liked a number of strategies and made suggestions for improvement. One such strategy was the history events chart. As students read about a particular event, they write down answers to the questions of who, what, where, when, how, and why in order to summarize the key narrative events. They do the same with each event they read about. However, the compelling task — the one that addresses a specific disciplinary problem in reading history — is to determine what the relationship is between the first and second event, between the second and third event, and so on. Students are asked to think about the most likely connections and to write these on the chart. The historians were approving of this task because it mirrored the kind of thinking that historians do. That is, historians infer cause-and-effect relationships when they study events and what precedes and follows them. These relationships are not necessarily visible in the events themselves, nor are they always made explicit in high school history texts, so they must be surmised. And, if they *are* made explicit in the text, students generally regard the connection as "truth" rather than as the construction of the writer. The task, then, not only mirrored historians' thinking but also offered the opportunity for students to construct the cause-and-effect relationships themselves.

At the time of this writing, the high school teachers have tried out several promising strategies in the classroom, including the ones described above. One of the history teachers engaged in a quasi-experimental study of another history strategy — one he called "the multiple-gist" strategy. In this strategy, students read one text and summarize it, read another text and incorporate that text into the summary, then read another text and incorporate that text into the summary, and so on. The summary has to stay the same length, essentially, and this forces a student to use words such as *similarly* or *in contrast* when incorporating texts that can be compared or contrasted with each other. His preliminary results reveal that students who learned the multiple-gist strategy wrote longer, more coherent answers to essay questions.

In summary, what we learned from the second year of the study was that the disciplinary teams advocated strategies that mirrored the kinds of thinking and analytic practices common to their discipline. While they politely acknowledged the value of more general strategies such as KWL (thinking about what you *know* and what you *want* to learn prior to reading, and what you *learned* after reading), they did not discuss using these strategies in teaching the content.

Conclusion

Literacy levels of adolescent students have languished in recent years, despite clear improvements in the reading performance of younger students. Although schools have managed to maintain the same levels of literacy attainment in the adolescent population that have been accomplished since the early 1970s, schools have not improved adolescent literacy levels since that time. This is unfortunate, as various social changes have increased the need for advanced literacy in America's economic, social, and civic life, and without increasing literacy attainment, many students are at risk of marginalization when they leave school.

Historically, instructional efforts in literacy have focused on highly generalizable skills and abilities, such as decoding, fluency, and basic comprehension strategies that can be applied to most texts and reading circumstances across the content areas. This is reasonable with younger children, but it becomes increasingly problematic as students advance through the grades because many literacy skills and texts are highly specialized and require actions that are relatively unique. Traditional efforts to encourage every content-area teacher to be a reading teacher by pressing them to teach general-purpose strategies have neither been widely accepted by teachers in the disciplines nor particularly effective in raising reading achievement on a broad scale. More recent treatments and the data from this study suggest that as students move through school, reading and writing instruction should become increasingly disciplinary, reinforcing and supporting student performance with the kinds of texts and interpretive standards that are needed in the various disciplines or subjects.

This article describes a project that we undertook with Carnegie Corporation support. We began this project by asking how disciplinary experts approached reading and how those approaches might be translated into instruction for high school students. This project has helped us rethink the basic content-area literacy curriculum that needs to be taught to preservice teachers in secondary education, and it has revealed the benefits of having a conversation among disciplinary experts, literacy experts, high school teachers, and teacher educators. Instead of trying to convince disciplinary teachers of the value of general reading strategies developed by reading experts, we set out to see if we could formulate new strategies or jury-rig existing ones so that they would more directly and explicitly address the specific and highly specialized disciplinary reading demands of chemistry, history, and mathematics.

Formulating an appropriate curriculum for secondary teacher preparation is a necessary, though insufficient, condition for improving literacy teaching for middle and high school students. There is also a clear need for explicit literacy certification standards for teachers who teach in the disciplines, closer relationships between the faculties of education and the liberal arts and sciences (who too often separately prepare these teachers), and sufficient resources to allow preservice teachers to practice their teaching in varied disciplinary situations and classroom contexts. We believe the key to such changes, however, is a literacy curriculum that directly guides students to better meet the particular demands of reading and writing in the disciplines than has been provided by traditional conceptions of content-area reading.

References

Alvermann, D. E., O'Brien, D. G., & Dillon, D. R. (1990). What teachers do when they say they're having discussions of content area reading assignments: A qualitative analysis. *Reading Research Quarterly, 25*, 296–322.

American College Testing. (2006). *Reading between the lines: What the ACT reveals about college readiness in reading.* Iowa City, IA: Author.

Arc, G., Phillips, K. R., & McKenzie, D. (2000). *On the bottom rung: A profile of Americans in low-income working families.* Washington, DC: The Urban Institute.

Barry, A. L. (1994). The staffing of high school remedial reading programs in the United States since 1920. *Journal of Reading, 38*, 14–22.

Barton, P. E., & Jenkins, L. (1995). *Literacy and dependency: The literacy skills of welfare recipients in the United States.* Princeton, NJ: Educational Testing Service.

Bazerman, C. (1998). *Shaping written knowledge: The genre and activity of the experimental article in science.* Madison: University of Wisconsin Press.

Beck, A. J., & Harrison, P. M. (2001). *Prisoners in 2000.* Washington, DC: U.S. Department of Justice, Bureau of Justice Statistics.

Bereiter, C., & Bird, M. (1985). Use of thinking aloud in identification and teaching of reading comprehension strategies. *Cognition and Instruction, 2,* 131–156.

Berkman, N. D., DeWalt, D. A., Pignone, M. P., Sheridan, S. L., Lohr, K. N., Lux, L., Sutton, S. F., Swinson, T., & Bonito, A. J. (2004). *Literacy and health outcomes* (Evidence Report/Technology Assessment No. 87). Rockville, MD: Agency for Healthcare Research and Quality.

Blair, L. (1999). Reading across the region. *SEDLetter, 11*(1). Retrieved October 31, 2007, from http://www.sedl.org/pubs/sedletter/v11n01/

Carnevale, A. P. (1991). *America and the new economy.* San Francisco: Jossey-Bass.

Darling-Hammond, L. (1999). *Teacher quality and student achievement: A review of state policy evidence.* Tacoma, WA: Center for the Study of Teaching and Policy.

De La Paz, S. (2005). Effects of historical reasoning instruction and writing strategy mastery in culturally and academically diverse middle school classrooms. *Journal of Educational Psychology, 97,* 139–156.

Deshler, D. D., Palincsar, A. S., Biancarosa, G., & Nair, M. (2007). *Informed choices for struggling adolescent readers.* Newark, DE: International Reading Association.

Fang, Z. (2004). Scientific literacy: A functional linguistic perspective. *Science Education, 89,* 335–347.

Frost, S. (2003). Foreword. In M. L. Kamil, *Adolescents and literacy: Reading for the 21st century.* Washington, DC: Alliance for Excellent Education.

Geisler, C. (1994). *Academic literacy and the nature of expertise: Reading, writing, and knowing in academic philosophy.* Mahwah, NJ: Lawrence Erlbaum Associates.

Grigg, W., Donahue, P., & Dion, G. (2007). *The nation's report card: 12th-grade reading and mathematics 2005* (NCES 2007-468). Washington, DC: U.S. Department of Education, National Center for Education Statistics.

Halliday, M. A. K. (1998). Things and relations: Regrammaticising experience as technical knowledge. In J. R. Martin & R. Veel (Eds.), *Reading science: Critical and functional perspectives on discourses of science* (pp. 185–235). London: Routledge.

Halliday, M. A. K., & Martin, J. R. (1993). *Writing science: Literacy and discursive power.* Pittsburgh, PA: University of Pittsburgh Press.

Hand, B., & Prain, V. (2002). Influences of writing tasks on students' answers to recall and higher-level test questions. *Research in Science Education, 32,* 19–34.

Hynd-Shanahan, C., Holschuh, J., & Hubbard, B. (2005). Thinking like a historian: College students' reading of multiple historical documents. *Journal of Literacy Research, 36,* 141–176.

Kirsch, I., de Jong, J., Lafontaine, D., McQueen, J., Mendelovits, J., & Monseur, C. (2002). *Reading for change: Performance and engagement across countries. Results from PISA 2000.* Paris: Organization for Economic Co-operation and Development.

Kirsch, I. S., Jungeblut, A., & Jenkins, L. (1993). *Adult literacy in America: A first look at the results of the National Adult Literacy Survey.* Washington, DC: U.S. Department of Education, National Center for Education Statistics.

Kutner, M., Greenberg, E., Jin, Y., Boyle, B., Hsu, Y., & Dunleavy, E. (2007). *Literacy in everyday life: Results from the 2003 National Assessment of Adult Literacy* (NCES 2007-480). Washington DC: U.S. Department of Education, National Center for Education Statistics.

Levy, F., & Murnane, R. J. (2004). *The new division of labor: How computers are creating the next job market.* Princeton, NJ: Princeton University Press.

Martin, J. R. (1993). Life as a noun: Arresting the universe in science and humanities. In M. A. K. Halliday & J. R. Martin (Eds.) *Writing science: Literacy and discursive power* (pp. 221–267). Pittsburgh, PA: University of Pittsburgh Press.

Mitchell, G. R., Carnes, K. H., & Mendosa, C. (2006). *America's new deficit: The shortage of information technology workers.* Washington, DC: U.S. Department of Commerce, Office of Technology Policy.

Nokes, J. D., Dole, J. A., & Hacker, D. J. (2007). Teaching high school students to use heuristics while reading historical texts. *Journal of Educational Psychology, 99,* 492–504.

O'Brien, D. G., Stewart, R. A., & Moje, E. B. (1995). Why content literacy is difficult to infuse into the secondary school: Complexities of curriculum, pedagogy, and school culture. *Reading Research Quarterly, 30,* 442–463.

Perle, M., Grigg, W., & Donahue, P. (2005). *The nation's report card: Reading 2005 (NCES-2006-451).* Washington, DC: U.S. Department of Education, National Center for Education Statistics.

Perle, M., & Moran, R. (2005). *NAEP 2004 trends in academic progress: Three decades of student performances* (NCES 2005-464). Washington, DC: U.S. Department of Education, National Center for Education Statistics.

Pickett, J. P. (Ed.). (2000). *American Heritage Dictionary of the English Language.* Boston: Houghton Mifflin.

Pressley, M. (2004). The need for research on secondary literacy education. In T. L. Jetton, & J. A. Dole (Eds.), *Adolescent literacy research and practice* (pp. 415–432). New York: Guilford Press.

Rayner, K., & Pollatsek, A. (1994). *The psychology of reading.* Mahwah, NJ: Lawrence Erlbaum Associates.

Schleppegrell, M. J. (2004). *The language of schooling: A functional linguistics perspective.* Mahwah, NJ: Lawrence Erlbaum Associates.

Shanahan, T. (1992). Reading comprehension as a conversation with an author. In M. Pressley, K. R. Harris, & J. T. Guthrie (Eds.), *Promoting academic competence and literacy in school* (pp. 129–148). San Diego: Academic Press.

Shanahan, T. (1998). Readers' awareness of author. In N. Nelson & R. C. Calfee (Eds.), *The reading-writing connection* [Ninety-seventh yearbook of the National Society for the Study of Education] (pp. 88–111). Chicago: University of Chicago Press.

Shanahan, T., & Barr, R. (1995). Reading Recovery: An independent evaluation of the effects of an early instructional intervention for at-risk learners. *Reading Research Quarterly, 30,* 958–996.

Snow, C. E. (1987). The development of definitional skill. *Journal of Child Language, 17,* 697–710.

Solomon, Y., & O'Neill, J. (1998). Mathematics and narrative. *Language and Education, 12*(3), 210–221.

U.S. Department of Education. (2005). *Analysis of state K–3 reading standards and assessments: Final report.* Washington, DC: Education Publications Center.

U.S. Department of Education. (2007). *Guide to U.S. Department of Education programs.* Washington, DC: Office of Communications and Outreach.

VanSledright, B., & Kelly, C. (1998). Reading American history: The influence of multiple sources on six fifth graders. *Elementary School Journal, 98,* 239–265.

Venezky, R. L., Kaestle, C. F., & Sum, A. (1987). *The subtle danger: Reflections on the literacy abilities of young adults.* Princeton, NJ: Educational Testing Service.

Redefining Content-Area Literacy Teacher Education: Finding My Voice through Collaboration

RONI JO DRAPER
Brigham Young University

In this essay, Roni Jo Draper reflects upon her professional journey as a content-area literacy teacher educator, describing how she first became a literacy teacher educator and how she later came to collaborate with a group of teacher educators who specialize in disciplines such as music, theater, and mathematics. Drawing upon ethnographic data from the group's participatory action research project, she explains how their collaboration shaped her understanding of her own professional role and expanded her definitions of texts, content-area literacy, and literacy itself. Informed by insights she gained through the project, Draper argues that content-area literacy instruction should promote mastery of the intellectual discourse within a particular discipline. She also suggests ways to increase collaboration between literacy and content-area specialists working in the field of teacher education.

I am a content-area literacy teacher educator. My vocation is to help content-area teachers infuse their content instruction with literacy instruction (O'Brien, Stewart, & Moje, 1995). While some have argued that content-area literacy teacher educators ought to rename their work in this area as work in adolescent literacy in order to keep adolescents in focus when discussing literacy instruction (see Moje, Young, Readence, & Moore, 2000), I have chosen to keep the focus on content-area literacy. I do this not because I value content over students, but because content-area literacy should not be directed toward one particular age group — in this case, adolescents. Rather, content-area literacy should be addressed throughout the education of all children and youth. This is particularly crucial now, when content-area teachers must educate increasing numbers of students with linguistic differences, and thus teachers must face the dual task of teaching content and literacy. Despite this declaration, my remarks in this article are clearly focused on the preparation

Harvard Educational Review   Vol. 78   No. 1   Spring 2008
Copyright © by the President and Fellows of Harvard College

of secondary teachers and their future work with adolescent students because that represents the focus of my professional role at the university.

Literacy educators have not settled on a singular aim of content-area literacy instruction. Some descriptions suggest that content-area literacy should be a *goal* of instruction, whereas others suggest that it should be a *tool* to enhance or enable learning. For example, when Simpson (1954) admonished that "no matter how poorly or how well high school students can now read, every high school teacher can help them to read with better understanding the textbook and the other materials that are required in his course" (p. 3), he was clearly advocating literacy as a goal. However, McKenna and Robinson (1990) have described it more as a tool, explaining that "the notion of content literacy . . . suggests that students' understanding of the content presented in all subjects could be substantially enhanced through appropriate writing assignments or through supplemental reading," and thus that "content literacy does not require content-area teachers to instruct students in the mechanics of writing" (p. 185). Similarly, Vacca and Vacca (2005) have argued that the "term *content literacy* refers to the ability to use reading, writing, talking, listening, and viewing to learn subject matter in a given discipline" (p. 7). Fisher and Ivey (2005), writing for literacy teacher educators, have stated clearly that "'every teacher a teacher of reading' is not working" (p. 6). They have suggested that literacy teacher educators instead move the discussion of content-area literacy away from a focus on teaching reading and writing — literacy as a goal — to a focus on reading and writing as tools for learning by "*capitalizing* on reading and writing versus *teaching* reading and writing" (emphasis in original, p. 6). However, such a focus on content-area literacy as a tool suggests that any reading and writing done by students, as long as it is in the service of learning, is legitimate. In contrast, a focus on content-area literacy as a goal suggests that instruction around texts in content-area classrooms must focus on texts appropriate for learning, communicating, and participating.

My job as a content-area literacy teacher educator entails promoting literacy and literacy instruction across the curriculum. I have increasingly acted to support content-area literacy as a goal of instruction because I believe that one who has content knowledge must have the skills related to using content-area texts to communicate and participate, as well as to learn. I have found myself working with preservice teachers from a variety of disciplines or, in some cases, an entire middle or high school faculty, trying to help them reconsider their role in promoting literacy and providing literacy instruction. I have explained, in words similar to Gray's (1925), that "each teacher who makes reading assignments [in their content area] is responsible for the direction and supervision of the reading and study activities that are involved" (p. 71). Like other content-area literacy teacher educators, I have faced teachers, both preservice and in-service, who question the efficacy of literacy instruction for their classrooms; who question their ability to promote literacy; and who question whether doing so will take time away from content instruction (Ratekin,

Simpson, Alvermann, & Dishner, 1985; Stewart & O'Brien, 1989). These questions have prompted me to seek more convincing arguments for content-area literacy than the traditional tool-versus-goal dichotomy.

My search for a clear aim for content-area literacy instruction and ways to promote content-area literacy with secondary teachers has been aided by collaborations with content-area teacher educators from a variety of disciplines (e.g., music, theater, and mathematics). We have conceptualized our work together as a form of participatory action research (Kremmis & McTaggart, 2000; Reason, 1994). One of the basic tenets of participatory action research is that participants serve simultaneously as coresearchers and corespondents. As such, we have established co-ownership of our research and have opened ourselves to interrogation as we have simultaneously interrogated each other. Participatory action research is preferred when individuals seek ways to do research *with* others rather than *on* others, with the goal of understanding and improving practice. In this case, our goal was to investigate content-area literacy and to improve our work with preservice teachers.

Through my collaborations with other teacher educators from areas outside of literacy, I have come to question universal claims made by some content-area literacy educators, such as:

- literacy instruction should happen in all classrooms regardless of content;
- literacy instructional methods can be modified for instruction in all content areas; and
- all content-area teachers would benefit by taking a course in content-area literacy methods.

While these are not all the claims, they capture the essence of those commonly made by content-area literacy teacher educators. These claims imply that literacy methodologies, with slight adjustments, can be used in "any reading-based lesson in any subject at any level" (Manzo, Manzo, & Estes, 2001, p. 45). Indeed, through my collaborations I have come to question anew the purpose of content-area literacy instruction, the promises made about the potential of content-area literacy instruction, and the universality of instructional practices recommended to teachers in order to enact content-area literacy instruction across all content areas.

Ultimately, these questions have led me to rethink what it means to be a content-area literacy teacher educator. My rethinking has been aided by my collaboration with teacher educators in other fields. These collaborations eventually caused me to doubt the value of advice I could offer to *all* teachers, regardless of the content. For example, after several weeks of observing my colleague Dan as he taught a mathematics course for preservice elementary teachers, I said to him:

> I know a lot of methods for teaching people how to read and comprehend. . . .
> I'm not in a position right now of knowing if that would help. . . . I'm not getting
> a sense [that] maybe it would help if [you taught with] a different kind of activ-

ity to help students get [the mathematics]. . . . So that makes me question, well, maybe the reading [instructional] strategies that I have — not that they won't apply, or they don't apply, but maybe there are other ways to [teach students how to read and write mathematics] that are just as effective. (personal communication, March 8, 2001)

Dan's mathematics instruction was based on his understanding of both mathematics and social constructivist pedagogies, as advocated by school mathematics reforms and standards documents (National Council of Teachers of Mathematics [NCTM], 1989, 2000). As I watched his instruction each week, I was struck by how masterful he was in helping students develop rich images for fractions, make sense of the various operations with fractions, and comprehend other mathematical concepts. I also watched as he helped his students learn how to describe and justify their thinking with drawings and other writing. I could not imagine that Dan would be able to improve the instruction with any guidance I might offer him as a literacy educator. The realization that I seemingly had nothing to offer a mathematics instructor caused me to rethink my position as a content-area literacy educator. I began to "be critical of my own biases," namely, my belief that appealing to content-area literacy instructional methods can improve mathematics instruction. I went even further, questioning my purpose as a content-area literacy teacher educator. If Dan's students were engaging in deep mathematics discussions, learning mathematics by developing images, and describing and justifying their thinking with manipulatives, pictures, and written explanations — activities that I considered literacy — *and* he did this all without considering literacy explicitly or tapping into literacy instructional practices, what could I offer to improve the mathematics learning and literacy of his students?

My doubt has led to inquiry about the nature of content-area literacy and my role as a content-area literacy teacher educator. In the process, I have realized that my inquiry would require me "to be at all times ready to dump [my] whole cartload of beliefs" (Peirce, 1955, pp. 46–47). In this article, I describe how I have come to rethink content-area literacy instruction and lay out the two broad positions I have taken as a result of my work with my teacher-education colleagues. I will contextualize these positions within my work with my collaborators and against my past writing about content-area literacy — both of these a focus of my personal and private theory-making — and within the greater literature about literacy and literacy instruction, with an emphasis on connecting my private theories to public theories.

My Journey to Content-Area Literacy

I came to content-area literacy by way of mathematics teaching. I find mathematics beautiful. I became a teacher because I believed I could demystify mathematics for young people and help them appreciate the beauty I found in the subject. Since "everyone knows that there is no reading in mathematics classes," while a preservice mathematics teacher I sat in my required content-area reading class (like many of my peers) wondering why I was required to take the course. But I enjoyed it. The professor was dynamic and passionate, and I found myself trying to make connections between the ideas presented in class and my burgeoning understanding of mathematics teaching. In the next semester I began student teaching at a local middle school, where my cooperating teacher hoped I could help him and the other mathematics teachers figure out how to help students read their new math textbooks. Not knowing quite what to do, I sought guidance from my former content-area reading professor.

I continued to work with this professor during my first years of teaching. So, while I tried to engage in meaningful instruction as a mathematics teacher at a local high school, I also continued to take graduate courses in literacy, despite being accepted into a mathematics master's program. I came to view content-area literacy as a way to help my high school students — many of them Latino/a students who were learning English as an additional language — make sense of mathematics and be able to communicate their understanding. Eventually I switched from the graduate program in mathematics to secondary education, with a focus on literacy education. My goal was to become a mathematics teacher educator after completing my master's degree. However, life (and providence) intervened, and I found myself completing a doctoral program in curriculum and instruction with a focus on literacy studies, ultimately becoming a content-area literacy teacher educator.

After completing my graduate studies, I felt prepared to offer content-area teachers ideas for supporting the literacy development of adolescent students in every content-area classroom. I believed I had useful answers to instructional problems and I was ready to share them freely. Like other literacy teacher educators, because of the privileged status literacy enjoys during this era of No Child Left Behind and high-stakes testing, my opinion has been sought by school administrators. I have been asked to make presentations for middle and high school teachers for entire districts. I am an instructor in a professional development program designed to help secondary teachers (approximately thirty each year) add a reading endorsement to their teaching certification so they will be highly qualified to teach reading classes in middle and high schools. Indeed, this is a great time to be a literacy teacher educator.

Despite my preparation, I have found myself as a content-area literacy teacher educator with no classes to teach at my institution. I was hired into a department (teacher education) that offered support to the various secondary preparation programs distributed throughout the campus in content-area departments, but I did not directly oversee any of the various secondary programs except social studies. Unlike the institution where I had done my undergraduate and graduate studies, a content-area literacy methods course was not usually required for secondary teaching candidates, except preservice English teachers.

I realize that my circumstances are not typical. Over 60 percent of U.S. states do require a content-area literacy course as part of the preparation of secondary teachers (Romine, McKenna, & Robinson, 1996). Despite the fact that my home state, Utah, does not require a content-area literacy course for licensure as a secondary teacher, all other institutions that prepare secondary teachers within the state require the course. I doubt that many universities hire a content-area literacy teacher educator when courses are not required. However, my circumstances have prompted me to rethink what it means to be a content-area literacy teacher educator. Literacy teacher educators must take care to promote literacy in a way that includes content — knowledge about the physical, social, and aesthetic world — or they will find that they are promoting a literacy that is empty and vacuous. The education of all children depends on the collective, collaborative efforts of all educators, not just those who have chosen to make literacy their focus.

Studying Self

In order to make sense of my journey, I have engaged in a form of autobiographical self-study (Bullough & Pinnegar, 2001). Autobiographical self-study research allows the researcher to locate herself in her chosen field by exploring theory through practice. Thus, engaging in self-study provides a means of exploring my own development as a teacher educator and reflects my commitment to that development (Bullough & Pinnegar, 2001; Loughran, 2007). In addition, disciplined and systematic self-study work has the potential to inform other teacher educators by connecting public issues and theories to local struggles and personal theories. In this case, my struggle was to understand the nature of my work or who I am as a content-area literacy teacher educator in light of the shifting definitions of terms like *literacy, texts, reading, writing,* and *content-area literacy.* Ultimately, my aim in engaging in this inquiry has been to reconsider and reconceptualize my work as a teacher educator, thereby improving my own practice and perhaps also providing suggestions for the practice of other teacher educators (Feldman, 2003).

Content-Area Teacher-Education Narratives

Because of the situation in which I have found myself as a teacher educator — without a program or courses to teach — I have engaged in several collaborations with content-area teacher educators. Our mutual goal has been to work jointly to consider the problems related to preparing secondary teachers to simultaneously teach content and support the literacy development of adolescents. While one could argue that these collaborative activities constitute my scholarship as a teacher educator and not my practice, I have come to see my work with other teacher educators as defining my practice as a content-area literacy teacher educator. Indeed, I have shifted my practice from direct work with preservice teachers to working with other teacher educators.

To this end, a couple of years ago I organized a group of secondary teacher educators from across the campus (biology, physical science, art, music, mathematics, and history) to study content-area literacy. For the past two years, the Content-Area Literacy Study Group (CALSG) has met approximately twice a month in one- to two-hour meetings. During these meetings we have discussed theories related to content-area literacy, read and discussed articles on various topics related to literacy, and considered instructional activities related to content-area literacy instruction and their possible usefulness in various content-area classrooms. The goal of the group was ultimately to make changes to the various programs, either through additional courses or by changing the content of existing courses to help preservice teachers learn theories and instructional strategies related to content-area literacy instruction. Because we conceptualized the work of the CALSG as a form of participatory action research (Kremmis & McTaggart, 2000; Reason, 1999), we collected data on our work together, including audiotapes of meetings. These tapes were then transcribed and distributed to all the members of the group to use in our joint inquiry.

As part of my work with the CALSG and other collaborative efforts on campus, I have been provided access to the enacted curricula of other teacher educators (Eisner, 1979).[1] For this study I have highlighted three curricular examples from my work with three content-area teacher educators: Paul, a music teacher educator; Amy, a theater teacher educator; and Dan, a mathematics teacher educator. In Paul's and Amy's case, these curricula were specifically redesigned to address literacy issues and prepare preservice secondary teachers to support the literacy of their future adolescent students. Through these enacted curricula, I was able to consider ideas described by teacher educators as related to literacy while they discussed literacy in connection with content-area aims and methodologies. In Dan's case, the enacted curriculum was part of a content course (as opposed to a methods course, as with Amy and Paul) for preservice elementary teachers. In this case, I viewed the enacted curricula of a mathematics content-area teacher as he created a classroom based on the most recent theories and instructional practices available to help students understand mathematics. I watched carefully for how literacy was taught and supported, even though I knew that literacy was not an explicit goal of the course. My work with Paul, Amy, and Dan has provided me with opportunities to reconsider my conceptions of literacy and literacy instruction in relation to the conceptions of content-area learning and instruction expressed by my colleagues through their enacted curricula.

Paul: Music Teacher Education

Paul and I became acquainted when he accepted an invitation to participate in the CALSG. Paul initially came to our meetings in order to protect the music program and to ensure that any policies that were adopted relative to preparing teachers to teach literacy did not distract from the aims of music education. When early discussions of the group were focused around adopting a broadened definition of text, and thus literacy, Paul became interested in continuing the discussion.

During the second semester of our work together in the CALSG, Paul invited me to observe his teaching. He team-taught an introduction to music education class for preservice secondary music teachers (strings, choral, and band) in their first semester in the professional teacher-preparation program. Paul's role on the team of music teacher educators was to provide a philosophical foundation for music education. As a result of our discussions, Paul made changes to his lectures by describing an expanded notion of music literacy beyond simply reading musical scores and music theory, and then arguing that music literacy was the goal for all students in schools. I observed him teaching and recorded field notes of his instruction. Paul and I met briefly after each session to discuss his teaching. These debriefings allowed me to ask questions about Paul's intentions and how he felt the class had gone. I also asked about how the session I observed differed from past sessions or from sessions in which he had taught similar material with a narrower literacy perspective — one that did not embrace an expanded notion of literacy that included the conductor, the ensemble, or the musical performance. I created memos of our debriefings immediately afterward (generally locating a quiet place near Paul's classroom before returning to my office). I e-mailed my observations and memos to Paul in order to get clarifications and to ensure that I had accurately captured his comments.

Amy: Theater Teacher Education

Like Paul, Amy accepted the invitation to participate in the CALSG. Because of Amy's background in theater, film, and media and her commitment to broad notions of text that include digital texts, images, the human body, sets, and other objects associated with film and theater, she initially attended the meetings to argue that other members of the group (particularly me) should embrace similarly broad notions of text. We soon became allies, since I had been calling for similarly broad notions of text to include objects used to communicate, learn, and practice mathematics, including symbols, equations, formulas, drawings, manipulatives, and graphs.

During the second year of our work together, Amy invited me to observe her as she taught the methods of teaching theater course that the preservice theater teachers needed to complete in the semester before student teaching. She had made changes to the content and the assignments for the course in order to help her preservice teachers consider their roles as literacy teachers. I visited the eight class sessions that Amy had redesigned to discuss literacy and literacy instruction for theater classrooms. During these observations, I created field notes of Amy's teaching, which I shared with her. Amy also audiotaped the class sessions and had the tapes transcribed. As I did with Paul, I held a short debriefing session after each observation in which we questioned each other about the day's class. Generally, I was interested in why Amy chose particular activities, what her instructional goals were for the day, and how she felt the day had gone. Amy was interested in my perception of how she was doing with the literacy aspect of her instruction, whether her explanations were accurate and clear, and whether she had missed any opportunities to discuss literacy with her preservice teachers. These debriefings were audiotaped and transcribed.

Dan: Mathematics Teacher Education

Dan and I met during my first year at the university before the formation of the CALSG. That was also Dan's first year on the faculty, and we became acquainted during professional development activities for new faculty sponsored by the university. Dan, as a mathematics teacher educator, taught both content and methods courses. I asked him if I could observe his teaching of a content course for preservice elementary teachers, explaining that I was particularly interested in how he addressed literacy during his teaching of mathematical content. Dan assured me that he did not attend to literacy at all and suggested that his class would not be very interesting; however, either due to my persistence or his goodwill, he eventually agreed to collaborate with me on a research project in which we investigated literacy instruction for mathematics classrooms based on Dan's standards-based mathematics classroom (see Draper & Siebert, 2004, for a detailed description of our collaboration).

I attended all of Dan's course sessions and created field notes of his instruction. I shared the field notes with Dan, and he checked them for accuracy and completeness. All class sessions but one were videotaped, and several were transcribed as a part of the original research study. (For the purpose of this current study, we used transcriptions of the audio recordings of class sessions.) Dan and I met four times during the semester to discuss his teaching. Before our meetings we each read the field notes; then during the meetings we discussed our perceptions of what was occuring in Dan's class. I shared with him how I viewed his teaching relative to literacy instruction, and he explained his teaching based on his understanding of current theories related to mathematics instruction. These meetings were audiotaped and transcribed.

Rethinking Content-Area Literacy

I sought to collaborate with Paul, Amy, and Dan in order to study content-area literacy and to discover ways in which my collaborators and I could better support content-area literacy instruction on campus. These collaborations allowed me to confront content-area literacy theories and instructional practices from the perspectives held by Paul, Amy, and Dan — perspectives outside of content-area literacy — and ultimately caused me to rethink my own position as a content-area literacy teacher educator. This reevaluation has been made possible by reviewing my own descriptions of content-area literacy found in my past writings, along with the instructional materials I have used with preservice and in-service teachers. I have also returned to the data (i.e., field notes, transcriptions of meetings and classes, and interviews) that I collected with my collaborators to examine my shift in thinking about content-area literacy, and, thus, my role as a content-area literacy teacher educator. Finally, each of them read drafts of this article and offered clarifications to ensure that I have accurately described our work together.

First, I reexamined the data to locate incidents in which I had to rethink content-area literacy theories and instructional practices. These incidents often were marked by my own memos or questions within the field notes that acknowledged the limitations of my views. For example, in field notes that I created during Paul's teaching, I included the following question to myself: "How would you do this without a music background?" This question and others like it mark an acknowledgment of my own limited views. The conversations I had with Paul, Amy, and Dan, particularly those in which I asked them to explain why they had engaged in a particular practice in their classrooms, made it clear to me that they had thoughtful, disciplined reasons for making the instructional decisions that guided their work with preservice teachers — reasons that were rarely part of my consideration as a content-area literacy teacher educator.

In the end, it was the content-area expertise that each of my collaborators brought to our work that forced me to reflect on my own thinking and practices. Paul as a music educator, Amy as a theater educator, and Dan as a mathematics educator came to the collaboration with a clear sense of the aims of their disciplines and, thus, the practices that should be implemented in classrooms to reach those aims with children and youth in public schools. Moreover, each of them, while open to my ideas about content-area literacy, had the wherewithal to challenge my views, particularly those related to instructional practices. As we worked together, each of them was firm without being resistant, gentle without being condescending. In fact, all of them would likely say that they did not offer critique. However, their knowledge, practice, and questions offered me a way to critically reconsider my own position, understanding, and practice. Specifically, this has required me to question the aims of content-area literacy instruction and the efficacy of content-area instructional practices to the extent that they are generic across all disciplines.

Content-Area Literacy Education Must Allow Broad Definitions of Text

Perhaps because I am a former mathematics teacher, I have long embraced broad notions of text and, thus, literacy. For example, very early in my thinking about literacy, I included equations, solutions to equations, and proofs among the texts that must be read and written in a mathematics classroom

(Draper, 2002b). Therefore, in my writing I have advocated a broad notion of text. Citing Neilsen (1998), I stated that texts "include anything that provides readers, writers, listeners, speakers, and thinkers with the potential to create meaning through language" (p. 523). However, in reading this definition now, I find myself less comfortable with my reliance on language. Indeed, my definition of text was broad enough to include objects that one might read, write, hear, or speak. But my focus on language is highly problematic for fields such as music and theater that rely on other forms of meaning in addition to language. Paul helped me see this when he explained to his class that music offers a way to access "the inner life . . . and stuff you can't talk about very well." He valued music, and other forms of art, because, as he explained to his class of future music teachers, it "pierces the under layers of consciousness" that are often inaccessible to language (personal communication, October 9, 2006).

Certainly, broad notions of text have been embraced by members of the literacy community. For example, Wade and Moje (2000) have defined texts as "organized networks that people generate or use to make meaning either for themselves or for others" (p. 610). In this definition, texts need not be print, they need not be permanent, and they need not focus solely on language. Similarly, Conley's (2008) most recent content-area literacy methods textbook contains a list of texts that include "Internet Web pages, trade books, music, movies and other media, magazines, and newspapers" (p. 125). Indeed, several of these texts — music, movies, and even Web pages — rely on print and nonprint objects that are not solely language based (New London Group, 2000). However, not all content-area literacy methods textbooks acknowledge this range (e.g., Vacca & Vacca, 2008), and even those that do frequently drop the point as soon as it is made and use only traditional forms of print- and language-based text as part of descriptions of text, literacy, and literacy instructional practices. Instead, their descriptions and examples remain centered around traditional print texts (e.g., Conley, 2008; Readence, Bean, & Baldwin, 2004). This "privileging" of print- and language-based texts and literacies may be problematic, particularly in a time when literacy educators are calling for teachers to engage students with multiple forms of representation and expression (Kist, 2001; New London Group, 2000).

Broad notions of text have consequences for literacy. Embracing these broad notions necessitates an expanded definition of literacy, moving away from simply reading and writing print material and including a wide variety of activities — viewing, designing, listening, producing, performing, critiquing, evaluating, and improvising — with a variety of texts. However, literacy educators have not agreed on a singular definition of literacy (Harris & Hodges, 1995), and literacy educators consider the multiplicity of definitions of literacy simply inevitable (Harris & Hodges, 1995). Nevertheless, literacy educators must get straight what they mean by literacy in order to be useful to educators who have little background in, and may find limited use for, literacy education.

Gee's (1989, 1996) notion of Discourse, and, thus, literacy may prove useful in thinking about text use and participation in content-area classrooms. Briefly, Gee (1996) defines Discourses as "ways of being in the world, or forms of life which integrate words, acts, values, beliefs, attitudes, and social identities, as well as gestures, glances, body positions, and clothes" (p. 127). As such, he explains that a Discourse is a "sort of identity kit" (p. 127) — a way of belonging and being recognized as belonging to a particular group. Gee's notion can be useful for content-area teachers who may be striving to help students take on new identities or to think and act like musicians, actors, directors, or mathematicians. As such, content-area classrooms can be seen as helping students master or control a particular Discourse by helping students learn how to appropriately act and interact with the texts used to communicate and participate within disciplinary communities of practice (Wenger, 1998, p. 127).

Indeed, Gee (1989) defines literacy as "control of secondary uses of language" (p. 23) or "mastery of a secondary Discourse" (1996, p. 143), where secondary Discourses are those that are acquired and learned in addition to the primary Discourse made available by one's family. Ignoring for a moment Gee's inclusion of language in his definition, this definition can be useful for thinking about learning and participation in content-area classrooms. In fact, this notion of mastering or successfully appropriating an identity that renders oneself recognizable as a member of a group (e.g., musicians, actors, directors, mathematicians) requires literacy educators to consider how the community of practice itself determines the appropriate texts and the appropriate uses of those texts — not literacy educators who may not be members of that particular community of practice and, thus, not members of that particular Discourse community.

Consider the following two incidents that occurred between my collaborators and me. These incidents illustrate the nature of the experiences that have prompted me to reconsider content-area literacy instruction as they have illuminated the limitations in my thinking. I saw how my lack of facility with the specific texts (both print and nonprint) in use and my lack of understanding of the discipline (or the community of practice or Discourse community) limited the guidance I might be able to offer content-area teachers about how to support the literacies of their students.

Non-Print Literacies

The first incident occurred between Paul and me. I had been discussing invisible forms of literacy instruction (Vacca, 2002) as a part of our biweekly CALSG discussions of literacy. Invisible forms of instruction are considered implicit as opposed to visible forms of instruction, which are considered explicit (see also Krashen & Terrell, 1983). As such, invisible forms of literacy instruction allow students to participate with texts in authentic ways and develop literacy skills through that participation. As part of our discussion, I offered the following music example:

[The teacher] can say, "We're about to listen to a piece of music that's similar to the piece that you've been practicing. I want you to think about some of the challenges you've had trying to perform that." Then the teacher would play the music. And then the teacher would stop and say, "Okay, take a moment and reflect on what you were feeling and thinking. What kinds of things were happening for you?" So then, in that moment, the teacher would be doing invisible [instruction]. The teacher would be forcing the kids to recall what they did last week . . . and then having them reflect on [the music] afterward. (Meeting transcript, September 28, 2006)

In this example, the teacher prompts students to set a purpose for their reading and to reflect while reading (skills associated with competent readers), allowing the students to experience skilled reading without explicit instruction. I then described various instructional activities that allow teachers to promote invisible literacy instruction, including anticipation guides.[2] My hope was that the content-area teacher educators around the table, including Paul, would be able to hear my descriptions of the instructional activities and modify them to fit their content areas. I had been describing an anticipation guide and had an example available to share with the group:

The idea behind a lot of these classroom strategies . . . is not to teach kids explicitly how to do the reading, but to provide opportunities for kids to practice the behaviors of competent readers with the idea that if they do that enough, then they will start acquiring those practices for themselves and bring [them] to the [other] texts that they read (Vacca, 2002). (Meeting transcript, September 28, 2006)

Paul's response gave me pause. He simply said, "I'm going to have to really think about how this would look" (personal communication, September 28, 2006).

A couple of weeks later, during my observation of Paul's class, I watched him get his class of preservice teachers to create music texts (original adaptations and performances of a song) as a form of invisible literacy instruction. Paul had stressed to students that a musically literate individual can do more than simply perform music according to the directions of the conductor (in middle and high schools, this is generally the music teacher). His goal was to model for the preservice teachers how to support their future students' ability to create music texts.

First he broke the class into five groups of about seven students each and explained, "You have three minutes to accomplish the following: You are going to create a version of 'Twinkle, Twinkle, Little Star.' . . . You have to make it through all the words at least once, and you must have a tonal center" (Field notes, October 18, 2006). He then gave each group a word that they had to use to guide the sound of their song: *urgent, exuberant, forlorn, relaxed,* and *exasperated.* His final instructions indicated that while he did not want the class to completely abandon the melody, they were "free to depart from it."

Students quickly formed their groups. The group that I was observing closely was talking, humming, and singing. One student said, "Yeah, that could be our bass line." Later one student critiquing another said, "That is not exuberant." After a few minutes, each group performed for the class. The music they created was incredible; I had never had so much fun listening to "Twinkle, Twinkle, Little Star."

In my notes that day I wrote to myself, "How would you do this without a music background?" I recalled my suggestion to Paul regarding invisible literacy instruction in a music classroom. Watching his classroom, I was glad that he had not taken my suggestion and used it in his class; I was particularly pleased that Paul did not try to adapt an anticipation guide for his classroom. What Paul did in supporting his class in creating music texts was far better than what I had suggested, or would have ever suggested. Paul focused on the *production* of text, where I had only focused on the *consumption* of text. Paul ended the session with the music teaching majors by asking them what literacies were necessary for middle and high school students to participate in this activity. They also brainstormed additional activities that would allow adolescents to create their own music texts.

I came to realize through my collaboration with Paul that although I can embrace broad definitions of texts and literacies, I remain limited in the sound pedagogical recommendations I am able to make for helping students learn to read and write those texts in discipline-appropriate ways. In fact, when content-area teacher educators adopt a multiliteracies framework (New London Group, 2000), they likely remain less able than their content-area education colleagues to prepare teachers to support those various literacies. While I can intellectually appreciate that there are a variety of literacies involved with various disciplines, I do not have enough experience with the particular texts to know the specific literacies and how to support the acquisition of those literacies.

Print Literacies

The lesson I learned with Paul — to avoid making instructional suggestions about texts you know little or nothing about — was reinforced by Amy. In this case the text was a script — traditional print. I had not made suggestions about how to teach theater texts. However, Amy had been present during our discussion of visible and invisible literacy instruction, and about a month later I observed her teaching her preservice theater teachers about the idea of visible and invisible literacy instruction.

Amy began the lesson by explaining to her preservice theater teachers that she was going to model invisible literacy instruction. She then said to the class, "I want you to observe Kami making a peanut butter and jelly sandwich."[3] She then turned to Kami: "Pretend you are making it for the man you love."

Kami quipped, "That will take a lot of imagination!"

To which Amy replied, "Imagination is the key to acting."

Kami stepped behind a table that was set up in the acting space. The rest of the class, serving as an audience, remained seated in desks arranged in a semicircle. Kami placed a paper towel on the table and put peanut butter on one piece of bread, using the other piece of bread to wipe her knife clean. She then spread the jelly on the bread that already had the peanut butter and again used the other slice of bread to clean her knife. She completed her sandwich and cut it diagonally. Finally, she cleaned up by replacing the lids on the jars and closing the bag of bread.

After some applause, Amy said to the class, "Let's articulate some of the things we observed."

Trish began, "She cleaned her knife on the other side of the bread."

Interrupting, Kami explained, "So you don't get peanut butter on the sponge."

Pam, returning to her observation, pointed out, "She was careful about mixing the peanut butter and jelly."

Amy accepted these and other observations and then introduced another scene. "Doug, put on your actor hat and here is a scenario. You are working graveyard shift at your construction job and you have to be there in five minutes, but you aren't going to have a break, so your goal is to make this peanut butter sandwich."

Doug stepped behind the table and quickly got to work making his sandwich. He grabbed two slices of bread and spread peanut butter on both slices, wiping the knife clean. He then poured the jelly on each slice. Doug finished by folding each slice of bread in half to make two small sandwiches.

Doug took his bow, and Amy asked the class, "How did that goal change what happened in the scene?"

Kami said, "He didn't clean up."

Trish added, "He poured the jelly."

Amy repeated the scene again with Trish and Pam. For this scene, Trish was late for work and had to make a peanut butter sandwich for her little sister, Pam. Amy added, "Pam is an obstacle because she hates peanut butter and jelly sandwiches."

Once the students finished the scene, Amy explained that actors use tactics to meet objectives. She defined objectives and tactics and explained that "we don't want to create a dead-end tactic." She then asked two more students, Doug and Kami, to act out a final peanut butter and jelly scene. "This time," Amy explained, "Doug wants to go out to eat, but Kami just wants to make a peanut butter sandwich." The other students were instructed to "look for objectives and tactics."

Shortly after Doug and Kami began, Amy froze the scene and the class discussed what objectives and tactics they saw occurring. Amy then said, "Pam, recommend a tactic." Pam suggested, "Flirt." The scene continued with Doug flirting with Kami to get her to drop the knife and go out to eat.

Amy called the class back together. She pointed out that she had modeled invisible literacy instruction, which would prepare students for locating objectives and tactics while reading a play script — an important theater literacy. At this moment in Amy's instruction, I realized fully that if I were given the script and then asked to make recommendations about how to provide instruction that would support adolescents' reading of the script, I would not suggest ideas for helping students locate objectives and tactics. As I expressed in my memo in the field notes, "The purpose of the reading is influenced by understanding the discipline. I would not know to [look] for objectives and/or tactics." While I would have likely helped students establish a purpose for reading, I would not have known to tell students that one purpose an actor might have for reading a script is to locate the objectives and tactics. In this case, it was not my inability to decode and comprehend print text — as was the case with the texts I encountered in Paul's classroom — that would interfere with my instructional practices; it was my lack of understanding of theater Discourses that would cause me to miss important opportunities to help my students read a script like an actor.

Content-Area Literacy Instruction Must Focus on Gaining Facility with Content-Appropriate Texts

Because of my background in mathematics and my experience as a mathematics teacher, I have felt confident in my ability to make suggestions about instructional practices in mathematics classrooms. Indeed, I am aware of and conversant with many mathematical texts, particularly those used in middle and high school classrooms. I have read all of the standards documents (several more than once); I have read closely mathematics methods textbooks, three of them for my dissertation study (see Draper, 2000, 2002a); I have read literature written by mathematics teacher educators about instruction for mathematics classrooms. However, because I have not always articulated content-area literacy as a goal for content learning, I have been guilty of suggesting the use of print texts that have distracted from the aims of mathematics instruction.

For example, I, like other content-area literacy teacher educators, have suggested that mathematics teachers use writing to support student learning in mathematics classrooms — an example of literacy as a tool. In particular, I have suggested that they use learning logs as a way to assess student learning and to create a dialogue between teachers and students, and as a way for students to articulate their thinking about mathematics (McIntosh & Draper, 1997a, 1997b, 2001). While I still support writing in mathematics classrooms, I have come to understand that in order to do the most good, I must support the writing of particular kinds of mathematics texts.

Dan has often expressed this point to me, and the following incident helped me to begin to see it. As a regular part of Dan's mathematics course for preservice teachers, he required them to write explanations of the mathematical phenomena and operations they were learning in class. Furthermore, he expected them to create particular concept-oriented explanations. About one month into the mathematics course I was observing, Dan explained to the class that "after reading the exam, some of you are getting really good at making explanations, but I thought some of you need more information on how to write a good explanation" (personal communication, February 7, 2001). Then Dan displayed an overhead transparency titled "Characteristics of a good explanation." He clarified the points he included on the transparency. The main points of his presentation were as follows:

- Good explanations are based on images or models rather than symbols.
- Every number is carefully linked to some quantity or relationship between quantities in the image or model.
- Every operation is described in terms of actions performed on the image or model.

Dan also discussed the questions the students should ask themselves while creating an explanation. He pointed out, "Now notice that these questions don't focus on '*How* did I get the answer?'" Rather, the questions focused on justifying *why* each step works and what it means. Dan ended the discussion by contrasting the characteristics of good explanations with those of poor explanations.

After this discussion, Dan divided the class into pairs to read each other's papers and give feedback about the explanations. He wrote the directions on the board:

1. Everyone read [an addition] and [subtraction] explanation from the homework for everyone in the group.
2. [Discuss] good things (name two and be specific).
3. Restate their ideas.
4. Give suggestions (be kind and be honest).

Many literacy educators will notice, as I did, that Dan engaged his students in writing instruction focused on the writing process — drafting, editing, and revising. He also had his students participate in peer editing. Clearly, his goal for this lesson was that his students gain facility in creating a mathematical explanation. Literacy was the goal. However, it was a particular literacy in that he remained focused on creating a particular kind of mathematics text. He was not satisfied that his students were simply writing; he also insisted that they write explanations that articulated accurate representations of the mathematics by requiring them to base their explanations on images of quantities and operations. Furthermore, Dan insisted that the explanations fit the conventions of mathematical writing — in this case, mathematical proof. Dan was not satisfied when his students' explanations simply described the algorithm they used to compute the correct answer.

When I review the work I have done in writing in mathematics, it is clear that I have been satisfied with mere descriptions of algorithms. For example, I have suggested learning log prompts such as, "Explain in words how to solve the problem" (McIntosh & Draper, 2001, p. 556). In the discussion that accompanied the prompt and the student example of writing (which was taken from my mathematics classroom), my coauthor and I pointed out that it was unclear "whether [the student] completely understands why she is doing each step" (p. 556). However, the prompt I provided did not require her to make clear *why* each step works. Thus, I missed an opportunity to focus on understanding mathematics (not to mention the issue of my privileging print literacy). Moreover, descriptions of algorithms do not represent mathematical Discourse any more than they characterize poetry writing or other similar literary genres, and, thus, they should be deemphasized in mathematics classrooms.

Trite slogans like "writing across the curriculum" do little to make clear that content-area teachers should focus on helping their students acquire and learn content-area literacies or master content-area Discourses. Furthermore, the slogans may send the message that reading or writing, regardless of the text, should be celebrated in every content-area classroom. Dan has made it clear to me on several occasions that he is not in favor of using precious instructional time to help students write poems, raps, or other kinds of texts that do not resemble the kinds of texts used to participate or communicate mathematically. Instead, mathematics instruction must help students become fluent in the texts consistent with mathematical Discourse and the aims of mathematics education. Similarly, writing that does not focus on making sense of the mathematics or merely requires students to put words to their algorithms should not be recommended for mathematics classrooms just so mathematics teachers can fulfill the "writing-to-learn" mandate.

Lessons Learned through Content-Area Educator Collaboration

Content-area literacy has not been universally embraced by content-area teachers. However, my collaborations with Paul, Amy, and Dan have helped me see that perhaps content-area literacy in a very general or generic sense is not useful for content-area classrooms. Our study had shown me that content-area literacy is more valuable to content-area teachers when it makes space for nonprint/non-language-based texts, and when teachers use print texts in discipline-appropriate ways. The focus should be on helping students gain facility with the texts already present and valued in content-area classrooms. Content-area literacy educators may say that this is precisely the message sent to content-area teachers. However, a close examination of the messages surrounding content-area literacy does not bear this out (Siebert & Draper, in press). For example, when literacy instructional activities are described specifically for mathematics classrooms, they generally advocate a kind of mathematics instruction that is deemphasized by mathematics reformers, such as memorizing algorithms.

Paul, Amy, and Dan have found value in considering the issues related to content-area literacy. However, they have done so while maintaining a clear vision of the aims of content instruction. For Paul, a focus on print texts is not compelling for the goals he is trying to accomplish in music education. Amy, on the other hand, knows that print texts are important for theater education. However, the literacies that accompany those texts are quite specific. And for Dan, content-area literacy that does not help him consider ways to help his students access a rich understanding of important mathematical concepts is useless. These subtleties may seem insignificant. However, they must be addressed if content-area literacy theories and instructional practices are going to realize their full potential to help students — regardless of class, culture, or linguistic background — access the knowledge and acquire the skills necessary to participate in various Discourse communities. Paul, Amy, and Dan have each tapped into the theories and practices related to content-area literacy as evidenced by the way in which they have incorporated content-area literacy ideas into the classes they teach to preservice teachers. I have also felt validated by my content-area teacher educator colleagues in that they have found my literacy ideas worthy of their consideration and valuable in their work with preservice teachers.

Conclusions

For my dissertation study, I conducted a qualitative content analysis of methods books written to prepare teachers to teach mathematics, science, and social studies (Draper, 2000, 2002a). I expressed hope that these types of "conversations across disciplines" would help "literacy educators . . . understand recent research, recommendations, and implications of content teaching and learning," and that "content-area educators . . . [might] consider doing some deep thinking and learning about adolescent literacy issues" (Draper, 2000, pp. 195–196). I believed that part of the reason content-area teachers resisted ideas about literacy and literacy instruction was that they could not see how the ideas fit with what they were learning about content instruction from their methods textbooks and professors. I conceptualized the problem then as one of coherence, or lack thereof. My hope in collaboration was that content-area teacher educators and literacy educators would adopt each other's language to some degree and then present their disparate ideas in a way that would allow preservice teachers to make the appropriate connections.

My thought was that content-area teacher educators were unwittingly undermining the work of literacy teacher educators, and that if they would just make some minor adjustments (e.g., not using writing as a punishment for students who disrupt the classroom), then preservice teachers would have a better chance of understanding how to infuse their content instruction with relevant literacy instruction. It did not occur to me then, as it does now, that literacy teacher educators may be unwittingly undermining the work of content-area teacher educators. Experiences with Paul, Amy, and Dan remind me that I have the potential to do harm to content instruction by making recommendations that distract from or distort the content. I have come to realize that because I am not a member of any of the particular Discourse communities that occur in school, I am not familiar with the texts or how those texts are used.

Ultimately, my experiences with Paul, Amy, and Dan have forced me to reconsider my purpose as a content-area literacy teacher educator. While I initially sought to create these collaborations because I believed in literacy and did not have the opportunity to teach a separate literacy course, I have come to appreciate our work together as my contribution to the preparation of secondary teachers on campus. I continue to believe that all teachers must be prepared to support the literacy development of their students, yet I am no longer convinced that *all* preservice teachers need to take a separate literacy course. Indeed, I cannot imagine that I could do a better job of preparing teachers to support adolescents' music literacies than Paul. I am likewise convinced that for theater, which relies to a large extent on print literacies, Amy is in a much better position to equip future theater teachers with the necessary techniques to engage their students in reading and writing those texts. In fact, Amy is in a much better position to describe to preservice theater teachers how the multiple texts (e.g., script, body language, costume and set design, music, theater production) relate to one another and how to help adolescents learn how this multiplicity of texts works together (and thus must be read and written together) in theater settings. I have appreciated the opportunity to collaborate on the content and methods of several content-area methods courses, and my role as a consultant on these courses works well for me and my colleagues.

Paul, Amy, and Dan have benefited from our collaborations as well. Each of them has gained ideas and ways of talking about content instruction that they can share with future teachers. They each discuss "literacy as a lens" for viewing content instruction and instructional problems within content-area classrooms. Paul and Amy have sought my guidance for changes they have made to their methods courses. They look forward to making a place for content-area literacy within their methods courses because they appreciate the power it gives them to discuss both the aims of content instruction and appropriate instructional practices. In fact, Paul, Amy, and Dan have also made a place for literacy in the scholarship aspect of their professional assignments by coauthoring presentations and publications on the topic.

Changing the location of my practice from teacher education to teacher educator education presents challenges for me and for my institution. The primary challenge that must be addressed is getting widespread participation in the study of literacy from teacher educators who prepare secondary teachers. Indeed, given the traditions of teacher education and the fact that content-area teacher educators are likely not seeking out ways to add to their curricula for preservice teachers, how might content-area teacher educators welcome collaborations with the content-area literacy teacher educators and consider it worthy of their time and energy? What considerations must be taken to ensure *true* collaboration rather than simply cooperation or instrumental action, where one collaborator seeks to impose his or her views on the other participants? How does the institution "count" the work of the content-area literacy teacher educator when his or her work does not fit into conventional full-time equivalence allocations? Moreover, what do these collaborative efforts look like at institutions that *do* offer a separate content-area literacy methods course?

Perhaps the CALSG offers a model for teacher educators to consider. Under this model, I have a one-course load reduction each semester that enables me to work with content-area teacher educators from all over campus. I facilitate our meetings by locating places to meet, establishing a schedule, and choosing reading material for us to discuss. In order to encourage content-area teacher educators to participate, particularly those who have scholarship responsibilities, I suggested that the group engage in a form of participatory action research (Kremmis & McTaggart, 2000; Reason, 1999). Therefore, from the first meeting of the CALSG we have been engaged in inquiry — audio-taping meetings; collecting artifacts such as course syllabi, descriptions of assignments, meeting agendas, and notes; and observing instruction. I have facilitated the inquiry by visiting courses, creating field notes of the instruction, and having one-on-one conversations with professors about the content of their courses. Our inquiry has led to several national and international research presentations and to the preparation of manuscripts for publication. We are currently working on a book proposal together.

I have also strived to build our collaboration in the CALSG on the precepts of democratic participation, which are consistent with collaborative forms of research like participatory action research (Draper, Hall, & Smith, 2006). This form of participation is in line with Dewey's (1916) description that "a democracy is more than a form of government; it is primarily a mode of associated living, a conjoint communicated experience" (p. 87). Dewey (1927) also explained that when the conjoint activity has consequences that are "appreciated as good by all" and when the realization of those good consequences is a desire that all are willing to work toward, a democratic community is formed (p. 149). Thus, a democratic community is formed when individuals work together on a common problem to find a solution that is beneficial to all. As Bernstein (1998) has explained, "the virtues of openness, fallibility, experimentation, ongoing criticism, and imagination are what Dewey took to be characteristic virtues of a community of inquirers" (p. 149). These characteristic virtues, which Dewey maintained are requisite for a democratic community, are those that we sought to appropriate in our work together in the CALSG.

Our common problem has been the preparation of secondary teachers. Moreover, we are all concerned about the education of adolescents and want

to prepare teachers who can create safe and educative opportunities for adolescents. As such we have worked together in the CALSG to build trust with
one another by listening to each other's concerns and expertise; we have been
open to alternative opinions; individuals have made changes to their practice
and reported those changes to the group; and individuals have continued to
focus on changing their own work and not the work of others. This has been
particularly challenging for me. I have had to remain patient and open to
allowing each participant to make his or her own sense of the ideas and to
implement the ideas in his or her own way. However, I believe it is my commitment to the process — rather than the product — that allows the group to
work so well together. In fact, this year (our third year) we welcomed five new
members to the group.

We will continue to work to overcome the challenges associated with collaboration and teacher education. These challenges and others must be addressed
in order to make the collaborative efforts between teacher educators effective.
Indeed, both content-area and literacy teacher educators must not abandon
the possibility of collaborative work simply because the challenges loom large.
Instead, we must gather up our courage and humility and seek ways to overcome those challenges if we hope to transform the preparation of middle and
high school teachers and, thus, the lives of the adolescents with whom they
will eventually work.

Notes

1. The enacted curricula, as described by Eisner (1979), are the curricula as implemented by a teacher during the practice of teaching. This is in contrast to the curricula described in textbooks or curricular outlines, or as represented in unit and lesson
   plans created by the teacher.
2. Anticipation guides consist of four to five true/false questions based on a passage students are going to read. Students answer the questions prior to reading the passage
   and discuss their answers with their peers. Students then read the passage with the
   express goal of verifying or refuting their answers. After reading, students discuss any
   changes that they must make to their answers. Anticipation guides require students to
   reflect on their background knowledge and read with a purpose.
3. All student names are pseudonyms.

References

Bernstein, R. J. (1998). Community in the pragmatic tradition. In M. Dickstein (Ed.), *The
revival of pragmatism: New essays on social thought, law, and culture* (pp. 141–156). London: Duke.

Bullough, R. V., Jr., & Pinnegar, S. (2001). Guidelines for quality in autobiographical forms
of self-study research. *Educational Researcher, 30*(3), 13–21.

Conley, M. (2008). *Content area literacy: Learners in context.* Boston: Pearson.

Dewey, J. (1916). *Democracy and education: An introduction to the philosophy of education.* New
York: Free Press.

Dewey, J. (1927). *The public and its problems.* Athens, OH: Swallow Press.

Draper, R. J. (2000). *How secondary preservice mathematics, science, and social studies methods text-books support content-area literacy instruction: A qualitative content analysis.* Unpublished dissertation, University of Nevada, Reno.

Draper, R. J. (2002a). Every teacher a literacy teacher? An examination of the literacy-related messages in secondary methods textbooks. *Journal of Literacy Research, 34,* 357–384.

Draper, R. J. (2002b). School mathematics reform, constructivism, and literacy: A case for literacy instruction in the reform-oriented math classroom. *Journal of Adolescent and Adult Literacy, 45,* 520–529.

Draper, R. J., Hall, K. M., & Smith, L. K. (2006). The possibility of democratic educational research to nurture democratic educators. *Action in Teacher Education, 28*(2), 66–72.

Draper, R. J., & Siebert, D. (2004). Different goals, similar practices: Making sense of the mathematics and literacy instruction in a standards-based mathematics classroom. *American Educational Research Journal, 41,* 927–962.

Eisner, E. W. (1979). *The educational imagination: On the design and evaluation of school programs.* New York: Macmillan.

Feldman, A. (2003). Validity and quality in self-study. *Educational Researcher, 32*(3), 26–28.

Fisher, D., & Ivey, G. (2005). Literacy and language as learning in content-area classes: A departure from "every teacher a teacher of reading." *Action in Teacher Education, 277*(2), 3–11.

Gee, J. P. (1989). What is literacy? *Journal of Education, 171*(1), 18–25.

Gee, J. P. (1996). *Social linguistics and literacies: Ideology in discourses* (2nd ed.). London: RoutledgeFalmer.

Gray, W. S. (1925). A modern program of reading instruction for the grades and high school. In G. M. Whipple (Ed.), *Report of the National Committee on Reading: 24th yearbook of the National Society for the Study of Education, part 1* (pp. 21–73). Bloomington, IL: Public School Publishing.

Harris, T. L., & Hodges, R. E. (Eds.). (1995). *The literacy dictionary: The vocabulary of reading and writing.* Newark, DE: International Reading Association.

Kist, W. (2001). Beginning to create the new literacy classroom: What does the new literacy look like? In J. A. Rycik & J. L. Irvin (Eds.), *What adolescents deserve: A commitment to students' literacy learning* (pp. 226–240). Newark, DE: International Reading Association.

Krashen, S. D., & Terrell, T. D. (1983). *The natural approach: Language acquisition in the classroom.* Oxford: Pergamon.

Kremmis, S., & McTaggart, R. (2000). Participatory action research. In N. K. Denzin & Y. S. Lincoln (Eds.), *Handbook of qualitative research* (2nd ed., pp. 567–606). Thousand Oaks, CA: Sage.

Loughran, J. (2007). Researching teacher education practices: Responding to the challenges, demands, and expectations of self-study. *Journal of Teacher Education, 58*(1), 12–20.

Manzo, A. V., Manzo, U. C., & Estes, T. H. (2001). *Content area literacy: Interactive teaching for active learning* (3rd ed.). New York: John Wiley & Sons.

McIntosh, M. E., & Draper, R. J. (1997a). Logging on daily. *Writing Teacher, 10*(2), 26–29.

McIntosh, M. E., & Draper, R. J. (1997b). *Write starts: 101 learning logs for the mathematics classroom.* Palo Alto, CA: Dale Seymour.

McIntosh, M. E., & Draper, R. J. (2001). Using learning logs in mathematics: Writing to learn. *Mathematics Teacher, 94,* 554–559.

McKenna, M. C., & Robinson, R. D. (1990). Content literacy: A definition and implications. *Journal of Reading, 34,* 184–186.

Moje, E. B., Young, J. P., Readence, J. E., & Moore, D. W. (2000). Reinventing adolescent literacy for new times: Perennial and millennial issues. *Journal of Adolescent and Adult Literacy, 43,* 400–410.

National Council of Teachers of Mathematics. (1989). *Curriculum and evaluation standards for school mathematics.* Reston, VA: Author.

National Council of Teachers of Mathematics. (2000). *Principles and standards for school mathematics.* Reston, VA: Author.

Neilsen, L. (1998). Playing for real: Performative texts and adolescent identities. In D. E. Alvermann, K. A. Hinchman, D. W. Moore, S. F. Phelps, & D. R. Waff (Eds.), *Reconceptualizing the literacies in adolescents' lives* (pp. 3–26). Mahwah, NJ: Erlbaum.

New London Group. (2000). A pedagogy of multiliteracies: Designing social futures. In B. Cope & M. Kalantizis (Eds.), *Multiliteracies: Literacy learning and the design of social futures* (pp. 3–37). London: Routledge.

O'Brien, D. G., Stewart, R. A., & Moje, E. B. (1995). Why content literacy is difficult to infuse into the secondary school: Complexities of curriculum, pedagogy, and school culture. *Reading Research Quarterly, 30,* 442–463.

Peirce, C. S. (1955). The scientific attitude and fallibilism. In J. Buchler (Ed.), *Philosophical writings of Peirce* (pp. 42–59). New York: Dover.

Ratekin, N., Simpson, M. L., Alvermann, D. E., & Dishner, E. K. (1985). Why teachers resist content reading instruction. *Journal of Reading, 28,* 432–437.

Readence, J. E., Bean, T. W., & Baldwin, R. S. (2004). *Content area literacy: An integrated approach* (8th ed.). Dubuque, IA: Kendall/Hunt.

Reason, P. (1994). Three approaches to participative inquiry. In N. K. Denzin & Y. S. Lincoln (Eds.), *Handbook of qualitative research* (pp. 324–339). Thousand Oaks, CA: Sage.

Reason, P. (1999). Integrating action and reflection through co-operative inquiry. *Management Learning, 30,* 207–226.

Romine, B. G. C., McKenna, M. C., & Robinson, R. D. (1996). Reading coursework requirements for middle and high school content area teachers: A U.S. survey. *Journal of Adolescent and Adult Literacy, 40,* 194–198.

Siebert, D., & Draper, R. J. (in press). Why content-area literacy messages do not speak to mathematics teachers: A critical content analysis. *Literacy Research and Instruction.*

Simpson, E. A. (1954). *Helping high-school students read better.* Chicago: Science Research Associates.

Stewart, R. A., & O'Brien, D. G. (1989). Resistance to content area reading: A focus on preservice teachers. *Journal of Reading, 32,* 396–401.

Vacca, R. T. (2002). Making a difference in adolescents' school lives: Visible and invisible aspects of content area reading. In A. E. Farstrup & S. J. Samuels (Eds.), *What research has to say about reading instruction* (3rd ed., pp. 184–204). Newark, DE: International Reading Association.

Vacca, R. T., & Vacca, J. A. (2005). *Content area reading: Literacy and learning across the curriculum* (8th ed.). Boston: Allyn and Bacon.

Vacca, R. T., & Vacca, J. A. (2008). *Content area reading: Literacy and learning across the curriculum* (9th ed.). Boston: Allyn and Bacon.

Wade, S. E., & Moje, E. B. (2000). The role of text in classroom learning. In M. L. Kamil, P. B. Mosenthal, P. D. Pearson, & R. Barr (Eds.), *Handbook of reading research: Volume III* (pp. 609–628). Mahwah, NJ: Erlbaum.

Wenger, I. (1998). *Communities of practice: Learning, meaning, and identity.* Cambridge, England: Cambridge University Press.

The author would like to express her appreciation to Paul Broomhead, Amy P. Jensen, and Dan Siebert for their generosity and willingness to teach her.

Cognitive Strategy Instruction for Adolescents: What We Know about the Promise, What We Don't Know about the Potential

MARK W. CONLEY
Michigan State University

"Strategy instruction" is quickly becoming one of the most common — and perhaps the most commonly misunderstood — components of adolescent literacy research and practice. In this essay, veteran teacher educator Mark Conley argues that a particular type of strategy instruction known as cognitive strategy instruction holds great promise for improving adolescents' reading, writing, and thinking across content areas. However, he further suggests that we do not yet have the research needed to adequately understand and maximize the potential of cognitive strategy instruction in secondary content-area classrooms. After situating cognitive strategy instruction in the larger context of research on adolescent literacy and school-to-work transitions, Conley provides classroom examples of cognitive strategy instruction, demonstrates the need for meaningful integration of cognitive strategies in teacher education, and recommends specific directions for future research needed to understand and maximize the benefits of cognitive strategy instruction for adolescents.

The national agenda for adolescent literacy is currently dominated by concerns about cognitive strategy instruction. Cognitive strategies are constructive interactions with texts, both written and digital, in which good readers and writers continuously create meaning (Pressley, 2006). Cognitive strategies include activities such as asking questions to interrogate texts, summarizing, activating prior knowledge, and organizing and engaging prior knowledge with newly learned information. Numerous reports from blue-ribbon panels and research and policy centers implicate poor understandings of cognitive strategies as the primary reason why adolescents struggle with reading and writing (Deshler, Palincsar, Biancarosa, & Nair, 2007; Graham, 2006; Snow & Biancarosa, 2003).

Harvard Educational Review Vol. 78 No. 1 Spring 2008

Other authoritative reports promote research-based instructional practices for developing cognitive strategies in adolescents as the pathway for literacy reform in middle and high schools (Biancarosa & Snow, 2004; Graham & Perin, 2007; Heller & Greenleaf, 2007; National Governors Association, 2005).

To successfully operate in college and in the workplace, now and in the future, adolescents will need to master cognitive strategies for reading, writing, and thinking in complex situations where texts, skills, or requisite knowledge are fluid and not always clearly understood. However, there can be little consensus about cognitive strategies and their function in complicated real-life contexts. There are disagreements, for example, about how strategies identified as effective with young children might be useful for adolescents. There are disagreements about the role of cognitive strategies as a tool for teachers and/or students. In order for adolescents to truly benefit from cognitive strategy instruction, research is needed to clarify how cognitive strategies operate in content-area classrooms to prepare adolescents for their future. Using this research, teacher educators could better prepare teachers to teach cognitive strategies to their students. The purpose of this article is to explain the importance of cognitive strategy instruction, to suggest ways that cognitive strategies are misunderstood or misconstrued, and to provide direction for research that could help us finally deliver on the promise of cognitive strategy instruction for adolescents.

Why Cognitive Strategies Will Continue to Be Important

Cognitive strategies are an integral part of preparing adolescents for success in college and the workplace. For example, many college professors would like students to come to college already equipped with higher-level thinking and problem-solving abilities (ACT, 2006). In the ACT National Curriculum Survey, college professors complained that high school teachers are overly fixated on teaching topics rather than on teaching students how to think, and that high school students are ill prepared to take on the complex kinds of strategic thinking required for college.

Two benchmark reports highlighting the connection between workplace demands and literacy skills — the Secretary's Commission on Achieving Necessary Skills (SCANS) Report and the Essential Skills and Workplace Literacy Initiative[1] — provide evidence that an understanding of cognitive strategies is fundamental for success in the workplace of today and tomorrow (Human Resources and Skills Development Canada, 2007). While the Bureau of Labor Statistics, the Educational Testing Service, and other organizations are continuously documenting adult- and labor-related literacy demands, these two reports are notable because they were initiated specifically in response to the new challenges created by the transformation of the workplace from a manufacturing base to an information-technology base. The reports suggest that classrooms promoting tools for reasoning while using complex texts, confronting difficult issues, and responding to a range of purposes are more useful in preparing students for a meaningful future than those that teach students isolated bits of knowledge or walk them through some pedagogical steps.

The SCANS Report was initiated by the U.S. secretary of labor in the early 1990s in order to identify the skills adolescents and young adults need to succeed in the workplace. The purpose was to encourage high-skill and high-wage employment, especially as the economy changed from manufacturing to an information-technology base. The findings of the report were intended to guide secondary and postsecondary educators in the development of a workforce for the future. Based on an analysis of fifteen job categories, the SCANS Report identified five workforce competencies (U.S. Department of Labor, 1991), including allocating time, money, material, and staff resources; working collaboratively on teams with effective interpersonal skills; managing and evaluating information effectively; understanding, designing, and adapting systems; and applying technology to specific tasks. The report also included basic skills in reading, writing, and mathematics; speaking and listening; thinking skills, including thinking creatively, making decisions, and solving problems; and personal qualities, such as individual responsibility and integrity.

The Essential Skills and Workplace Literacy Initiative from the Human Resources and Skills Development Canada is a more recent and more comprehensive effort to document workplace skills. The initiative identifies and ranks various workplace tasks on a number of different dimensions for over two hundred occupations. The entire system is based on three conceptions of literacy (Kaestle, Campbell, Finn, Johnson, & Mikulecky, 2001): *prose literacy*, or the knowledge and skills needed to understand and use information from texts that include editorials, news stories, poems, and fiction; *document literacy*, or the knowledge and skills required to locate and use information contained in job applications, payroll forms, transportation schedules, maps, tables, and graphs; and *quantitative literacy*, or the knowledge and skills required to apply arithmetic operations, either alone or sequentially, using numbers embedded in printed materials. Using this framework as a lens, the cognitive strategies required from one occupation to the next can differ dramatically. For instance, a machinist needs to interrogate a text in order to understand formulae or procedures for carrying out unfamiliar metal-working tasks. A paramedic might scan the *Compendium of Pharmaceuticals and Specialties* to anticipate how to care for a patient (Human Resources and Skills Development Canada, 2007). Differences in interrogating, scanning, interpreting, and evaluating multiple kinds of texts are all aspects of the complexity of cognitive actions that characterize various occupations.

Despite this prevailing assumption that, somehow, preparation in cognitive strategies in elementary and secondary education should lead to success in college and the workplace, there is little agreement about how this should happen. As detailed as these reports are about cognitive skills and technological tasks, we still know very little about how teachers may use cognitive strategy instruction in preparing students for a meaningful future. The reports provide no indication of how content-area teachers can combine their conceptions of content, pedagogy, and learning with workplace-related cognitive reasoning. Although many middle schools and high schools have experimented with incorporating the findings from these reports, it continues to be difficult to envision cognitive strategy instruction for adolescents in ways that develop workplace skills. Often, the debate centers on what curricula should be pushed aside so that teachers can focus more deliberately on workplace skills such as interpersonal skills or a greater facility with technology. At what point do schools stop teaching English, mathematics, science, and social studies in order to focus on the particulars of the cognitive strategies necessary to succeed in the occupations? Or do we continue as we always have, assuming that the disconnect between secondary education and the workplace will somehow right itself as adolescents progress through the system and into professional schools? We really know very little about the potential for cognitive strategy instruction for adolescent literacy because of ongoing uncertainty about how experiences in education could or should build from one context to the next. And yet, staying the course is what these reports invite us to do.

Challenges Facing Researchers

Researchers interested in cognitive strategy instruction face a number of dilemmas, not the least of which concerns the lack of consensus about the nature and workings of cognitive strategies. For example, there is a significant but overlooked difference between using cognitive strategies as a "teaching tool" versus using cognitive strategies as a "learning tool." Also, the ways in which cognitive strategies are connected to the purposes, topics, and goals of a content area are not well understood.

Consider the following two classroom stories that illustrate the teaching of a cognitive strategy using a graphic organizer. While these stories are hypothetical, they are grounded in my experience as a teacher educator. In the first story, the goal is to teach students to follow the steps of a teaching activity through repeated exposure. In the second, the primary goal is to develop the students' strategic tools for reasoning by using a graphic organizer as a cognitive strategy. Note how the stories differ with respect to how students are taught to use the graphic organizer and the role it plays within the broader context of the lesson.

Ms. Gunnings's Classroom: Doing Graphic Organizers

Ms. Gunnings decides to use a graphic organizer to help her tenth-grade students activate their prior knowledge and organize new information while she teaches a science lesson about pollution. She prepares an organizer, like the one in Figure 1, and plans to use it to guide her students through an instructional conversation.

FIGURE 1   *A Graphic Organizer about Pollution*

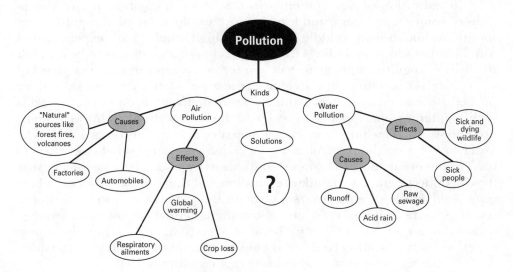

"So, can anyone tell me about pollution?" Ms. Gunnings asks. She writes the word *pollution* on an overhead projector. As her students tell what they know, Ms. Gunnings fills in the organizer. Sometimes she uses items on her planned organizer to ask questions: "What are some of the causes of water pollution?" At other times she uses the planned organizer to create meaningful categories from students' responses: "So, how are breathing problems, problems with crops, and global warming all alike with respect to air pollution?" Students respond that they are all the results or effects of air pollution. When the discussion ends, students read a chapter in their science textbooks about pollution. Later they add information from the chapter to the class organizer that they have copied into their individual science notebooks.

This version of events illustrates Ms. Gunnings's decision to use a graphic organizer as an instructional activity introducing and developing key concepts about pollution. In this story, Ms. Gunnings teaches her students how to record graphic organizers in their notebooks and add details to those organizers as a way of later recalling information for quizzes and tests. Because her students have experienced this use of graphic organizers many times, they know that their role during the instructional conversations and reading is to provide answers and record the information in the resulting organizer. As such, they are involved in Ms. Gunnings's strategic decisions about using graphic organizers. An important question, however, is whether students are learning to be cognitively strategic through Ms. Gunnings's teaching of graphic organizers. A long-held assumption among some curriculum theorists is that yes, indeed they are. The assumption is that, exposed to multiple iterations of graphic organizers, the students will eventually learn to organize their own thinking. To some this justifies identifying what Ms. Gunnings is doing and what students are learning as *teaching a cognitive strategy*. This view has been prevalent in textbooks about adolescent literacy practices for many years (Conley, in press).

However, it is difficult to imagine how students are learning to be strategic, creating meaning on their own, or thinking for themselves through Ms. Gunnings's lesson. More likely, Ms. Gunnings's students have internalized only the steps in a teaching activity rather than a reasoning process they can employ on their own. Evidence that students are not internalizing cognitive strategies through repetition usually emerges when students are asked to complete another assignment where using a cognitive strategy is a reasonable expectation. Instead, students may go through the motions of their assignments without stopping to think.[2]

Ms. Gunnings's Classroom: Developing Cognitive Tools

In this next version, Ms. Gunnings considers her goals for teaching the science content and for developing scientific reasoning. She wants her students to understand pollution as a scientific phenomenon with potentially devastating natural and social implications. More importantly, she wants students to develop an informed, critical stance about pollution, including understanding ways that scientific information can be manipulated for different purposes. To achieve these goals, Ms. Gunnings plans to continuously engage her students by drawing on their personal experiences with pollution, using media coverage of current events and identifying issues within the community. She selects articles about water pollution from *Newsweek* magazine, research reports from *Science Daily*,[3] political speeches about global warming, updates on China's struggle with air pollution in anticipation of the Olympic Games, and position papers from Greenpeace. Ms. Gunnings selects this range of text resources in order to provide discrepant points of view so her students can make multiple comparisons between their prior knowledge and the various texts. For their part, students will need to evaluate claims and supporting evidence across these resources in order to form conclusions about the causes, consequences, and potential ways to address pollution. She plans a culminating event for her pollution unit consisting of a simulation in which students will make recommendations to the United Nations about addressing world pollution.

In this version of the story, Ms. Gunnings views a graphic organizer as the ideal tool to support students' inquiry and cross-text comparisons. The organizer is continually consulted by Ms. Gunnings to demonstrate how to make initial claims and interrogate texts. Ms. Gunnings then invites the students to use their graphic organizers to compare their own experiences and assumptions with the assertions and evidence collected from the texts. In this version, Ms. Gunnings deliberately sets out to teach students how to use a graphic organizer as a cognitive tool to develop and organize their thinking. Ultimately, the goal of this second lesson is not the design of a particular graphic organizer or participation in a series of steps; instead, the goal is to help students create mental structures or models to support their thinking and learning.

Ms. Gunnings introduces the lesson topic, pollution, and asks students to make observations based on their own experiences. Next she names the cognitive strategy: "We are going to use a graphic organizer to record your observations." She provides her students with a brief explanation for how the strategy is useful for learning: "Graphic organizers are a way of picturing what you know. You can make a graphic organizer to think about what you already know and to use when you are learning something new. You can add more as you learn more, and you can change what you think. I'll show you how." Ms. Gunnings models how to create a graphic organizer, thinking out loud as she builds its components. "Water pollution is caused by sewage. I read about that in the local newspaper the other day when they talked about inspecting the river for signs of dumping. Notice how I think about my reasons as I add new information." As she models her thinking, Ms. Gunnings draws her part of the organizer on the overhead and encourages students to ask questions as she models the strategy. After listening carefully to their questions and asking a few of her own, she is satisfied that they are ready to reflect on what they know by adding to the graphic organizer she started.

Ms. Gunnings then transfers responsibility for the new strategy to her students. "Let's see you add more to our class graphic organizer by thinking about what you know about pollution. Turn to your partner and talk about another example of pollution. Make a mini graphic organizer based on your conversation, and we will add it to the class graphic organizer I have already started. Remember to think about your reasons for adding the new information." As students turn to their partners to discuss and prepare their individual organizers, Ms. Gunnings eavesdrops on their conversations, stepping in to ask questions, adding some new information, or correcting any misconceptions. One student pair writes *new car smell* under air pollution, and Ms. Gunnings asks, "What does that have to do with pollution?" Her student responds, "I saw on television that the new car smell is actually the gases coming off of the plastic on the dashboard and that those gases are poisonous. So that is a form of air pollution too!"

After the paired discussions and practice with individual graphic organizers, Ms. Gunnings asks students to add information to the class organizer that she started. The students add their own assertions about pollution along with reasons for their contributions to the collective class organizer. At one point, a student volunteers that a number of people believe some kinds of pollution are not real, as with global warming from carbon emissions, or even air or water pollution. The class decides to add a category entitled "Pollution: Myth or Reality?" to the organizer. This category is extremely important as Ms. Gunnings engages her students in the competing points of view in the texts she selected. Ms. Gunnings continually refers students back to the class organizer as they encounter different claims and evidence. She probes for reasons to check on students' thinking. She also encourages students to develop confidence in their own perspectives rather than deferring to any one of the texts. By the end of the unit, the class graphic organizer has changed many times as students' perspectives and reasoning about pollution have become more sophisticated and richly supported.

The key difference in these two accounts is between treating strategy instruction as rehearsal — doing a teaching activity step by step, over and over again, in the hope that somehow it will stick with students — versus considering cognitive strategy instruction as a deliberate action to develop in students a critical understanding of subject matter ideas *and* a cognitive approach to learning. In the first account, teaching a strategy is almost entirely about a teacher's performance of a teaching activity; in effect, *doing graphic organizers.* In the second account, teachers and students, respectively, have different but intimately connected roles through concept and strategy development, use, and application. Ms. Gunnings connected her subject-matter goals — helping students understand and compare various perspectives on pollution — with a teaching activity suitable for the intellectual task at hand, helping students constantly compare their prior knowledge with various texts, all of which are open to challenge. Ms. Gunnings was explicit while explaining her thinking and using graphic organizers as a tool. She thought aloud as she filled out the class graphic organizer and provided students with practice and feedback as they filled out mini graphic organizers of their own. Rather than doing graphic organizers merely as a series of steps, the second account situates graphic organizers as a component of students' cognitive tool kit.

Setting out to build adolescents' cognitive tools raises the teaching and learning bar higher than just adopting activities to teach reading and writing. As the second account of Ms. Gunnings's classroom illustrates, the decisions can be quite complex. There are remarkably different assumptions about teaching and learning and ways to establish an appropriate learning context. Developing a graphic organizer to extract meaning from a single text is quite different from developing critical stances about an issue by wading through multiple texts that represent scientific concepts and reasoning and reflect differences in perspective, interpretation, and bias.

Many would agree that the second account is much closer to what is required in daily life, sifting through various kinds of information produced for purposes of conveying or persuading. Consider not only the issue of pollution, but also the reasoning required for job-related tasks in the modern technological office, or even participation as a voter during elections. Few adults would argue that developing a graphic organizer is a worthwhile learning goal in and of itself for everyday living. On the other hand, many adults might agree that forming a mental model, like a graphic organizer, can be invaluable for sorting through readings and media to form an opinion or take action. As such, the second account of Ms. Gunnings's classroom holds the potential not only for a well-integrated, purposeful use of a graphic organizer, but also for the development of cognitive strategies useful for later learning. The well-integrated and purposeful application of cognitive strategies combined with explicit instruction and guided practice increases the likelihood that cognitive strategies will be useful later on.

Despite these accounts, we know relatively little about how to promote this more integrated, complex version of cognitive strategy instruction. For many years, courses in content-area literacy (sometimes referred to as adolescent literacy courses) have been based on the assumption that teachers should supply the connections between content knowledge and cognitive strategy implementation. The courses often just provide the instructional activities, focusing on the strategies themselves without providing teachers with opportunities to learn how to use those strategies in service of deeper student thinking. For many years, I have observed teachers struggling to make these connections. One of the reasons for this struggle is that research and practice have offered far more examples that resemble the first version of Ms. Gunnings's classroom and not the second. Consequently, it can be difficult for content-area teachers to see how cognitive strategy instruction can be applied, particularly when research and practice offer simple solutions to learning goals, opportunities, and problems that teachers view as both important and complex.

Current research simply doesn't provide many examples of how to effectively teach cognitive strategies in the content areas in middle and high schools. Most of our current knowledge about cognitive strategy instruction comes from research on young children with relatively simple academic tasks. Pressley and his colleagues are responsible for much of the basic research on cognitive strategies as a foundation for reading comprehension and have contributed several influential reviews (Pressley, 2000; Pressley & Hilden, 2006). Oft cited is the connection between *word-oriented* cognitive strategies necessary for comprehension and *comprehension-oriented* cognitive strategies that aid reading comprehension.[4] Word-oriented strategies include sounding out words (sometimes referred to as decoding); learning to recognize sight words (words frequently encountered and instantly recognized without having to figure them out, such as "from," "the," "and," "because"); using semantic context clues to evaluate whether decodings are accurate; and building vocabulary knowledge. Comprehension-oriented cognitive strategies include activating one's relevant prior knowledge and using prediction; generating questions during reading; constructing mental images representing the meanings in texts; summarizing and clarifying the meanings in texts; and analyzing the structural components of narrative and informational texts (Pressley, 2006).

There is growing evidence that adolescents struggle with word-oriented cognitive strategies, often referred to as fluency (Rasinski, Padak, McKeon, Wilfong, Friedauer, & Heim, 2005), but there is a lack of consensus on how to teach word-oriented cognitive strategies at this level. The staff developer's or literacy professor's worst nightmare is standing before an audience of middle or high school teachers while trying to instruct them about word-level cognitive strategies. This fear stems from conflicts between secondary teachers' perceived roles and the teaching of basic reading skills. When confronted with the prospect of teaching word-oriented cognitive strategies, many secondary teachers ask, "How is teaching reading and decoding related to my job as a subject-matter teacher?"

One would expect that research focusing on comprehension would be more consistent with secondary teachers' views. However, we still may not know enough about how comprehension-oriented cognitive strategies are connected to and useful for learning in various subject-matter domains, with different kinds of concepts, and for various purposes. For example, does the difference in format and writing style in English literature, compared with physics, demand a different set of comprehension skills and cognitive strategies? One model that addresses this tension is the Strategic Instruction Model developed at the University of Kansas, which consists of an array of task-specific cognitive strategies potentially applicable in many different secondary content area classrooms (Schumaker & Deshler, 2006). A cognitive strategy within this research is defined as "an individual's approach to a task. It includes how a person thinks and acts when planning, executing, and evaluating performance on a task and its outcomes" (Deshler & Schumaker, 1988). Examples include forming mental pictures of events described in a reading passage, forming questions about information and finding answers to those questions later in the reading, paraphrasing the main idea and important details, and connecting words and word meanings to prior knowledge. Many studies, individually and in combination, have demonstrated the power of these cognitive strategies in helping adolescents learn more successfully (Deshler & Schumaker, 2006).

However, the value of cognitive strategies like the ones in the University of Kansas model still relies on teachers' decisions, particularly about subject-matter goals and anticipation of the challenges adolescents face while learning. Teachers may choose to use cognitive strategies and yet may persist in assuming that text meanings are fixed and ready for a reader to "unlock" the meaning, as featured in the first version of Ms. Gunnings's classroom. As the second version of Ms. Gunnings's classroom illustrates, single texts are not always the point of instruction, nor are meanings in texts literally fixed. Subject-matter goals often call for the use of interpretive or critical reading. In most content areas, gaining a general understanding of a text may be an early stage in a more sophisticated process of questioning and deliberation. Critical reading is a common expectation in social studies or English courses in middle and high school. Science educators frequently mistrust texts because the texts communicate misconceptions. In mathematics, main ideas, numbers, and details are only brief stops along the way to more sophisticated mathematical understandings. Because of the gap between the simple state of cognitive strategy research and the complexity of subject-matter teaching and learning, many experienced teachers may not be able to make the best use of cognitive strategy instruction. Clearly, there is a need to better understand cognitive strategies, their function, and their application in diverse and complex subject matter contexts.

Unfortunately, the approach over time from the literacy profession has been to provide relatively simple and generic strategy solutions for the teaching of complex content-area topics, purposes, and goals. *Content-area literacy* is the term used to describe instructional activities that integrate reading, writing, speaking, and listening into subject-matter contexts (McKenna & Robinson, 1990). Teaching activities within content-area literacy include using semantic maps, graphic organizers, anticipation guides, three-level guides, journaling, and I-searches, along with many others. Many of these activities are referred to in content-area literacy textbooks as strategies.[5] A compendium of these activities is in its sixth edition (Tierney & Readance, 2004), while many of the best-selling textbooks in content-area literacy are widely used and are in their eighth or ninth editions (Bean, Readance, & Baldwin, 2007; Vacca & Vacca, 2007). In short, there are many books on the market that offer dozens of simple content-area, comprehension-oriented instructional activities that do not necessarily lead to a deeper use of cognitive strategies.

Content-area literacy textbooks often blur or omit distinctions between instructional actions by teachers and cognitive actions students learn and apply in strategic ways. Moreover, they often emphasize generalist approaches to instruction, where one activity fits all subjects and all adolescents (Conley, in press). Teachers who follow these recommendations run the risk of engaging in activities that walk students through steps, like the first version of Ms. Gunnings's use of a graphic organizer, rather than teaching students how to adapt cognitive strategies for their own purposes.

Chris Tovani's (2004a, 2004b) work represents a departure from the typical approach within this genre. Tovani, a former English teacher, adopts many of the same insights found in the cognitive strategies research, especially with regard to considering how teaching is connected to strategy development in students. For example, Tovani provides specific recommendations and examples of how teachers can model the reasoning they want students to learn how to do. The strategies Tovani emphasizes come from cognitive strategies research, such as developing a purpose for reading, connecting the new to the known, thinking aloud, asking yourself a question and trying to answer it, monitoring comprehension, knowing what to do when one gets stuck (fix-it strategies), making a connection between the text and real life, making a prediction, noticing patterns in text structure, and visualizing a text's meaning (Pressley & Hilden, 2006). Engagement in these activities is explained both from the teacher's perspective with regard to instructional actions and from the student's point of view as a learner.

In many ways, Tovani's treatment is a distinct improvement over the content-area literacy genre because she distinguishes and yet connects teachers' instructional actions to students' development of cognitive strategies. Still, teachers are mostly responsible for supplying the missing yet critical features of the context, including the content-area learning goals and purposes; understandings about specific learning opportunities and challenges related to the particulars of the content; and decisions about texts and pedagogy to advance students' reasoning.[6] Because of this, many teachers might still struggle with how to envision content-area goals, imagine challenges for students' learning, and bridge gaps appropriately between content knowledge and students' needs through integrated cognitive strategy instruction. Some teachers might still gravitate toward the first version of Ms. Gunnings's classroom rather than the second version because of challenges associated with making all of the necessary content-area and pedagogical connections.

In my own reworking of the content-area literacy genre, I have aimed for a better accounting of instructional activities in support of cognitive strategy development (Conley, 2008). I reviewed the research on cognitive strategies and related instruction and the original[7] research on teaching activities that appear most often in the content-area literacy textbooks. I then matched cognitive strategies with the original intent of the teaching activities. Next, I regrouped and re-explained each of the teaching activities with regard to their potential for developing in students an understanding of cognitive strategies. For example, to teach students about questioning as a cognitive strategy, I grouped guided reading (Stauffer, 1975), question-answer relationships (Raphael & Pearson, 1985), and the ReQuest (Manzo & Manzo, 1990) teaching activities. The ReQuest procedure is an example in which a teacher asks questions and then, with little or no explanation, turns the questioning over to the students (Manzo & Manzo, 1990). The reexplaining was critically important, since most of these activities involved simple step-by-step rehearsal but not explicit teaching of cognitive strategies. In reimagining the teaching activity, I added explanation, modeling, and guided practice as essential components of cognitive strategy instruction, mirroring Ms. Gunnings's lesson in the second example.

Although my work, like Tovani's, draws a closer relationship between teaching and learning that deliberately supports the development of cognitive strategies, it is not nearly enough. It still does not provide teachers with explicit connections between cognitive strategy instruction and complex subject-matter goals and purposes. The one-strategy-fits-all approach persists. It is as if the first version of Ms. Gunnings's classroom was improved with more explicit attention to what students might do with the teaching activity.

The field of content-area literacy is still far from delivering on a more complex view of developing deep understandings for content as well as cognitive tools. As a science educator colleague of mine likes to point out, teaching and learning about an invisible process like carbon exchange is not the same as teaching about visible phenomena such as the workings of an ecosystem. The same could be said about the comparison between teaching quadratic equations and three-dimensional geometry in mathematics, or teaching the literary canon and the anti-canon in English. In contrast to generic recommendations from content-area literacy, cognitive strategy instruction should not be the same in each case. Instead, we need instructional recommendations that support teachers in selecting, adapting, and teaching a different strategy specifically and appropriately for each learning context, especially if the goal is to support students in internalizing and adapting cognitive tools of their own.

Challenges Facing Teacher Educators

Teacher education currently lacks a focus on the meaningful integration of cognitive strategy instruction, especially with regard to connecting cognitive strategy instruction to student thinking and learning across the content areas. I have been working with both beginning and experienced secondary teachers across the content areas on ways to improve adolescent literacy for nearly thirty years. In recent years, I have taken on the goal of deepening our vision for what it means to promote learning. An important part of this goal involves developing understandings about cognitive strategy instruction for learning in the content areas. Achieving this goal has been far from easy.

Each semester in a course devoted to adolescent literacy, I am greeted by a new group of twenty-year-old prospective teachers representing every content area, including mathematics, science, social studies, English, agricultural science, art, and music. I call them the "passionately naive" because their enthusiasm is inspiring while their understandings for the complexity of schooling are just beginning. The first five weeks of the course are reserved for preparing beginning teachers for eight weeks of tutoring in local urban middle schools. For many years, I taught this course as a content-area literacy class, promoting a long list of content-area literacy teaching activities for use across content areas. This menu satisfied my students' urgent need to learn how to do activities that would help them assume the role of a teacher. I was forced to rethink my approach to the course when many of my prospective teachers returned from their tutoring experiences saying that they were unable to use any of the class activities. Their reasons included having few opportunities to "plug in" a reading activity when the content-area lesson did not call for one, or the fact that the activities somehow did not meet the struggling adolescents' needs.

I studied my prospective teachers' online journals about their tutoring experiences in the urban middle schools. Many reported struggling with understanding and motivating adolescents, knowing how to start instruction, asking the right kinds of questions at the right times, figuring out what works, and building relationships (Conley, Kerner, & Reynolds, 2005). The course was reorganized using these themes, related readings, and renewed reflections on the tutoring. After working with this framework for a time, I became troubled again. These teacher candidates struggled to connect motivation, teaching, and learning. They appeared to have limited understandings of these concepts or their connections to each other. For example, one of my graduate student instructors observed that teacher candidates defined motivation as having a book in hand and a smile, and yet they rarely mentioned students. Many teacher candidates reflected on how they looked and acted and what their students said and did, but not about what they learned. "How can they understand adolescent literacy," I asked myself, "if they don't understand much about motivation or learning?" In many ways, the confusion of these prospective teachers mirrored the ambiguity in the field about the role of cognitive strategies in teaching and learning.

Recent research on our program supported by the Carnegie Adolescent Literacy Preservice Initiative has provided another picture of the reasons underlying our prospective teachers' struggles. Along with colleagues in science education, we interviewed our science teacher candidates while they watched three videos, including a lesson conducted by a gifted and experienced high school science teacher, a clinical interview with a young student about his understanding of photosynthesis, and a tutoring session between a struggling eighth grader and one of my students in the adolescent literacy course.

Our initial findings show that, well into our teacher-education program, prospective teachers hold fast to their views of teaching and learning based on their own experiences as students. This often means hanging on to an authoritative narrative of science knowledge handed down to them by past teachers. Many of our prospective teachers view their job as passing down this knowledge — the story of science as they know it — just as it was handed down to them. Tools of inquiry demonstrated by the gifted science teacher in the demonstration video and recommended within science education as part of a cognitive tool kit for scientific reasoning are quickly reinterpreted by our beginning teachers as possible steps for transmitting their own science knowledge to their students. At the same time, our teacher candidates struggle with what they know or do not know about the content, and they sometimes have difficulty articulating what they want students to know. Yet they report their own needs as more closely associated with learning how to *do* the activities of teaching as a way of becoming a teacher, rather than thinking about what they want their students to know about science content.

According to our teacher candidates, students should be ready and willing to accept the transmission of knowledge, although many of our prospective teachers admit to having some fear that adolescents are not so willing. Teacher candidates want students to be happy and engaged and yet are fearful that they might become unmotivated. They note that the student in the clinical interview about photosynthesis is a home gardener, a great starting point for motivation, yet they fail to notice his misconceptions about plant nutrition. They note the cooperation of the struggling eighth grader yet are convinced he must know more than he is volunteering, assuming his difficulties have more to do with motivation than with low reading skill. These observations have led us to conclude that beginning teachers cope with the complexity of teaching by compartmentalizing and not connecting important problems, such as teaching content, teaching scientific reasoning, and understanding students (Tuckey & Anderson, in press).

This picture raises many problems with regard to preparing beginning teachers to embark on cognitive strategy instruction. The prominent position politically and from a policy perspective has been to inject information about content-area literacy teaching activities into preservice literacy courses. Nearly every state requires one — if not two or even three — courses in literacy for secondary preservice teachers. Providing lots of literacy-related teaching activities assuredly feeds prospective teachers' need to learn *how to do* teaching. The product of these mandates, however, might likely be entire cadres of beginning teachers all practicing the methods demonstrated in the first version of Ms. Gunnings's classroom, doing pedagogy co-opted for purposes of handing down authoritative knowledge from textbooks. This likelihood is increased when one considers that many beginning teachers feel rewarded by an educational system they believe did the same for them — handed them authoritative knowledge. Without clear understandings of subject-matter knowledge and goals, without learning about the challenges associated with various content area concepts, and without a measure of cognitive and emotional empathy for adolescents, how will prospective secondary teachers ever translate knowledge about strategy instruction into effective practice? The challenge ahead is to consider cognitive strategy instruction for preservice teachers in the context of this question and our own research.

The Research We Need

Despite the promises within the policy world, there is no "magic bullet" with regard to cognitive strategy instruction for adolescents. Part of the problem is that we simply do not know enough about cognitive strategy instruction and its educational role over time. We do not have a clear picture of how students can learn, apply, and transfer their understandings of cognitive strategies into increasingly complex subject-matter and workplace domains. Because of the murky and complex picture presented here, policies and funding directed toward developing cognitive strategies for adolescents represent little more than a shot in the dark. The potential for improving adolescent literacy through cognitive strategy instruction might best be addressed through research focused on how cognitive strategies can be developed over time; how cognitive strategy instruction "works" in the context of adolescence; how relationships between cognitive strategies and the knowledge, strategy, and discourse demands in the content areas function in higher education and the workplace; and, finally, how teachers can learn to integrate cognitive strategy instruction effectively within the complex domains and perspectives found in the content areas. This is the research we need.

How can and should cognitive strategies be developed over time for different purposes and in different contexts?

This is a question that has long haunted researchers who study cognitive strategy instruction. However, the concern of the research is often cast as one of sustaining understandings of specific cognitive strategies (Pressley & Hilden, 2006). Far less frequently represented is the concern for how the development and application of cognitive strategies need to change and adapt to different learning purposes and contexts. The issue of change and adaptation of strategies raises a range of other questions. For example, does an understanding of relatively simple cognitive strategies used for reading in elementary school create a foundation for other kinds of strategy learning and application later on in middle and high school? Might some kinds of cognitive strategy instruction interfere with learning in more complex subject-matter domains?

Consider a cognitive strategy such as summarization (Palincsar & Brown, 1984). For younger and older students, summarizing can be an effective way to self-check, to see if information from reading makes sense. A compelling argument is that teaching summarization in the early grades would pay dividends for adolescents because if their understanding of the strategy could be sustained, they could use it for sense-making across the curriculum. But what happens when the curriculum increases the challenge to the point where summarization is not sufficient? Envisioning this possibility is fairly easy, given critical and discourse perspectives within science (Anderson, 2007), social studies (Evans, 2006), English (Goebel, 2004), and mathematics (Sfard, 2001), as well as the complex array of tasks that span the workplace (Mikulecky, 2007). When confronted with the new challenges, will adolescents find a way to adapt summarization to the new and different purposes? Will they even recognize what is required of them in the new contexts? Will they hang on to summarization at the expense of the new challenges? What kinds of cognitive strategy instruction will be required to help adolescents persist in building their strategy learning?

What are the relationships between cognitive strategy teaching and learning and what we know about adolescence?

Despite nearly a decade of research on adolescents and their literacies, we know very little about the connections between adolescence and strategy development. This is a critical omission for both adolescent literacy researchers and for those interested in cognitive strategy instruction. Adolescent literacy researchers have provided a rich profile of adolescence, helping us understand the importance of discourse, knowledge, and the multiple literacies that adolescents develop by virtue of experiences at home, in their community, and at school (Alvermann, Hinchman, Moore, Phelps, & Waff, 2006). This research documents problems that emerge when teachers ignore adolescents' funds of knowledge. It problematizes the notion of struggling readers. Rather than claiming that adolescents are unskilled, as the term suggests, these researchers point to ways the education system fails to recognize adolescents' multiple literacies, especially those that adolescents acquire from out-of-school experiences such as using the Internet and playing computer games.

Yet this research and its accompanying rhetoric fail to envision a promising future for adolescents (Conley, 2007). While it celebrates adolescence in the moment, there is little if any concern for how adolescents can transform their experiences into success at school or later in life. As a result, we know little about how to develop adolescents' understandings of cognitive strategies. This raises several important questions: How do students' experiences in their families, in their communities, and with their peers equip them for understanding cognitive strategies? Is there a sense that adolescents become strategic from these experiences? Could those experiences be productively mined for further strategy instruction? Are there adolescent experiences that conflict with notions about cognitive strategies? For example, are cognitive strategies defined by adolescents as school-based knowledge in ways that might cause them to reject their use in other contexts?

Researchers in cognitive strategy instruction have long worried about what happens when cognitive strategies are developed in more complex domains (Pressley & Hilden, 2006). Most of this research has been done with simple recall or memory tasks, and in nowhere near as complex an environment as a middle or high school classroom. An important finding from this research is that motivation is an important condition for effective instruction (Pressley, Kersey, Bogaert, Mohan, Roehrig, & Bogner-Warson, 2003). Specifically, learning cognitive strategies requires motivation and persistence. As subject-matter and workplace texts and tasks become even more complex, the challenges for motivation and cognitive strategy instruction increase. The research on adolescent literacy provides a number of reasons why adolescents might not be motivated to learn cognitive strategies, such as the competing worlds of peers and out-of-school experiences. But adolescent literacy research also offers clues to what it might take to engage adolescents in cognitive strategy instruction, including combining cognitive strategy instruction with specific instructional strategies for building motivation. Concept-Oriented Reading Instruction (Guthrie, Wigfield, & Perencevich, 2004; Swan, 2004) is one example where researchers have begun to explore the relationship between adolescents, motivation, and strategies like activating prior knowledge. Given that adolescent literacy researchers have established that adolescence is a particularly important time for identity formation and exploration, it is essential that cognitive strategy research takes into account the motivational challenges and opportunities that may underlie the effectiveness of strategy instruction for adolescents.

What are the relationships between cognitive strategies and the knowledge, strategy, and discourse demands in the content areas, in higher education and in the workplace?

Cognitive strategy researchers and literacy educators tend to prescribe simple solutions to complex subject-matter, higher education, and workplace domains.

Strategies are used, for example, to create summaries or to write questions, but there is rarely, if ever, a concern about the topical task or philosophical diversity that characterizes learning within and across disciplines and throughout the workplace. This gap is particularly evident when comparing the basic strategy research in which six or seven strategies are championed for reading with differences in expectations at the high school and college levels, or when comparing the diverse array of workplace tasks and implied cognitive demands of job-related skills (Human Resources and Skills Development Canada, 2007).

There are several problems that emerge from maintaining this gap between simple cognitive strategies for younger children and the increasingly complex and diverse cognitive demands of the content areas, higher education, and the workplace. One problem concerns equipping students with cognitive strategies that simply may not be adequate for the demands of more complex and diverse domains. Preparing adolescents with cognitive strategies that assume homogenized and unvarying kinds of knowledge and tasks creates the possibility that they will be unprepared for more difficult challenges and will be limited in their options later in life. Researchers have argued and even demonstrated that cognitive strategies are a good foundation for school-to-work transitions (Deshler & Schumaker, 2006). However, this foundation will be inadequate if the development of cognitive strategies is unaccompanied by a view of the content areas, higher education, and the world of work as complex and diverse.

Recognizing this complexity raises yet another set of questions: Does this mean that the knowledge, tasks, discourses, and skills of all of the content areas, higher education, and workplace domains need to be catalogued so that cognitive strategies can be explicitly taught? If so, is there an applied curriculum for very young children, through adolescence, and beyond? Are there essential core strategies from which all of the others emanate? And, the perennial cognitive strategy question, what about transfer? Should a core of strategies be taught and learned, accompanied by strategies for transferring learning across different domains?

How can teachers learn to integrate cognitive strategy instruction effectively within the complex domains and perspectives found in the content areas?

If the research on strategy instruction has demonstrated anything, it is how difficult it can be for teachers to engage in cognitive strategy instruction, particularly at the secondary level. The preparation of secondary teachers tends to focus on development of content knowledge. Although the content areas are diverse in philosophical intent, they all share a common perspective that the purpose of teaching is to promote content acquisition (Conley, in press). Among the teacher candidates in our study, most interpret teaching as passing on authoritative knowledge to (hopefully) willing recipients. However, there are many troubling aspects of our story. One is that the teacher candidates tend to see the need to build their students' knowledge but not their capac-

101

ity to learn. Another is that teacher candidates do not have a broad view of the need to know students or to connect students' understandings to their teaching. These circumstances naturally reduce any consideration for cognitive strategy instruction and how it might be helpful, other than for picking up more activities for their teaching bag of tricks.

The implications of this picture are challenging. Teacher educators need a way to redirect the priorities of teacher candidates to focus on understanding adolescents in rich ways by integrating goals for content learning with developing adolescents' capacities and identities. This is no easy task. Traditional approaches to preparing content-area teachers emphasize content acquisition. State teacher-preparation standards that emphasize teaching activities, as in the content-area literacy textbooks, state tests, and core curricula, all conspire to keep the focus squarely on subject-matter and step-by-step pedagogy. These circumstances support the ongoing complaint made by secondary teachers that they do not have time to teach cognitive strategies. These conditions could also be a reason for the frequent complaints by administrators, policymakers, teacher educators, and even parents that secondary teachers do not "see" students. Given the predominant focus on developing content knowledge through content-area literacy activities that fail to engage students in deeper thinking, policymakers need to consider what gets sacrificed under these conditions. By focusing so much attention on building knowledge while using unproven if not uncertain pedagogical tools, policymakers could severely constrain opportunities for teachers to build pupils' capacity to learn in and beyond the content areas.

Despite these challenges, we are beginning to redesign courses and field experiences to create a greater likelihood that adolescents and their lifelong learning will be at the center of our teacher candidates' concerns. Some of our ideas consist of targeted tutoring experiences where our teacher candidates conduct in-depth student interviews and then observe students as they encounter various kinds of knowledge and tasks throughout the school day. We will also develop pedagogy that supports and challenges our teacher candidates as they observe instruction, seeking to expand their view from the authoritative subject-matter perspective to an understanding of how teachers listen to and are responsive to students. We are preparing a context in which our teacher candidates can consider how subject-matter teaching and cognitive strategy instruction go hand in hand.

Will cognitive strategy instruction be worth the effort?

Finally, we have to ask the question: Will it be worth the effort? Will we eventually know enough about cognitive strategy instruction and how it can deliver on the promises? Teachers are bombarded by external demands, from the implementation of new core curricula to mandated testing. It seems unfair and unrealistic to ask teachers to set aside valuable planning and instructional time to focus on cognitive strategy instruction when we know so little about what it is or could be, about how to implement it, or even about how to judge its effectiveness with regard to the current standards for test performance. Given the current policy environment for secondary schooling, it is no surprise that the ongoing response from teachers is that they do not have the time or the energy to take on one more thing, much less an initiative without a proven record of success, particularly for adolescents.

On the other hand, the idea of building capacity for learning from the early grades through adolescence and adulthood is educationally appealing. Is it possible to develop cognitive strategies in young children that could be expanded and elaborated? Can we find a balance between content, general, and specific strategies, and teach students how to adapt these strategies for different purposes and contexts? Can research identify a curriculum that would provide a vision for how cognitive strategy instruction could work from early childhood through adolescence and adulthood? We just do not know. But if research could answer these questions, the issues surrounding the potential or value of cognitive strategy instruction might be resolved.

From time to time, research provides glimmers of what might be possible. In a recent study, researchers introduced cognitive strategies to high school English-language learners, including planning and goal setting; activating prior knowledge; forming interpretations; and reflecting, relating, and evaluating (Olson & Land, 2007). These strategies are similar to ones I have identified as important for successful performance on high-stakes tests (Conley, 2004). These strategies also happen to be useful in many real-life situations. Not surprisingly, students who internalized these strategies performed better on both high-stakes tests and placement tests for community college English classes than students who were not introduced to the strategies. According to this research, the close integration of the cognitive strategies with content-area purposes and material is a key element for student achievement (Olson & Land, 2007). We need additional research like this, which specifically connects cognitive strategy instruction to adolescents and content-area contexts and thereby supports student achievement.

Conclusion

This essay started by describing the promise of cognitive strategies for adolescents. There is indeed increased interest in adolescent literacy as evidenced by blue-ribbon-panel reports, foundation support, and legislative initiatives. There is a solid record of research both in adolescent literacy and in cognitive strategy instruction that would suggest that an integrated effort toward implementing cognitive strategy instruction for adolescents would pay big dividends in learning (Biancarosa & Snow, 2004; Graham & Perin, 2007; Heller & Greenleaf, 2007; National Governors Association, 2005).

But there is so much more that we do not know about the potential of using cognitive strategies. Research is needed to clarify the role and development of cognitive strategies in teaching adolescents about complex subject matter and preparing them for workplace domains. We need a vision of a cognitive strategy curriculum that will develop, sustain, and adapt students' strategic learning capabilities from early childhood through adolescence and beyond. This vision needs to be intimately connected to the diverse yet specific knowledge, tasks, and discourse demands of various subject areas, higher education settings, and occupations. As we develop this vision, we also need to attend to the challenges and constraints that limit the potential for secondary teachers to commit to cognitive strategy instruction. For this to happen, a better balance must be struck between knowledge, adolescents, and practice so that adolescents and their learning are not left out of the equation. Without an understanding of how cognitive strategies may be effectively integrated into efforts to improve adolescent literacy, it is hard to argue for more money, policy, or legislation focused on intervention. With efforts directed toward research and the questions articulated here, we may eventually develop a better understanding of how cognitive strategy instruction for adolescents could actually deliver on its potential for adolescent literacy.

Notes

1. Visit the website for the Essential Skills and Workplace Literacy Initiative at http://srv108.services.gc.ca/english/general/home_e.shtml
2. I have observed this frequently when teachers try to develop strategies for test taking, such as highlighting or diagramming test questions, as a way for students to get organized to respond to test questions. When the test begins, the tools students might use to implement a cognitive strategy, including highlighters or scratch paper, sit ignored on their desks as students rush through their questions without any outward evidence that they are using a cognitive strategy.
3. Visit *Science Daily* online at: http://www.sciencedaily.com/news/earth_climate/pollution
4. There is often confusion about terminology between *cognitive strategies* and *comprehension strategies*. Different cognitive strategies can have different purposes, sometimes for discovering word meanings, but also for constructing meanings of entire passages. Because of their purpose in constructing meaning from larger portions of text, the latter types are often referred to as *comprehension-oriented cognitive strategies*, or, in short, *comprehension strategies*.
5. Very few, if any, textbooks use the term *cognitive strategies*, preferring instead to use the generic term *strategies*. The intended meaning for the use of the term *strategies* is not always clear.
6. An activity that is very popular with teachers is Tovani's notion of double-entry journals or diaries. The steps for double-entry journals are described and illustrated, and there are justifications for why teachers should use them. There are examples coming from different content areas. Teachers are responsible for doing the work of identifying and articulating subject matter purposes and developing well-integrated, purposeful strategy instruction.
7. Research cited in the content-area literacy textbooks often goes back eighty years or more. My concern was that the translation of the research into the textbooks could miss the original intent of the research. So, it was important to read and cite the original research rather than depend only on the information in the textbooks.

References

ACT. (2006). *ACT national curriculum survey.* Iowa City, IA: Author.

Alvermann, D., Hinchman, K., Moore, D., Phelps, S., & Waff, D. (2006). *Reconceptualizing the literacies in adolescents' lives.* New York: Erlbaum.

Anderson, C. (2007). Perspectives on science learning. In S. Abell & N. Lederman (Eds.), *Handbook of research on science education* (pp. 3–30). Mahwah, NJ: Erlbaum.

Bean, T., Readance, J., & Baldwin, S. (2007). *Content area literacy: An integrated approach.* Dubuque, IA: Kendall Hunt.

Biancarosa, G., & Snow, C. (2004). *Reading next — A vision for action and research in middle and high school literacy: A report from Carnegie Corporation of New York.* Washington, DC: Alliance for Excellent Education.

Conley, M. (2004). *Connecting standards and assessment through literacy.* Boston: Allyn and Bacon.

Conley, M. (2007). Reconsidering adolescent literacy: From competing agendas to shared commitment. In M. Pressley, A. K. Billman, K. H. Perry, K. E. Reffitt, & J. M. Reynolds (Eds.), *Shaping literacy achievement: Research we have, research we need* (pp. 77–97). New York: Guilford.

Conley, M. (2008). *Content area literacy: Learners in context.* New York: Allyn and Bacon.

Conley, M. (in press). Improving adolescent comprehension: Developing comprehension strategies in the content areas. In S. Israel & G. Duffy (Eds.), *Handbook of research on reading comprehension.* New York: Erlbaum.

Conley, M., Kerner, M., & Reynolds, J. (2005). Not a question of "should," but a question of "how": Integrating literacy knowledge and practice into secondary teacher preparation through tutoring in middle schools. *Action in Teacher Education, 27*(2), 22–32.

Deshler, D., Palincsar, A., Biancarosa, G., & Nair, M. (2007). *Informed choices for struggling adolescent readers: A research-based guide to instructional programs and practices.* New York: Carnegie.

Deshler, D., & Schumaker, B. (1988). An instructional model for teaching students how to learn. In J. Graden, J. Zins, & M. Curtis (Eds.), *Alternative educational delivery systems: Enhancing instructional options for all students* (pp. 391–411). Washington, DC: National Association for School Psychologists.

Deshler, D., & Schumaker, B. (2006). *Teaching adolescents with disabilities: Accessing the general education curriculum.* Thousand Oaks, CA: Corwin.

Evans, R. (2006). The social studies wars, now and then. *Social Education, 70*(5), 317–325.

Goebel, B. (2004). *An ethical approach to teaching Native American literature.* Urbana, IL: National Council of Teachers of English.

Graham, S. (2006). Strategy instruction and the teaching of writing. In C. MacArthur, S. Graham, & J. Fitzgerald (Eds.), *Handbook of writing research* (pp. 187–207). New York: Guilford.

Graham, S., & Perin, D. (2007). *Writing next: Effective strategies to improve writing of adolescents in middle and high schools.* Washington, DC: Alliance for Excellent Education.

Guthrie, J., Wigfield, A., & Perencevich, K. (2004). *Motivating reading instruction: Concept-oriented reading instruction.* New York: Erlbaum.

Heller, R., & Greenleaf, C. (2007). *Literacy instruction in the content areas: Getting to the core of middle and high school improvement.* Washington, DC: Alliance for Excellent Education.

Human Resources and Skills Development Canada. (2007). Essential skills and workplace literacy initiative. Retrieved June 12, 2007, from http://srv108.services.gc.ca/english/general/home_e.shtml

Kaestle, C., Campbell, A., Finn, J., Johnson, S., & Mikulecky, L. (2001). *Adult literacy and education in America.* Washington, DC: National Center for Education Statistics.

Manzo, A., & Manzo, U. (1990). *Content area reading: A heuristic approach.* Columbus, OH: Merrill.

McKenna, M., & Robinson, R. (1990). Content literacy: A definition and implications. *Journal of Adolescent and Adult Literacy, 34,* 184–186.

Mikulecky, L. (2007). Workplace literacy. In B. Guzzetti (Ed.), *Literacy for the new millennium* (Vol. 4). Westport, CT: Greenwood.

National Governors Association. (2005). *Reading to achieve: A governor's guide to adolescent literacy.* Washington, DC: NGA Center for Best Practices.

Olson, C., & Land, R. (2007). A cognitive strategies approach to reading and writing instruction for English language learners in secondary school. *Research in the Teaching of English, 41*(3), 269–303.

Palincsar, A., & Brown, R. (1984). Reciprocal teaching of comprehension-fostering and monitoring activities. *Cognition and Instruction, 1,* 117–175.

Pressley, M. (2000). What should comprehension instruction be the instruction of? In M. Kamil, P. Mosenthal, P. Pearson, & R. Barr (Eds.), *Handbook of reading research* (Vol. III, pp. 545–561). Mahwah, NJ: Erlbaum.

Pressley, M. (2006). *Reading instruction that works: The case for balanced teaching.* New York: Guilford.

Pressley, M., & Hilden, K. (2006). Cognitive strategies: Production deficiencies and successful strategy instruction everywhere. In D. Kuhn & R. Siegler (Eds.), *Handbook of child psychology* (Vol. 2, pp. 440–480). Hoboken, NJ: Wiley and Sons.

Pressley, M., Kersey, S., Bogaert, L., Mohan, L., Roehrig, A., & Bogner-Warson, K. (2003). *Motivating primary grade students.* New York: Guilford.

Raphael, T., & Pearson, P. (1985). Increasing student awareness of sources of information for answering questions. *American Educational Research Journal, 22,* 217–237.

Rasinski, T., Padak, N., McKeon, C., Wilfong, L., Friedauer, J., & Heim, P. (2005). Is reading fluency a key to successful high school reading? *Journal of Adolescent and Adult Literacy, 49*(1), 22–28.

Schumaker, J., & Deshler, D. (2006). Teaching adolescents to be strategic learners. In D. Deshler & B. Schumaker (Eds.), *Teaching adolescents with disabilities: Accessing the general education curriculum* (pp. 121–156). Thousand Oaks, CA: Corwin Press.

Sfard, A. (2001). Learning mathematics as developing a discourse. In R. Speiser & W. Maher (Eds.), *Proceedings of the 21st conference of PME-NA* (pp. 23–46). Columbus, OH: Clearinghouse for Science, Mathematics, and Environmental Education.

Snow, C., & Biancarosa, G. (2003). *Adolescent literacy and the achievement gap: What do we know and where do we go from here?* New York: Carnegie Corporation.

Stauffer, R. (1975). *Directing the reading-thinking process.* New York: Harper and Row.

Swan, E. (2004). Motivating adolescent readers through concept-oriented reading instruction. In T. Jetton & J. Dole (Eds.), *Adolescent literacy research and practice* (pp. 283–303). New York: Guilford.

Tierney, R., & Readance, J. (2004). *Reading strategies and practices: A compendium.* New York: Allyn and Bacon.

Tovani, C. (2004a). *Do I really have to teach reading? Content comprehension, grades 6–12.* Portland, ME: Stenhouse.

Tovani, C. (2004b). *I read it, but I don't get it.* Portland, ME: Stenhouse.

Tuckey, S., & Anderson, C. (in press). Literacy in science: Using agency in the material world to expand the conversation. In M. Conley, J. Freidhoff, M. Sherry, & S. Tuckey (Eds.), *Adolescent literacy: The research we have and the research we need.* New York: Guilford.

U.S. Department of Labor. (1991). *What work requires of schools: A SCANS report for America 2000.* Washington, DC: U.S. Department of Labor.

Vacca, R., & Vacca, J. (2007). *Content area reading: Literacy and learning across the curriculum.* New York: Allyn and Bacon.

The Complex World of Adolescent Literacy: Myths, Motivations, and Mysteries

ELIZABETH BIRR MOJE
MELANIE OVERBY
NICOLE TYSVAER
KAREN MORRIS
University of Michigan

In this article, Elizabeth Birr Moje, Melanie Overby, Nicole Tysvaer, and Karen Morris challenge some of the prevailing myths about adolescents and their choices related to reading. The reading practices of youth from one urban community are examined using mixed methods in an effort to define what, how often, and why adolescents choose to read. By focusing on what features of texts youth find motivating, the authors find that reading and writing frequently occur in a range of literacy contexts outside school. However, only reading novels on a regular basis outside of school is shown to have a positive relationship to academic achievement as measured by school grades. This article describes how adolescents read texts that are embedded in social networks, allowing them to build social capital. Conclusions are framed in terms of the mysteries that remain — namely, how to build on what motivates adolescents' literacy practices in order to both promote the building of their social selves and improve their academic outcomes.

It is popular these days to raise concerns about the adolescent literacy crisis. But what does it mean, really, to talk about adolescent literacy? Who are adolescents? What is literacy? What is a crisis? In our work with young people across a variety of spaces, contexts, and social, racial, and ethnic groups, we have noted both vastly different and remarkably similar approaches to skills in reading and writing a range of different texts. We find, in fact, that even within a tightly defined population of young people in one neighborhood, a predominantly Latino/a community in a large midwestern city, many different ways of and reasons for reading and writing can be discerned. We posed specific ques-

Harvard Educational Review Vol. 78 No. 1 Spring 2008

tions to the youth participants of our study, which are discussed throughout this article. Consider, for example, their responses to the interview question, "Why do you read what you read?"

- My uncle wants to take me to hunting classes so he gave me his hunting books, so I could start reading them. I just started reading them yesterday . . . It's 'cause I never went hunting before so I can just do something for fun that I could do with my uncle, instead of just feeling left out 'cause he always talks about hunting, and he likes to go hunting and he likes to hunt for deers and stuff, so now I can, like, talk to him about that too.
- Mysteries, because I like — it's so fun how they investigate and then, like, you try to guess who it is, and then sometimes you're right, and at the end it tells if you were right. And then you get so excited, like, "Oh yeah, I was right," you know.
- For fun, see, 'cause my dad sometimes brings in magazines — newspapers, I mean. The Latin newspapers, like maybe once a month or something . . . I would just go to the sports section and see what's up and that's it . . .
- Well, one, just Bill Clinton's book is real big, so I figure, "Hey, I could tackle that one." *A Lesson Before Dying* (Gaines, 1997), it was just something I picked up and couldn't put down.
- [*Game Informer*] 'cause I can know which games are coming out and if they're good or not.
- [I don't read] often. I only, like, when I don't got nothing to do, or when I think, like, I get bored of playing video games, I just grab a book and start reading it. I lay on my bed, and I put it on top, and I start reading it.

Responses to this question were so varied, in fact, that it was difficult to choose just which ones to include for this introduction. Virtually any set of responses would have represented the fact that while some youth read a great deal, others hardly read at all. Some read print novels, while others gravitate toward Internet texts and still others like a good magazine. Some do not read much but they love to write. Moreover, as we document in this article, the reasons the youth in this study give for their literacy practices are equally diverse. They read because they are part of social groups or because they are in search of role models or information. They write for self-expression, to get through periods of crisis, to document their beliefs, or to communicate with other youth. Thus, we see the world of adolescent literacy as complex, not only because both "adolescent" and "literacy" are ill-defined constructs, but also because young people are so different from one another. And yet, although the specifics of their literacy practices are different, they do share some important patterns. Our goal in this article, then, is twofold: We wish to complexify notions of what it means to talk about adolescent literacy, but we also want to draw attention to some overarching patterns in at least one group's literacy practices. Our larger purpose is to shed light on what, why, and how youth read so that educators can adopt policies and practices that address the range of youth interests, needs, and skills, and also to support youth in developing sophisticated academic, community, and workplace literacy practices.

To these ends, we offer analyses of what, how often, and why young people from one urban community choose to read. These analyses address the myths — and realities — of adolescent literacy in one community. We focus on the motivating (and demotivating) features of the texts these young people choose, and we examine the connection between out-of-school practices and in-school achievement. Conclusions are framed in terms of the remaining mysteries of adolescent literacy development, but we also suggest implications for practical moves, research designs, and policy interventions that may be helpful in enhancing adolescents' literate development.

Theoretical and Empirical Perspectives on Adolescent Literacy

Adolescent literacy represents an ill-defined area of study in the field of education, with debates over what counts as literacy, who counts as an adolescent (with even a seemingly simple concept such as age debated), and on what adolescent literacy research should focus.

What Counts as Literacy: A Sociocultural Perspective

To address the definitional question of adolescent literacy, it is first necessary to define literacy more generally. Definitions of literacy range from perspectives that limit it to the ability to read and write alphabetic print (Goody, 1999) to those that posit literacy as any form of oral and/or written communicative practice (Resnick & Gordon, 1999). A sociocultural perspective on literacy acknowledges the role of print and other symbol systems as being central to literate practice, but recognizes that the learning and use of symbols is mediated by and constituted in social systems and cultural practices (Heath, 1983; Scribner & Cole, 1981; Street, 1984).

To this sociocultural view on literacy practice we add a critical stance, arguing that power, identities, and agency play important roles in whose social and cultural practices are valued — and, thus, whose literacy practices are valued and whose are not (Moje & Lewis, 2007). Literacy is not just any social practice, but one that requires making sense of a variety of codes — symbolic, visual, oral, and embodied (Kress, 2003). Having access to socially constructed and conventionalized codes is central to being part of a community and means having access to certain kinds of power; it also allows people to adopt the self (or identity) they feel is appropriate or demanded by a particular relationship, space, or time (see Moje, 2004, on "enacting" identities).

Although literacy focuses on making sense of written symbols, other ways of communicating (e.g., oral language, photographs, drawings, body language, and dress) also play a central role in making and representing meaning in conjunction with written symbols. Without each of these forms of representation, reading and writing would be limited tools. The research represented in this paper revolves heavily around how youth use print texts in the context of other activities in their lives, but at the same time, we cannot ignore the role of other forms of representation that shape how young people read and write print and other symbols. For example, one type of text that many of the youth in our study read is *manga* (Japanese comics on paper), which is an intricate combination of words and image. Because we are interested in their reading of manga, we are also interested in their watching of *anime* (Japanese animated cartoons, typically shown on television) and any other television, movies, conversation, art, or music that support meaning-making when reading manga. The same relationships between print and nonprint forms hold for the other types of texts we document. Thus, our research interest begins with the reading of written symbols but does not ignore other forms of representation that contribute to making sense of those written symbols.

What Is an Adolescent?

With this theoretical stance on literacy in mind, we turn to the question of what an adolescent is. Although the label *adolescent* is the source of some debate (see Lesko, 2001), it is generally accepted that people between the ages of ten and twenty are within the range of adolescence. A number of educators consider adolescent literacy to begin at the fourth-grade level, when text demands shift from a predominance of narrative, or story-based, texts to increasing encounters with expository, or informational, texts. This is a reasonable assumption, but allowing for such an age and grade span in the definition of adolescence overlooks at least two important factors that should be considered when thinking about adolescent literacy, particularly when much of the research conducted is cross-sectional in design (i.e., focuses on one age cohort at a time). One factor is the role of physical and cognitive development on youth literacy practices. The other is the role of secondary school contexts, with their changing classes and teachers, disciplinary divisions, and increasing controls (see Eccles, Lord, & Midgley, 1991; Eccles, Wigfield, Midgley, Reuman, MacIver, & Feldlaufer, 1993, on the developmental mismatch between secondary school settings and adolescents' needs). As a result, our work focuses on youth between grades six and twelve, with an approximate age range of twelve to eighteen. We focus on that age range in order to document how school and community contexts, as well as young people's changing independent status and their advancing cognitive development, may play a role in their thinking about and practices of literacy. Our study design allows for both cross-sectional and, eventually, longitudinal analyses of these physical, social, and contextual changes over time.

What Is Adolescent Literacy?

The unique construct of *adolescent literacy* also requires definition. John Guthrie and Jamie Metsala (1999) describe proficient youth literacy in these terms:

A highly achieving student, whether at grade four, eight, or twelve, must not only comprehend passages of text but must also (1) integrate information across multiple texts, (2) critically relate paragraph meanings to personal experience, (3) employ knowledge from texts to evaluate science observations or historical documents, and (4) compose complete messages in the form of stories and reports for actual audiences. (p. 382)

Data from the National Assessment of Educational Progress (NAEP) (Donahue, Daane, & Grigg, 2003) suggest, however, that although a considerable percentage (approximately 70% across the age range) of young people aged ten to eighteen are able to read and write at basic levels or above, few are able to read and write with proficiency (23% to 30%) and even fewer (3% to 6%) at advanced levels. National attention has focused on those adolescent readers who perform below the basic level on these achievement measures and on the well-documented fact that the below-basic category is occupied by a disproportionate percentage of ethnic and racial minority youth and youth who live in poverty. Thus, the label *struggling reader* (and, to a lesser extent, *writer*) has emerged as a catchphrase associated with adolescent literacy. More recently, however, perhaps due to reports released by ACT, Inc., (2006) indicating that only 51 percent of graduating high school students read well enough to succeed in college, attention has turned to youth who read at basic but not proficient or advanced levels.

Interest is also increasing in adolescents who are successful readers and writers of narrative and general expository texts but who struggle with the demands of the specialized or disciplinary texts they encounter in middle and high school. Germane to this focus on disciplinary texts, many scholars define proficient adolescent literacy skills more specifically as the ability to read, interpret, critique, and produce the discourse of a disciplinary area (Bain, 2006; Hand, Wallace, & Yang, 2004; Lee, 2005; Wineburg, 2001; Wineburg & Martin, 2004). These scholars argue that to learn in a content area, young people need access to the conventions of disciplinary knowledge production and communication. Such knowledge, they argue, gives young people the power to read critically across various texts and various disciplines. Thus they become critical readers and thinkers.

From this perspective, young people in secondary school are expected to participate in the discourses of the disciplines, to incorporate these discourses into other discourses and identities they experience throughout the secondary school day, and to forge, or at least try out, new identities as they take up these discourses (Gee, 2001; Luke, 2001; Luke & Elkins, 1998). This suggests that teachers of content areas need to provide young people with opportunities to examine the discourses of the subject-area texts in relation to the discourses of everyday life (i.e., the ways they read, write, and speak with friends, family, and in the community) (Moje, Collazo, Carrillo, & Marx, 2001).

Still others claim that adolescent literacy skills for the twenty-first century must revolve around navigating multiliteracies (Luke & Elkins, 1998; Luke,

2002; New London Group, 1996) or having the ability to read many different types of texts, each imbued with the discourses of a particular community or affinity group (i.e., a group of like-minded people who engage in shared practices). The New London Group (1996) argues that education should be as much about learning to be metadiscursive as it is about teaching conventional codes and scripts. Metadiscursivity is the ability to engage in many different discourse communities, to know how and why one is engaging, and to recognize what those engagements mean for oneself and others in terms of social positioning and larger power relations. Metadiscursiveness provides access to many different literacies because readers and writers can understand the different discourses that authors bring to bear on a text or can produce such discourses themselves. Scholars of "new literacies" further argue that the technologies for accessing, creating, and producing codes and scripts, whether conventional or alternative, should be a site of instruction (Leu, 2005). These scholars suggest that the digital media themselves shape what gets written and how such texts should be read, and that young people need to develop both skills in using these technologies and strategies for navigating the technologies when their skills break down.

Raising the question of what it means for adolescents to really be literate in a new century also raises questions about whether school-based — or academic — literacy skills are the best metric by which to measure adolescent literacy skills. Although NAEP data suggest that many young people are not proficient in the literacy skills necessary for proficient and advanced literacy achievement, a number of adolescent literacy researchers who have studied youth engaged in literacy outside of school have observed what appears to be proficiency with sophisticated texts, even among youth identified as "struggling" in school (Alvermann, Young, Green, & Wisenbaker, 1999; Cowan, 2005; Knobel, 1999; Mahiri, 2003; Moje, 2000). Such studies have suggested that some literacy activities may be more motivating and engaging to youth than others, compelling youth to persist even in the face of challenging texts. Another interpretation is that school texts and practices are typically static and even demotivating; thus, youth do not exert any effort to make sense of them, even when the texts are not terribly challenging (see Leander & Lovvorn, 2006).

Whatever the explanation, these studies highlight the complexity of literacy activities youth engage in outside of school, demonstrating that many young people are able to read across a variety of symbol systems, including print, such as those represented on the Internet's instant messenger (cf. Lewis & Fabos, 2005), or in video and computer games (Alvermann, Hagood, & Williams, 2001; Leander & Lovvorn, 2006; Mahiri, 1994). Others have documented that youth can produce complex texts in a variety of media, including print on paper and in digital environments (Camitta, 1993; Chandler-Olcott & Mahar, 2003; Gustavson, 2007; Ingalls, 2005; Knobel & Lankshear, 2002; O'Brien & King, 2002). In each case, researchers have noted that the youth studied appear to be highly motivated to engage in and complete the activities under study, even when the literacy activities appeared to challenge some of their skills. Studies of youth engaged in digital or new literacies suggest that many of the text forms that hold young people's interest have been designed to engage youth. Gee (2003), for example, argues that video games create identities into which readers can step, set goals for the different players to achieve, and provide lexical and other supports to guide gamers/readers as they engage with the texts. In their analysis of youth text choices out of school, Ellis, Moje, and VanDerPloeg (2004) demonstrate that even conventional print texts offer personas that call out to the reader, engaging their subjective experiences in ways that school texts do not.

"Motivated literacy" (McCaslin, 1990), then, is a construct worth studying in more depth. Scholars can ask not only whether adolescents are motivated to engage in particular activities, but also whether the types of texts and contexts available to them influence their abilities to engage in basic, proficient, and advanced levels of literacy skill. A number of scholars have studied motivation and engagement in reading (Alexander, 2003; Alexander, Kulikowich, & Jetton, 1994; Alvermann et al., 1999; Guthrie & Wigfield, 2000), whereas other researchers have studied motivation more generally (Blumenfeld, Kempler & Krajcik, 2006; Eccles et al., 1993). Each emphasizes the importance of understanding motivation and engagement as an aspect of reading comprehension and general school achievement. Wigfield, Eccles, and Rodriguez (1998), in particular, highlight the importance of understanding motivation and engagement in relation to social context and the interactions in which young readers and writers find themselves. Alexander, Kulikowich, and Jetton (1994) investigated the intersection of learner interest with subject matter domain knowledge and strategic processing in reading. Similarly, Moje, Dillon, and O'Brien (2000) argued that reading (and all literacy acts) is the result of an intricate intersection of learner knowledge and interest, textual factors, and social, cultural, and disciplinary contexts.

Given the importance of motivated readers and motivating texts and contexts to literate proficiency, it seems that arguments for the development of proficient, strategic, metadiscursive adolescent readers and writers must be informed by studies of adolescent motivation and engagement. Does the motivation to obtain a particular type of information shape adolescents' abilities to integrate information across texts, relate text meanings to personal experience, employ knowledge from texts to evaluate observations or documents, and compose messages for actual audiences? It may be that the contexts and texts of classrooms are not engaging enough to draw young people in, or that everyday literacy skills are cognitively different from those required in academic learning settings. Perhaps the different social and cultural arrangements of home, community, peer social network, and school constrain the transfer of literacy skills from one context to another. Or, are the literate demands of schooling not relevant to the literate demands of the world adolescents have come to value?

Each of the questions posed above is an open question in adolescent literacy research and theory. Although research on adolescent literacy learning in school has been conducted for the last fifty years — and research on outside-of-school literacy has increased dramatically in the past twenty years — few studies have united these two contexts to explore adolescents' engagement in literacy practices and development of literate skills over time and across contexts. In particular, there are few large-scale studies of adolescents' out-of-school practices, and there are few in-depth studies of adolescents' academic literacy proficiencies.

To begin addressing those questions, we report here on our ongoing, longitudinal, integrated-methods study of youth reading and writing practices in one community, focusing on the following research questions:

- What do young people in one community read and write outside of school?
- What is the relationship between what they read and write outside of school and their achievement in school?
- What motivates youth to read and write outside of school?

Research Design and Methods

The theoretical frame for this study of adolescent literacy assumes that literacy is socially situated and mediated; therefore, our research design reflects a socio-cultural orientation to understanding the social and cultural practices of literacy. At the same time, we are interested in representing the literacy practices of a normative sample of adolescents. Thus, the study design incorporates methods that allow us to document and analyze the practices, skills, and motivations of large numbers of youth, while also documenting and analyzing how and why youth read by focusing on a smaller subsample of the larger population.

Specifically, in this study, we administer a large-scale literacy practices and motivations survey, as well as a large-scale reading diagnostic. School records and writing samples are also collected for the overall sample. We then conduct multiple types of interviews and collect artifacts from a subsample of these youth, and we follow an even smaller subsample ethnographically by collecting data over time in schools and in the community served by the focal schools. Our methods of analysis, too, always derive from and speak to a socio-cultural orientation; we employ statistical, constant-comparative, and discursive-analytic methods, with the goal of allowing our data sources and methods to inform each other. These procedures are discussed in detail in the following sections.

Participants and Sites

Data in this analysis are drawn from an ongoing longitudinal study in a predominantly Latino/a community in a large Midwestern city (population 950,000). Moje began research in this community nine years ago with a community ethnography focused on youth literacies, identities, and cultures. In 2004, Moje added a large-scale survey component combined with continuing ethnographic work. Two waves of data were collected at the time this article was prepared. The Wave 1 sample includes 329 sixth-, eighth-, and ninth-grade students in one private religious school and two public schools in the early spring of 2005. The Wave 2 sample for this article includes 716 seventh-, ninth-, and tenth-grade students from three public schools and one public charter school in early spring of 2006.[1] Each of these schools serves the community under study and thus were recruited for participation.

The ethnic/racial composition of the sample is 72.1 percent Latino/a, 20.9 percent African American, 5.6 percent European American, and 1.4 percent other, with some slight variation by year of the study.[2] Slightly more than half (56.1%) are female. Students range in age from 10.8 to 17.0 years of age, and nearly two-thirds of the students speak Spanish at some level (i.e., some identify as fluently bilingual, others identify as Spanish monolingual, and still others identify as speaking only some Spanish). The percentage of economically disadvantaged youth ranges from 73 to 91 percent, depending on the school setting. According to U.S. Census data, the majority of residents in these students' neighborhood(s) live below the federal poverty line. Table 1 presents student demographics for the full Wave 2 sample.

Our sampling procedure is to recruit all students in the target grades from all schools, including students who receive specialized student services (e.g., emotionally impaired, honors, corrective reading, English as a second language classes). Our demographic data indicate that we have achieved a sample representative of the ethnic/racial, gendered, linguistic, and achievement-level populations of each school.

The subsample for the present study includes seventy-nine youth, which represents 10 percent of the overall sample. For this subsample, we make an effort to recruit youth who represent different patterns of literate practice in terms of reading frequency, nature of texts read, and motivations for in-school and out-of-school reading and writing activities. We also attempt to recruit members of both sexes and a proportionally representative sample of the different ethnic and racial groups represented in our larger sample. However, gender representation in the subsample is skewed toward females, who currently represent 65 percent of the interview sample (but only 56 percent of the overall sample). The subsample also does not currently include any European American youth. Finally, we recruit the subsample from across school contexts, and we continually add youth to the subsample as the study progresses.

The research team is comprised of researchers of varying years and levels of expertise, many of whom are former middle or high school teachers or community youth workers. The team is diverse in ethnicity, gender, and disciplinary and methodological background. Several team members are fluent in both English and Spanish, the dominant languages of the community.

TABLE 1   *Student Demographics for the Full Sample*

Student Characteristics — FULL SAMPLE (n = 716)

Variables	Percent	Mean (S.D.)
Age (years)		14.9 (1.28)
Female	56.1	
Male	43.9	
Race		
White	5.6	
Black	20.9	
Latino	72.1	
Other	1.4	
Seventh Grade	21.6	
Ninth Grade	41.1	
Tenth Grade	37.3	
School 2	14.7	
School 3	62.2	
School 4	7.0	
School 5	16.2	
Spanish Speakers[a]	63.0	
Language Mainly Spoken at Home		
English	18.4	
Spanish	42.4	
Both	39.3	

[a] Includes Spanish-Only and Spanish-English Bilingual Students.

Procedures and Methods of Data Gathering

Data sources for the larger study include (a) computer-based surveys, (b) computer-based reading diagnostics, (c) school record data, (d) semi-structured interviews, (e) reading and writing process interviews, and (f) ethnographic interviews and observations. The diagnostics and surveys are administered to the entire sample, whereas we conduct interviews and observations only with the subsample of the population. In what follows, we outline the data sources analyzed for this report.

— Surveys

We administered computerized surveys to intact or whole school classes during regular class time. The survey examines a broad range of student perceptions of, motivations for, and practices with literacy across a range of contexts and texts. Questions focus on the four academic content areas of school (science, social studies, mathematics, and English language arts) and on multiple contexts outside of school. Questions about student background characteristics focus on school, grade, gender, age, race/ethnicity, birthplace, preferred language, and language spoken in the home.

Youth respond to sequentially presented survey questions on individual laptop computers. Administrations range over two to three class sessions, depending on the length of the regular class period in each of the three school settings. The overall survey covers a range of motivations for reading and writing in and out of school, text types read and written, educational and employment aspirations, and sense of racial and ethnic identities. In what follows, we provide details about the survey measures of interest in this report, focusing on out-of-school literacy practices. Survey items focusing on out-of-school literacy practices tap students' frequency of reading and writing across a broad range of text types outside of school. Students are asked how often they read and write for pleasure as part of a larger set of activities, such as doing homework, engaging in family activities, and hanging out with friends. The reading and writing for pleasure questions are followed by the question, "What are you reading when not in school? During the last month, how many times did you *read* any of the following?" Seventeen types of texts, including novels, e-mail, newspapers, and comic books, among others, are offered as choices. For writing, we ask youth, "What are you writing when not in school? During the last month, how many times did you *write* any of the following?" Text choices include e-mails, poetry, music lyrics, and stories, among others. All responses were recorded on a 1–7 Likert-type scale, with 1 representing *never* and 7 representing *every day for more than an hour.* The list of choices was based on findings from a previous study conducted in this community (VanDerPloeg & Moje, 2004), and was updated from Wave 1 to Wave 2 as students indicated other texts they read with some frequency.[3]

— Interviews and Observations

Drawing from the overall sample, we recruited students to participate in a series of interviews. To date we have administered seventy-nine semi-structured interviews and fifty-two reading-process interviews, and have followed fifteen youth ethnographically. We report here on only the thirty-eight semi-structured interviews analyzed to date, but draw from the ethnographic data of all fifteen youth to frame the interview findings.

Semi-Structured Interviews. Our semi-structured interview takes an individual youth through a series of questions that focus on prompts offered by a collection of seventy-eight different book covers, magazine covers, newspaper front pages, screen shots of Internet sites, handwritten notes and poetry, music lyrics, and more. Text prompts are drawn from texts nominated by the overall sample on a free-response task included on our survey, although we have also added materials based on previous ethnographic work conducted in this community (Moje, 2006a; VanDerPloeg & Moje, 2004).

We ask youth participants to look through the entire collection; to nominate their first, second, and third choices for reading; and then to explain their choices. After this task, we ask them to look through the choices again, this time categorized by type (books, magazines, websites, etc.), and we ask them to choose from within a category. Each of these tasks is then repeated for writing, again using picture prompts. We also ask the participants to look at photos of people reading and writing different kinds of texts (books, magazines, newspapers, computer images, etc.) and ask them to choose which image looks most like something they would do, and then explain why. The photos show individuals, pairs, and groups of people reading and writing, and the people in the images represent different ages, genders, and ethnic/racial groups, insofar as can be indicated by physical characteristics.

Ethnographic Interviews. Ethnographic interviews occur *in situ*, with questions stemming from the activities in which youth are engaged at the time. Although the interviews are not constrained by a structured set of questions, the researchers prompt students to talk about particular literate practices as they occur. To date, we have accompanied youth to their homes, on bowling outings, bookstore visits, shopping trips, library trips, afterschool programs, and summer program activities.

School Record Data. We request school record data in the form of class grades, TerraNova test scores, state test scores, attendance records, and free/reduced-price lunch status from the schools and district. To date, we have grades and test scores for one public school at Wave 1; grades for the private school at Wave 1; and cumulative grades for the public charter school at Wave 2.

Analytic Methods

Descriptives. Student responses on the reading and writing for pleasure survey were compared across several items with t-tests and analysis of variance (ANOVA) procedures using the Tukey post-hoc test, which allowed us to determine which group averages were statistically different from one another. These calculations explore how students differ in their reported frequency of pleasure reading and writing beyond differences based on gender, race, and grade level.

Regressions. After conducting ANOVAs on survey responses across schools, we determined that there were no significant differences in youth responses by school, so we could use one school to examine relationships between student achievement and the frequency and nature of youth reading practices outside of school. We used the school record data we had at each wave — Schools 1 and 2 at Wave 1, and School 5 at Wave 2. We tested these relationships using correlations and multiple linear regression methods.

For the Wave 1 analysis, we used grades as a dependent variable, arguing that grades represent a measure of students' achievement, if not actual ability.

Because we wanted to test the relationship between reading out of school and in-school achievement, grades were the most reasonable measure. We created a year-end cumulative grade point average based on class grades reported by the schools, both of which used a 4.0 scale, in English, science, social studies, and mathematics. The cumulative GPA was calculated by taking the average of grades earned in each content area. We also analyzed frequencies against grades in English and science classes to determine if there were differences by subject matter achievement. Math and social studies grades were not analyzed due to missing data. Cases without grade information were deleted from the analysis, resulting in 208 cases from the total sample of 218. In the first three models, bivariate correlations led us to use the frequency of *writing for pleasure* and *reading for pleasure* as independent variables, controlling for student gender and ethnicity. The final three models incorporated the independent variables of reading novels and poetry outside of school, controlling for student gender and ethnicity.

For Wave 2 regressions, we again created a cumulative GPA by taking the average of student grades in math, science, social studies, and English. In this case, we did not analyze against discrete grades because they were non-normally distributed. Cases without grade data were deleted from the analysis, resulting in 96 cases from the total School 5 sample of 115 in Wave 2. In this model, we employed a three-tiered out-of-school variable to represent reading and writing frequencies (1 = never; 2 = once a month to once a week; 3 = 3 to 4 times per week or more). Bivariate correlations between frequency of literacy practices and school achievement led us to use frequency of reading novels, reading music lyrics, and writing graffiti as three independent variables, controlling for student gender and ethnicity.

Constant Comparative Analyses. Methods for analyzing the interviews and observations included constant comparative analysis (CCA) (Glaser & Strauss, 1967). Constant comparative analysis involves coding across three stages: open, axial, and selective coding. In the open-coding stage, categories and subcategories are noted and labeled, and initial connections among categories are noted. Our open-coding stage for this particular analysis yielded several codes of why and how youth read and wrote, including social networks (e.g., families, peers, popular culture affinity groups); identities (e.g., racial/ethnic, gendered, linguistic); school practices, entertainment, social capital, and information (utilitarian and personal interest); self-improvement (e.g., negative and positive examples, resilience, information); and genres (e.g., suspense, fantasy).

In the axial-coding stage, we reduced the codes to four of those listed above — social networks, identities, self-improvement, and information — with the idea that each of these was connected to the larger construct of *generation of social capital*, which we had determined to be the axis code, or category. Each code was compared to other codes, looking for overlap, points of convergence or divergence, and outright contradictions. Axial coding allowed us to assess whether the codes should be identified as categories, collapsed into other codes, or further separated into subcodes.

For example, codes of social networks and social capital might seem so closely related that they appear redundant; through axial coding, however, we determined that these codes signaled different, and equally important, points about *where* text choices originated (social networks such as peer groups, families, church) versus *why* some texts were sought out by youth (because they provided information, discourses, and practices that served as forms of social capital).[4] This axial-coding process also required us to reexamine data at later points, thus safeguarding against premature typification (Erickson, 1992) of data patterns. In the selective-coding stage, we revisited the data organized into central categories, checked for data saturation, searched for discrepant cases, and assessed generalizability of patterns across the sample.

Throughout the CCA process, we prepared theoretical memos and integrative theoretical memos in order to link data to relevant extant theory and empirical research; to test, generate, and document initial hypotheses for later analysis; and to communicate theories being generated across the research team. We conducted several layers of independent analyses, each with different team members participating. In each case, coders noted the same codes (in many cases, with no prior training in the coding system), although language use differed at times (e.g., one coder might use the words *social capital*, whereas another might refer to *information useful for creating or building social relations*, and another might code using the label *funds of knowledge*). We discussed the nuanced differences in these theoretical terms and agreed on standard coding labels in recurring team meetings and via memo writing.

Results: Countering Myths and Exploring Motivations

What and How Often Do Youth Read and Write "For Pleasure"?

Given the popular belief that youth "don't read" (National Endowment for the Arts [NEA], 2007), we thought it important to begin with a simple descriptive statistic: 92 percent of the 716 youth surveyed in this community — one that is described as high-poverty and/or underresourced — report reading some kind of text outside of school three to four times per week or more. They also write with some frequency (82 percent report writing some kind of text three to four times per week or more). What they read and write, however, varies. The majority of youth in this community do not often read novels or write stories, but many youth do read and write other kinds of texts, and they read and write with regularity. In what follows, we provide some flesh to the bones of this claim that youth read and write, and we paint a picture of what adolescent youth in one community do read and write, how often, and why.

Reading and Writing for Pleasure. As indicated, our survey includes a series of questions about activities in which youth engage when not in school, with *read-*

ing for pleasure and *writing for pleasure* included as two of the activities youth are asked to rate. In response to the question asking students how often they read for pleasure in the last month, about one-fifth (21.3%) of students selected *never* (Figure 1). The remaining 80 percent varied in how they identified. Of those students who did indicate that they read for pleasure, the average frequency was 3.87 (SD = 1.56), or just under once per week (a 4 on our scale). Thirty percent of the students reported reading for pleasure weekly, and 12.3 percent of students reported reading for pleasure every day.

Females were more likely to report reading for pleasure (M = 3.58, SD = 1.86), than males (M = 2.85, SD = 1.67, p < .001). African American students (M = 3.77, SD = 1.88) reported reading for pleasure more frequently than Latino students (M = 3.17, SD = 1.77, p < .01) and White students (M = 2.50, SD = 1.62, p < .01). Students across grades responded with similar frequencies of reading for pleasure outside of school (see Table 2). There were no differences in average frequency of reading for pleasure outside of school based on race, or the language spoken mainly in the home.

To the question of writing for pleasure in the last month, 28 percent of students responded *never* (Figure 1). Of those students who did report writing for pleasure, the average frequency of writing was 3.93 (SD = 1.57), or slightly less than once per week. Twenty-nine percent of students indicated that they wrote for pleasure weekly, and 11.9 percent of students reported writing for pleasure every day.

Females were also more likely to report writing for pleasure (M = 3.62, SD = 1.88) than males (M = 2.46, SD = 1.65, p < .001). Seventh graders (M = 3.48, SD = 1.88) averaged higher frequencies of writing for pleasure outside of school than ninth- (M = 3.03, SD = 1.92, p < .05) and tenth-grade students (M = 2.98, SD = 1.80, p <. 05). There were no differences in average frequency of writing for pleasure outside of school based on race, or the language spoken mainly in the home (see Table 2).

The finding that these youth read and write for pleasure once a week or less may seem to contradict the claim that 92 percent of the youth in our sample claimed to read something three to four times per week. The contradiction lies in what the words "reading and writing for pleasure" appear to mean to students. We ran bivariate correlational analyses of responses to this item against responses to each of our questions about specific text types to assess what the construct of *reading/writing for pleasure* signified to the youth in our study. Responses to the *reading for pleasure* item correlated only to responses to the questions that asked students how often they read novels, short stories, picture books, and plays. Reading for pleasure was correlated with the students' frequency of novel reading (r = .515, p < .01), poetry (r = .383, p < .01), and information books (science, nature, history) (r = .346, p < .01). Pleasure reading was weakly correlated with digital reading, including e-mails (r = .083, p < .05) and websites (r = .094, p < .05). A similar relationship was found in outside-school writing. Writing stories was correlated with responses on writ-

FIGURE 1   *Frequency of Reading and Writing for Pleasure — Percent of Student Responses (n = 716)*

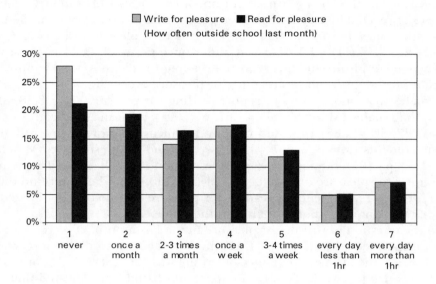

ing for pleasure (r = .403, p < .01), whereas writing e-mails, chats, shout-outs,[5] and blogs was less correlated (r = .177, p < .01).

These findings suggest that when the youth in this sample think of reading for pleasure, they think of reading literature; when they think of writing for pleasure, they usually think of writing stories. In some cases, they may even associate the words *reading* and *writing* with compulsory reading, as suggested by one young man who, when asked during an interview what he read for fun, responded: "I don't like reading just for fun unless it's something I like."

Thus, surveys that base youth pleasure-reading statistics on questions about reading for pleasure may be tapping only the reading of conventionally published print literature, or even of school-like reading assignments, and not the reading of magazines, informational texts, digital or electronic texts, or texts written by other youth, whether teen 'zines (see Knobel & Lankshear, 2002), letters and notes, or text messages. Some may question, however, whether these reading and writing practices have much impact on the kind of reading that matters in school; in other words, are these practices critical to understanding adolescent literacy?

A Second Look at Literacy Practices Outside School

We assert that such practices *do* matter for both school achievement and for young people's emotional and cognitive development. We also predicted how youth might interpret questions about reading and writing for pleasure, and therefore, we asked students to provide more specific information about their reading and writing of particular texts.

TABLE 2   *Students' Self-Reported Frequencies of Reading and Writing for Pleasure by Gender, Grade, Race, and Language*

Student Reading and Writing Outside of School (n = 716)

Variables	Mean (S.D.) Range (1–7) [a]
Read for Pleasure — All Students	3.26 (1.81)
Gender: Female [c]	3.58 (1.86) ***
Male	2.85 (1.67)
Grade: Seventh [d][e]	3.53 (1.65)
Ninth	3.25 (1.92)
Tenth	3.11 (1.77)
Race: White [b][d]	2.50 (1.62) ***
Black	3.77 (1.88) **
Latino	3.17 (1.77)
Language Spoken in Home: English [d]	3.42 (1.74)
Spanish	3.24 (1.84)
Both	3.18 (1.72)
Write for Pleasure — All Students	3.11 (1.87)
Gender: Female [c]	3.62 (1.88) ***
Male	2.46 (1.65)
Grade: Seventh [d][g]	3.48 (1.88)
Ninth	3.03 (1.92)
Tenth	2.98 (1.80)
Race: White [d][f]	2.64 (1.78)
Black [f]	3.47 (1.96)
Latino	3.05 (1.84)
Language Spoken in Home: English [d]	3.31 (1.94)
Spanish	3.02 (1.84)
Both	3.08 (1.80)

[a] 1 = never, 2 = once a month, 3 = 2–3 times a month, 4 = once a week, 5 = 3–4 times a week, 6 = every day less than 1 hour, 7 = every day more than 1 hour.

[b] White compared to Black (p < .001), Black compared to Latino (p < .01), all other racial differences not significant in reading.

[c] Differences calculated via t-test.

[d] Differences calculated via one-way ANOVA with Tukey post-hoc.

[e] Seventh compared to tenth (p < .10), all other grade differences not significant for reading.

[f] White compared to Black (p < .10), Black compared to Latino (p < .10), White compared to Latino not significant in writing.

[g] Seventh compared to ninth (p < .05), seventh compared to tenth (p < .05), ninth compared to tenth not significant in writing.

~ p < .10, * p < .05, ** p < .01, *** p < .001

FIGURE 2   *Average Responses of Frequency Outside School Reading by Text/Genre (n = 716)*

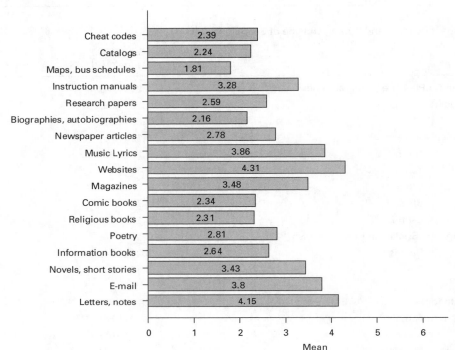

Reading and Writing Practices Outside of School. Data from the questions that tapped frequency of youth reading multiple text types demonstrated that, on average, students identified *reading* websites (M = 4.31, SD = 1.94) outside of school most frequently, followed by letters and notes from other people (M = 4.15, SD = 1.83), music lyrics (M = 3.86, SD = 2.08), e-mail (M = 3.79, SD = 2.10), magazines (M = 3.48, SD = 1.70), and novels, short stories, and plays (M = 3.43, SD = 1.99) (see Figure 2). However, it is important to note that most of the distributions were non-normal, with the majority of youth sitting at the low ends of the distribution, and, therefore, the mean responses should be interpreted with caution. Nevertheless, all calculations of text-reading frequency suggest that these six types of texts were read with the most frequency by the largest numbers of youth in the sample. In other words, these appear to be the most popular types of texts youth read.

In regard to *writing* outside of school, the type of texts students reported writing most often were e-mails, chats, shout-outs, and blogs (M = 4.05, SD = 2.07), and letters or notes (on paper) (M = 4.04, SD = 1.92), followed by music lyrics (M = 3.24, SD = 2.13) and graffiti or tagging on paper (M = 3.05, SD = 2.14). Creative writing in the form of stories (M = 2.44, SD = 1.71) and

FIGURE 3   *Average Self-Reported Frequencies of Writing Outside of School by Text/Genre (n = 716)*

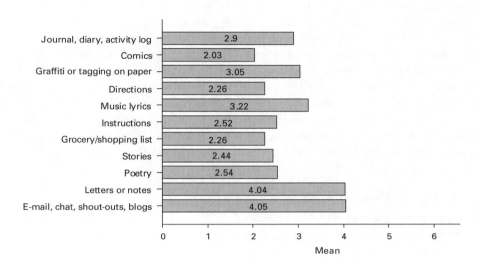

poetry (M = 2.54, SD = 1.85) averaged less than once a week. Again, aggregate student responses often did not reflect normally distributed histograms (see Figure 3), and, therefore, the means should be interpreted with caution. That said, the same note applies as with the reading of texts: By all calculations, these are the texts youth wrote most often.

Although each of these forms of text is important to understanding students' reading and writing practices, space constraints prevent us from discussing each response in depth. Therefore, we highlight two types of text that seem central to youth reading, albeit for different reasons: websites/e-mail and novels. We chose digital texts because, despite a basically bimodal distribution, they are read and written with some frequency, and even students with little access expressed interest in and knowledge of digital text forms. We chose novels because of their similarity to school texts.

Digital Reading and Writing. Only 28 percent of students reported reading websites every day outside of school in the last month (10.1% reporting less than one hour, and 17.8% reporting more than one hour), while 11.5 percent of students reported that they did not access websites outside of school. Thirty-six percent of students read websites outside of school once a week or less. Evidence of a digital divide is more prominent in reading e-mail outside of school. More than one-quarter of students (26.5%) reported that they did not read e-mail outside of school in the last month. Twenty-nine percent of students read e-mail once a week or less. The remaining students (28.9%) reported reading e-mails outside of school every day.

The frequency of writing e-mails, chats, shout-outs, and blogs again shows a digital divide among the students. A substantial portion of students (18.8%) reported never writing online outside of school in the last month, while a larger portion (27.9%) reported writing online every day. About one-third of students write online in e-mails, chats, etc., once a week or less, while the remaining 19.5 percent of students write online three to four times a week.

According to Lenhart, Madden, and Hitlin (2005), nearly 90 percent of American teens ages twelve to seventeen are online Internet users, and half of these wired youth access the Internet on a daily basis. However, our interview, survey, and ethnographic data provide a striking contrast to such claims. Consider this excerpt from an interview with one young woman from our subsample, Valeria,[6] a sixth-grade Latina who represents the 36 percent of youth who read on the Internet once a week or less:

(V = Valeria; I = Interviewer)

I: How often do you use the computer?

V: Like, I don't use it much, 'cause I don't have a computer, so I don't use it much.

I: At school do you use it?

V: No.

I: No, you guys don't go to the computer lab?

V: No.

I: Really? OK, so you don't use the Internet to get information —

V: — Only when we have projects I go to the library, but it's just, like, or I go to my cousin's house, but I don't, like, use it, like, much. I might use it, like, a month and then a month, one day in a month, or not even a day.

I: Do you ever surf the web and just look for stuff, or [is it] usually just connected to a project for school kind of thing?

V: It's usually — I never usually play on the computer. I always use the computer to take information out.

Valeria's experiences are not the exception in our sample. Among youth interviewed who said they did not use the Internet, the most common explanation was lack of access. But, not one youth eschewed Internet use. In fact, for youth with Internet access, the technology proved to be a major source of reading material and writing audiences, as illustrated in the youth responses presented in a later section of this article. Thus, access to technology appeared to be the main roadblock to more consistent use among a subset of our sample.

These findings merit further, fine-grained research on the accessibility and use of technology for this population of adolescents and others like them. Although the experiences of the youth in this city cannot be generalized to all youth, these youth are not unlike youth in other large urban settings, especially in areas of high poverty. Given the large number of the nation's youth who live in such settings, educators should question the increasingly popular notion that all youth are wired. Does high use among middle- and upper-middle-class youth mask the poor access of young people in high-poverty communities, whether urban or rural?

Novels and Other Literature. Novel reading outside of school presents a highly skewed distribution, with 24 percent of students reporting that they have not read a novel, short story, picture book, or play in the last month. Only 17.2 percent of students reported reading these types of fictional texts every day (see Figure 1). On average, females (M = 3.84, SD = 2.00) spent significantly more time reading novels than males (M = 2.92, SD = 1.87, p < .001). In sum, novel reading was not a major source of activity among the youth of this community, although it should be noted that 30.2 percent of the respondents did indicate reading novels three to four times a week or more. However, 25 percent of the youth interviewed gave *lack of time for reading* — and often, homework as the cause of this lack — as a deterrent to reading more regularly. Lack of interest in reading novels was a close second to lack of time. These low levels for novel reading will have more importance as we discuss the results of our regression analyses of the relationship between out-of-school reading practices and school achievement.

What's more, on an open-ended survey question about book reading, 68 percent of the 682 youth who answered (among 716 survey respondents) were able to name and write about a favorite book. One point that we found particularly compelling is the number of times school-based texts were named as favorite books on the open-ended portion of the survey. *The Outsiders* (Hinton, 1967), *Holes* (Sachar, 1998), and *Hatchet* (Paulsen, 1987) were among the most-popular youth texts (with *The House on Mango Street* [Cisneros, 1991] and a number of Shakespearean texts and Greek myths also top vote-getters). In other words, although the youth of this community did not report reading novels extensively, they did not typically disparage reading novels. They do, in fact, read this type of text, and school may be one important source of their text choices.

Although these data are representative of only one portion of the adolescent population and thus not generalizable to all adolescents, the fact that 30 percent of these youth — young people who live in a high-poverty setting and are often described as reading in the basic or below-basic range — read novels regularly provides evidence that adolescents are not unmotivated to read. These encouraging statistics about youth reading also suggest that we need to look more closely at the texts offered to young people in school, and at the ways texts are offered (i.e., how texts are assigned, discussed, and used in classrooms), rather than simply ascribing low motivation to youth when it comes to reading this type of material.

Another Way of Looking: Exploring Effects of Outside-School Reading and Writing

With the above findings in mind, and prompted by reading research that suggests a relationship between the amount of time children spend reading outside of school and their school achievement (Stanovich, 1986), we turned to the question of whether these literacy practices had any relationship to school achievement. After determining that there were no significant differences in survey responses by school attended, we ran multiple linear regression analyses on out-of-school reading frequencies by text type for youth with school record data available.

Wave 1 Out-of-School Reading and Achievement. Analyses at Schools 1 and 2 in Wave 1 (n = 209) indicated that frequency of reading outside of school as measured by the question "reading for pleasure" related positively to English grades (β = .180, p < .001), science grades (β = .138, p < .01), and cumulative GPAs (β = .156, p < .001), after controlling for student gender and ethnicity. The frequency of novel reading did not have a significant relationship to science grades or cumulative GPAs. Writing did not relate to cumulative or science achievement, and, in fact, had a slightly negative relationship to English achievement, although with only marginal significance (β = −.077, p < .10), after controlling for student gender and ethnicity (see Table 3).

We also examined the relationship between frequency of reading particular text types and grades in English and science. Of the text types, only novel reading showed any relationship, and then only to English class grades, and this relationship was only marginally significant (β = .067, p < .10). Poetry reading did not have a significant relationship to any of our outcome variables (See Table 4).

Wave 2 Outside-School Reading and Achievement. To further examine these relationships, we examined data from one school in the Wave 2 data set, School 5 (n = 96), which was the only Wave 2 school for which we had school record data at the time of this analysis. Based on the outcomes of this second regression analyses, we found that, holding constant all independent variables in the model, increased novel reading again predicted an increase in cumulative GPA (β = .138, p < .05), while reading music lyrics (β = −.135, p < .05) and writing graffiti (β = −.099, p < .05) were negative predictors of achievement, as measured by cumulative GPA (see Table 5).

Although the influence of novel reading seems to be consistent from Wave 1 to Wave 2, further analysis is needed to understand the relationship that these types of outside-school reading and writing activities share with achievement. Writing graffiti, for example, may not have a direct relationship on achievement, but rather, it may be a proxy for a larger pattern of counter-school cultural behaviors, which, in turn, influence achievement for a host of reasons (e.g., negative teacher expectations or low student attendance).

TABLES 3–4   *Summary of Wave 1 Regression Analysis Estimating the Effect of Reading and Writing Outside of School on Academic Achievement as Measured by Grades on a 4.0 Scale (Schools 1–2; n = 209)*

TABLE 3   Relationship between Reading and Writing for Pleasure and Academic Achievement

Independent Variables	Model 1 DV = English Grade	Model 2 DV = Science Grade	Model 3 DV = Cum. GPA [b]
Constant	1.584 ***	1.416 ***	1.453 ***
Reading for Pleasure	.180 ***	.138 ***	.156 ***
Writing for Pleasure	−.077~**	−.063***	−.059***
Female	.242 ~**	.260***	.181***
Hispanic American[a]	.115***	.267***	.270***
African American[a]	.050***	.526***	.309***
R-Square	.107 ***	.071 ***	.091 ***

[a] Reference group is Caucasian Americans.

[b] An average of student grades in English, science, and math.

~ $p < .10$, * $p < .05$, ** $p < .01$, *** $p < .001$

TABLE 4   Relationship between Reading Novels and Poetry and Academic Achievement

Independent Variables	Model 4 DV = English Grade	Model 5 DV = Science Grade	Model 6 DV = Cum. GPA [b]
Constant	1.661***	1.566 ***	1.624 ***
Reading Novels [c]	.067 ~**	.043***	.052***
Reading Poetry	.037***	−.029***	.004***
Female	.158***	.261***	.157***
Hispanic American [a]	.167***	.331***	.301***
African American [a]	.166***	.621 ~**	.404***
R-Square	.050 ~**	.037***	.036***

[a] Reference group is Caucasian Americans.

[b] An average of student grades in English, science, and math.

[c] Full category in the computer survey response includes "Novels, short stories, picture books, plays."

~ $p < .10$, * $p < .05$, ** $p < .01$, *** $p < .001$

Race and gender were not significant predictors of achievement in this model, nor was youths' home language. We also tested the relationship between school achievement and weekly online access (reading e-mails and websites and writing e-mails, chats, shout-outs, and blogs outside of school at least once

TABLE 5   *Summary of Wave 2 Regression Analysis Estimating the Effects of Reading and Writing Outside of School on Academic Achievement (School 5; n = 96)*

Reading and Writing Texts Outside of School as Predictors of Academic Achievement

Independent Variables	Fitted Coefficient
Constant	2.702 ***
Reading Novels, short stories, picture books, plays	.138 ***
Reading Music Lyrics	−.135 ***
Writing Graffiti or Tagging on Paper	−.099 ***
Female	.169***
Hispanic American[a]	−.101***
African American[a]	1.091***
R-Square	.181 ***

[a] Reference group is Caucasian Americans.

[b] An average of student grades in English, science, and math.

~ p < .10, * p < .05, ** p < .01, *** p < .001

DV: Cumulative GPA.

a week or more), and found no relationship. Finally, youths' responses to the question about the frequency of reading and writing for pleasure did not show a relationship to achievement, which may result from the fact that the average frequency of reading and writing for pleasure for this subsample is low, and very few students included daily reading and writing behaviors, such as Internet reading, writing in a journal, etc., when reading or writing for pleasure (see Table 5).

With limited school record data available, our results can only be considered exploratory, but the findings suggest questions for future research. Specifically, these results are both surprising and unsurprising. The documented positive relationship between novel reading and achievement meshes well with past studies. Through a synthesis of research on time spent reading, Stanovich (1986) concluded that the more students read, the better readers they become (i.e., the "Matthew effect"). Specifically, an increase in reading caused an increase in students' vocabulary knowledge, which in turn increased the students' reading ability, which motivated the students to read more, beginning the reading cycle once again. The amount of reading done in school was not the only factor that related to improved reading; students' out-of-school reading habits have also been documented as indicators of their reading ability (Anderson, Wilson, & Fielding, 1988).

However, the fact that novel reading was the only type of text reading associated with achievement in our data set is perplexing, given Stanovich's theory. If time spent reading is an important explanatory factor, then *all* reading should increase opportunities for incidental word learning or the building of background knowledge. The fact that novel reading was associated with over-all achievement, but not with achievement in classes other than English language arts, raises questions about whether the effect of out-of-school reading on achievement has more to do with how tightly a text type meshes with the discursive and rhetorical conventions of a discipline than it does with the simple act of reading. This finding could underscore one of the main differences between children's and adolescents' academic literacy learning: the impact of disciplinary discourse, conventions, and vocabulary on both content and literacy learning for older students. That is, general word reading and writing activities may not provide the incidental word and concept learning necessary for achieving high levels of success in upper-level, academic, content-area classes.

However, this finding could also suggest that achievement (as measured by grades achieved in middle and high school content areas) may not be as dependent on written language facility as it is in English classes. How much is text actually used in content-area classes other than English language arts? Could the lack of attention to texts in school classrooms be responsible for young people's moderate achievement on national tests, which are dependent to a great extent on language facility, even in content-area classes such as mathematics and science? These questions, relating to the impact of a host of out-of-school reading and writing practices on secondary school achievement in specific subject matter areas, merit further study.

Motivations for Youth Reading and Writing Outside School: In Their Own Words

With these large-scale analyses as a backdrop, we now turn to the words of the youth themselves to provide an analysis of what and why young people are motivated to read and write different kinds of texts outside of school. Do young people's motivations for reading and writing outside of school indicate possible explanations for the failure to see strong effects from these activities on school achievement?

Our major assertion about these young people's motivations to read and write outside of school is that reading and writing are situated in and constitutive of social networks and identities (either developed, or developing). As such, reading and writing provide important forms of social capital by providing information that allows for the maintenance of social networks, the development of subjective experiences and enactments of identity, and models for self-improvement and achievement of future goals. Text reading and writing also appear to allow for social and psychological adjustment, an important function in and of itself. For example, the youth in our study read and write for self-expression, to work through problems, or to seek information or models to help them live in their homes, schools, and communities. In other words,

131

reading and writing may do more than merely influence school achievement, as illustrated in the following data exemplars.

In what follows, we present data to exemplify the two major categories — reading as situated in social networks, and reading as generative of social capital — in which reading and writing are situated, each followed by data exemplars that indicate the types of social networks or the forms of social capital and social/psychological adjustment opportunities these reading and writing practices provide to youth. Before diving into these categories, however, we should underscore the overlap among and across categories. Reading as situated in social networks, for example, also often means reading that allows for racial or gendered identities to be constructed or enacted. Reading in affinity groups is most often gendered and raced. Reading and writing that express racial identities may also be forms of self-expression or self-improvement. Each of these concepts will be exemplified and explained in the sections that follow.

Although we separate data exemplars into categories for the purpose of analysis and for clarity of expression, we want to emphasize that these categories work together in young people's lives. In fact, our choices of exemplars are purposeful in that each exemplar typically represents at least one other category of analysis. Each exemplar also represents a pattern of practice among respondents, rather than a single instance. With these notes, we present the data that support our assertion about the motivations for and maintenance of reading and writing among youth in this community.

Reading and Writing as Situated in and Constitutive of Social Networks

Peers and Reading Groups. With few exceptions, each student indicated that peers were a source of reading material (either by giving recommendations for books/magazines or by providing actual texts). Several adolescents (all girls) reported that they belonged to informal reading and writing networks, and six young women reported more formal reading groups that coordinated book selections, organized the procurement of books, and discussed the reading. One was moderated by an adult, and the others were facilitated by the students themselves. Brianna, for example, was a member of a book club organized by the mother of a friend. The mother would provide lunch for the group and assign vocabulary words based on the reading to each member:[7]

(B = Brianna; I = Interviewer)

B: Last but not least [would] probably be *The Skin I'm In* by Sharon G. Flake. . . . I was in a book club and they chose. We all, like, voted on books we wanted to read, and it seemed like an interesting book. So the majority of people voted for that book, and I like the book so that's why I chose it. . . .

I: So tell me about this book club. Who's in it?

B: Some of my friends and some people. It was my friend's book club, and she invited some of her friends that I didn't know, and now they're my friends.

I: So how many people are in this book club?

B: About seven people.

I: OK, and they're all your age — seventh graders?

B: Some are a grade higher, a grade lower. . . .

I: And so, how often do you meet?

B: Well, the book club stopped a couple years ago. Well, last year, and they're starting back in January, but we met every Saturday. And then we would go to see the movies of the books . . . and last Saturday we went to see *The Lion, the Witch and the Wardrobe* because that was one of the first books that we read. . . . [We read] about twenty books, 'cause we read one a month, and if the book was short, then we read two.

Five other young women offered similar descriptions of their book-reading experiences within peer social networks, ranging from book clubs that meet once a month, to groups of girls checking out the same book at the library (e.g., *The Sisterhood of the Traveling Pants*) and discussing it during lunchtime in the school cafeteria, to reading scary stories aloud by candlelight with friends at a slumber party, to two girls who divided *The Coldest Winter Ever* into halves, reading their respective halves, and then discussing the total book.

Boys, in general, talked less about their experiences sharing books with organized groups. In fact, their mention of book-sharing is exemplified by seventh-grade Javier's rather qualified — and even half-hearted — description in an interview:

(J = Javier; I = Interviewer)

I: Do you share books with your friends?

J: Yeah, kind of; like when we go to the library and I tell them about joke books or books they might like to read.

I: So you find it and then you'll bring it over?

J: Yeah.

Writing Groups and Networks. Writing and sharing poetry is a popular activity among some youth — again, girls are in the majority on this dimension — whereas others share books and personal goals on a regular basis. For example, sixth grader Carlotta told an interviewer about being a member of a group that wrote and shared personal goals: "We all have a copy of it, and then we save it, and by the end of the year we see what goals we've accomplished." Two other young women wrote chapter and comic books with friends; four talked about sharing poems with friends; and one described a group notebook designated just for writing letters and poetry. Alita, also a sixth grader, described a different kind of group writing activity engaged in at school, a notebook that she and other girls circulated in her homeroom class. To comment on a particular entry in the notebook — texts that typically "talked bad" about people — one had to read from the beginning of the thread, which was similar to a discussion among members of a digital community. Alita's description suggests an awareness of the norms and conventions practiced among members of the group. In this way, the text was both part of and constitutive of a social network.

Family Reading and Writing Networks. Eight of the youth interviewed said that their parents encouraged their reading habits; in five of the cases, adults shared their own books with children. A few parents of children who read "urban books" disapproved of the themes of the books or wanted their children "to read different books from the books I read, you know, to expand [my horizons]," which suggests that parents were aware of and guided their children's reading choices. Javier, for example, reported that his mother encouraged him to read in Spanish so he wouldn't forget the language:

(J = Javier; I = Interviewer)

I: OK. Do you read things together with your family members?

J: No, only like when, like, I'm forgetting Spanish, or some hard-to-read Spanish, so my mom makes me read some Spanish books so I don't forget Spanish and stuff like that.

I: So then you might read with her?

J: Yeah, and if I get, like, a word wrong, she has me pronounce it.[8]

Students also report reading books to or with younger siblings or writing material for younger siblings to read. Eva, in seventh grade, described reading picture books to her siblings. When asked, "Do you ever write to help yourself or other people get things done, like, you know, instructions or recipes for family?" Pedro, a sixth-grade boy, responded, "I help my brother with instructions." Young women across the sample often referred to or were observed helping siblings with homework and reading to their siblings in the process. Jorge, a seventh grader, describes reading a video-game manual to teach his brother how to play the game:

(J = Jorge; I = Interviewer)

I: The Sonic Hedgehog video-game book? And why would you pick that?

J: I think it's interesting because my little brother, I think he wants me to help him pass the game . . . He doesn't know how to read, but he knows how to play.

I: How old is your little brother?

J: Like, four.

Affinity Groups and Reading and Writing. The two major affinity or community groups that dominated talk about texts involved cars or lowrider bikes on the one hand, and video games on the other. Four young men reported reading car magazines, car manuals, and looking at pictures of cars on www.[city name] Raza.com, [9] or talking to friends about cars. One seventh-grade youth, Sammie, described reading car and bicycle magazines, searching for car pictures online, watching movies about cars, and playing a video game about truck driving, as well as his future aspirations of working as an auto mechanic. In this interview excerpt, Federico, a sixth-grade student, explained that he read *Lowrider* magazine because he owned a lowrider bike and was fixing it up, a common affinity group activity among the young men in the sample:[10]

> (F = Federico; I = Interviewer)
>
> I: So the things that you do read, like *Lowrider* magazine and the dog stuff, where did you get that stuff from?
>
> F: *Lowrider*?
>
> I: Yeah, I mean, did somebody give you the magazines? Do you buy them? Do you go to the library?
>
> F: I go to my cousin's house and I just take them. . . . He keeps [*Lowrider*], like, he wants to know how to draw 'cause he's gonna be an engineer — those people that draw houses — that's why he gets that [*Lowrider*] . . . . He just copies pictures off of there; he draws them.

Federico's literate practice, like the other lowrider bike fans, was stimulated by his relationship with his cousin, his own interest in the bikes, and a utility value for the work that he was doing on his bike.

Two young women also identified car and bike clubs as affinity groups that shaped their reading choices. Juanita, a ninth grader, helped her brother-in-law work on cars and reported reading car magazines. Carlotta, in fact, named *Lowrider* magazine as her number-one reading choice:

> (C = Carlotta; I = Interviewer)
>
> I: *Lowrider* is number one?
>
> C: Uh-huh.
>
> I: You read that?
>
> C: Uh-huh.
>
> I: You like lowriders.
>
> C: I love lowriders; they're the best.
>
> I: You're the first girl that I've interviewed that likes *Lowrider* magazine! Do you work on cars at all?
>
> C: No, but like, in my street they have a community center, and when we get out of school — like, [at] the end of the school year — they're gonna put [in] a bike shop, and it's gonna be mostly for lowriders. And then I'm gonna be working in it; like, they're gonna assign us each what we're talking about — what we're gonna work on, and we're gonna get paid seven dollars an hour.

These two girls were outliers among other young women we interviewed in the sense that they actively read *Lowrider* magazine. Many other young women talked about lowrider bikes and cars, but they did not describe reading the magazine. Like the boys of the sample, these young women situated their reading in affinity groups and family relationships.

Gaming is another example of an affinity group activity that shapes reading practices, albeit in unique ways. Gaming texts are not generally read in groups like the book clubs described by some of the young women, yet the ideas and information in gaming texts are often discussed among friends who share a gaming affinity. Six youth in the sample explicitly identified gaming as a reason for reading: They use cheat codes available in paper and online venues to guide their gaming. Many other youth with regular Internet access mentioned playing games, but we distinguish the casual players from "gamers" who actually read to access instructions, supports (or "cheats"), and ideas for new games. Although they talk about games and even play them while in the same room, they often do not share codes because they want to compete with one another. Although they read as part of an affinity group, they do not share the information they read, as exemplified in Jorge's description of his gaming literacy practices:

(J = Jorge; I = Interviewer)

I: Do you know the names of the sites that you go to?

J: CheatPlanet.com.

I: All right; and what do you do at CheatPlanet.com?

J: I look for cheat codes for the games that I have.

I: And again, do you do that with every game, or just some of the games?

J: Every game.

I: Do you ever look at walk-throughs? . . .

J: Yes.

I: OK, what else are on these sites? Do you ever, like, go to message boards and talk with other fans about the game, or not really?

J: No.

I: No. So basically you just go there and get information, get your cheats, get your walk-throughs, and you're done . . . Have you ever read something and you said, "Oh, wow, this was really helpful," or "Oh, yeah, this will definitely help me pass the level," and then you show it to somebody else?

J: I don't like showing people . . . other people that have the same game. I want to beat it first.

I: Oh, I see . . . OK, so you keep all the secrets; you keep all the codes yourself so you can finish it first.

J: Yes.

I: All right, when you finish it, *then* do you tell them?

J: I help them out.

Popular Cultural Networks. Popular culture is a unique kind of network because it is not held together by a gathering of people, but rather by information, ideas, and practices generated in and from popular cultural texts. The best example of popular cultural networks may be online "fanfiction," in which participants write alternative storylines for popular television shows and movies. However, although many of the youth participants in our study had heard of the practice, few acknowledged writing fanfiction with any regularity. Still, when faced with a selection of unfamiliar texts, youth often used elements of popular culture (e.g., movies, television shows, musicians) to establish connections, as illustrated in this exemplar from Eva:

(E = Eva; I = Interviewer)

I: What would you choose to read as a third choice?

E: . . . *InuYasha* (Takahashi, 2003) [manga].

I: Why?

E: 'Cause I like the cartoon. I watch it with my sister when I'm at home. . . . I think that's a book, but it's on the cartoons. . . . Hey, *Harry Potter*. Hey, my friend had that book [points to *Esperanza Rising* (Ryan, 2000)]. We, I think we seen a movie on that *Esperanza* —

I: — *Esperanza Rising*?

E: I think we seen a movie on that . . . I think that's what they said on the front of it, the movie *Esperanza*. My friend was reading it, and she was telling me about it, but I can't remember what she said; and my friend was reading this book [*The Coldest Winter Ever* (Souljah,1999)] in class. Sister Souljah.

I: You pointed to *Harry Potter*. Have you read any of the Harry Potters, or do you just know Harry Potter?

E: I think I read one of them, which was called . . . It was a long book, so like, after that I didn't read no more *Harry Potter*. It was like . . . . Hey, look, that's *Sorcerer's Stone* (Rowling, 2001) right there [pointing to image in interview book] . . . . I seen the movie, too.

The motivation to read a book (or multiple books, as in Eva's case) after seeing a movie based on the book was mentioned time and time again by young people in the sample, as was the reading of manga that were directly connected to anime they watched on television. When browsing with youth in a local bookstore, many of the young people went immediately to the graphic novel section, where one young woman showed a team researcher a variety of different manga/graphic novels and explained which ones were based on television shows she watched.[11] In addition, young people's interest in elements of popular culture (e.g., music artists, actors, video games) can result in thematic reading across genres. For example, based on their interest in a particular music artist, students would read biographies, look up the artist's lyrics, and visit the artist's web page.

Reading as Generative of Social Capital

Reading and Writing as Racial/Ethnic Identity Development. Reading and writing certain texts also served as a way of enacting identities; that is, enacting the sense of self students felt was demanded or appropriate for a particular time, space, or relationship (Moje, 2004). In addition, reading and writing those texts served as a means of gaining information needed to enact or develop new identities. Findings in this category replicate past ethnographic studies in this community (Moje, 2004; VanDerPloeg & Moje, 2004) by highlighting the important role of racial and ethnic identities.

Our youth participants' racial and ethnic identities both helped to shape — and were shaped by — reading and writing in three ways. First, reading choices were influenced by an interest in learning about cultural heritage. In some cases, this desire came about from a perceived lack of racial/ethnic representation in their school curriculum. Carlotta mentioned an interest in reading a Cesar Chavez biography so that she "would be more informed [about] what he did for the Hispanics," and Alex, a seventh-grade youth, claimed that he read about ethnic culture to supplement what he learned in school: "You always hear about famous Black people and White people and barely hear any mentions of Mexicans." Charla, a seventh grader, echoed his comment by saying, "They don't really tell us, like, they tell us about Martin Luther King."

Second, youth read to locate current information about racial/ethnic groups. Much of this reading revolved around issues of immigration. Sammie, for example, stated that he reads the community newspaper, *Latino*, to obtain news about immigration, community issues, and Mexico. Alma, a tenth grader, echoed the desire to stay abreast of news and information related to her ethnic community, stating: "I am Mexican and would like to know what is happening." Jacque, a ninth grader who identified as Blackfoot Indian and African American, stated explicitly that she read to get information about "what's happening with the Mexicans":

(J = Jacque; I = Interviewer)

J: I probably will read this one [*Latino*] too . . .

I: All right, and what parts do you read of *Latino*?

J: Like, if there's a story about, like, what's happening now about the Mexicans, and, like, if they have anything about that, I'll read it, like, anything important.

I: What do you mean by "what's happening now with the Mexicans"?

J: Like, they're [going] to pass a thing, [and] I would like to know if they did pass it.

I: Oh, OK, yeah, I've heard about that, too. Would you go to the protests or no?

J: No, but I agree. I think they should earn their own freedom to be here because most of the time, they're the only ones who work. Like, they, most of the time there's like, they're owning most of the business here, so if it wasn't for them, no one would ever have business here. That's what I think, but I think they should keep fighting for that because they deserve it.

Jacque's discourse — particularly her use of the third person plural to refer to Mexicans — indicates that she sees herself as separate from other members of her community in ethnic terms, but she identifies with their "earning their freedom to be here," and indicates a desire to read for solidarity with Latino/as. Having named herself as multiracial and living in a predominantly Latino/a neighborhood of a predominantly African American community, Jacque's discourse and her reading practice serve to position her as an insider, even while they simultaneously help her to maintain her own individual racial identity. Her reading, then, seems especially attuned to questions of power, identity, and agency within her geographic community and her ethnic and racial groups.

Finally, of the Latino/a youth interviewed who referred to website reading, all mentioned sites that were somehow connected to their ethnicity. Amanda, a ninth grader, in particular, sought out Latino/a websites and claimed that she frequented at least six Latino/a chat rooms, including Amor Latino, Hablando Espanol, Mexicano, Latino, Boricua, and www.[city name]Raza.com.[12] Sites such as www.southwest[city name].com were also routinely read by youth, as we have documented in other ethnographic work. Southwest[city name].com is unique because it not only represents a Latino/a identity, but it also represents community issues and lowrider bike affinity groups, thus combining a number of social networks and identity enactments into one site.

Third, youth reading choices were often influenced by group members' desires to see a mirrored experience in the text or to bond with group members who generated the text. Sammie expressed an interest in *Always Running* (Rodriguez, 1993) because the main character is Mexican, and it looks like "an immigration thing."[13] His interest in the book was piqued by what he saw as a possible link to his ethnic and lived experience (i.e., that of immigration). Others made comments about particular books such as *The House on Mango Street* (Cisneros, 1991) because "it was, like, about [the] Latino experience," or *The Skin I'm In* (Flake, 1998), which many young Black women described as important to them in terms similar to those described by Monica, a fourteen-year-old African American girl:

(M = Monica; I = Interviewer)

I: What would make you pick that? Let's say you hadn't read it before. What made you pick it the first time when you first saw it?

M: Because it stood out to me as being a good book that talks about you should like the skin that you're in. You know . . . What I got out of it was where it talks about her having problems about being dark-skinned, and I know I have problems like that, so that's what really stood out, too.

Charla, also African American, echoed Monica's need to explore her racial identity as she explained, "I could learn how they feel 'cause sometimes I don't feel like I like the skin I'm in." And Brianna described her interest in reading *My Sisters' Voices: Teenage Girls of Color Speak Out* (Jacob, 2002) because, "I'd think it'd be about girls that have [gone] through struggles based on racial issues."

Finally, Latino/a youth in the sample also read and wrote as part of their desire to maintain native language, suggesting an overlap between ethnic (typically Latino/a, in this community) and linguistic identities. That is, ethnicity was represented by language, but language identities may have also been a distinct motivating factor in the young people's reading and writing choices (or in their resistance to reading and writing certain texts). As one seventh grader, Clara, indicated, "I just seen it [*Latino* magazine], and it was in Spanish, and it's helping build my Spanish . . . . I'm trying to build up my Spanish so I can get a little bit more better at it than I am now." Similarly, Eva described herself as going exclusively to Spanish-speaking chat rooms, even though she has some difficulty writing in Spanish and occasionally needs to look up words in the dictionary. Other youth were less self-directed in their attempts to maintain their natal language, but included it as a reason for reading, nonetheless. By contrast, it is interesting to note that although we interviewed several Spanish-dominant speakers, we did not document any youth referring to reading or writing as a way to learn English, perhaps because these English language learners were constantly immersed in texts that demanded English language fluency and did not feel the need to seek them out.

Reading and Writing as Gender Identity Development. A second prominent identity category revolves around gender identities. Most of the references to gender were made when female students selected texts that heavily featured the female voice (*Latina* or *My Sister's Voices*). In five instances, students were explicit about gender-related themes that they had gleaned from texts they read. For example, students expressed interest in a number of texts because the characters showed pride in being male/female. Tiana, a tenth grader, explained her interest in *Phenomenal Woman* (Angelou, 2000), by saying, "Just the fact that it's about a woman and me being a woman or growing up to be a woman, it's just the type of woman I want be, so that's what makes it special," whereas Burton, an African American ninth grader, found *A Lesson Before Dying* (Gaines, 1997) compelling because in it, "a teacher has to teach this guy how to be a man" and "two men forge a bond."

In other cases, text mirrored students' own experiences and, as such, spoke to them (see VanDerPloeg & Moje, 2004). For example, Brianna described

Clique as a book about "how your friends will turn on you . . . very realistic; I know a lot of girls who do that." Finally, in terms of gendered identities, students read texts that allowed them to explore relationships with the opposite sex. Alex described reading men's magazines as teaching him about "*Maxim* girls, cars, and games," whereas Jacque described reading books about sex and "what to do if he's not satisfying you . . . do not fake it. Just tell him so that way he can work on it." Two other young women described chatting on message boards for the main purpose of communicating with boys.

Reading and Writing for Self-Improvement. Reading and writing also served a number of purposes that allowed the young person to become stronger, more resilient, more informed, and more in control of their emotions. Writing as a therapeutic act was a major theme in the interviews. Of the thirty-eight interviews analyzed to date, eleven students reported writing poems, letters, or journals when they felt sad or angry. Two others described the use of personal writing to express feelings to themselves or to others, and one young woman, Clara, wrote poems when angered by her friend so that she could "keep it to myself [rather] than involve my friend, 'cause it comes to a whole conflict." Here, Patricia, a ninth grader, describes her motivation for writing as both a way to vent and, at times, to communicate her anger:

(P = Patricia; I = Interviewer)

I: OK, what makes you really want to write something?

P: Either — I don't know — sometimes when I'm mad or upset or tired.

I: OK, and what do you write when you're mad, upset, and tired?

P: Letters.

I: And who do you write the letters to? Are those the letters you write to your friends, or letters . . . [to] family?

P: No, I just the, like, the angry letters I never sent to anybody or . . . of course, I don't write about anybody, you know, but, like, angry letters . . . I never show it to them . . . Or, like, once when we start talking about all that, yeah, I show it to them but it would be, like, I didn't mean to write it like that or . . . Like, they don't get all that mad but they're like, OK, they know what makes me click.

This pattern in young people's reasons for writing was a dominant theme of the open-ended survey response in which students were to answer the question, "Are you a writer, and if so, then what kinds of things do you write?" Eighty-six percent of the respondents in Wave 1 answered that they were writers, and the majority described their reasons for writing as being rooted in self-expression. A comment, however, that was discrepant from this pattern is evident in ninth grader Adriana's response to the question, "What makes you not want to write something?"

(A = Adriana; I = Interviewer)

A: I don't know if like . . . political stuff. No, wait, I don't like writing about . . . stuff, but I talk about it with my friends, but I never write it. . . . Like, the president and all he's doing, sending our troops into Iraq. I don't write about it, but I talk about it.

I: OK; and so, would you ever talk about this political stuff in your ROTC class?

A: No.

I: Why not?

A: I find it too personal. It's my brothers who went to the war and [are] going again . . . I don't want to talk about it too much. . . . Yeah, I don't know; writing about it makes it seem too personal, so I don't like it.

Adriana's talk about writing reveals an interesting contrast to the majority of the other responses, and raises questions about how young people take up highly personal topics in school classrooms. Whereas Patricia wrote to vent feelings that she knows nobody will ever read unless she allows it, Adriana resisted writing about topics that cause her anguish. Adriana's words — "writing about it makes it seem too personal" — might be interpreted as a concern that putting down fears in print may make them real. This contrast in how young people think about writing, and/or what kinds of topics make acceptable fodder for self-expression, has important implications for how teachers might think about engaging students in writing (and reading) about sensitive social topics in classrooms. Although writing about the highly personal might seem like a powerful way to make academic topics interesting to young people, this approach may also turn off some youth.

A second commonly mentioned form of reading or writing for self-improvement and reflection revolved around explicit attempts to develop one's sense of self or subjectivity, and thus to enact certain identities. Burton, for example, described writing on his bedroom ceiling inspirational quotes that he picked up from books and conversations, such as: "I will . . ." (reminder to achieve his goals); "Proper physical exercise increases your chances for health; proper mental exercise increases your chances for wealth" (from *Rich Dad, Poor Dad*, Kiyosaki, 2002, p. 15); and a Malcolm X quote from his English textbook.

Ethnographic observations of the smaller subsample, together with past ethnographic work among youth in this community (Moje, 2006a), reveal that Burton was not the only one to keep written records of inspirational quotes. A number did just as Burton did: They decorated walls, lockers, and their own bodies with quotations that remind them to work hard, set goals, and to be certain kinds of people. As noted previously, Carlotta is a member of a group who meets to write as a way of setting and sharing personal goals. Additionally, Maria described writing as a way of enacting an identity that provided a positive example for her younger sister, and Clara used her writing as a way to reflect on the past, looking back on texts she had written to determine whether she had been upset "over nothing, or it was something important." In sum, interviews were filled with examples of youth writing to inspire or motivate themselves to work hard and stay focused on the "right" things in life.

Reading often served the same purpose. Alicia recommended the book *La Maestría del Amor* (Ruiz, 2001), which, she claimed, makes you "cherish what you have and not to want more," a mature sentiment for a twelve-year-old youth. Javier assessed his progress as a reader by looking at stories that he had read in fifth grade "to see what I used to study and how it has changed from what I'm doing now."

In a related vein, youth described seeing texts as providing examples of negative behaviors from which they could learn vicariously, or through which they could process actual experiences. Chrissa, a seventh-grade youth, echoed this notion regarding reading: "If you read about someone who is getting into trouble or doing drugs, they can teach you about a way of life and help you get on the right track instead of doing what they did."

Melissa, an eighth-grade student, claimed that "[*Chicken Soup for the Soul*] will tell you a story about that person and then it will tell you . . . why you shouldn't do it, and if you do it, this is what it's going to cost," whereas Alma described *Juventud en Éxtasis* by Carlos Cuauhtémoc Sánchez (1995), part of a widely read series of books among girls in the community, as being about "youth and the risks that they have." And eighth grader Ari stated that certain books "make you realize not to make the same mistakes that they did. Makes you think of what would happen if it was you. . . . And . . . what would you do in her place — or, the person's place." Jacque, referring to *The Coldest Winter Ever* (Souljah, 1999), argued that "When reading somebody else's mistakes — you can learn from them."

Two students offered the opposite reason for reading: the search for positive examples and inspiration, as indicated by Patricia, who responded to the question of why she read particular texts in this way:

> Inspiration? Like, in one of the stories, it showed about a woman that was, like, fat or chunky, and she wouldn't be able to run or walk or things like that, and she got the inspiration to walk or run, and it's like, if she could do it, I probably could too, or things like that, so . . .

Reading for positive models of resilience, inspiration, and guidance, then, was a dominant theme across age levels and across years, and it is especially noted among the young women. Indeed, *Chicken Soup for the Teenage Soul* (Canfield, Hansen, & Kirberger, 1997) is one of most often-cited books on the open-ended survey task (two mentions in Wave 1 and ten mentions in Wave 2), and this book routinely comes up in ethnographic observations. In one trip to a bookstore, for example, two young women asked one of the researchers for advice on which *Chicken Soup* book to buy (*Chicken Soup for the Teenage*

Soul or *Chicken Soup for the Teenage Soul: Love and Friendship* [Canfield, Hansen, & Kirberger, 2002]), and were delighted when one of the researchers suggested that they each buy a different book and then trade them.

Another form of reading for self-improvement demonstrated two respondents' awareness of how reading increases writing ability, an interesting — albeit weakly demonstrated — pattern, because few survey respondents noted a relationship between reading and writing in their response to two survey items that ask them whether their reading depends on their ability to write and vice versa. In interviews, Tiana stated that she liked to read poetry because "it makes me add to my writing the way they're writing . . . but it helps me better my writing," and Antonio echoed that sentiment, claiming that, "Sometimes if you see something and you say, 'Oh, I want to write something like that,' and you make the effort and do it." This pattern is not dominant, but it does demonstrate that at least some youth see relationships between reading and writing and, therefore, are strategic or metacognitive in their approach to writing. In sum, the range of reasons for reading to improve the self is powerful; whether or not these youth achieve higher grades in school as a result of their reading, the reading they do appears to have an important impact on their lives.

Reading and Writing for Information. The three categories detailed above could all be considered forms of information reading, if one considers that the young people described using texts to provide access to networks and relationships, models for self-improvement or resilience, and examples of and information about being certain kinds of people. But we also documented evidence of what might be more obviously considered information reading, in the form of reading to obtain facts, to prepare for college, or to follow news stories. The information reading we documented could be subcategorized in two ways: seeking information for utilitarian reasons, and for the satisfaction of personal interests.

Examples of seeking information for utility include activities as diverse as reading and translating (in speech or in writing) materials for family members and using the Internet to comparison shop. For example, in this excerpt, Valeria describes translating for family members and for other people (at times, for pay):

(V = Valeria; I = Interviewer)

I: Is there anything that you use to help your family get things done? Do you ever translate things . . . ?

V: Yeah. . . . Translat[ing] is hard sometimes . . . when we go to the store, when we go to the hospital . . . the doctor . . .

I: Are there any things that you have to read in another language?

V: Taxes, bills . . . forms like that I read . . . like, this couple was gonna get married, and I had to go with them to translate.

In addition to reading for translation purposes, some students used the Internet to search for information. Clara used the Internet to explore ideas for a school science project; Burton sought information about jobs and college; and Christopher, Burton, and Antonio each mentioned searching the Internet to comparison shop. Other youth read to follow news stories about current events, particularly ones of local or personal interest. One such interest was immigration reform, a topic discussed by four youth in semi-structured interviews.[14] Alma described her interests in immigration and in the world beyond her in this way:

(A = Alma; I = Interviewer)

I: What type of articles in the newspapers are you interested in? When do you read it?

A: Mmmm . . . It can be like about sports. And news, but like . . . politics or whatever, something that is interesting, not everything, but something that has happened. . . . Like, for example, the place that one lives in, what happens there. That's what I meant . . . I don't know, immigration topics, what's going on, the laws that will be put in. . . .

I: Like, for example, would a war in another country interest you?

A: Yes. . . . Because I would like to know, like, what are the countries or the people involved in the war? Could be. And the immigration thing, well, in my case, I am Mexican, and, well, I would like to know, like, what is happening.

Other reasons to read for information included reading to obtain news about the war or to follow a friend in the military; reading about personal interests, such as articles related to owning a pet; and reading about current events, as described in the following excerpt from an interview with Ari:

(A = Ari; I = Interviewer)

I: Do you use the Internet to read for information about your favorite actors and stuff? What do you read for on the Internet?

A: Um, besides MySpace . . . I just, like . . . on AOL news, if they have something of, like . . . a celebrity I like, I'll just click on it and read the article. . . . Or stuff about . . . that might interest me, like . . . about . . . about the environment, like how the . . . the water is . . . like, not . . . the ice melting and then maybe, I don't know, by what year, we might not — polar bears might be extinct.

I: OK. So you read about environment and global warming and stuff?

A: That worries me.

We find the potential match between the content of the texts some youth are reading outside of school and the content of their science and social studies classrooms especially interesting and possibly fruitful. Yet, most of these youth express a lack of interest in science and social studies, with science nominated as the least-useful and least-liked content area on our survey, with social studies a close second (Stockdill & Moje, 2007). Such findings should raise questions for adolescent literacy researchers and secondary school teachers alike about the disconnect that exists between youth interests in scientific and social issues outside of school and their interest and achievement in these areas within secondary schools. One aspect of this disconnect may be that the texts of school content areas are not embedded — or, at least, are not presented as embedded — in social networks relevant to the lives of youth. As the findings of our qualitative analyses suggest, youth read and write when they have a well-articulated purpose, a purpose that is usually centered in a network of social activity.

The Mysteries of Adolescent Literacy: Implications for Practice, Questions for Research

These findings of what, how often, and why youth read and write outside of school, together with findings on the relationship between out-of-school literacy practices and in-school achievement, present a number of important possible implications for education practice. The findings, however, also pose some remaining questions — mysteries — to be studied in future research. We want to underscore our contention, based on the preliminary findings of this research, that before policies are made regarding the best methods for improving adolescent literacy achievement, a stronger research base is needed to understand the relationship between what, why, and how youth read and write on their own and in school. That said, we do think there are many points to be learned from this analysis.

First, youth *do* read and write outside of school. If this report communicates nothing else, it should debunk the myth that youth — at least in the community studied here — are not reading and writing. They do read and write, but they may not read and write the kinds of texts that adults value. The host of reasons for reading and writing indicated by the youth of this one community suggest that it would behoove educators, policymakers, and school textbook publishers to attend to the types of texts that young people value and the reasons for which they read. We find it compelling that in both the surveys and interviews, youth indicate that they read texts in school that are situated in social networks they can identify with (e.g., urban settings, or youth who struggle with adversity). Offering youth high-quality adolescent literature, in addition to canonical texts of English language arts, does appear to make a difference in young people's reading lives.

We have often heard from teachers that "kids don't read." Our findings suggest that young people will read, but they may need suggestions for reading and writing activities, as well as a wider array of options within their chosen topic areas. The findings presented here provide a glimpse of what young people value in texts: They like to read books about people like them, and not only in terms of race, ethnicity, age, class, or gender (although these features are important). They also like to identify with characters who are resilient through struggles, people who are working through relationships, people trying to figure out who they are. They want to read books and write texts that offer them social capital in the form of information, ideas for self-improvement, models for identities, or ways to maintain existing relationships and build new ones.

Second, although our analyses demonstrate that this one group of urban youth does read and write outside of school, we must acknowledge that they may not be reading and writing widely or frequently enough to make a difference in their school achievement. Findings from preliminary analyses suggest that time spent reading novels does predict students' achievement, but that the reading or writing these youth engage in happens infrequently, or may be too different from school reading and writing to impact their achievement in domains other than English language arts. Thus, these data suggest that simply reading outside of school may not increase in-school academic achievement. It appears that genre, content, and subject area are important aspects to consider when evaluating the relationships between time spent reading and in-school achievement. In other words, school science learning is more likely to be bolstered by reading science texts, history learning by reading history, and so on. These findings must be supplemented with additional and more powerful analyses as data continue to be collected, but initial analyses raise key questions for future research.

Our qualitative findings suggest some explanations for the lack of relationship between out-of-school time reading and school achievement in content areas other than English class, as youths' purposes for reading out of school are more in line with the study of English language arts, and less connected to the kinds of texts and purposes they would typically encounter or be asked to produce in classes such as science or social studies. Reading and writing to explore or express emotions, for example, is not an activity typically valued in chemistry or economics classes. In fact, in previous studies we have documented that young people's emotions and opinions can interfere with their writing of social science essays. When they are asked to take a stand on social issues, young people often want to maintain their own impassioned stances toward social issues, rather than engaging in dispassionate critique using evidence (Moje, 2006b; Moje & Speyer, in press).

In other words, what and why young people read and write outside of school may affect their continuing literate development as they advance through school, especially in the disciplinary domains. This finding, however, presents a challenge: Knowing that much of the reading and writing youth are motivated to do on their own revolves around the maintenance of social networks, relationships, identity development, and self-improvement and self-expression, how do we engage young people in the texts of disciplinary domains outside of school (or in school, for that matter), which may often be far removed

147

from the concerns of their lives? How do we build educational interventions that acknowledge youths' strengths and interests, while also engaging them in content-based reading and writing?

Gee's analyses of video gaming (2003), together with our analysis presented here, may suggest some possible directions. As Gee argues, video-game programmers are skilled at building social worlds and networks into which youth are drawn. Often, the virtual social world of the game is connected to a live social network, thus providing increased motivation for reading and sense-making. Gee demonstrated that video games not only offer worlds to gamers, but also identities and goals. Our data suggest that social networks, identities, and established goals are key motivators for youth reading outside of school. Youth read inside social networks, in line with identities they recognize or wish to enact, and they look for ways to build social capital in order to meet particular goals of self-improvement and future aspirations. What are the corollaries to such social worlds, identities, and goals in the disciplinary domains? What would it mean to help a ninth-grade student connect to the social networks of biologists or historians? Do most educators feel connected enough to these social networks to be able to reconstruct them for youth?

A number of educational projects simulate the activities of disciplinary communities (such as project-based science or social studies simulations). But do they replicate the goals, identities, and discursive practices of those disciplinary social (and cultural) networks? According to Rogers Hall and Susan Jurow (2006), some do. They experimented with bringing practicing scientists into the classroom to engage in a critique of students' written representations (i.e., poster presentations) of scientific investigations. Such activities provide social networks for youth and model discursive practices of the disciplines in ways that the learning of technical terms and discourse conventions do not.

More to the point of adolescent literacy development, however, is whether subject matter texts make evident the disciplinary social networks, goals, and identities involved. According to studies such as Paxton's (1999), the social identities and work of the discipline as represented by the historian's voice are absent in typical history textbooks (see also Schleppegrell, 2004). Thus, in addition to building social networks that engage youth in the identity enactments, content representations, and literacy and language practices of the disciplinary domains, educators and publishers might consider developing different kinds of texts in those domains. In this case, we are referring to engineering new types of classroom texts, ones that recognize the need to situate reading and writing within social networks and invite young readers into a relationship with the text and the work of the discipline. Visiting scientists (or historians, mathematicians, literary theorists, or artists) may not be practical for all classrooms, but texts can be generated to provide simulations of those social networks and discursive practices.

The work of Annemarie Palincsar and Shirley Magnusson (2001), in which researchers constructed a fictional scientist's log that young children read and critiqued as they carried out their own investigations, offers a compelling example of the possibilities for engaging readers in deep content reading and writing that connects them to other learners and investigators. Similarly, Lee's (2007) recent study of the use of history textbooks — revised to demonstrate the thinking of the historians — suggests that making social networks, goals, and identities visible can make a difference in how young people read (and possibly, write) in content areas. Some of these texts might employ digital platforms, thus allowing for interaction with actual social networks of members of the disciplines. Our data suggest that young people would read such texts with enthusiasm.

However, this idea raises concerns related to a third key finding of our research. In this community — one not unlike many other high-poverty settings — Internet activity does *not* seem to be responsible for distracting youths' attention from school reading and writing, as some would argue. Nor is Internet activity particularly supportive of school achievement. In fact, when compared to statistics of daily youth Internet use reported by others (Lenhart, Madden, & Hitlin, 2005), our data suggest that the digital divide has not closed. If the popular conception of equal digital access dominates, then educational and social policies may overlook the need to continue working toward more-equitable digital access for all people.

We wish to conclude by emphasizing that, even without a demonstrated impact on school achievement, the literacy practices of youth documented in our study are significant and powerful in their lives. In other words, the value of youths' out-of-school practices should not be assessed only by the influence of the practices on school achievement. The qualitative data we present demonstrate that youth read and write for social, emotional, intellectual, and spiritual purposes. Their reading and writing practices foster communication, relationships, and self-expression among peers and family members; support their economic and psychological health; and allow them to construct subjectivities and enact identities that offer them power in their everyday lives. These consequences of literate practice in the everyday world should not be diminished by the quest to improve the school achievement of all young people, even as educators pursue the important goal of closing the achievement gap. Indeed, future studies of adolescent literacy development should continue to examine how educational practice and policy can draw from and support — without co-opting, exploiting, or diminishing — the powerful literacy practices of young people's everyday lives.

Notes

1. A third wave of data collection has just been completed, resulting in a stronger longitudinal sample. These data, however, had not been analyzed at the time of paper preparation.
2. These ethnic/racial identity data are both self-reported by the youth in the study and verified by school reports. As part of the survey, we ask youth to report their ethnic/

racial identity according to U.S. Census categories, as well as to answer open-ended questions about how they identify. The open-ended questions yield more complex information about how youth prefer to represent themselves, but the self-report categories provide access to their primary representations at a given point in time. (Most, it should be noted, are stable over the two years of the study, with slight variation in representation of specific national identity for those who claim a Latino/a identity.)

3. Namely, *cheat codes*, or tips to enable video/computer game players to play a game or figure out a clue in a game, were added because they were written in so often, and the phrase *graphic novels* was added to *comic books*.

4. These constructs have an important iterative relationship; that is, social capital provides access to social networks, and social networks provide opportunities to build social capital.

5. In this instance, *shout-outs* are messages that youth write to each other in Internet chat rooms and other electronic media. The origin of the term is found in popular music, in which references or "nods" are made to artists, well-known people, or to people of personal importance to the performer.

6. All names are pseudonyms.

7. Exemplars are edited for clarity or to achieve brevity, but not for content. Throughout the transcripts, extended ellipses are used to indicate pauses in speech. Short ellipses at the end of a line indicate speech trailing off, and dashes at the end and beginning of lines of speech indicate that one speaker has interrupted another speaker's speech. An ellipsis after a period, question mark, or comma indicates that text has been edited out for brevity or clarity.

8. It is worth noting that although Javier denies reading with his family, throughout this particular interview and a second reading-process interview, he describes a number of other instances in which he reads with various family members.

9. Masked to maintain anonymity.

10. It is more common for these youth to own bikes than cars, primarily because of their age and the relative cost differences, although lowrider bikes can run into the several-thousand-dollar range.

11. In truth, anime typically derive from manga, rather than the paper-based comics deriving from animated versions. However, the young people in our study are often introduced to the texts via the television programs they watch, and thus see the manga as derived from anime.

12. Masked to maintain anonymity.

13. Sammie's comment makes clear that he has not actually read *Always Running*, which is an autobiographical narrative of gang life in Los Angeles.

14. We also noted this focus in reading-process interviews in which we asked students to think aloud about content and reading processes as they read academic texts and texts of their choosing, but, due to space constraints, we have not included those analyses in this paper.

References

ACT, Inc. (2006). *Reading between the lines: What the ACT reveals about college readiness in reading*. Iowa City, IA: Author.

Alexander, P. (2003). Profiling the adolescent reader: The interplay of knowledge, interest, and strategic processing. In C. Fairbanks, J. Worthy, B. Maloch, J. V. Hoffman, & D. Schallert (Eds.), *53rd yearbook of the National Reading Conference* (pp. 47–65). Milwaukee, WI: National Reading Conference.

Alexander, P. A., Kulikowich, J. M., & Jetton, T. L. (1994). The role of subject-matter knowledge and interest in the processing of linear and nonlinear texts. *Review of Educational Research, 64,* 201–252.

Alvermann, D. E., Hagood, M. C., & Williams, K. B. (2001). Image, language, and sound: Making meaning with popular culture texts. *Reading Online, 4*(11).

Alvermann, D. E., Young, J. P., Green, C., & Wisenbaker, J. M. (1999). Adolescents' perceptions and negotiations of literacy practices in after-school read and talk clubs. *American Educational Research Journal, 36,* 221–264.

Anderson, R. C., Wilson, P. T., & Fielding, L. G. (1988). Growth in reading and how children spend their time outside of school. *Reading Research Quarterly, 23,* 285–303.

Angelou, M. (2000). *Phenomenal woman.* New York: Random House.

Bain, R. (2006). Rounding up unusual suspects: Facing the authority hidden in the history classroom. *Teachers College Record, 108,* 2080–2114.

Blumenfeld, P. C., Kempler, T. M., & Krajcik, J. S. (2006). Motivation and cognitive engagement in learning environments. In K. Sawyer (Ed.), *The Cambridge handbook of the learning sciences* (pp. 475–488). New York: Cambridge University Press.

Camitta, M. (1993). Vernacular writing: Varieties of literacy among Philadelphia high school students. In B. V. Street (Ed.), *Cross-cultural approaches to literacy* (pp. 228–246). Cambridge, England: Cambridge University Press.

Canfield, J., Hansen, M. V., & Kirberger, K. (1997). *Chicken soup for the teenage soul: 101 stories of life, love, and learning.* Deerfield Beach, FL: Health Communications.

Canfield, J., Hansen, M. V., & Kirberger, K. (2002). *Chicken soup for the teenage soul: Love and friendship.* Deerfield Beach, FL: HCI Teens.

Chandler-Olcott, K., & Mahar, D. (2003). "Tech-savviness" meets multiliteracies: Exploring adolescent girls' technology-mediated literacy practices. *Reading Research Quarterly, 38,* 356–385.

Cisneros, S. (1991). *House on Mango Street.* New York: Vintage Books.

Cowan, P. M. (2005). Putting it out there: Revealing Latino visual discourse in the Hispanic academic summer program for middle school students. In B. V. Street (Ed.), *Literacies across educational contexts: Mediating learning and teaching* (pp. 145–169). Philadelphia: Caslon.

Cuauhtémoc Sánchez, C. (1995). *Juventud en éxtasis.* Mexico City, Mexico: Ediciones Selectas Diamantes.

Donahue, P., Daane, M., & Grigg, W. (2003). *The nation's report card: Reading highlights 2003* (No. NCES 2004452). Washington DC: U.S. Department of Education, Institute for Education Sciences, National Center for Education Statistics.

Eccles, J. S., Lord, S., & Midgley, C. (1991). What are we doing to early adolescents? The impact of educational contexts on early adolescents. *American Journal of Education, 99,* 521–542.

Eccles, J. S., Wigfield, A., Midgley, C., Reuman, D., MacIver, D., & Feldlaufer, H. (1993). Negative effects of traditional middle schools on students' motivation. *Elementary School Journal, 93,* 553–574.

Flake, S. (1998). *The skin I'm in.* New York: Jump at the Sun/Hyperion Books for Children.

Ellis, L. M., Moje, E. B., & VanDerPloeg, L. (2004, April). *Listening for the call and response: Hearing the second personas in texts and the youth who resignify them.* Paper presented at the annual meeting of the American Educational Research Association, San Diego, CA.

Erickson, F. (1992). Ethnographic microanalysis of interaction. In M. D. LeCompte, W. L. Millroy, & J. Preissle (Eds.), *The handbook of qualitative research in education* (pp. 201–225). San Diego: Academic Press.

Gaines, E. (1997). *A lesson before dying.* New York: Vintage.

Gee, J. P. (2001, December). *Reading in "new times."* Paper presented at the National Reading Conference, San Antonio, TX.

Gee, J. P. (2003). *What video games have to teach us about learning and literacy.* New York: Palgrave Macmillan.

Glaser, B., & Strauss, A. (1967). *The discovery of grounded theory: Strategies for qualitative research.* New York: Aldine.

Goody, J. (1999). The implications of literacy. In D. A. Wagner, R. L. Venezky, & B. V. Street (Eds.), *Literacy: An international handbook* (pp. 29–33). Boulder, CO: Westview.

Gustavson, L. (2007). *Youth learning on their own terms.* New York: Routledge.

Guthrie, J. T., & Metsala, J. L. (1999). Literacy in North America. In D. A. Wagner, R. L. Venezky, & B. V. Street (Eds.), *Literacy: An international handbook* (pp. 381–384). Boulder, CO: Westview Press.

Guthrie, J. T., & Wigfield, A. (2000). Engagement and motivation in reading. In P. B. Mosenthal, M. L. Kamil, P. D. Pearson, & R. Barr (Ed.), *Handbook of reading research* (Vol. III, pp. 403–419). Mahwah, NJ: Lawrence Erlbaum Associates.

Hall, R., & Jurow, S. (2006, April). *Hybrid interactional practices: Expanding the disciplinary expertise of a middle school mathematics classroom.* Paper presented at the American Educational Research Association, San Francisco.

Hand, B., Wallace, C., & Yang, E. (2004). Using the science writing heuristic to enhance learning outcomes from laboratory activities in seventh-grade science: Quantitative and qualitative aspects. *International Journal of Science Education, 26,* 131–149.

Harrison, M., & Harrison, H. H. (2006). *Mother to son: Shared lessons from the heart.* New York: Workman.

Heath, S. B. (1983). *Ways with words: Language, life, and work in communities and classrooms.* Cambridge, England: Cambridge University Press.

Hinton, S. E. *The outsiders.* New York: Puffin Books.

Ingalls, R. (2005). *Taking a page from their books: Negotiating containment and resuscitating rhetoric in writing across academic and spoken-word genres.* Unpublished doctoral dissertation, University of Michigan, Ann Arbor.

Jacob, I. (Ed.). (2002). *My sisters' voices: Teenage girls of color speak out.* New York: Owl Books/ Henry Holt and Company.

Kiyosaki, R., & Lechter, S. L. (2002). *Rich dad, poor dad: What the rich teach their kids — that you can learn too.* New York: Time Warner.

Knobel, M. (1999). *Everyday literacies.* New York: Lang.

Knobel, M., & Lankshear, C. (2002). Cut, paste, and publish: The production and consumption of zines. In D. E. Alvermann (Ed.), *Adolescents and literacies in a digital world* (pp. 164–185). New York: Peter Lang.

Kress, G. (2003). *Literacy in the new media age (literacies).* New York: Routledge.

Leander, K. M., & Lovvorn, J. F. (2006). Literacy networks: Following the circulation of texts, bodies, and objects in the schooling and online gaming of one youth. *Cognition & Instruction, 24,* 291–340.

Lee, C. D. (2005, December). *Re-conceptualizing disciplinary literacies and the adolescent struggling reader: Placing culture at the forefront.* Paper presented at the annual meeting of the National Reading Conference, Miami, FL.

Lee, M. (2007). *Promoting historical inquiry using secondary sources.* Unpublished doctoral dissertation, University of Michigan, Ann Arbor.

Lenhart, A., Madden, M., & Hitlin, P. (2005). *Teens and technology: Youth are leading the transition to a fully wired and mobile nation.* Washington, DC: Pew Internet & American Life Project.

Lesko, N. (2001). *Act your age! A cultural construction of adolescence.* New York: Routledge-Falmer.

Leu, D. (2005, December). *New literacies, reading research, and the challenges of change: A deictic perspective of our research worlds.* Paper presented at the National Reading Conference, Miami, FL.

Lewis, C., & Fabos, B. (2005). Instant messaging, literacies, and social identities. *Reading Research Quarterly, 40,* 470–501.

Luke, A. (2001). Foreword. In E. B. Moje & D. G. O'Brien (Eds.), *Constructions of literacy: Studies of teaching and learning in and out of secondary schools* (pp. ix–xii). Mahwah, NJ: Lawrence Erlbaum Associates.

Luke, A., & Elkins, J. (1998). Reinventing literacy in "new times." *Journal of Adolescent & Adult Literacy, 42,* 4–7.

Luke, C. (2002). Re-crafting media and ICT literacies. In D. E. Alvermann (Ed.), *Adolescents and literacies in a digital world* (pp. 132–146). New York: Peter Lang.

Mahiri, J. (1994). Reading rites and sports: Motivation for adaptive literacy of young African American males. In B. J. Moss (Ed.), *Literacy across communities* (pp. 121–146). Cresskill, NJ: Hampton Press.

Mahiri, J. (Ed.). (2003). *What they don't learn in school: Literacy in the lives of urban youth.* New York: Peter Lang.

McCaslin, M. M. (1990). Motivated literacy. In *Literacy theory and research: Analysis from multiple paradigms. The thirty-ninth yearbook of the National Reading Conference* (pp. 35–50). Chicago: National Reading Conference.

Moje, E. B. (2000). To be part of the story: The literacy practices of gangsta adolescents. *Teachers College Record, 102,* 652–690.

Moje, E. B. (2004). Powerful spaces: Tracing the out-of-school literacy spaces of Latino/a youth. In K. Leander & M. Sheehy (Eds.), *Spatializing literacy research and practice* (pp. 15–38). New York: Peter Lang.

Moje, E. B. (2006a). Motivating texts, motivating contexts, motivating adolescents: An examination of the role of motivation in adolescent literacy practices and development. *Perspectives, 32*(3), 10–14.

Moje, E. B. (2006b, March). *Enhancing content-area literacy and learning in secondary schools: Perspectives from research and strategies for practice.* Paper presented at the State of Michigan Governor's Summit, Lansing, MI.

Moje, E. B., Dillon, D. R., & O'Brien, D. G. (2000). Reexamining the roles of the learner, the text, and the context in secondary literacy. *Journal of Educational Research, 93,* 165–180.

Moje, E. B., Collazo, T., Carrillo, R., & Marx, R. W. (2001). "Maestro, what is 'quality'?": Language, literacy, and discourse in project-based science. *Journal of Research in Science Teaching, 38,* 469–496.

Moje, E. B., & Lewis, C. (2007). Examining opportunities to learn literacy: The role of critical sociocultural literacy research. In C. Lewis, P. Enciso, & E. B. Moje (Eds.), *Identity, agency, and power: Reframing sociocultural research in literacy* (pp. 15–48). Mahwah, NJ: Erlbaum.

Moje, E. B., & Speyer, J. (in press). The reality of challenging texts in high school science and social studies: How teachers can mediate comprehension. In K. Hinchman & H. Thomas (Eds.), *Best practices in adolescent literacy instruction.* New York: Guilford Press.

National Endowment for the Arts. (2007). *To read or not to read* (No. 47). Washington, DC: National Endowment for the Arts.

New London Group. (1996). A pedagogy of multiliteracies: Designing social futures. *Harvard Educational Review, 66,* 60–92.

O'Brien, D., & King, J. R. (2002). Adolescents' multiliteracies and their teachers' needs to know: Toward a digital detente. In D. E. Alvermann (Ed.), *Adolescents and literacies in a digital world* (pp. 40–50). New York: Peter Lang.

Palincsar, A. S., & Magnusson, S. J. (2001). The interplay of first-hand and text-based investigations to model and support the development of scientific knowledge and reasoning. In S. M. Carver & D. Klahr (Eds.), *Cognition and instruction: 25 years of progress* (pp. 152–193). Mahwah, NJ: Erlbaum.

Paulsen, G. (1987). *Hatchet.* New York: Bradbury Press.

Paxton, R. J. (1999). A deafening silence: History textbooks and the students who read them. *Review of Educational Research, 69,* 315–339.

Resnick, L., & Gordon. (1999). Literacy in social history. In B. V. Street, R. L. Venezky, & D. A. Wagner, (Eds.), *Literacy: An international handbook* (pp. 16-21). Boulder, CO: Westview.

Rodriguez, L. J. (1993). *Always running: La vida loca, gang days in LA* (1st ed.). Willimantic, CT: Curbstone Press.

Rowling, J. K. (2001). *Harry Potter and the sorcerer's stone.* New York: Scholastic.

Ruiz, D. M. (2001). *La maestria del amor: Una guia practica para el arte de las relaciones.* San Rafael, CA: Amber-Allen Publishing.

Ryan, P. M. (2000). *Esperanza rising.* New York: Scholastic.

Sachar, L. (1998). *Holes.* New York: Farrar, Straus and Giroux

Schleppegrell, M. J. (2004). *The language of schooling: A functional linguistics perspective.* Mahwah, NJ: Lawrence Erlbaum Associates.

Scribner, S., & Cole, M. (1981). *The psychology of literacy.* Cambridge, MA: Harvard University Press.

Souljah, S. (1999). *The coldest winter ever.* New York: Pocket Books.

Stanovich, K. E. (1986). Matthew effects in reading: Some consequences of individual differences in the acquisition of reading. *Reading Research Quarterly, 21,* 360–407.

Stockdill, D., & Moje, E. B. (2007). *Adolescents as readers of culture, history, economics, and civics: The disconnect between student interest in their world and social studies schooling.* Ann Arbor: University of Michigan.

Street, B. V. (1984). *Literacy in theory and practice.* Cambridge, England: Cambridge University Press.

Takahashi, R. (2003). *InuYasha* (Vol. I). San Francisco, CA: VIZ Media LLC.

VanDerPloeg, L. S., & Moje, E. B. (2004, December). *Urban Youth Reading for "Real": Intersections of Race, Ethnicity, Relationships, and Urban Experience.* Paper presented at the National Reading Conference, San Antonio, TX.

Wigfield, A., Eccles, J. S., & Rodriguez, D. (1998). The development of children's motivation in school contexts. In P. D. Pearson & A. Iran-Nejad (Eds.), *Review of research in education* (Vol. 23, pp. 73–118). Washington, DC: American Educational Research Association.

Wineburg, S. S. (2001). *Historical thinking and other unnatural acts: Charting the future of teaching the past.* Philadelphia: Temple University Press.

Wineburg, S. S., & Martin, D. (2004). Reading and rewriting history. *Educational Leadership, 62*(1), 62.

The project described was supported by Grant Number R01HD046115 from the National Institute of Child Health and Human Development/ACF/ASPE/IES. The content is solely the responsibility of the authors and does not necessarily represent the official views of the National Institute of Child Health and Human Development, the National Institutes of Health, the ACF, ASPE, or the Institute of Education Sciences.

Toward a More Anatomically Complete Model of Literacy Instruction: A Focus on African American Male Adolescents and Texts

ALFRED W. TATUM
University of Illinois at Chicago

In this article, Alfred Tatum argues that the current framing of the adolescent literacy crisis fails to take into account the in-school and out-of-school challenges confronting many African American male adolescents today, particularly those growing up in high-poverty communities. Using the metaphor of literacy instruction as a human body, he argues that in the absence of sound theory about the importance of texts for African American male adolescents, even the best instructional methods will fall flat, like a body without a head. He offers a more anatomically complete model in which instructional methods are governed by theories about how literacy can help young men of color respond to their immediate contexts, and in which professional development gives legs to these methods by preparing teachers to engage all students. Finally, in a case study of one Chicago youth, Tatum illustrates both the power that relevant texts can hold for young men of color and the missed opportunities that result when students do not encounter such texts in their schools.

According to many standardized assessments, educators in the U.S. continually fail to advance the literacy development and academic achievement of African American male adolescents, particularly the ones who live and go to schools in high-poverty communities. There is an absence of interdisciplinary depth, theoretical grounding, and focus on responsive pedagogy required to provide effective literacy instruction for these young men. For example, when policymakers plan literacy reforms, they often do not consider research on resilience (Henderson & Milstein, 2003; Werner & Smith, 1992), life outcome perspectives (Mizell, 1999), the relationship between masculinity and schooling (Gilbert & Gilbert, 1998; Young, 2000), the relationship between neigh-

Harvard Educational Review   Vol. 78   No. 1   Spring 2008

borhood quality and schooling (Ceballo, McLoyd, & Toyokawa, 2004), and how social processes of race, class, and gender are interwoven with literacy (Greene & Abt-Perkins, 2003; Lesko, 2000; Swanson, Cunningham, & Spencer, 2003). In efforts to reverse trends of poor reading outcomes among this group, the multiple in-school and out-of-school contexts that African American male adolescents have to negotiate are often ignored when developing or adopting instructional plans, selecting curricula, or examining students' placement in low-level or remedial courses.

My experience over the past fourteen years as a teacher, researcher, and professional developer in middle and high schools leads me to assert that many school leaders are not openly and critically discussing issues of race, language, gender, social class, and adolescent literacy. Discussion of race and social class creates tension in schools, and is often devoid of the critical analysis such a dialogue deserves. I am often asked to explain why I feel the need to write about African American adolescent males when the data are clear about their dismal reading achievement and the deleterious outcomes these young men experience in school and society. It is because there is an urgent need to address both the literacy needs and life outcomes of African American male adolescents in order to improve the conditions of these young men in school and society. It has become perfunctory to describe African American males using high school dropout, incarceration, and unemployment statistics, without also providing the necessary careful analysis done by social scientists and educators to unearth the root causes of these outcomes (Roderick, 1994). Questions related to educational malfeasance toward poor adolescents, particularly African American males, are not asked, and our educational discourse suffers as a result.

In this article, I describe the need for a more anatomically complete model of literacy instruction for African American male adolescents. After describing the model, I explain how the adolescent literacy crisis and its framing can potentially interrupt the implementation of such a model for young men of color. The last section of the article focuses on a qualitative case study with a sixteen-year-old African American male and highlights the centrality of meaningful texts to any literacy model that aims to advance the literacy development of African American male adolescents.

By expressly focusing on African American males in this article, I do not intend to undermine the significance of addressing the literacy needs of *all* adolescents in the United States, where an adolescent literacy crisis has been identified (Biancarosa & Snow, 2006). A false polarization is often evoked when efforts are aimed specifically to address the literacy needs of African American male adolescents. It is often intimated that a concentrated focus on African American males suggests that the literacy needs of African American adolescent girls or other adolescents are less important or do not require the same attention. This is simply not the case. It is the case, however, that literacy reform efforts aimed at improving African American male adolescents' reading achievement and life outcomes have been woefully inadequate and have underestimated the depth of their literacy needs in both racially segregated and racially integrated schools. Therefore, I have been working for the past eight years to develop a model for advancing the literacy development of African American male adolescents. Though the model is theoretically grounded in the literacy needs of these young men, it does not exclude other populations and may even be useful in promoting the literacy development of all students.

My work began as an eighth-grade social studies teacher on Chicago's South Side, working with struggling adolescent readers. In trying to improve their reading achievement, I was confronted with myriad challenges, including students' accumulation of failure, poor concepts of reading, and lack of self-efficacy stemming from years of ineffective instruction. Offsetting the resistance toward reading among my African American male students was particularly challenging. Four of the eighth-grade boys I taught during my third year of teaching simply refused to read. I began to engage their voices as a teacher-researcher to find ways to break down the barriers that disenfranchised these boys, who had been assigned to a low-level reading track (Tatum, 2000). Over time, I realized that the four major barriers to their engagement with reading were the fear of being publicly embarrassed if they failed in front of their peers, their limited vocabulary knowledge, the lack of attention their former teachers placed on reading books and engaging with texts, and their perceptions that teachers expected them to fail.

Since that time, I have conducted two qualitative case studies exploring the root causes of reluctance among some African American male adolescents. The first was a case study of a professional development initiative aimed at identifying the aspects of professional development that teachers found most useful for advancing the literacy development of seventh- and eighth-grade African American students (Tatum, 2002, 2003). The second was a case study of an African American teenage male, in which I sought to identify texts and textual characteristics he found effective for becoming a better reader and shaping his own identity (Tatum, in press). Some aspects of the latter study are described in this article. Currently, I am in my nineteenth month of working to help close the reading achievement gap in a large, racially integrated high school where the African American males are among the lowest-performing readers and have not made Adequate Yearly Progress under No Child Left Behind in the past five years. Additionally, my own status as an African American male who was educated in several of Chicago's inner-city schools in high-poverty neighborhoods, and who later became a teacher and reading specialist in similar communities, informs the call I make to move toward a more anatomically complete model of literacy instruction for adolescents (Tatum, 2003, 2005).

The more anatomically complete model of literacy instruction that I propose integrates effective instructional practices informed by the extant reading research on adolescent literacy (Alvermann, Hinchman, Moore, Phelps, & Waff, 2006; Biancarosa & Snow, 2006; Jetton & Dole, 2004; Rush, Eakle, &

Berger; 2007), by research on African American males (Fashola, 2005; Polite & Davis, 1999), and by research on boys and literacy (Brozo, 2002; Smith & Wilhelm, 2002). My model also gives attention to multiple conceptualizations of literacies and identities, some of which are situated within power structures such as class, gender, and race (Collins & Blot, 2003; Street, 1995). Finally, it aims to support teachers in structuring their students' day-to-day activities in a way that maximizes their engagement with meaningful, relevant texts.

As displayed in Figure 1, the model I am advancing has multiple theoretical, instructional, and professional development strands. *Theoretical strands* constitute the head of the model and focus on defining the role of literacy instruction for adolescents in their present-day contexts, creating curriculum orientations that empower them, and using a culturally responsive approach to literacy teaching. Each of these strands is glaringly omitted in many school literacy reform efforts. The *instructional strands* comprise the body of the model and focus on research-based reading practices. The *professional development strands* serve as the legs of the model and focus on in-school teacher professional development and teacher preparation.

At present, most literacy reform efforts focus primarily on the instructional strands (body), and thus constitute what I refer to as an anatomically *incomplete* model of literacy instruction. For example, Chicago Public Schools, the third-largest school district in the United States, uses a literacy reform framework that focuses primarily on word study, fluency, comprehension, and writing. Yet according to recent National Assessment of Educational Progress (NAEP) data, only 17 percent of Chicago's eighth-grade students scored at a proficient level in reading, performing better than only three large urban districts in the United States. While reading strategies offer much-needed support for struggling adolescent readers (Heller & Greenleaf, 2007), the corpus of these strategies aimed at improving the reading achievement of African American adolescent males remains insufficient.

Many teachers who have a strong foundational knowledge for teaching reading still experience difficulty teaching African American male adolescents who attend schools in high-poverty communities. During an e-mail exchange, a veteran educator informed me that she had more than twenty-five years of experience teaching reading strategies but found she was ineffective with the African American ninth-grade males in her classes. She acknowledged that she did not have sufficient competence with other components of literacy instruction, which I refer to here as "vital signs," that could contribute to her effectiveness with African American male adolescents.

Multiple Vital Signs of Literacy Instruction

A more anatomically complete model of literacy instruction pays attention to four categories of literacy vital signs — vital signs of *reading*, vital signs of *readers*, vital signs of *reading instruction*, and vital signs of *educators* — all essential

FIGURE 1   *A More Anatomically Complete Model of Literacy Instruction*

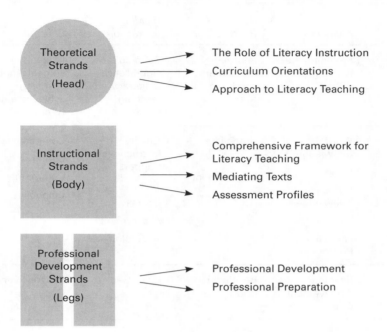

elements for improving students' reading achievement. The vital signs refer to aspects of instruction that should be cultivated in classrooms and tailored to the characteristics of educators and students. As shown in Table 1, the vital signs categories correspond to four parallel gaps affecting students' literacy-related outcomes: a reading achievement gap, a relationship gap, a rigor gap, and a responsiveness gap.

The vital signs of *reading* provide the necessary working tools (e.g., decoding, self-questioning and comprehension-monitoring techniques, summarizing, and other strategies) that students need to handle texts independently, and they constitute a necessary minimum set of tools for all literacy efforts. Attending to the vital signs of reading by focusing on students' reading skills is important in addressing the reading achievement gap. The vital signs of *readers* direct educators' attention to students' lived experiences, both in school and outside of school, and are useful for considering ways to improve the human condition. When educators attend to the vital signs of readers — the everyday lives of the students they teach — they begin to build supportive relationships with their students and thereby address the relationship gap.

The third set of vital signs, those of *reading instruction*, are intimately related to rescuing and refining the significance of literacy teaching for adolescents in this current era of accountability. In other words, they are useful for conceptualizing the rationale for literacy teaching and enhancing academic rigor

TABLE 1   *Multiple Vital Signs of Literacy Instruction*

	Reading	Readers	Reading Instruction	Educators
Rationale	Providing the working tools (What)	Improving the human condition (Why)	Refining the significance of literacy teaching (How)	Interacting with students, not scorecards of achievement (Who)
Vital Signs	Word Knowledge Fluency Strategy Knowledge Writing Language Proficiency	Home Life Culture Environment Language Economics	Quality Instructional Support Text Context Assessment Technology	Competence Caring Commitment Culpability
Aims to Correct	Reading Achievement Gap	Relationship Gap	Rigor Gap	Responsiveness Gap

in the classroom. Attention to the vital signs of reading instruction should cause educators to reflect on texts, quality instructional supports, assessments, and the potential uses of technology in an attempt to shape rigorous learning experiences for adolescents.

The vital signs of *educators* are related to shaping educational contexts characterized by caring, commitment, competence, and culpability. Adolescents benefit when they know that they belong in the learning environment, when they experience psychosocial membership, and when they feel they are in the presence of an adult advocate who is not going to give up on them (Goodenow, 1993; Price, 2000). In this sense, attention to the vital signs of educators is a critical step toward addressing the responsiveness gap. Moving toward a more anatomically complete model of literacy instruction that pays attention to these vital signs requires an understanding of the current adolescent literacy crisis and how African American adolescent males are situated within it.

Overview of the Adolescent Literacy Crisis

The term *adolescent literacy crisis* is the current descriptor used in the United States to encapsulate the more than two-thirds of all eighth- through twelfth-grade students who are reading below a proficient level. Reading achievement is clearly marked along economic, ethnic, and gender lines. The confluence of historical antecedents, social class, community membership, language, race, ethnicity, and gender; their interplay with institutional structures (e.g., schools and government); and the shaping of these institutional structures by educators and policymakers have contributed to a crisis in literacy education that is difficult to unravel. Although this crisis begins to take form in the earlier grades, it becomes more pronounced during adolescence and contributes to the fact that more than 7,000 U.S. students drop out of high school each school day (Alliance for Excellent Education, 2006).

The landscape of adolescent literacy development and proposed solutions to the adolescent literacy crisis in the United States are influenced by, at minimum, seven elements (see Table 2). The market economy, advances in technology, and globalization have a gripping influence on the politicized discourse about adolescent literacy. The roles of reading and writing for adolescents, particularly high school students, are viewed in direct relationship with the economy. According to a recent report by the National Center on Education and the Economy (2006):

> This is a world in which a very high level of preparation of reading, writing, speaking, mathematics, science, literature, history, and the arts will be an indispensable foundation for everything that comes after for most members of the workforce. It is a world in which comfort with ideas and abstractions is the passport to a good job, in which creativity and innovation are the key to a good life, in which levels of education — a very different kind of education than most of us have had — are going to be the only security there is. (p. 6)

Although an economic focus and attention to twenty-first-century literacy skills have become paramount in the national dialogue, we lack a clear definition of literacy instruction for adolescents in the United States that will translate into successful classroom practice. Without this clear definition, overwhelming and embarrassing inconsistency in literacy instruction occurs and can be expected to continue across schools. Literacy experiences and the ways that literacy instruction is conceptualized and practiced are characteristically different for adolescents attending schools in economically depressed environments and for adolescents who come from affluent homes and attend schools in affluent neighborhoods. The same differences exist in mixed-income school environments in which students' literacy experiences and academic schedules are governed by reading achievement data. Arguably, shortsighted or quick-fix solutions to the adolescent literacy crisis will continue to result in different literacy experiences and life-outcome trajectories for adolescents on opposite ends of the economic continuum.

Situating the African American Adolescent Male in the Crisis

The focus on economic projections oversimplifies the role of literacy education in the lives of African American males, who constitute 7 percent of the

TABLE 2 *Seven Critical Elements Shaping the Landscape of Literacy Instruction in the United States*

Accountability NCLB AYP NAEP	Accountability has a gripping influence on the national dialogue about adolescent literacy. Discussions and literacy reform efforts are framed by No Child Left Behind, Adequate Yearly Progress, and National Assessment of Educational Progress outcomes.
Standards Professional organizations States Content areas	Professional organizations such as the International Reading Association and the U.S. states have developed standards to shape literacy practices. These standards are often found in lesson plans and are made visible in classrooms during instruction, as mandated by school and/or district administrators.
Teacher Preparation and Teacher Professional Development	Teacher education programs are increasingly held accountable for poor adolescent literacy, while at the same time there has been a proliferation of teacher professional development focused on literacy instruction across the United States. Increasingly, there are more literacy coaches assigned to middle schools and high schools to support struggling readers.
Gap Focus Reading achievement gap Racial achievement gap Opportunity gap Preparation gap	Closing the reading achievement gap between White students and students of color has been discussed for the past forty years. Increasingly, schools are gauging their success by their ability to close the reading achievement gap. The gap is often discussed in terms of race, opportunity, or preparation.
Diversity Shifting demographics English-language learners (ELLs)	Schools are experiencing major shifts in their demographics: Urban areas become destabilized as students move to surrounding suburban school districts, and increased numbers of immigrants to the United States have led to a dramatic increase in the number of ELLs in America's classrooms.
Social Class Poverty Parenting	Reading data are aggregated to examine the performance of students from homes with low socioeconomic status. Research also looks at the effect of parents' levels of education on students' literacy.
Race Impact Dialogue	Although the dialogue is not robust in literacy reform efforts, there is a racialized component to the gap in reading achievement. There is a reading achievement gap between middle-income African Americans and middle-income Whites.

school-aged population. First, an economic focus fails to account for the day-to-day realities of African American males, particularly the young men living in high-poverty communities where long-term economic projections are overshadowed by immediate concerns like violence, classism, and poor schooling — conditions that cause many of them to feel dehumanized and devalued. Literacy education has to have a strong gravitational pull for African American male adolescents in their present-day contexts. Externally driven rationales for literacy instruction rooted in macrosociological concerns — such as taking on the challenges of life in a global economy, or stabilizing communities that are imploding because of concentrated poverty — fail to interrupt students' existing "maladaptive solutions" (Spencer, 1999).

Unfortunately, the African American male presence in reading research is dismal (Lindo, 2006). Up to this point, studies involving African American males have focused on factors that characterize these young men as *at-risk*. These studies have also ignored their racialized and gendered identities and have focused on comparing their academic outcomes to those of other students (Davis, 2001; Gilbert & Gilbert, 1998; Price, 2000). A meta-analysis is needed that examines how instructional practices, texts, and classroom contexts can be shaped to advance the literacy development of African American male adolescents, particularly the ones who experience difficulty with school-based reading (Tatum & Fisher, in press). The current absence of adequate research is contributing to policy, curricular, and pedagogical misalignments that are not effective for these young men. The lack of research on African American male adolescents contributes to three major issues:

1. Many educators are failing to increase African American male adolescents' engagement with texts, and subsequently, their overall reading achievement scores.
2. Specific texts and text characteristics that engage African American adolescent males are strikingly absent from the curriculum (Tatum, 2006).
3. Educators find it difficult to use texts to counter in-school and out-of-school context-related issues that heighten the vulnerability level of African American males.

The goals of literacy for African American male adolescents remain trapped in an achievement-score quagmire. At the same time, solutions to the adolescent literacy crisis are grounded in economic referents, such as the market economy and the need for future workers. These foci have unintended, negative consequences for schools' efforts to promote the literacy of African American male adolescents. First, they position adolescent literacy development as an in-school phenomenon related to standardized scores. Secondly, the crisis, as it is currently framed, affects the definition of adolescent literacy. A limited view of the crisis results in observable practical and theoretical vacillations among educators, policymakers, and educational publishers. The search for solutions to the adolescent literacy crisis remains scattered; teachers of adolescents lack clarity about what competencies outside their disciplines they need to develop; and the support provided by professional developers remains as varied as the professional developers themselves. The lives of many adolescents, particularly adolescent males of color, are treated as expendable, both within and outside of schools.

In subsequent sections of this article, I draw from a qualitative case study I conducted that supports my proposed model of a more anatomically complete model of literacy instruction. This study examined how choosing the right texts is central to advancing the literacy development of African American male adolescents. By illustrating the importance of engaging African American adolescent males with texts they find meaningful, the case study affirms the need for a more anatomically complete model of literacy instruction in schools.

African American Males and Texts

The impact of texts on the lives of African American adolescent males cannot be underestimated. Historically, texts have been central to the literacy development of African American males, with eminently clear connections among reading, writing, speaking, and actions (Tatum, 2005). Historical accounts of the lives of African American men are laden with references to enabling texts. An *enabling text*, as I define it, is one that moves beyond a solely cognitive focus — such as skill and strategy development — to include a social, cultural, political, spiritual, or economic focus. I was able to identify such texts by examining biographical and autobiographical documents written by Black male archetypes from the past century.

As part of my examination, I constructed textual lineages (Tatum, 2007) of Black male archetypes' literary experiences. *Textual lineages* are diagrams of texts that individuals found meaningful and significant, as evidenced by documents they have written. I constructed the lineages by placing the first pivotal text the archetypes identified at the top of the diagram. I then recorded other texts in the order they were discussed in the individuals' biographical and autobiographical narratives. For example, Eldridge Cleaver, who wrote the memoir *Soul on Ice* (1968), shared "how he devoured [the book, *Negroes with Guns* by Robert Williams] and let a few friends read it, before the [prison] library dug it and put it on the blacklist" (p. 71) (see Figure 2). He described other texts as "books that one wants to read — so bad that it [causes] a taste [in] the mouth" that only the books can satisfy (p. 70). Cleaver also complained that he could not get his hands on texts that were satisfactory to a man trying to function in the society and time in which he lived.

Subsequent to constructing the textual lineages of more than thirty Black male archetypes — among them Nat Turner, Frederick Douglass, Malcolm X, Huey Newton, and Tupac Shakur — I constructed my own textual lineage using texts that were significant to me in middle and high school (see Fig-

FIGURE 2   *Eldridge Cleaver's Textual Lineage, Constructed from Reading Cleaver's*
Soul on Ice *(1968) (The shaded boxes denote texts that recur in the textual lineages*
of African American males from the 1960s onward)

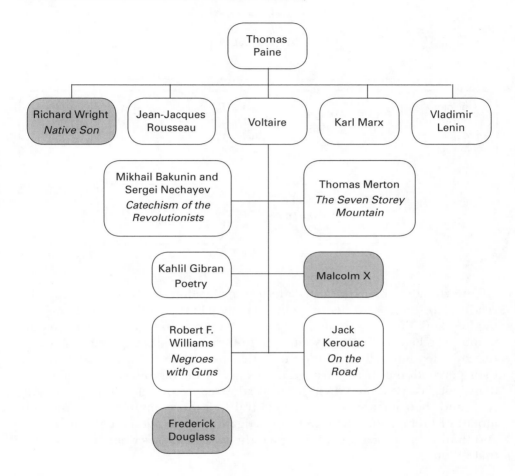

ure 3). I also collected 243 textual lineages from African American males in
middle and high schools in an attempt to identify the characteristics of texts
they found meaningful and significant, and to compare these characteristics
to those identified in the examination of the textual lineages of Black male
archetypes and myself (Tatum, in progress). Early analysis suggests that there
are four characteristics of texts that African American males find meaningful
and significant:

1. They contribute to a healthy psyche.
2. They focus on a collective struggle.
3. They provide a road map for being, doing, and acting.
4. They provide modern awareness of the real world. (Tatum, 2007)

FIGURE 3   *Tatum's Textual Lineage from Middle and High School*

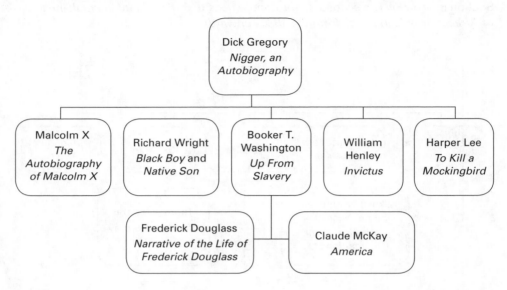

Unfortunately, many African American male adolescents who struggle with reading are unable to identify texts that they find significant. As evidenced by the blank lineage submitted by an eighth-grade boy in an urban middle school (see Figure 4), these young men often lack a growing textual lineage. Instead, they generally encounter texts that are *disabling* — texts that reinforce their perception of being struggling readers. While disabling texts ignore students' local contexts and their desire as adolescents for self-definition, *enabling* texts and their characteristics are central to a more anatomically complete model of literacy instruction. To investigate how an adolescent encounters and thinks about such texts, I designed the case study described in the section that follows.

A Qualitative Case Study

In an attempt to identify characteristics of texts and ways to effectively mediate texts with African American male adolescents, I designed a ten-month, in-depth qualitative case study (Merriam, 1998) to identify and describe the aspects of texts that Quincy, the pseudonym of a sixteen-year-old African American male, found most useful for improving his reading and shaping his identity. Quincy's mother approached me through a mutual friend and asked me to help save her son's life. The mother feared that Quincy, who was retained three times in a K–8 school because of his failure to meet the minimum reading score for promotion to high school, would be dead or incarcerated in three years if he did not become a better reader.

FIGURE 4   *Textual Lineage of an Eighth-Grade Boy Attending an Urban Middle School*

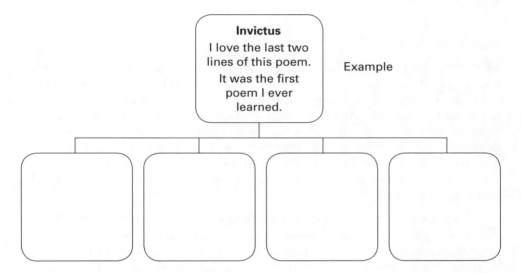

Directions: In each box below, place the title of a book, essay, or poem that you think you will always remember. Place only one title in a box. Explain why you think you will always remember the book, essay, or poem. Look at the example.

The study was framed by a phenomenological variant of ecological systems theory (Spencer, Dupree, & Hartmann, 1997) that takes into account structural and contextual barriers to identity formation and the implication of these barriers for psychosocial processes such as self-appraisal. This theoretical framework was useful because Quincy's view of himself and of how others viewed him seemed to be interrupting his literacy development, and structural and contextual barriers to his identity formation could not be ignored. At the time of the study, Quincy lived in one of Chicago's inner-city neighborhoods, which he described in the following way:

> I know the West Side of Chicago is ghetto . . . On my little three block[s], Mona, Mavis, and Monte, where I stay at, there may be a lot of kids, but all blocks got drugs on them. . . . It's like a drug house or something. In that three-block area you see cars, everything, police cars comin' through twenty-four seven.

Along with having to withstand the negative community contexts, Quincy was also struggling to overcome some the psychological overload thrust upon him by his family, as evidenced by his sharing the comment, "They all think I

167

am dumb." His family members' views became more pronounced after Quincy dropped out of school during the middle of his freshman year.

Additionally, Quincy suffered from an underexposure to reading materials in school and at home. He had never read anything that affected him and he had never read a complete book. Essentially, he was striving for identity without the benefit of having read texts that could potentially inform his identity development. During our first interview, he shared, "To say the truth, I ain't read a book." He then informed me that his teachers did not assign books at school.

Data Collection

The study was designed to gather Quincy's views on how texts (i.e., poems, essays, speeches, books, and news clippings) affected the way he viewed himself as he negotiated his home and community contexts. I attempted to identify texts that would provide Quincy with capital to become resilient amid some of his negative environmental conditions. Consistent with the anatomically complete model in which an understanding of a student's context drives instructional decisions, I planned to use these texts to provide explicit reading skill and strategy instruction. Quincy consented to participate in the study by agreeing to do the following:

1. Read books, articles, newspaper clippings, and speeches I recommended. He was given the final decision about the material he chose to read.
2. Participate in twenty 90-minute audio-taped discussions about the reading materials that took place every other Saturday morning at a bookstore or library near his home.
3. Write reflections in a journal during the last ten minutes of each discussion.
4. Participate in four 30-minute interviews to reflect on the discussions. The interviews were scheduled at ten-week intervals.

Data Analysis

I analyzed discussion and interview transcripts line by line in order to name and identify characteristics of texts or in-school and out-of-school variables that affected Quincy's engagement with texts. I generated codes or used *in vivo* codes (Strauss & Corbin, 1998) after each discussion. I attached researcher's memos to the codes to add attributes or question their potential multiple meanings, to develop a more specific focus, and to prepare questions to ask the case-study participant in subsequent discussions (Glesne & Peshkin, 1992). I then grouped the codes based on their ability to describe the case-study participant's perspectives about texts and text types he found most useful for addressing his literacy needs, as well as variables that interrupted his engagement with texts. Using an approach similar to that of Ivey (1999), I tri-

TABLE 3   *Texts Quincy Read During the Case Study*

Books
>   *"Yo, Little Brother . . ."* (Davis & Jackson, 1998)
>   *Handbook for Boys: A Novel* (Myers, 2002)
>   *Monster* (Myers, 1999)
>   *Willie Lynch: Why African Americans Have So Many Issues* (Sims, 2002)

Poems
>   "Does the World Care if I Exist" (Tatum, 2005)
>   "Life through My Eyes" (Shakur, 1999)

Speeches
>   Bill Cosby's (2004) Address to the NAACP on the Fiftieth Anniversary of *Brown v. Board of Education*
>   Martin Luther King Jr.'s (1963) "I Have a Dream"

Excerpts
>   "Letter to My Nephew" from James Baldwin (1963), *The Fire Next Time*
>   "Black Power" from Martin Luther King Jr. (1967), *Where Do We Go from Here: Chaos or Community?*

angulated data across sessions by rereading the transcripts from our previous discussions, along with the participant's written reflections, before reading new transcripts and reflections. I also shared my thinking with Quincy during each session to resolve any misunderstandings I might have held about the data. For example, I would ask him if I was representing his thoughts clearly.

Results

During the study, Quincy read or attempted to read four books, two speeches, two poems, and excerpts from two books (see Table 3). His text-related discussions provide valuable insights for shaping educational contexts and selecting and mediating text with an African American male adolescent who struggles with reading. Three major themes emerged in the study: perceived supports, meaningful engagement with texts, and self-organizing processes.

Perceived Supports

During the first interview I conducted with Quincy, we discussed teachers' perceptions of African American males. I wanted to know how he believed others viewed him. Excerpts from our conversation are included below:

> *Tatum:* When you come in contact with people who are not African American, how do you think they perceive you?
>
> *Quincy:* . . . I was in school with all Whites; they treated me the same way they treated all the other people. So basically, I don't see nothing wrong. I think they do a good job.

Tatum: So you would agree that they do not have a negative perception of you?

Quincy: No, only thing that is wrong, they just didn't know how to handle the African American kids.

Tatum: Are you talking about the teachers?

Quincy: Yeah . . . They are, like, scared or something. I don't know what it is, but I think African American teachers know what to do. They look at our work and they see our grades and tell us what we need to do, unlike other teachers. They give us afterschool help, give us help on this and this and this, give us some private time, and help you out. The other teachers, they do a good job too, but they're not like African American teachers. My point: African American teachers — when we act up, they know how we are, they know what it is, and the other teachers, they be quick to send you out for a quick descent to the principal and get suspended for something.

Tatum: Do you have specific examples?

Quincy: I don't know what it was, but I kept asking the teacher for help, and she's like, you're doing good in this class; you don't need help. And I told her all I need help is with one problem, and you can go finish whatever you were doing. And she thought I was really being smart, and she sent me out. And the rest of the class tried to get me out of trouble, but she made a big deal and I got suspended for it.

Tatum: You said something interesting to me. You said that some teachers don't know how to handle African American kids; some of them might be scared. Talk about that a little more.

Quincy: 'Cause they just think we're worthless. They think we are just going to give up. We won't do what we need to do right. They try to help us, but they won't constantly help us to get us on track. Like the rest of the class, we fall behind, but they don't take the time when they can get the class started on work. They just go on grades and try to get their stuff together, but they just need to come over and give us a little sermon. But they just don't do that.

Quincy perceived that the support of classroom teachers was lacking, and assessed this lack of support as a form of rejection stemming from teachers' perceptions of African American students as worthless. A month into the study, he continued to describe the lack of support, this time in the midst of a reading event, as we discussed the text, "*Yo, Little Brother . . .*" (Davis & Jackson, 1998), a book he found favorable. He made the following comments about the book:

I don't know what made me read it, but I was, like, totally involved in what he's saying, what the guy was saying. To tell you the truth, I read this book in one day. I ain't started it until that Monday, and I sat down 'cause I wasn't going to read it at first, but I sat down, and said, let me read this book. So as I flip over the pages and I start out reading, I'm like, I like this book for a reason, so I'm going to try to read, and then I seen this say "Street Smarts" right at the top. I know I know a lot about the street, so I just read to see what they was talking about. Then some of the things they was saying was true . . . As I was going along I wanted to stop, but I couldn't. I was like, I started it, and I ain't going to sleep 'til about six in the morning. That's how into it I was, and I didn't know I could get into a book like that. To tell you the truth, I forgot I was reading . . . This is a good book, it help you out a lot.

I wanted Quincy to compare this text to the types of materials he read in school, and to determine if he would prefer to read more of such texts in school. Excerpts from the interview are shown below:

Tatum: Do you read these types of materials in school?

Quincy: No, I do not.

Tatum: Do you think you should be reading these types of materials in school?

Quincy: . . . I think it would be a waste of time.

Tatum: To read something like this?

Quincy: Yes, even though it would help a lot of people.

Tatum: It helps a lot of people, but it would be a waste of time. Help me through this confusion.

Quincy: It is something that we should be reading in school, but the teachers would read it and use it like a story. They ain't going to explain what it means. They going to give us things to write about it and all, but they ain't going to really explain it like the book is. The kids that don't understand what they see in here, they ain't going to really know what they are talking about. If they are going to start a book like this, they gotta let them know what [it] means. Especially what [it] means.

Quincy's comments suggest that the text he found meaningful outside of school would be less valuable if it became part of the school curriculum, because he believed teachers would fail to discuss its significance. This is one of the shortcomings that result from not using a more anatomically complete model of literacy instruction that brings attention to instructional and theoretical strands, which can inform how we discuss texts with adolescents. Quincy's remarks suggest that in his school, such texts would be mediated in ways that pay attention to the vital signs of *reading* (e.g., school-based writing assignments, assessment questions) but ignore the vital signs of *readers* and *reading instruction* — namely, shaping classroom contexts to pay attention to students' lived experiences and providing opportunities for meaningful engagement with texts.

Meaningful Engagement with Texts

Commenting again on *"Yo, Little Brother . . ."* (Davis & Jackson, 1998), the book Quincy read prior to our second meeting, he explained why certain pages of the text resonated with him. After reading in the book about Driving While Black (DWB), he used the text to make sense of a DWB experience he had had while en route to a luncheon:

171

Tatum: Why do you think those pages of the text stood out to you?

Quincy: Because my friend's dad drove me and two other guys, and we all were Black in the car, and we really weren't doing nothing. We were going the speed limit and all, and as he was driving, the police pulled him over and all of us. He made us get out of the car, thinking we had drugs and stuff on us, even though we all had suits on. He searched us, then he searched the car, and the guy asked the officer why it was he was stopped. And then I heard this with my own ears, he was like "DWB," but I don't know what that means.

Tatum: Who said DWB?

Quincy: The officer.

Tatum: Was he White or Black?

Quincy: I think he was White. I don't really remember. When he said that, I really didn't know what he means until I read this. When I thought about it, DWB, I don't know how it popped back to [the day of] my luncheon, but then I realized what DWB was.

Quincy's year-old personal experience with police misconduct resurfaced after reading the text, which ultimately helped him make sense of an incident that had embarrassed him. Describing how he felt about being stopped and searched by the police, he said, "I was a little embarrassed, to tell the truth. I was on my way to a luncheon and I didn't want to get messed up or nothing. I wanted to stay clean all the way there." This dehumanizing and devaluing of the African American male adolescent is often overlooked by literacy models that are solely grounded in cognitive reading processes. By failing to consider these societal ills, such models may inadvertently undermine African American males' meaningful engagement with texts.

The types of texts students are asked to read, the structure of the texts, and students' limited reading skills also interrupt meaningful engagement with texts. This was evident in Quincy's failure to complete the text, *Willie Lynch: Why African Americans Have So Many Issues* (Sims, 2002), which he selected to read between our second and third sessions. He was unable to get past the first two pages. I discovered that he had been trying to read the preface of the book, which I had not anticipated:

Tatum: I gave you five different titles to choose from the last time. Why did you select this text?

Quincy: Because I wanted to see what he was talking about.

Tatum: What stood out to you as you read the text?

Quincy: I really didn't get into it. I started reading the first two pages. I just wanted to understand.

Tatum: Talk about that a little more.

Quincy: I started reading, and as I was reading, I just couldn't get into this book.

Tatum: Can you explain why it did not hold your attention?

Quincy: Man, I just didn't get into it. I tried reading it a couple more times. Maybe it was just, maybe it was just the [preface].

Tatum: Did you move beyond the preface? Do you know the purpose of the preface?

Quincy: No.

Quincy could not get into the book "'cause every time [he] took a break [he] gotta read over what [he] read." To continue the session, I read part of the text with Quincy and provided him with strategies for decoding the text and monitoring his comprehension, areas I had assessed to be his weaknesses. He became engaged with the text during the session:

Tatum: I want you to read page forty-six.

Quincy: "Year after year we allow our boys to attend inferior public schools and then we wonder why they don't like school. African American boys don't like school because school educators, administrators and the American educational system do not like African American boys."

Tatum: Do you think this is true?

Quincy: No.

Tatum: Why aren't you going to one of the highest-achieving schools?

Quincy: Because . . . (long pause)

Tatum: Do you feel that you are receiving an inferior education as opposed to a superior education?

Quincy: Not really.

Tatum: Talk about that.

Quincy: They are teaching us some things, but they ain't teaching us the best they could.

This session suggests a very important caveat to consider when mediating texts with struggling adolescent readers. The content of the text alone may not be sufficient to move them toward engagement. Instructional supports that include explicit strategy instruction and ways of finding an entry point or entry passage to the text may be necessary to get adolescents engaged. In this conversation, I asked Quincy questions about his own educational experiences in order to make the argument in the text more concrete. Quincy became more engaged when these supports were provided. For instance, in this conversation, he challenged and then expanded upon the author's assertions. I look back at this session and this text as the tipping point when Quincy starting viewing texts as a tool to think about his own life. He stated at the end of this session and the subsequent sessions, "I got to get it right. I got to get my life right."

Self-Organizing Processes

Quincy's engagement with texts had increased by the sixteenth week of the case study. By this time, he had reenrolled in an alternative high school after sitting out for several months. In our meetings, he began to ask more questions about the texts and engage in more reflection, whereas at the beginning of the study, he would simply identify parts of the texts that stood out to him and read those parts during our time together. I often initiated those discussions by asking Quincy questions to help him gather his thoughts about the readings. During our seventh session, however, Quincy initiated the discussion with a question based on his reading of the poem, "Does the World Care if I Exist" (Tatum, 2005), which is excerpted here:

> Does the world care if I exist?
> Or, am I just America's problem?
> Don't they know I am dying like no other?
> No, they just fear me, they can't hear me
> Hell, you can't even teach me how to read — Mr. and Mrs. Teacher
> Then you flunk me, and blame it on me
> Some of it's my fault
> Probably some of my momma's fault as well
> But you're at fault, too
> I don't want your pity or your crying
> Teach me how to man-up, and be a man
> Help me to stop dying
> If you don't this nation will continue to spill over with the black man's blood
> You'll have to build more jails.
> It is now your time to act
> If you don't act
> I now believe that, *America does not care if I exist,* is a fact.
> No more peace until we all get a piece (American pie)
> Damn, my time expired. I'm gone . . . (p. 7)

As we entered the library to have our discussion about the poem, he asked, "I wanna know what made you, like, write. What made you describe that type of boy?" Excerpts from the interview follow:

Tatum: I wanted to write to help people understand that a lot of African American males do not believe the world cares if they exist. Also, this poem reflects my own childhood and the experiences of a lot of other young men that grew up on the South Side of Chicago. This is how I saw a lot of the young brothers I grew up with . . . What was it about the poem that led you to that question? Is there something that stood out to you?

Quincy: I don't know, 'cause it's like, in the beginning, I read the title and it was like, did the world care if I exist? What I see now is, like, when African Americans go to jail, they don't care if they exist, basically. If they really cared, they would do more positive things to help them not go to jail. And like in the middle or the end, wherever it was, when he was like, "you would have to build more jails because of the" — like, I don't know what he means by the "Black male's blood," or what that means.

Tatum: It's saying that this nation will continue to spill over with the Black male's blood. That means you will find more African American men murdering African American men. The blood of African American men will fill America's streets if we don't do something different to address their multiple needs.

Quincy: OK. There was another part I liked. They talking about the teachers in the school. He was saying, like, part of it was his fault, his parents' fault, and the teachers' fault. That is how he worked his way out of it, 'cause he has got to do the work his self, he can't just depend on nobody else. It is [the] majority of the teachers' fault, because, like, they teach us what they supposed to teach; they don't teach anything that is going to help the students.

Tatum: Help me understand what you mean.

Quincy: OK, what I mean by that is, like a list of assignments — it is just like you get assigned a list of assignments that you want the class to learn, but it ain't like what the class *needs* to learn.

Tatum: What are some things that students need to learn?

Quincy: Since I have been going to school lately, it is like the teachers don't even care. It's like they just teach the things just thrown on grade level just to get out of class. Go to the next shelf, make sure you get the grades. Like teaching stuff you already know. Why don't they just go to something new? Sometimes it is just good to work hard; you know what I am saying? If you give us some easy work when we know we are going to finish that in less than a minute, give us something that we have got to sit down and think about.

Tatum: Is that happening in your new school?

Quincy: Don't laugh; this might be funny, but don't laugh. My teacher teaching us literature, right, but he doing measurements and stuff. Ain't literature something like reading? We didn't even have no books. The only thing we got books for is the science.

This poem led Quincy to examine his existence in the alternative high school setting, and further, it led to a meaningful exchange of ideas between us, initiated by Quincy's questions. He questioned curriculum orientations and analyzed the plight of African American males and their shared culpability in their social demise. Quincy did not understand why teachers refused to challenge him and his African American classmates. Sadly, the time that was allocated for literature instruction was co-opted by math because of the absence of other texts. He asked me not to laugh, but I think his warning would have been more targeted if he had told me not to explode with anger or cry.

Quincy continued to ask questions about the texts during our discussions. In our last session together, he read the following excerpt from Martin Luther King Jr.'s discussion of Black power (Hord & Lee, 1995):

But we are also Americans. Abused and scorned though we may be, our destiny is tied up with the destiny of America. The Negro must face the fact that America is now his home, a home that he helped to build through blood, sweat, and tears. Since we are Americans the solution to our problem will not come through seeking to build a separate black nation within a nation, but by finding that creative minority of the concerned from the ofttimes apathetic majority, and together moving toward that colorless power that we all need for security and justice. (p. 295)

The last text-based question Quincy asked me was, "What did he mean by 'creative minority'?" After sharing my thoughts on the phrase "creative minority," I asked him why he had asked the question. Quincy said, "I just wanted to understand it." He began to seek understanding from texts as he thought about his own life. He found that the texts and our discussions of them led him to some self-correcting processes, such as reenrolling in school after dropping out and forming a better relationship with his mother (Tatum, in press).

Early in the study, Quincy shared his belief that he was poorly served by his literacy experiences in school because teachers failed to "read" him. When I asked him how teachers could read him without living his experiences, he offered:

It like the same thing Tupac (Shakur, 1999) is saying in "life in his eyes." I mean, you gotta see what you see in your eyes, what you see every day. It's like a good book or something. You reading it at home and you think somebody else might like it. You ask them to read the title. If you tell a student that you really liked a book and it was good, they gonna notice it and give it a chance, the first couple of pages, or chapter or something. They don't like it; they will let you know . . . You can hear conversations sometimes. What they are going through . . . I ain't doubting teachers don't care; they care. If they didn't care, they wouldn't be there, but it just that they are doing what they want to do. They doing what they think they need to teach; they ain't doing what the students need. They ain't reading us.

In his final comments, Quincy referred to Tupac's (Shakur, 1999) poem, "Life through My Eyes," a text we read and discussed during the study. In it, Tupac states,

Fun and games R few but treasured like gold 2 me,
cuz I realize that I must return 2 my spot in poverty.
But mock my words when I say my heart will not exist
unless my destiny comes through and puts an end 2 all of this. (p. 11)

Quincy dropped out of the study after his mother kicked him out of the house and told him to move in with his father, who had recently been released from prison. The potential to use literacy instruction and texts to empower this African American male adolescent was not realized. Sadly, his recent reentry into high school had done nothing to jumpstart that potential, and, in fact, seemed to squander it.

During the study, Quincy was slowly becoming more convinced about the power of texts, particularly the enabling texts he selected from the choices I provided. When he reenrolled in the alternative high school, he expected to be able to read these kinds of texts in school, but he discovered that the same old material he had been provided before he had dropped out was still the standard fare. Quincy believed me as I discussed how texts could help him shape a positive life trajectory. He also discovered something about himself as he read the material — texts that I hope will become a part of his textual lineage.

The stakes are much higher for Quincy now. He has a son and another child on the way — two kids who will be raised by a father who has yet to receive a high school diploma.

Concluding Thoughts

In this article, I discussed the need for a more anatomically complete model of literacy for African American male adolescents, particularly the ones living under the weight of a widening gulf of social, economic, and educational disparity. I assert that literacy instruction can serve as a mechanism to shape a more egalitarian, just society by paying attention to the varied needs of adolescents now living in high-poverty communities. It is naive to believe, or mendacious to suggest, that the broader societal aims that should be associated with literacy instruction can be reached by focusing on research-based skills and strategies alone. There are multiple tangible and intangible influences on adolescent literacy development. In-school factors and out-of-school factors function in concert with students' external and internal resources, and they all combine to impact their literacy development.

Educators and policymakers must assiduously question how policy, pedagogical practices, and research will benefit and advance the literacy development of both the poorest and the most privileged adolescents in this nation. The economically privileged and economically disadvantaged adolescents of today will be bound together to solve the nation's political, social, and educational problems. Literacy development has to be conceptualized in such a way that it addresses the needs of *all* adolescents, including African American male adolescents. It also has to be conceptualized to preserve American democracy and the American economy, which are now threatened by the large number of high school dropouts who will not be able to find sustainable employment or participate in the political process.

There is a need to include the voices of African American adolescent males in literacy research. While qualitative research provides powerful data, large-scale research studies are needed to specifically examine the literacy development of African American adolescent males. This can be accomplished by conducting carefully controlled studies in schools where we find African American adolescent males who struggle with reading. The results of these studies can then be combined with the best practices found in descriptive and qualitative studies. This approach will potentially guard against essentializing African American male adolescents' literacy experiences in the United States.

Additionally, more attention needs to be given to text types, characteristics of texts, and the role of texts in advancing the literacy development of African American males. There is ample historical precedent for the role of texts in shaping the lives of African American males in the United States. Educators often overlook this precedent when making curricular decisions purportedly designed to improve the reading outcomes of African American males.

It may be helpful to adopt a life course perspective (Mizell, 1999) that aligns neatly with cultural-ecological theories addressing out-of-school and in-school contexts, students' identities, and the structural barriers that exist in a highly stratified class-based and race-based society. But taking on such a perspective requires a broader conceptualization of literacy instruction for African American male adolescents, who can be both resilient and vulnerable at the same time. I suggest that educators and school reformers adopt a more anatomically complete model of literacy instruction that integrates theoretical, instructional, and professional development strands — head, body, and legs, respectively — as a comprehensive approach to advancing the literacy development of African American male adolescents. Moving toward a more anatomically complete model of literacy development can expand the lens of the adolescent literacy field, inform and shape the direction of educational research, and advance the literacy development of African American male adolescents in ways that will benefit them in school and society.

References

Alliance for Excellent Education. (2006). *Who's counted? Who's counting? Understanding high school graduation rates.* Washington, DC: Author.

Alvermann, D. E., Hinchman, K. A., Moore, D. W., Phelps, S. F., & Waff, D. R. (Eds.) (2006). *Reconceptualizing the literacies in adolescents' lives* (2nd ed.). Mahwah, NJ: Erlbaum.

Baldwin, J. (1963). *The fire next time.* New York: Dial Press.

Biancarosa, C., & Snow, C. E. (2006). *Reading next — A vision for action and research in middle and high school literacy: A report to Carnegie Corporation of New York* (2nd ed.). Washington, DC: Alliance for Excellent Education.

Brozo, W. (2002). *To be a boy, to be a reader: Engaging teen and preteen boys in active literacy.* Newark, DE: International Reading Association.

Ceballo, R., McLoyd, V., & Toyokawa, T. (2004). The influence of neighborhood quality on adolescents' educational values and school effort. *Journal of Adolescent Research, 19*(6), 716–739.

Cleaver, E. (1968). *Soul on ice.* New York: Dell.

Collins, J., & Blot, R. K. (2003). *Literacy and literacies: Texts, power, and identity.* Cambridge, England: Cambridge University Press.

Cosby, W. (2004, 17 May). Address at the NAACP's commemoration of the fiftieth anniversary of *Brown v. Board of Education.* Retrieved December 7, 2007, from http://www.americanrhetoric.com/speeches/billcosbypoundcakespeech.htm

Davis, A., & Jackson, J. (1998). *"Yo, little brother . . .": Basic rules of survival for young African American males.* Chicago: African American Images.

Davis, J. (2001). Transgressing the masculine: African American boys and the failure of schools. In W. Martino & B. Meyenn (Eds.), *What about the boys?* (pp. 140–153). Philadelphia, PA: Open University Press.

Fashola, O. S. (Ed.). (2005). *Educating African American males: Voices from the field.* Thousand Oaks, CA: Corwin Press.

Gilbert, R., & Gilbert, P. (1998). *Masculinity goes to school.* New York: Routledge.

Glesne, C., & Peshkin, A. (1992). *Becoming qualitative researchers: An introduction.* White Plains, NY: Longman.

Goodenow, C. (1993). The psychological sense of school membership among adolescents: Scale development and educational correlates. *Psychology in the Schools, 30,* 79–91.

Greene, S., & Abt-Perkins, D. (2003). *Making race visible: Literacy research for cultural understanding.* New York: Teachers College Press.

Heller, R., & Greenleaf, C. (2007). *Literacy instruction in the content areas: Getting to the core of middle and high school improvement.* Washington, DC: Alliance for Excellent Education.

Henderson, N., & Milstein, M. (2003). *Resiliency in schools: Making it happen for students and educators.* Thousand Oaks, CA: Corwin Press.

Hord, F. L., & Lee, J. S. (Eds.). (1995). *I am because we are: Readings in Black philosophy.* Amherst: University of Massachusetts Press.

Ivey, G. (1999). A multicase study in the middle school: Complexities among young adolescent readers. *Reading Research Quarterly, 34*(2), 172–192.

Jetton, T., & Dole, J. (Eds.). (2004). *Adolescent literacy research and practice.* New York: Guilford.

King, M. L., Jr. (1963, Aug. 28). I have a dream. Retrieved December 7, 2007, from http://www.americanrhetoric.com/speeches/mlkihaveadream.htm

King, M. L., Jr. (1967). *Where do we go from here: Chaos or community?* Boston, MA: Beacon.

Lesko, N. (2000). *Masculinities at school.* Thousand Oaks, CA: Sage.

Lindo, E. (2006). The African American presence in reading intervention experiments. *Remedial and Special Education, 27*(3), 148–153.

Merriam, S. (1998). *Qualitative research and case study applications in education.* San Francisco, CA: Jossey-Bass.

Mizell, C. A. (1999). Life course influences of African American men's depression: Adolescent parental composition, self-concept, and adult earnings. *Journal of African American Studies, 29*(4), 467–490.

Myers, W. D. (1999). *Monster.* New York: HarperCollins.

Myers, W. D. (2002). *Handbook for boys: A novel.* New York: Amistad.

National Center on Education and the Economy. (2006). *Tough choices or tough times: The report of the New Commission on the Skills of the American Workforce.* San Francisco: Jossey-Bass.

Polite, V., & Davis, J. (Eds.). (1999). *African American males in school and society: Practices and policies for effective education.* New York: Teachers College Press.

Price, J. (2000). Peer (dis)connections, school, and African American masculinities. In N. Lesko (Ed.), *Masculinities at school* (pp. 127–159). Thousand Oaks, CA: Sage.

Roderick, M. (1994). Grade retention and school dropout: Investigating the association. *American Educational Research Journal, 31*(4), 729–759.

Rush, L., Eakle, J., & Berger, A. (Eds.). (2007). *Secondary school literacy: What research reveals for classroom practice.* Urbana, IL: National Council of Teachers of English.

Shakur, T. (1999). *The rose that grew from the concrete.* New York: Pocket Books.

Sims, M. (2002). *Willie Lynch: Why African Americans have so many issues.* Chicago: Author.

Smith, M., & Wilhelm, J. (2002). *"Reading don't fix no Chevys": Literacy in the lives of young men.* Portsmouth, NH: Heinemann.

Spencer, M. B. (1999). Social and cultural influences on school adjustment: The application of an identity-focused cultural ecological perspective. *Educational Psychologist, 34*(1), 43–57.

Spencer, M. B., Dupree, D., & Hartmann, T. (1997). A phenomenological variant of ecological systems theory (PVEST): A self-organization perspective in context. *Development and Psychopathology, 9*(4), 817–833.

Strauss, A., & Corbin, J. (1998). *Basics of qualitative research: Grounded theory procedures and techniques* (2nd ed.). Newbury Park, CA: Sage.

Street, B. (1995). *Social literacies: Critical approaches to literacy in development, ethnography and education.* London: Longman.

Swanson, D., Cunningham, M., & Spencer, M. B. (2003). Black males' structural conditions, achievement patterns, normative needs, and "opportunities." *Urban Education, 38*(5), 608–633.

Tatum, A. W. (2000). Breaking down barriers that disenfranchise African American adolescents in low-level reading tracks. *Journal of Adolescent & Adult Literacy, 44*, 52–64.

Tatum, A. W. (2002). Professional development for teachers of African American adolescents. *Illinois Reading Council Journal, 30*(1), 42–52.

Tatum, A. W. (2003). *Advancing the literacies of African American adolescents: A case study of professional development.* Unpublished doctoral dissertation, University of Illinois at Chicago.

Tatum, A. W. (2005). *Teaching reading to African American adolescent males: Closing the achievement gap.* Portland, ME: Stenhouse.

Tatum, A. W. (2006). Engaging African American males in reading. *Educational Leadership, 63*(5), 44–49.

Tatum, A. W. (2007). Building the textual lineages of African American male adolescents. In K. Beers, R. Probst, and L. Rief (Eds.), *Adolescent literacy: Turning promise into practice* (pp. 81–85). Portsmouth, NH: Heinemann.

Tatum, A. W. (in press). African American males at risk: A researcher's study of endangered males and literature that works. In S. Lehr (Ed.), *Shattering the looking glass: Issues, controversy, and trends in children's literature.* Norwood, MA: Christopher Gordon.

Tatum, A. W. (in progress). *Rebuilding the textual lineages of African American male adolescents.* Portsmouth, NH: Heinemann.

Tatum, A. W., & Fisher, T. A. (in press). Nurturing resilience among adolescent readers. In S. Lenski and J. Lewis (Eds.), *Addressing the needs of struggling middle level and high school readers.* New York: Guilford.

Werner, E. E., & Smith, R. S. (1992). *Overcoming the odds: High-risk children from birth to adulthood.* New York: Cornell University Press.

Young, J. P. (2000). Boy talk: Critical literacy and masculinities. *Reading Research Quarterly, 35*(3), 312–337.

Implementing a Structured Reading Program in an Afterschool Setting: Problems and Potential Solutions

ARDICE HARTRY
ROBERT FITZGERALD
KRISTIE PORTER
MPR Associates, Inc.

In this article, Ardice Hartry, Robert Fitzgerald, and Kristie Porter present results from their implementation study of a structured reading program for fourth, fifth, and sixth graders in an afterschool setting. As the authors explain, schools and districts often view an extended school day as a promising way to address the literacy needs of their lowest-performing students by devoting more time to reading instruction. While structured reading programs may help teachers use afterschool instructional time more effectively, the degree to which these programs improve student outcomes depends on the effectiveness of their implementation. Focusing on program implementation in one district as part of a randomized controlled trial, the authors find that successfully implementing a structured reading program in an afterschool setting depends on thoughtful preparation, suitable resources, and ongoing attention.

According to the most recent results from the National Assessment of Educational Progress, the "Nation's Report Card," only one in three U.S. eighth graders is reading at the proficient level or above, and both White students and students of color in eighth and twelfth grades scored lower in reading in 2005 than in 1992 (Grigg, Donahue, & Dion, 2007; Perie, Grigg, & Donahue, 2005). In addition, the gap between the reading levels of White and Asian students on one hand, and African American and Hispanic students on the other, has not narrowed since 1992. The persistence of these trends has led to a national push to boost literacy levels, particularly among adolescent students and students of color. The concern about literacy development, however, extends from elementary school to college. Less than half of ACT-tested high school graduates in 2005 demonstrated readiness for college-level read-

Harvard Educational Review Vol. 78 No. 1 Spring 2008

ing, and there has been ongoing concern about the so-called "4th grade slump in reading abilities" that is evidenced by students who emerge from primary reading instruction with a mastery of basic reading processes but an inability to read for ideas, information, and concepts (National Council of Teachers of English, 2007, p. 1). Add to the preceding facts that more than three thousand students drop out of high school every day — often because they do not have the literacy skills to keep up (Kamil, 2003) — and it becomes painfully obvious why many believe that adolescent literacy is in critical need of attention.

Many school districts are turning to afterschool programs as a way to provide additional instructional time to struggling readers. The question hundreds of districts are asking themselves is not *whether* to provide students with extra help in reading, but *what type* of reading program they should provide. Unfortunately, districts find few good answers to this question. In this article, we describe how one school district implemented a structured reading program in an afterschool setting. We hope this discussion will help districts — particularly those facing poor achievement results — as they consider whether afterschool reading programs might be feasible to implement and beneficial to their students.

In 2005, MPR Associates, an independent research firm, received funding from the William T. Grant Foundation to evaluate the effectiveness of a reading program provided in an afterschool setting. One year later, we received a grant funded by the U.S. Department of Education's Office of Elementary and Secondary Education (OESE), under subcontract with Southwest Educational Development Laboratory (SEDL), to conduct a replication study of the same program. Both studies were conducted in partnership with a public school district in the Boston metropolitan area. The primary objective of these impact studies was to compare a highly structured academic intervention called READ 180 with standard and generally less-structured afterschool program activities to determine the program's effectiveness. Developed and owned by Scholastic, Inc., READ 180 targets students in grades four through twelve and, as of April 2007, was being used in over twelve thousand classrooms across the country (Scholastic, 2007). Though the READ 180 curriculum is commonly used during the school day, Scholastic has found that many schools and school districts are contemplating its use as a supplemental, afterschool program. One reason may be that READ 180 attempts to incorporate some of the best practices for afterschool programs, as will be discussed in more detail below.

In this article, we present one set of findings from a randomized controlled trial intended to investigate the use and effectiveness of READ 180 in afterschool settings. The part of the study that is not reported here measured the difference in reading achievement between students who participated in READ 180 in an afterschool program and students who participated in the district's regular afterschool program. The other part of the study, which is discussed in detail on the following pages, was an implementation-fidelity study designed to assess the extent to which the READ 180 program was implemented as originally intended and to discover the factors that impeded or promoted its smooth and successful implementation. Overall, our objective was to determine whether READ 180 could be implemented successfully in an afterschool setting. To address this overarching question, we explored the following specific research questions:

- What types of preparation and planning were required to deliver the reading program as designed? What obstacles were encountered prior to launch of the program, and how did district or Scholastic personnel respond to these obstacles?
- What resources and personnel were required in order to deliver the reading program as designed? Were there resources that seemed central to faithful program implementation?
- What were the key challenges the district and/or schools faced during the course of the year in implementing the reading program? How were those challenges resolved?
- How much additional time-on-task in reading are students likely to spend during a year of participation in a READ 180 afterschool program?

Our goal in this article is to assist school districts in understanding the factors that impede or promote effective implementation of a structured academic program offered in an afterschool setting. Our findings suggest that structured reading programs can be implemented effectively in afterschool settings, but that they require strong preparation, the right resources, and ongoing attention to the program.

Previous Research

Our interest in researching READ 180 in an afterschool setting was prompted by several major questions related to certain key aspects of the program. First, the research was motivated by the growing concern for and attention being paid to adolescents' literacy development. In fact, adolescent literacy has been undergoing a renewal of research interest, "due in large part to continued failures to close the achievement gap between privileged and not-so-privileged high school students" (Snow & Biancarosa, 2003, p. 2). The Carnegie Corporation of New York, along with a number of other foundations, formed the Adolescent Literacy Funders Forum (ALFF) to focus efforts on solving this problem. According to an article in *Carnegie Results*, "All the reading experts agree. America is having an awful time teaching its middle school and high school students how to read with comprehension" (Grosso de Leon, 2005, p. 1). The article also points to a decline in science and math achievement that closely parallels a similar decline in reading achievement, and it suggests that the two trends may be related, given that reading is a fundamental prerequisite for all academic achievement.

An important first step toward renewing the attention paid to adolescent literacy has been identifying critical elements in effective programs (Biancarosa & Snow, 2004), as well as other syntheses of expert opinion on effective approaches (cf., Alvermann, 2002; Carnahan & Cobb, 2004). In *Reading Next* (2004), Biancarosa and Snow distill the report of a panel of expert researchers in the field, in which were delineated fifteen "promising elements of effective adolescent literacy programs" (p. 12). The panel posited that while these elements have a substantial base in research and professional opinion, not enough research has been done that clearly demonstrates what works with adolescents. They suggested a set of planned variation studies that would test different combinations of elements. The elements are organized into two categories — instructional improvements and infrastructure improvements — and several in each category are relevant to this research: 1) direct, explicit comprehension instruction; 2) motivation and self-directed learning; 3) strategic tutoring; 4) diverse texts; 5) a technology component; 6) ongoing formative and summative assessment; and 7) extended time for literacy (p. 12).

The summary of research on the key elements cited above echoes to a large degree a policy statement commissioned by the International Reading Association (Moore, Bean, Birdyshaw, & Rycik, 1999). The authors of this statement suggest that, among other things, adolescents require a wide variety of reading material that appeals to their interests; instruction that builds their skills and fosters their desire to read increasingly complex materials; and assessment that reveals their strengths as well as their needs (Phelps, 2005).

Adolescent students who struggle with the development of their literacy skills for anywhere from one to twelve years may also have major hurdles to overcome in terms of their self-esteem and feelings of competence. In another summary of research on adolescent literacy commissioned by the National Reading Conference, Alvermann (2002) argues that positive perceptions of self-efficacy are central to motivation and can be increased by providing students with clear goals for what they are to learn, as well as feedback on the progress they are making. She also cites literature (Kamil, Intrator, & Kim, 2000) indicating that technology environments that heighten motivation can increase students' sense of competency. In addition, she refers to an extensive review by Guthrie and Wigfield (2000) of the ways that instruction influences reading engagement and achievement. The review indicates that while various instructional practices widely considered important do not seem to affect student outcomes directly, the level of student engagement acts as a mediating factor through which instruction directly influences outcomes.

This study was also motivated by questions about extended time for learning. One option that has been explored by many districts and supported by federal legislation is afterschool programs. In the emerging field of research on these programs, a representative document is one commissioned by the Nellie Mae Education Foundation, *Critical Hours: Afterschool Programs and Educational Success* (Miller, 2003). According to this report, evidence clearly suggests that effective afterschool programs make a difference for student learning. Specifically, they result in greater engagement in learning and higher academic performance. Miller's review of numerous studies showed that students who attended high-quality programs increased their social competence, academic performance, and civic engagement. Furthermore, the students who benefited most were the ones who were the most at risk, including students from low-income backgrounds and from non-English-speaking families.

Afterschool programs serve many purposes, from providing supervision during the afternoon to offering enrichment activities in which students could not otherwise participate. Since the passage of the No Child Left Behind Act (NCLB), many schools and districts have turned to afterschool programs as a way to supplement the regular school day and offer academic programs that will help increase students' reading and mathematics scores (see, among others, Miller, 2003). Offering more time for instruction, many believe, can help students who are performing below proficiency in school to "catch up" to their peers. This philosophy is explicit in the U.S. Department of Education's 21st Century Community Learning Centers "notice of priorities," which states that for children who are "not reading as well as they should, Community Learning Centers can provide extended time in which to overcome the obstacles that have in the past prevented them from becoming good readers" (Federal Register, 1997, p. 63774, as cited in James-Burdumy, Dynarski, Moore, Deke, Mansfield, & Pistorino, 2005). Yet the question of what types of programs should be offered during these additional minutes remains widely contested.

Previous studies have indicated that structured, high-quality activities in afterschool programs can improve student outcomes. In a review of sixty-eight studies, Hammond and Reimer (2006) found that the creation of "appropriate, consistent structure" (p. 35), where flexibility is balanced with well-developed procedures, often led to positive outcomes, especially in programs with an academic focus. Similarly, in a meta-analysis of previous research, Lauer, Akiba, Wilkerson, Apthorp, Snow, and Martin-Glenn (2004) found "evidence of the effectiveness of a well-defined curriculum and structured approach" (p. 47). In examining a single program, the Massachusetts After-School Research Study identified several "quality indicators" for afterschool programs, including activities that are "appropriate, challenging, and stimulate critical/higher order thinking, are part of a larger project, have evidence of prior preparation, and have clear instructions" (Miller, 2005, p. 3).

These studies suggest that there is broad support for the hypothesis that extended learning time increases academic achievement, but support for this theory is far from universal. For example, Kane (2004) has argued that additional time is typically too limited. If students do not learn during the six hours they spend in class, he has asked, how can an additional hour or two make any difference? In focusing on student-centered concerns, other critics (Noam, 2004; Weisburd, 2005) have argued that at-risk students do not need an afterschool program that looks like an extension of their school day.

Instead, these researchers recommend trying different approaches, with an emphasis on appealing activities and academic programs that allow students to be physically active rather than sitting at their desks.

Central to these criticisms is the belief that what takes place during afterschool hours should be different from what happens during the regular school day. Afterschool programs work well when they engage students, offer well-considered and structured activities, and provide additional time to help students in academics (Hammond & Reimer, 2006). These are demanding criteria, and programs that meet these criteria may be difficult to implement in the afterschool setting. Our research followed the implementation of a program that appears to meet these criteria and asked the question, "Can a structured yet engaging reading program be implemented effectively in the afterschool setting?"

The Problem of Implementation

In the current era of accountability, districts have to think long and hard about where to invest their limited program funding. The preliminary findings from our study of the impact of READ 180 in an afterschool setting suggest that participation in READ 180 led to statistically significant gains in oral reading fluency for fourth graders (Visher & Fitzgerald, 2006). In the second year of the impact study, we found that READ 180 students performed substantially better than control-group students on a norm-referenced test. Although it is too early to say whether READ 180 can have a positive impact on test scores, and, if so, for which populations of students, other previous research indicates that this program might be a feasible option for districts to adopt (see Scholastic, 2006, for a summary of previous research).

Once a program is adopted, implementation begins. When new curricula or programs are introduced to a school, teachers and administrators often have high expectations for their success. The practices may seem promising, and the theory behind the activities may appear meaningful. Yet, schools and districts frequently have difficulty aligning these practices with their own planning as they face challenges in scheduling, materials, technology, or personnel. These issues, which may seem minor during the planning process, in reality can derail the potential for students to learn from the new program. This is the problem of implementation.

Implementation fidelity — how closely the program's delivery matches the intent of the program designer — includes such factors as the qualifications of teachers who are actually delivering the program to students, how much time students spend on task during the afterschool program, and barriers or unforeseen problems, such as problems with technology or scheduling. Given that READ 180 was originally designed for the regular classroom day and not for an afterschool setting, we set out to focus on these fidelity concerns in our study.

The implementation study was based on three methods of data collection:

1. A series of site visits that included classroom observations and interviews with afterschool program teachers
2. Surveys of students and teachers
3. Measures of student engagement from each afterschool site, including data on daily attendance

These data were triangulated, examined for convergence on certain themes, and analyzed for answers to the research questions set forth above. These methods are described in detail in the section on methodology.

Rationale

The implementation study described in this article had two main purposes. The first was to monitor schools' fidelity of implementation in order to contextualize and interpret our findings about the program's impact on student achievement.[1] The second purpose of the implementation study — the one that is the focus of this article — was to assess whether READ 180 could be implemented well in an afterschool setting.

The Intervention: READ 180

Scholastic developed READ 180 based on the work of Ted Hasselbring at Vanderbilt University. Beginning in 1985, with a grant from the U.S. Department of Education, Hasselbring developed a prototype of reading software that used individual student performance data to differentiate instruction. Ten years later, the Vanderbilt software was modified into a program for the lowest-performing readers in schools in Orange County, Florida. Scholastic became involved in 1997–1998 when the corporation collaborated with Vanderbilt University and Orange County schools to test and refine the program. Scholastic launched READ 180 in 1999–2001, and it was immediately implemented in hundreds of schools across the country. As noted above, it is estimated that READ 180 is currently being used in over 12,000 regular classrooms across the U.S. (Scholastic, 2007).

The READ 180 instructional model is intended to provide a well-structured way for teachers to organize reading instruction and classroom activity (Scholastic, 2006). A READ 180 session begins and ends with whole-group, teacher-directed instruction. During the time between the whole-group meetings, students break into three small groups that rotate among three stations: small-group direct instruction by the teacher, a READ 180 software or computer rotation, and independent and modeled reading. Each rotation is meant to target different reading skills. During *small-group direct instruction*, students at similar reading levels sit with their teacher at a small table, and the teacher uses manuals provided by Scholastic to deliver individualized instruction that meets students' specific needs. In the *software or computer rotation*, students are allowed to work independently at a computer workstation that provides them with "intensive, individualized skills to practice" (Scholastic, 2006, p. 10). Finally, in the *independent and modeled reading rotation*, students have a chance to read READ 180 paperbacks or listen to READ 180 audio books alone or in pairs. The independent and modeled reading rotation is meant to "build fluency and reading comprehension through modeled and independent reading" (Scholastic, 2006, p. 10). Before they begin the program, students take a proprietary, embedded test, the Scholastic Reading Inventory (SRI). This test yields Lexile scores, which measure the difficulty level of the reading materials and the students' reading ability on the same scale, allowing students to select materials that are challenging, yet within their reading ability.

READ 180 appears to possess many of the elements that have been identified as helpful to adolescent readers. As mentioned above, programs that are engaging for students, that encourage their self-esteem and sense of self-efficacy as readers, and that provide feedback on their progress are more likely than programs that do not include these features to benefit adolescents who are learning to read more skillfully. READ 180 is designed to provide students with positive reading experiences. Many adolescents who are beginning readers are forced to read books written for much younger children; the books in the READ 180 program, however, are written specifically for adolescents. Students in the program are supposed to read books that are challenging but not too difficult for their reading ability. Nevertheless, the topics are designed to appeal to adolescents and hold their attention. Students are provided feedback on their reading at regular intervals in the form of computer-generated progress reports; these reports include information on books read, words mastered, and growth in students' Lexile levels. Students are also intended to find the computer technology engaging, and they are able to work at the computer with a sense of privacy. All these factors point toward a program that should be successful with adolescents.

READ 180 has been the subject of a number of prior studies, some of which suggest that the program can lead to modest gains in test scores (Scholastic, 2006). Other research, however, indicates that READ 180, along with other technology-based programs, may have a limited impact on student achievement (Dynarski, Agodini, Heaviside, Novak, Carey, Campuzano, et al., 2007). In addition, a study conducted by Policy Study Associates in Fairfax County, Virginia, found that "levels of implementation of the READ 180 instructional model are associated with different levels of improvement in reading comprehension" (Scholastic, 2006, p.18).

READ 180 in Afterschool Programs

Although READ 180 has been used in regular-school-day classrooms for over ten years, it is new to the afterschool setting. Several design elements of READ 180 suggest that it could be adapted for an afterschool context. First, it is designed to be engaging for students, as evidenced by its materials on topics of interest to middle schoolers and its use of an interactive computer program. Second, although its lessons were originally created to last for ninety minutes, the schedule can be modified to be more conducive to the shorter time frame of the afterschool setting. Third, the materials and activities of the program are designed to require limited teacher-preparation time; this is particularly true of the newest version of the program, called READ 180 Enterprise Edition (Scholastic, n.d.). As in the district we studied, many afterschool teachers also teach during the regular school day and have little time to prepare lessons for an afterschool program. A curriculum that contains predesigned lesson plans and other planning materials is therefore very appealing for afterschool teachers.

Scholastic typically provides ongoing training for teachers who use READ 180. As is true for all school districts that purchase the program, teachers in our study received two days of training from a Scholastic representative prior to the launch of the program. The training covered the basics of the program, the materials, and instruction on using the computer (Scholastic, 2005). Teachers also had access to Scholastic RED, an online training and professional development program. Throughout the school year, Scholastic conducts "Teachers' Cadre" meetings in which READ 180 teachers from across the district meet for an afternoon to discuss issues that have arisen and learn how to implement additional elements of the program.

Methodology and Data

Study Design

In order to participate in the study, schools had to have adequate facilities, enroll a minimum number of students, and commit to using READ 180 in their afterschool programs. Because READ 180 is designed for students who are reading at least two grade levels below their expected ability, the study required schools in which large numbers of students were reading below grade level. It was also helpful if afterschool programs already existed at the schools in order to limit the problems of implementation to those associated specifically with READ 180. With cooperation from Scholastic, we undertook a national search to identify and recruit a school district with a sufficient number of schools that met the criteria. The resulting study emerged from collaboration between MPR, Scholastic, and the school district itself.

Because we were studying a reading program designed for early adolescents who are reading below grade level, students in grades four through six who were reading below proficiency (based on the Massachusetts Comprehensive Assessment System [MCAS] reading or language arts assessments) were eligible to enroll in the district's afterschool program. Participation in the afterschool program was voluntary, and parents were informed about the nature of the study. Written (i.e., active) parental permission was received from all parents prior to enrolling students in the study.

In Year 1 (2005–2006), a total of 294 students from three schools were enrolled in the afterschool program; in Year 2 (2006–2007), a total of 312 students from four schools were enrolled. The students received a battery of reading pre-assessments at baseline[2] and then were randomly assigned to either a group that used READ 180 (the treatment group) or a group that received the regular district afterschool programming (the control group). The afterschool program ran from the end of October to the beginning of May each year, and at the end of the treatment period, students took a battery of post-intervention assessments. The same set of assessments was administered to both control and treatment groups.

The Setting and Sample

The school district that hosted this study serves a city of approximately 100,000 people and is located in the Boston metropolitan area. The district, which enrolls children from prekindergarten through twelfth grade, consists of approximately twenty-five schools and is one of the largest districts in the state of Massachusetts. Its population is diverse, with 46 percent African American, 38 percent White, and 12 percent Hispanic students. Almost 60 percent of students receive free or reduced-price lunches, and 5 percent are English language learners (ELLs).

A total of seven schools participated in the READ 180 study: three in the first year (2005–2006) and four in the second year (2006–2007). The demographics of the seven schools in this study closely reflect the overall makeup of the school district but vary in significant ways from the state of Massachusetts as a whole. In the research study schools, African American students made up about 43 percent of the population; White students represented about 42 percent; and Hispanic students made up about 10 percent of the total enrollment in both school years. In the state as a whole, African American students accounted for about 8 percent of the total population, while White students constituted about 72 percent. About 57 percent of students in our study schools were classified as low-income, compared with fewer than 29 percent of students in the state. Also, about 13 percent of students in our study schools were classified as ELLs, compared with 5 to 6 percent of students in Massachusetts. This overrepresentation of low-income students and English language learners was an explicit goal of the study.

Afterschool students in the program were poorer and more likely to be members of racial/ethnic minorities than were students in the overall school population: more than half (53%) were Black, 16 percent were Hispanic, and about 75 percent were low-income. Table 1 presents selected demographic characteristics of the students enrolled in the study, by treatment-group status.

The average class size was similar for students in the READ 180 and the control-group classes. In 2005–2006, the average afterschool class size was 15.0 students for both groups. In 2006–2007, the READ 180 classes averaged 13.0 students while the control group averaged 13.4 students. In both cases, there

TABLE 1   *Selected Student Demographic and Academic Characteristics, by READ 180 or Control-Group Membership*

	Control (%)	Read 180 (%)	Total (%)	n
Gender				
Female	56.1	52.3	52.6	318
Male	43.9	47.7	47.6	288
*Race/ethnicity**				
White, not Hispanic	26.7	23.6	25.1	152
African American, not Hispanic	51.7	54.7	53.2	322
Hispanic, all races	15.3	16.7	16.0	97
Other	6.3	4.9	5.6	34
English Language Learner				
No	92.6	92.5	92.6	561
Yes	7.4	7.5	7.4	45
Special education status				
No	78.0	77.0	77.5	470
Yes	22.0	23.0	22.5	136
Eligible for free or reduced lunch				
Not eligible	24.3	25.9	25.2	152
Eligible	75.7	74.1	75.0	454
Grade				
4	35.9	34.4	35.1	213
5	39.9	41.0	40.5	246
6	24.0	24.6	24.3	147

* Ethnicity information was not available for one student who withdrew from the program at the beginning of the school year.

was generally just one teacher per classroom. In a few cases, a student teacher was available to help in READ 180 classes one or two days per week.

— Attrition: Students Who Withdrew

For the two study years combined, the schools jointly recruited 606 students to participate. During the school years, 116 students (19%) withdrew from the program, bringing the total number of students served throughout an entire year to 490. Parent requests (including moving) accounted for 96 percent of the withdrawals. The remaining 4 percent of students were either suspended from school or left due to medical reasons.

Twenty-two students moved out of the district during the course of the study; treatment- and control-group students moved at an equal rate, as would be expected given that the groups were randomly assigned. However, of the 95 students who withdrew from the afterschool program but remained in the district, 36 were from the READ 180 program and 59 were from the control group, a statistically significant difference at the .01 level ($\chi^2 = 7.32$ on df = 1, p = 0.007).

Instructional Model

For the current study, the sixty-minute instructional model was used in all participating schools. Because the total afterschool program ran for only 120 minutes (which is true of many afterschool programs around the country), and the parameters of the study required that two groups of students pass through the model on any given day, Scholastic worked with the district to reduce the ninety-minute model to a sixty-minute model. During the first year of the study, the revised schedule limited the frequency of whole-group and wrap-up sessions while maintaining the twenty-minute small-group rotation. During the second year, the model was modified to include a whole-group session on alternate days, with two rotations instead of three undertaken each day in an attempt to incorporate as many of the original program components as possible and to maintain fidelity of implementation.

The Counterfactual: Control-Group Activities

Our implementation study focused primarily on the factors that impede or enhance effective implementation of a structured reading program in the afterschool setting. As such, much of the relevant data we collected pertains to the activities of the treatment group. However, we also collected some data on control-group activities in order to understand the afterschool experiences of students who were not assigned to the treatment group.

The control group, which was assigned to the district's standard afterschool program, experienced a variety of afterschool activities, many of which included a small academic component. Students in the control group would begin their afterschool day with twenty to thirty minutes of homework help and then would participate in various activities designed by district afterschool curriculum personnel. The control-group activities contained academic elements but also included "enrichment" activities that tended to involve art, cooking, and sports as major components.

Data Collection and Measures

The data from this study were collected across two school years. Students in control and treatment groups received the same assessments, except that students who were in the treatment group were administered an additional five questions about READ 180 on the survey. For the most part, the same data were collected in both years. We collected many of these data during site visits, which included interviews with key stakeholders and classroom observations. During the site visits, only READ 180 teachers were interviewed, and we used a rubric only in our observations of READ 180 classrooms; in control-group classrooms, we completed a brief observation questionnaire. We surveyed all teachers at both the beginning and the end of the year. Finally, we collected daily attendance rosters, computer log-on times, and monthly attrition data for all students. This section describes these measures.

— Interviews

We interviewed key stakeholders in the study sites at the beginning and end of each school year. We interviewed the principal and site supervisor together, and then conducted a group interview with the afterschool READ 180 program teachers. Since the main purpose of the interviews was to understand the teacher's opinions about implementation, these interviews were semi-structured. Although researchers had prepared a list of questions, they allowed the conversation to flow naturally. Information was collected on all major questions, but teachers were allowed to discuss new topics as they arose. The interviews covered ease of implementation of the program itself; any issues related to technology, facilities, or schedules; issues related to the impact study and random assignment; and anticipated results of READ 180.

— Observations

In 2005–2006, we observed every READ 180 afterschool classroom for an entire one-hour program session twice during the year. In 2006–2007, most READ 180 classrooms were observed for the entire hour, three times during the year. Teachers were told in advance that we would be visiting to observe fidelity of implementation. To conduct these observations, we adapted for our study a rubric that Scholastic provides to help schools ensure quality implementation. The classroom observation protocol provides a framework for assigning points for classroom setup, fidelity of rotations, and classroom management. Classroom setup includes the availability and accessibility of READ 180 materials, the classroom layout, and the availability of functioning technology. This construct is worth a total of twelve points. During each rotation, we observed the number of minutes the rotation lasted and the level of student engagement. In addition, each type of rotation necessitated its own specific fidelity measures. For example, during the small-group instruction, we observed whether the teacher explicitly spoke about connections between skills taught in the READ 180 block and other reading tasks; whether teachers appeared to assess students' understanding of materials; and whether teachers used READ 180 resources. Fidelity of rotations was worth a total of nine points (three points for each rotation). Finally, classroom management included sections on ease of transitions and on whether there was disruptive behavior and/or student engagement.[3]

— Surveys

We surveyed teachers from both the control group and the READ 180 group at the beginning and end of the school year. The fall surveys collected information about teachers' credential status and educational background and asked about their perceptions of the goal of afterschool programs (e.g., recreation or academic enrichment). At the end of the year, READ 180 teachers answered questions about their perceptions of the effectiveness of the READ 180 program.[4]

— Attendance and Attrition Data

For all students in the afterschool program, researchers collected attendance data and calculated attrition rates. We used attendance as a measure of student engagement in the afterschool program. Attendance was taken daily, and we had access to individual student-level attendance data. For this measure, we tracked the number of possible days each student could have attended the afterschool program (i.e., the number of days the program was open for business) and the number of days each student actually attended the program. For each month the program was open (October through May), we calculated an individual attendance rate for each student. Because some schools were open a different total number of days than other schools, we used attendance rates, rather than absolute number of days of attendance, as our measure.

Results and Discussion

The afterschool programs in this district were able to implement READ 180 for an hour each day, but it took a lot of work prior to the start of the program, the right resources, and ongoing monitoring to implement the program. Advanced planning ensured that the infrastructure was in place to receive students and that the entire school staff, whether involved with the afterschool program or not, was part of a team that would support the program and its students. Having the "right resources and personnel" meant having certified teachers (as recommended by Scholastic), but it also meant ensuring that technology coordinators were available to troubleshoot equipment malfunctions, as well as recruiting additional personnel for each classroom to work with students outside of the small-group setting. Also, as additional problems arose throughout the year, the schools needed to have a system in place so that they could respond quickly to these challenges. The following section examines these aspects of implementation in more detail.

What types of preparation and planning were required in order to deliver the reading program as designed?

Delivering the READ 180 program requires more than having new books and paper materials on hand; it also requires technology, classroom setup, and organization. Accomplishing all of this is complicated enough in a regular school day, but it creates new logistical problems in the afterschool setting, as the program may not be housed in classrooms that use READ 180 during the school day, or because multiple classes may need access to the equipment during a short period of time. In addition, READ 180 uses technology (although the computer component is a small part of the overall student day), so the schools need to be sure that technology workers are available throughout the afternoon to help solve problems. Overcoming these challenges takes strong preparation.

— Preparing the Facilities and Developing the Schedule
If an army marches on its stomach, then a school operates by its bus schedule. Afterschool programs usually need to accommodate time for snack, transition (such as restroom breaks), homework, and other activities before the buses roll at the end of the day. Although these activities may seem minor, they can make or break an afterschool program by constraining the amount of time left for instruction. For example, in our study, the buses left the school sites at 5:00 PM on the dot, which meant that all classroom instruction had to be completed by 4:50 PM at the very latest, to give students the opportunity to pack up their materials and come to the front of the building to board the buses. Since the school day ended at 2:50 PM, this gave students only 120 minutes in which to leave their regular-day classes, move into their afterschool program, eat a snack, visit the bathroom, do homework, and complete the day's instructional activities. If snack and bathroom break took too long at the beginning, teachers were unable to make up for lost time at the other end of the day, as buses wait for no one.

In addition, students in many elementary schools are not allowed to move from classroom to classroom independently but must move in a group with a teacher or other adult escort. In our study, we found that the schools struggled to find ways to accommodate students' immediate needs while also attending to their instructional needs. As one teacher put it, "A kid can't read if he's squirming in his seat."

The four schools that were able to ensure that students spent more than fifty minutes receiving instruction and the least amount of time in transition undertook extensive preprogram preparations. First, they considered the physical layout of their school. Because the distance between the regular-day classroom and the afterschool program can affect the number of instructional minutes available, the schools looked for ways to shorten the distance students needed to cover to reach their afterschool classrooms. They worked with the regular-day schoolteachers to release students early for the afterschool program, or enlisted the help of aides to bring snacks to the afterschool classroom, rather than requiring students to meet first in the cafeteria.

Efficient use of classroom time was a significant challenge for schools and teachers. Over the two years, we observed that students were in class for fewer than the sixty minutes set aside for the READ 180 program. Of those sixty minutes, approximately ten or eleven minutes, on average, were used for transitions — setting up the program, moving between READ 180 rotations, and cleaning up at the end of the day. The amount of time spent in transition varied from teacher to teacher: At the low end, one teacher had developed a routine so that her students received almost fifty-eight minutes of instructional time, out of a sixty-minute period. On the high end, another teacher spent about eighteen out of sixty minutes in transitions. In our study, most afterschool teachers did not teach in their regular-day classroom, but moved into a different classroom for the afterschool program. This required the teachers to make additional transitions, and they often felt that they were intruding on another teacher's time for classroom setup. One teacher said, "I'm very picky about how my room is arranged, so I always try to leave the room exactly as we found it. But that takes time."

There were also many cases in which multiple teachers would use a single READ 180 classroom. One would teach a class during the first hour of the afterschool program, and then a second teacher would teach a class during the second hour. These teachers had to pack up and move quickly between classrooms. The schools that managed this process most successfully prepared individualized packets by teacher, so that during transitions, teachers only needed to grab a single bag containing all of their required materials. In addition, the schools had portable "homework" boxes, with rulers, pencils, and other equipment students might need to complete their homework, reducing the time students needed to move between classrooms.

— Technology and Teacher-Preparation Time

One notable difference between the first and second year of our study was the change in the amount of preparation time reported by teachers. In the first year, teachers used READ 180 Version 1.6, which required them to prepare their own lessons, make copies of all worksheets, and prepare for the afterschool program as they would for the regular classroom day. For the second year, however, the new version of READ 180, called the Enterprise Edition, was bundled with Scholastic's *rBooks*, which are workbooks with daily lesson plans. (More detailed information about these programs is available from Scholastic.) Teachers could rely on the program materials and did not have to spend as much time on preparation.

In the first year, most of the READ 180 teachers reported that the amount of preparation time needed for each session was far greater than they had originally anticipated. During interviews, about half of the teachers said that the amount of time they spent preparing for the following week's lessons declined over the year, as they began to learn more about how the program worked and what supporting materials were available from Scholastic. The other half felt that the amount of preparation time did not change. Teachers reported spending anywhere from two to four hours per week preparing lessons, although a few reported that eight hours were required to "really prepare right." Because all of the teachers also taught during the regular school day, the amount of preparation time became a problem for some of them. In fact, at least two claimed that they spent their regular-day preparation time planning instead for the afterschool READ 180 program. "Prep time is the biggest issue," said one teacher, "and it might be the reason why I don't do READ 180 [in the afterschool program] next year."

In the second year, when schools used the READ 180 Enterprise Edition, few teachers mentioned preparation time as a concern. When asked about the amount of preparation time required, they almost invariably said that they needed only a limited amount of time to prepare because the *rBooks* supplement laid out the day's activities so well. Teacher logs indicated that most teachers spent between 1 and 3 hours a month for preparation time, and, although one teacher spent 23 hours in the first month and about 18 hours in each subsequent month, the average of 4 hours per month in Year 2 was substantially less than what was reported anecdotally during Year 1.

What resources seemed to improve implementation?

Many afterschool programs struggle to find and keep qualified staff (Miller, 2005), and this problem is often exacerbated because Scholastic recommends that only certified staff teach READ 180. In our study, we looked at the qualifications of teachers, the number of additional adults in the classroom working with the students, and the extra roles required for the afterschool program.

The teachers in both years met the certification requirements for the READ 180 program. A total of thirty teachers were involved in teaching the READ 180 program across the two years of the study. Twenty-five had regular or state standard certificates; two had probationary certificates, which indicated that they had completed all of the certification requirements and were completing a probationary period to receive a regular state certificate; and three had provisional certificates (i.e., licenses through an alternative certification program).

Because teachers need to be able to concentrate on small-group instruction during the rotations, Scholastic suggests placing a paraprofessional assistant in each READ 180 classroom. However, due to financial constraints, the district and schools were generally unable to accommodate this suggestion. In some classrooms, college students working as interns were able to fill the role of a paraprofessional, helping students with technology malfunctions or sitting with students who had particular behavioral problems. During our observations, it appeared that having a second adult in the classroom led to smoother implementation of the structured reading program. Although the average implementation score in classrooms with a second adult was slightly higher than in those classrooms without one (7.4 compared to 7.1 out of a total of 9.0, a difference that is not statistically significant), only 7 of the 52 classrooms we observed had an additional adult, making it difficult to draw any conclusions about the difference.

Also, because working computers, equipment, and servers are needed to keep the computer rotation — and thus, the READ 180 period — running smoothly, a district technology manager was assigned to address technical problems. In addition to having access to a district technology manager, one school had an afterschool supervisor who also served as the on-site technology expert and was always available during the afterschool program. The other schools reported that having an in-house technology person would have helped them handle technology issues more efficiently.

What were the key challenges the district or schools faced?

Despite all of the preparation that successful schools undertake before beginning the afterschool year, problems do arise. In addition, the quality of the program can decay or depreciate if not given ongoing attention. In this district, the schools found themselves responding to a variety of challenges, from teacher and student burnout, to technology problems, to increasingly heavy homework burdens.

— Teacher and Student Fatigue

There has been concern among afterschool program educators that teacher fatigue is an impediment to using structured academic interventions in afterschool settings (James-Burdumy et al., 2005). Teachers are at greater risk of suffering from burnout when they teach in both the regular-day and the afterschool programs, particularly when the afterschool program contains a significant academic component. We examined data that could be considered potential indicators of teacher fatigue, including the use of substitute hours in the afterschool program, teacher surveys, and interviews made during our on-site visits. Our results suggest that teacher burnout may not be as substantial an obstacle to implementing structured afterschool programs as we had feared.

Although there are many reasons other than fatigue for why substitutes might be required to fill in for regular afterschool staff, high levels of substitute hours could reflect teacher fatigue. While comprehensive data on substitute hours were unavailable for Year 1 of the study, we did interview substitutes and learn that they, in general, worked fewer days than anticipated by the schools. The exceptions were two who substituted for a teacher taking an extended medical leave. Data for Year 2 were available and showed no significant difference between READ 180 and the control group in the number of hours worked by substitutes during the school year.

Teachers remained enthusiastic about the READ 180 program through the end of the school year, as reflected in their survey responses. They said during interviews that a highly structured program is good for students, even in the afterschool setting. With a program such as READ 180, students move frequently between activities so they are less inclined to get bored, but they are still subject to a structure that keeps them disciplined.

Some teachers, however, did mention that the afterschool program created a long day for both teachers and students; to support that claim, teachers noted that some students did, in fact, appear more restless than they did during the regular school day. Teachers responded to student fatigue by making ongoing adjustments to the READ 180 program. Most of the changes described below did not affect the underlying program model but allowed for enough change to retain student interest. Other modifications, such as shortening or eliminating small-group instruction, required altering the structure of the program.

The variety of materials kept students engaged for much of the year. Teachers generally reported (and site visits corroborated) that students found the READ 180 books engaging throughout the course of the year. In an end-of-year interview, one principal stated the belief that "READ 180 students had far more enthusiasm for their afterschool program" than did the students in the control group. To help ensure that students' interest remained high, teachers also introduced innovative activities such as "team-reading" or linking the books that students read during independent reading time to their small-group instruction.

— Technology Issues

Many of the challenges the schools faced were technology-related. While technology can be disruptive when it does not function properly, it is particularly problematic when a program is as dependent upon technology as READ 180. On the whole, most students were able to use the technology components on a regular basis, although both computers and audio players caused difficulties for the individual teachers and the district as a whole.

The most frequent complaints we heard from teachers about READ 180 regarded computer problems, some of which were internal to the district and some of which were "bugs" in the READ 180 system itself. Because the computer rotation was the students' favorite activity, and the teachers felt that it was the most effective component of the program, it was very frustrating when the computers did not function properly.

These problems were exacerbated during the afterschool program because, although teachers and site supervisors at all three schools in Year 1 reported that district personnel were very helpful in resolving technology issues, many problems had to wait until the next day to be reported. According to staff reports, rarely was someone immediately available from the district central office to help resolve issues during the afterschool period.

How much additional time-on-task in reading were students likely to spend?

Because the main purpose of an academic afterschool program is to increase the amount of instructional time students receive, it is critical that time-on-task remains high throughout the year. In addition, the time must be spent on the program (the model itself), rather than on other activities. This combination of time-on-task and fidelity to design constituted one of the central aspects of our data collection and analysis. We considered whether the model was implemented as designed. How much time did students spend receiving direct instruction, working with the computer, and reading independently? How much time was lost to transitions (before the afterschool program, during the READ 180 model, and after the end of the session)? Finally, we examined whether there were differences in attendance between afterschool students who participated in the READ 180 program and those who did not.

— Fidelity and Time-on-Task

READ 180 is driven by technology as a way of efficiently providing a structured but flexible program to students. Students are expected to spend twenty minutes each day using the computer and the READ 180 software. While logged on to the computer, students can participate in a variety of activities, each emphasizing a different reading skill. Students move from the activities to embedded assessments of fluency, comprehension, and vocabulary. Once they successfully complete the tests at the end of each section, they are free to pursue another topic.

During the computer rotation, all students must have access to working computers, software, microphones, and headphones. Students also need to be engaged in the computer activities, not distracted by their fellow students, homework, the Internet, or other activities unrelated to READ 180. On the whole, our site visits revealed that the computer rotation was implemented with high levels of fidelity and was popular with both students and teachers. The average scores (on a scale of 0 to 3, with 3 representing a very high level of implementation) for the computer rotation ranged from 3.0 in November 2005 to 1.70 in November 2006, with an overall average of 2.40. These data are presented in Table 2.

When the computers were working, students rotated through the session and remained actively engaged. What lowered the scores were faulty technology and short rotation times. Nonetheless, the level of student engagement remained high. In 114 out of 120 rotations observed over the two years, all students were on-task throughout the rotation.

Based on surveys and interviews, it was clear that teachers and administrators regarded the computer rotation as the "heart" of the READ 180 program. During an interview one teacher stated, "Students seemed eager to come to the program, and almost all students were particularly excited about working on the computers." Several teachers also noted that most students especially liked the speaking and recording activities. When asked on the end-of-year survey to rate the effectiveness of the computer rotation, 21 out of the 27 READ 180 teachers surveyed (or 78 percent) rated the computer rotation as "very effective," while six teachers rated the rotation as "effective."[5] No teachers rated the computer rotation as "somewhat effective" or "not at all effective." Distributions of teachers' survey responses are presented in Table 5.

TABLE 2   *Average Fidelity Scores on the Computer Rotation. Scale ranges from*
0 to 3, with 3 representing a very high level of implementation. (n = 22 classrooms)

	November	April	Total
2005–2006			
School A	3.0	2.3	2.7
School B	3.0	3.0	3.0
School C	3.0	3.0	3.0
TOTAL	3.0	2.8	2.9
2006–2007			
School D	1.8	1.8	1.8
School E	2.0	2.0	2.0
School F	1.5	2.3	1.9
School G	1.5	3.0	2.3
TOTAL	1.7	2.2	1.9
OVERALL	2.3	2.5	2.4

Teachers also appreciated that over time, students became quite competent at getting the computers up and running and troubleshooting computer issues, which freed teachers to work with other students. Teachers also indicated that the computer sessions, more than the other rotations, enhanced students' self-esteem and confidence, because the software is designed to acknowledge the success that students achieve through the SuccessZone. Teachers felt that the certificates of achievement were motivating for students, especially for fourth and fifth graders. One teacher believed that this confidence was sustained beyond the computer rotation, explaining, "The students appear to be more willing to take risks in class and to participate in all reading activities. They definitely have more self-confidence in their abilities and enjoy participating in all reading activities."

During the small-group instruction rotation, students sat at a table with the teacher either working on skills such as finding the "big idea" and reading aloud, or otherwise receiving direct instruction. Students were usually grouped according to need, based upon teachers' observations as well as embedded assessments, such as the SRI and the Phonics and Word Study Skills assessments.

In both November and April of Year 1, classroom scores for small-group rotation (on a scale of 0 to 3, with 3 representing a very high level of implementation) averaged 2.40 across all classrooms. Teachers were observed using READ 180 resources and appeared to assess students' understanding of the materials on which they were working. These data are presented in Table 3.

TABLE 3   *Average Fidelity Scores on the Small-Group Rotation. Scale ranges from 0 to 3, with 3 representing a very high level of implementation. (n = 22 classrooms)*

	November	*April*	*Total*
2005–2006			
School A	3.0	2.7	2.8
School B	3.0	3.0	3.0
School C	2.7	3.0	2.8
TOTAL	2.9	2.9	2.9
2006–2007			
School D	1.8	2.0	1.8
School E	2.0	3.0	2.5
School F	1.5	2.0	1.8
School G	1.5	3.0	2.3
TOTAL	1.7	2.3	2.0
OVERALL	2.2	2.6	2.4

Classrooms received lower implementation scores mainly because students did not set reading and writing goals, and because about half of the teachers did not appear to explicitly connect the skills from the small-group instruction to other reading tasks. Because Scholastic requires these components for high implementation scores, their absence was notable. Despite this, students appeared to be on-task: In 111 of the 120 rotations observed over the two years, all students were on-task throughout the rotation.

During site visits, we noted some difficulty in conducting the small-group rotation. Teachers often had to leave the small group to help other students who were having trouble with the computers or with their independent reading. In a few instances, teachers started small-group instruction with an activity and then spent five to seven minutes of the rotation getting students set up on the computers, repairing headphones, finding books, or otherwise engaging in activities that pulled teachers away from the small-group instruction table. Although the students in the rotation were usually able to work on the assigned activity without further attention from the teacher, discipline problems sometimes arose.

In general, teachers believed that the small-group instruction rotation was very effective. On the end-of-year survey, nineteen out of twenty-seven teachers (or 70 percent) described the small-group rotation as "very effective," while six described it as "effective," and two described it as "somewhat effective." Again, the distributions of teacher responses are presented in Table 5. At one school, all three teachers agreed that small-group instruction allowed them to teach using their own strengths and individual teaching styles. In addition, teachers stated that the READ 180 materials were helpful, and they appreciated being able to work with students in small groups based upon their individual needs. During an interview, one teacher said she believed the small-group activities were most engaging for her students, due to the very fact that the groups *were* small. Students, she said, "compete over giving answers, and they all want to read out loud." The smaller size of the groups also gave more students a chance to participate.

During independent reading, students selected books of interest to them and appropriate for their Lexile reading level, and settled into comfortable chairs, pillows, or beanbags to read on their own. They could also listen to audio recordings, in which a reading "coach" helped guide them through the text. In order to have a high implementation score, the rotation had to last eighteen to twenty minutes, and all students needed to have access to READ 180 books at their reading level. All students needed to be engaged in reading, with or without audiotapes, and be undistracted by their peers. Students were encouraged to read aloud to each other, as long as they read appropriate READ 180 materials at their Lexile level.

Rotation scores (on a scale of 0 to 3, with 3 representing a very high level of implementation fidelity) were based upon the number of students in each rotation who appeared to be on-task — that is, engaged in one or more of the above activities. These data are presented in Table 4.

In about 65 percent of the rotations observed, all students were on-task throughout the rotation. In the remaining rotations, students were frequently distracted, doing homework, or engaging in private conversations.

Teachers reported that students read many books during the independent reading rotation. One teacher reported that each of her students read over a dozen books during the year. Opinions were mixed about the books. Most teachers thought that students found the books interesting and engaging — one commented, "I never had students complain that they couldn't find a book they wanted to read" — but others said that their students had read all the books of interest before the end of the year.

Of the three rotations, teachers regarded independent reading as the least effective. On the end-of-year survey, six out of twenty-seven teachers (or 22 percent) rated independent reading as "very effective," while fifteen rated it as "effective," and six rated it as "somewhat effective." Table 5 presents these results as well.

Independent reading might also be the most difficult rotation to administer in an afterschool setting because students are often tired and restless after their six- or seven-hour school day. As one teacher commented, "The kids are fried by the end of the day," and would sometimes complain about having to sit still and read. In interviews, teachers suggested that while the computer work kept students interested, and small-group rotations required teachers

TABLE 4   *Average Fidelity Scores on the Independent Reading Rotation.*
Scale ranges from 0 to 3, with 3 representing a very high level of implementation.
(n = 22 classrooms)

	November	April	Total
2005–2006			
School A	3.0	2.4	2.7
School B	3.0	3.0	3.0
School C	3.0	3.0	3.0
TOTAL	3.0	2.8	2.9
2006–2007			
School D	1.8	1.5	1.6
School E	2.0	2.0	2.0
School F	1.5	2.0	1.8
School G	1.5	3.0	2.3
TOTAL	1.7	2.1	1.9
OVERALL	2.2	2.5	2.4

to be physically nearby to ensure that students were on-task, students were on their own during independent reading time. After a long day, some students appeared to lack the stamina required to concentrate on books, however interesting and engaging those books might have been.

— Reducing Transition Time

During our site visits, we generally found high levels of fidelity to the design of the READ 180 program with regard to transition time. Overall, the average score across all rotations was 2.4 out of 3.0, or 80 percent of the maximum score attainable. This suggests that READ 180 was implemented in a way that was close to its original design. In addition, students appeared to be on-task with the computer and small-group activities, and were usually engaged in their independent reading rotation. The transitions between classes and rotations were smooth, with few disruptions. According to teacher and staff reports, initial implementation went smoothly for the most part. Over the year, teachers made small adjustments to the schedule that, in their professional opinion, were necessary to keep students engaged. Some of the changes included keeping students on the computer for longer periods and decreasing the amount of time for either the small-group instruction or the independent reading rotation.

TABLE 5   *Distribution of Teacher Ratings for Each Rotation*

	Very Effective (%)	Effective (%)	Somewhat Effective (%)	Not at all Effective (%)	N
2005–2006					
Computer	92	8	0	0	12
Small Group	75	25	0	0	12
Independent Reading	42	25	33	0	12
2006–2007					
Computer	67	33	0	0	15
Small Group	67	20	13	0	15
Independent Reading	7	80	13	0	15
OVERALL					
Computer	78	22	0	0	27
Small Group	70	22	7	0	27
Independent Reading	22	56	22	0	27

— Attendance

Attendance is a major concern of afterschool programs for a variety of reasons, all of which had implications for our study. Attendance and attrition are particularly acute problems in the afterschool setting because students are not required to attend, parents are less likely to view the program as integral to their child's education, and other afterschool activities often interfere with attendance. Yet, if students do not attend the program, they cannot benefit from it. Students can either officially withdraw from a program, or they can remain on the roster but fail to attend. In either case, students do not receive the suggested dosage of the program.

In addition to administering surveys and interviewing principals and afterschool supervisors, we collected data on student attendance from the afterschool program sites. We also downloaded information from the Student Management System (SMS), which is part of the READ 180 software. Results show that attendance rates for students who were assigned to READ 180 were higher overall than attendance rates for students in the control group. The difference between the two groups was statistically significant ($t = 3.4$, $p = 0.001$; see Table 6). When students who withdrew from the program were removed from the analysis, we found that READ 180 students still attended at significantly higher rates ($t = 2.3$, $p = 0.021$).

TABLE 6   *Percentage of Possible Days Attended by Control and READ 180 Participants, by Month (n = 587 students)*

	Control (%)	READ 180 (%)	t-test
October	87	89	0.8
November	81	87	3.0**
December	75	81	2.5*
January	70	79	3.3***
February	63	73	3.6***
March	65	74	3.0**
April	59	67	2.8**
TOTAL	70	78	3.4***

* p<0.05; ** p< 0.01; ***p< 0.001

Note: Excludes students who moved.

Attendance rates declined as the school year progressed, but rates for READ 180 students declined less rapidly than those of control-group students. With the exception of October, in every month, READ 180 students attended the afterschool program at significantly higher rates than the control-group students (see Table 6).

Many factors may contribute to these higher attendance rates, including parental interest in students' reading and student engagement in specific afterschool activities. However, if the goal of an afterschool program is to extend the instructional time for students, then the fact that students who received READ 180 attended at significantly higher rates is important. Only students who attend the afterschool program can receive additional instructional time, so schools and districts should take probable attendance rates into consideration when they select afterschool activities and programs. Students who received the structured academic program continued to attend at higher rates than other students throughout the year, and this finding contradicts the findings from another study of afterschool programs (Miller, 2005), which found lower attendance among students in the academic program. One explanation for our different results might lie in the fact that many students appeared to find the program engaging. One fourth-grade student wrote on her survey, "READ 180 is so fun, I'd like to do it again next year."

Conclusion

Under pressure to rapidly improve test scores in all disciplines, schools and districts are scrambling to find ways to help adolescents with low levels of reading achievement learn to read better. READ 180 has shown promise for improving adolescent reading in previous research (Scholastic, 2006), and this study has shown that it can be altered to fit into an afterschool setting. This study has also demonstrated that students who use READ 180 in afterschool settings may attend afterschool programs at higher rates than students who do not have access to the program. Schools and districts should be aware that adopting any program, but particularly one with a large technology component, requires a strong emphasis on implementation. Because the READ 180 program requires significant resources in terms of teachers and materials, it is very important that districts and schools consider whether they will be able to implement it fully and faithfully before investing in READ 180. By describing how one school district implemented READ 180 in its afterschool program, we have tried to highlight the obstacles and possible solutions of which schools and districts considering purchasing this program should be aware.

Our findings suggest that strong preparation is required before the program can be launched in schools. Issues such as the physical layout of the school, access to technology, and scheduling are paramount to a smooth initial implementation. Schools need to consider specific questions, such as:

- Which classrooms are conducive to the use of READ 180?
- Will teachers have to move to new classrooms for the afterschool program?
- How will that transition work?
- How will snack and homework time — not to mention bathroom breaks — be accommodated within the daily schedule?

Districts and schools must also consider the availability of necessary resources, including:

- Can the district or school afford to pay certified faculty to teach in the afterschool program?
- How much additional preparation time should those teachers receive?
- Will someone who is familiar with technology be available during afterschool hours to troubleshoot any problems that arise from the technology?
- Can the school provide an aide, such as a college student (intern) or paraprofessional, to assist with the READ 180 classes?

The overarching question addressed in this article is whether it is feasible to implement READ 180 successfully in afterschool programs. Based on our observations, the answer is "Yes." Although not without challenges, READ 180 was offered four days a week from October through the beginning of May in each year of our study, meaning that students were exposed to as much as 85 hours of supplemental reading instruction. The components of the program that Scholastic identifies as central to student learning — the specific materials, the computer-based activities, and the Lexile-leveled audio recordings with reading coaches — were included every day that the program was offered. Students remained, on the whole, very engaged in the program, and attendance was high, especially for an afterschool setting. Teachers were enthusiastic, as were their principals.

As schools and districts search for solutions that will bring struggling readers to grade level, they will continue to consider an extended school day as one way to provide these students with additional instruction in reading. Districts are looking for afterschool programs that not only produce higher test scores but also are appealing, can be adapted to the casual environment of afterschool programs, and can be implemented effectively. The results of this study suggest that READ 180 — a program about which students and teachers remained enthusiastic even after nearly a full year — can, with minor modifications, be implemented successfully in an afterschool setting.

Notes

1. Although the impact study was based on a randomized controlled trial that focused on student achievement outcomes, a finding of *no impact* could mean one of several mutually exclusive things: First, it could mean that the program was implemented well but is simply not effective. Alternatively, it could mean that the program delivered was not the same as the one initially designed, and, therefore, the finding of *no impact* does not necessarily mean that the program itself is ineffectual. Conversely, if one *does* find a positive impact, one wants to verify that the program was actually implemented as designed. We also wondered whether fidelity of implementation scores would be positively correlated with student test scores.
2. Assessments administered at baseline and at the conclusion of the intervention in the first year included the Dynamic Indicators of Basic Early Literacy Skills (DIBELS), the Group Reading Assessment and Diagnostic Evaluation (GRADE), and the Test of Word Reading Efficiency (TOWRE). Assessments administered at baseline and at the end of the intervention in Year 2 included the DIBELS, the Title Recognition Test (Cunningham & Stanovich, 1991), and the Early Reading Attitudes Survey (McKenna, Kear, & Ellsworth, 1995). We also had post-intervention assessment results from the SAT 10.
3. Classroom observation rubrics are available from the authors upon request. Although classroom management was scored (and worth nine points), this score was not included in the total for "implementation fidelity" because management can be excellent even when the program is not well implemented, thus confusing the total score. We also observed the control-group classes, but, because they varied widely in terms of activities, we did not have a "fidelity" rubric to score. Instead, we observed the classes by completing an observation form that asked about similar constructs, such as type of literacy activities, student engagement, access to equipment and materials, and elements of classroom management. Because this was a randomized controlled trial, we also ensured that control groups were not receiving the READ 180 program, which would have been a problem of contamination.
4. The teacher survey instrument is available from the authors upon request.
5. Three teachers did not return post-intervention surveys.

References

Alvermann, D. E. (2002). Effective literacy instruction for adolescents. *Journal of Literacy Research, 34*(2), 189–208.

Biancarosa, G., & Snow, C. E. (2004). *Reading next — A vision for action and research in middle and high school literacy: A report to Carnegie Corporation of New York.* Washington, DC: Alliance for Excellent Education.

Carnahan, D., & Cobb, C. (2004). *A conceptual model of adolescent literacy.* Naperville, IL: Learning Point Associates.

Cunningham, A., & Stanovich, K. (1991). Tracking the unique effects of print exposure in children: Associations with vocabulary, general knowledge, and spelling. *Journal of Educational Psychology, 83*(2), 264–274.

Dynarski, M., Agodini, R., Heaviside, S., Novak, T., Carey, N., Campuzano, L., Means, B., Murphy, R., Penuel, W., Javitz, H., Emery, D., & Sussex, W. (2007). *Effectiveness of reading and mathematics software products: Findings from the first cohort* (NCEE 2007-4005). Washington, DC: U.S. Department of Education, Institute of Education Sciences, National Center for Education Evaluation and Regional Assistance.

Grigg, W., Donahue, P., & Dion, G. (2007). *The nation's report card: 12th-grade reading and mathematics 2005* (NCES 2007-468). Washington, DC: U.S. Department of Education, Institute of Education Sciences, National Center for Education Statistics.

Grosso de Leon, A. (2005). *America's literacy challenge: Teaching adolescents to read to learn.* New York: Carnegie Corporation of New York.

Guthrie, J. T., & Wigfield, A. (2000). Engagement and motivation in reading. In M. L. Kamil, P. B. Mosenthal, P. D. Pearson, & R. Barr (Eds.), *Handbook of reading research* (Vol. 3, pp. 403–422). Mahwah, NJ: Erlbaum.

Hammond, C., & Reimer, M. (2006). *Essential elements of quality after-school programs.* Clemson, SC: National Dropout Prevention Center/Network.

James-Burdumy, S., Dynarski, M., Moore, M., Deke, J., Mansfield, W., & Pistorino, C. (2005). When schools stay open late: The national evaluation of the 21st Century Community Learning Centers Program: Final report. Washington, DC: U.S. Department of Education, Institute of Education Sciences, National Center for Education Evaluation and Regional Assistance. Retrieved August 9, 2007, from http://www.ed.gov/rschstat/eval/other/cclcfinalreport/cclcfinal.pdf

Kamil, M. (2003). *Adolescents and literacy.* Washington, DC: Alliance for Excellent Education.

Kamil, M. L., Intrator, S. M., & Kim, H. S. (2000). The effects of other technologies on literacy and literacy learning. In M. L. Kamil, P. B. Mosenthal, P. D. Pearson, & R. Barr (Eds.), *Handbook of reading research* (Vol. 3, pp. 771–788). Mahwah, NJ: Erlbaum.

Kane, T. J. (2004, January 16). *The impact of after-school programs: Interpreting the results for four recent evaluations* (Working Paper). New York: William T. Grant Foundation.

Lauer, P. A., Akiba, M., Wilkerson, S. B., Apthorp, H. S., Snow, D., & Martin-Glenn, M. (2004). *The effectiveness of out-of-school-time strategies in assisting low-achieving students in reading and mathematics: A research synthesis.* Aurora, CO: Mid-continent Research for Education and Learning.

McKenna, M. C., Kear, D. J., & Ellsworth, R. A. (1995). Children's attitudes toward reading: A national survey. *Reading Research Quarterly, 30*(4), 934–956.

Miller, B. M. (2003). *Critical hours: Afterschool programs and educational success.* Quincy, MA: Nellie Mae Education Foundation. Retrieved November 4, 2007, from http://www.nmefdn.org

Miller, B. M. (2005). *Pathways to success for youth: What counts in after-school* (Massachusetts After-School Research Study Report). Arlington, MA: Intercultural Center for Research in Education and National Institute on Out-of-School Time.

Moore, D., Bean, T., Birdyshaw, D., & Rycik, J. (1999). *Adolescent literacy: A position statement for the Commission on Adolescent Literacy of the International Reading Association.* Newark, DE: International Reading Association.

National Council of Teachers of English. (2007). *Adolescent literacy* (Policy Research Brief). Urbana, IL: Author. Retrieved December 18, 2007, from http://www.ncte.org/library/files/Publications/Newspaper/Chron0907ResearchBrief.pdf

Noam, G. G. (2004). *The four Cs of afterschool programming: A new case method for a new field* (Afterschool Matters Occasional Paper Series). New York: The Robert Bowne Foundation.

Perie, M., Grigg, W., & Donahue, P. (2005). *The nation's report card: Reading 2005* (NCES 2006-451). Washington, DC: U.S. Department of Education, Institute of Education Sciences, National Center for Education Statistics.

Phelps, S. (2005). *Ten years of research on adolescent literacy, 1994–2004: A review.* Naperville, IL: Learning Point Associates.

Scholastic. (2005). *Read 180 teacher implementation guide.* New York: Author.

Scholastic. (2006). *Compendium of Read 180 research.* New York: Author. Retrieved August 2, 2007, from http://216.182.167.201/products/research/pdfs/RF_R180_compendium.pdf

Scholastic. (2007). *From failing grades to all stars.* New York: Author. Retrieved December 14, 2007, from http://www.scholastic.com/aboutscholastic/news/press_04182007_CP.htm

Scholastic. (n.d.). *Read 180, America's premier reading intervention program for elementary through high school* (Enterprise Edition Manual). New York: Author.

Snow, C. E., & Biancarosa, G. (2003). *Adolescent literacy and the achievement gap: What do we know and where do we go from here?* New York: Carnegie Corporation of New York.

Visher, M. G., & Fitzgerald, R. (2006). *Can after-school programs boost academic achievement? An impact evaluation in an after-school program.* Unpublished manuscript, Berkeley, CA.

Weisburd, C. (2005, May). Academics after-school style. *The School Administrator.* Retrieved August 9, 2007, from http://www.aasa.org/publications/saarticledetail.cfm?ItemNumber=2519

The authors would like to thank Beverly Farr, Mary Visher, Andrea Livingston, Debra Jones, and Michael Vaden-Kiernan for their helpful comments on an earlier draft.

State Literacy Plans: Incorporating Adolescent Literacy

CATHERINE E. SNOW
TWAKIA MARTIN
Harvard Graduate School of Education

ILENE BERMAN
National Governors Association Center for Best Practices

In this article, Catherine Snow, Twakia Martin, and Ilene Berman describe professional development institutes offered in 2001 and 2002 by the Harvard Graduate School of Education and the National Governors Association Center for Best Practices to familiarize state-level policymakers with research on adolescent literacy and to guide states' development of effective literacy plans. The authors then review the literacy plans that four of the participating states developed in the years following their institute involvement and discuss ways in which the content of the literacy institutes is reflected in these states' plans. In conclusion, the authors call on higher education institutions to help state policymakers develop and evaluate initiatives intended to increase adolescents' reading skills. They also call for broader cross-state comparisons of states' strategies for improving adolescent literacy.

Attention to the achievement of secondary school students has moved to the center of policy consideration in recent years. This can be attributed in part to the data showing poor performance by U.S. students in international comparisons, such as those carried out under the auspices of the Programme for International Student Assessment (PISA; UNESCO Institute for Statistics, 2003, 2007). PISA results show U.S. students scoring among the best in the world in grade four, but much lower in comparison to other countries in grade eight, and among the lowest in the world in grade ten. In addition, many indicators of poor performance have been made public by the accountability focus of No Child Left Behind (NCLB) and NCLB-generated data, including high rates of underproficiency on state reading assessments (Center on Education Policy, 2007) and on the National Assessment of Educational Progress (Lee, Grigg, & Donahue, 2007; Perie, Grigg, & Donahue, 2005). The test-perfor-

Harvard Educational Review   Vol. 78   No. 1   Spring 2008

mance data have made clear that far too many U.S. students are being inadequately prepared for the demands of higher education, employment, and citizenship. Accordingly, some states — acknowledging the economic value of a highly educated workforce and understanding that literacy skills contribute to student achievement across the curriculum — have explicitly incorporated adolescent literacy goals into their plans for raising student achievement. This has meant going beyond states' traditional policy focus on reading instruction in the primary grades, enhanced since 2002 by federal Reading First grants, toward more comprehensive literacy plans that address literacy development in grades four through twelve. Recognizing that states bear the primary responsibility for education in this country, governors and other state leaders have begun to institute new policies in state K–12 literacy plans that provide guidance, incentives, and support to districts and schools for extending the state literacy focus through secondary school.

In this article, we describe an initiative undertaken at the Harvard Graduate School of Education in 2001 and in partnership with the National Governors Association Center for Best Practices (NGA Center) in 2002 to familiarize state-level education policymakers, as well as other key actors, with research that might help them shape effective literacy policies in their states. In contrast to much of the guidance available in 2001 and 2002, this initiative emphasized a focus on literacy practices designed to prepare students for the adolescent literacy challenges of comprehension, engagement, and content-area reading. We also illustrate both the challenges and possibilities of developing state-level plans for adolescent literacy by describing the range of policies that four participating states developed in the five to six years after their participation in the institutes.

During the summers of 2001 and 2002, teams from nine states attended literacy institutes at the Harvard Graduate School of Education. The institutes, which were funded by the Carnegie Corporation of New York and implemented by faculty (including one of the authors of this article), were designed to help the state teams review and analyze the literacy content of their preservice and in-service teacher-education standards and programs. The first literacy institute, called the Harvard Literacy Institute (HLI), took place in June 2001 and included participants from California, Florida, Illinois, Maine, and Ohio. The second institute, called the Institute for Statewide Literacy Initiatives (ISLI), was convened in June 2002 and included participants from Georgia, Louisiana, Nevada, New Jersey, and (for a second year) Florida.

An incentive for states' participation was the opportunity to formulate plans that would help them secure the federal Reading First funding for kindergarten through grade three, which at that point was just becoming available. State teams consisted of representatives from the state department of education, the governor's office, and leading institutions of higher education. Although obtaining guidance for developing Reading First applications was a primary motive for the states, the institutes' curriculum focused on the skills teachers need to provide initial literacy instruction (phonological awareness, phonics, fluency) and to prepare students during the primary and postprimary grades for later literacy development (supporting oral language skills, vocabulary development, comprehension, and world knowledge). During the weeklong institutes, participants were exposed to content about literacy development and instruction, and teams were charged with working together to formulate state literacy plans. Steps in the state plan development included constructing a set of goals before arriving at the institute, working on an action plan during the institute, and eventually presenting the action plan to other participants at the close of the institute.

Supported by funding and resources from the NGA Center,[1] four of the nine states that participated in one or both institutes — Florida, Louisiana, Maine, and New Jersey — subsequently formulated plans that extended their states' focus from the primary grades to the arena of adolescent literacy. One purpose of this paper is to describe the range of approaches developed by these four states to address the literacy needs of students in grades four through twelve. In addition, we explore the degree to which these four state plans reflect content delivered at the institutes, and we consider the possibility that the institute-fostered teamwork helped develop the relationships that made the adolescent literacy planning process feasible. The development of K–12 literacy plans in these four states suggests that access to research-based information and structured opportunities for team planning might promote improved educational policies in other states as well.

Obstacles to Successful Educational Change

The goal of Reading First is to prepare students to learn to read well by the end of third grade. Through the $1 billion-per-year federal program, states and districts with approved applications receive support to establish scientifically based reading programs in their classrooms from kindergarten through third grade. Although Reading First has been associated with many good outcomes (Scott, 2006), it is now widely recognized that the inoculation model it instantiates is insufficient for promoting the literacy outcomes our country desires. Reading First–supported changes must be complemented by giving ongoing attention to reading instruction in grades four and five, content-area literacy skills in grades six through twelve, and effective, targeted interventions for students falling behind at any point in their literacy development. A number of states have embraced this expanded agenda, in some cases with support from the NGA Center, which has awarded resources and provided technical assistance through two grant programs — Reading to Achieve: State Policies to Support Adolescent Literacy and High School Honor States — to help states develop adolescent literacy plans. However, other states, including two that participated in the literacy institutes at Harvard, have still not developed policies focused specifically on adolescent literacy challenges. This fact highlights the difficulty inherent in this work, even for states in which policymakers are well informed about the importance of improving adolescent literacy.

Reading First, the success of its implementation in various states, and, more importantly, questions about whether it has improved the key literacy outcomes of primary-grade and older students, can be seen as a specific case of a more general problem: When and how does social science research get used in policymaking (and, implicitly, why does it not get used more widely and more effectively)? The use and usability of research knowledge in policymaking has received systematic attention since the 1970s (e.g., Lindblom & Cohen, 1979; Rein, 1976; Weiss, 1978), continuing into this millennium (Fuhrman, 2001; Kirst, 2000), and has generated a body of scholarly work much too large to review here. However, recurrent themes in this literature highlight the challenge of communicating relevant research findings to policymakers (e.g., Lagemann, 1997; Shonkoff, 2000). Even effective communication is insufficient when it comes to ensuring that policy changes actually take place (Weiss, 1978; Weiss & Bucuvalas, 1980). The influence of research findings is rarely immediate but typically emerges over time, through a process that has been called "enlightenment" (Weiss, 1980).

In planning and implementing the literacy institutes, we were well aware of two of the elements the long history of policy-focused research had identified as crucial to effective research-based policy change: the need to provide knowledge in a usable form, and the need for workable structures, including willing and motivated participants, to translate this knowledge into real change (McDonnell, 1988). The goal of this paper is to show how the work of the literacy institutes directly addressed both the usability of knowledge and the formation of workable structures.

However, it is worth noting that the institutes also had the benefit of good timing. As it turned out, the message of the institutes anticipated a national shift in thinking about literacy policy as a K–12 concern rather than solely a K–3 issue. For example, in 2003 the Carnegie Corporation of New York started funding activities to bring issues of adolescent literacy into central focus, including the need to provide ongoing literacy instruction to postprimary-grade students, the need to provide remedial services to struggling adolescents, and the need to develop literacy standards for content-area teaching and for these teachers' literacy coaches. Four years earlier, in 1999, the Alliance for Excellent Education was founded to promote adolescent literacy achievement, decrease high school dropout rates, and improve college access.

In 2005, the Strategic Education Research Partnership established its first field site devoted to issues of middle school literacy in the Boston Public Schools. In addition, the International Reading Association established a special focus on adolescent literacy and generated professional development activities, reading materials, and guidance for teachers of adolescent readers.[2] The importance of adolescent literacy as a complement to early literacy was also communicated to policymakers and school-level practitioners in documents such as the NGA Center's *Reading to Achieve: A Governor's Guide to Adolescent Literacy* (Berman & Biancarosa, 2005) and the National Association of Secondary School Principals' report, *Creating a Culture of Literacy* (Phillips, 2005). In other words, although Reading First mandated and funded activities in the primary grades, states, districts, and professional associations began to realize that such a focus was too narrow. In fact, since 2002, the policy context has shifted sufficiently that a middle school counterpart to Reading First is under consideration as part of the reauthorization of No Child Left Behind. Without such a shift in the national discourse, it seems unlikely that states would have invested the necessary time and energy in the formulation of literacy plans that specifically addressed the literacy needs of adolescent students and their teachers. In that sense, the timing of the institutes may have added resonance and urgency to the message they provided.

Usability of Knowledge

A presupposition of current federal policies for education is that successful reform must be built on knowledge of how to *achieve* the desired ends — that is, reform needs to rest on a foundation of "research-based" approaches to promoting literacy achievement. The literacy institutes were designed to synthesize that knowledge in the domain of literacy instruction and make it available to the participants in ways that facilitated its further dissemination to other key actors in their states. We hoped that both the content presented at the institutes and the modes of presentation would serve as models states could replicate in local literacy institutes.

The goal of the institutes was to bring together state teams to review current research and best practices in preparing teachers to teach reading to elementary-aged students, with a focus on literacy outcomes in the middle school and high school years. The content of the institutes provided subject matter relevant to cross-grade literacy development and a context within which states could lay the groundwork for more comprehensive approaches to subsequent literacy improvement. Efforts were made to enhance the usability of the knowledge shared at the literacy institute by providing state teams with the lectures and activities in forms that could easily be used in state-level replication activities (e.g., easily accessed reading materials, CD-ROMs with lectures and examples, and streaming video). Teams were also provided with a briefing book compiled by the NGA Center, which included information and resources for policymakers seeking to build partnerships for improving teacher education and literacy achievement.

Institute content was developed during a two-day session by a design team of literacy researchers and educators; this team then served as the faculty for the institutes, delivering the material to participants through lectures and small-group discussions. The team incorporated research-based advances in understanding the process of reading development, the characteristics of optimal instruction, and the impact of factors such as current demographic shifts (e.g., an increase in the number of English-language learners, or ELLs) on the tasks that teachers face. In addition, the content emphasized the need to keep the challenges of later literacy tasks in mind while preparing primary-grade readers, as well as the need to provide teacher education focused on vocabulary, comprehension, assessment, oral language development, second-language learners' specific language-support requirements, and other topics not specific to Reading First objectives.

Table 1 specifies the themes of the institutes, which included phonological awareness, phonics, fluency, vocabulary, comprehension, assessment, ELLs, oral language, and writing. Table 1 also identifies which themes related specifically to the Reading First guidelines and which went beyond them to anticipate the kinds of concerns that would emerge with the later focus on adolescent literacy.

An example of a content focus from the institutes may serve to clarify how the material went beyond that defined by the parameters of Reading First. The team presented research on the role of oral vocabulary knowledge in reading comprehension and also demonstrated techniques that have been shown to be effective in teaching primary-grade students the vocabulary they will encounter in middle-grade texts. The team emphasized the differences that exist between native English speakers' and ELLs' knowledge of oral vocabulary (particularly all-purpose academic terms), and demonstrated the resulting implications for reading comprehension success (see papers in Wagner, Muse, & Tannenbaum, 2006, for examples of relevant content).

Formation of Workable Structures

We believe that another key element in effective reform is the establishment of a well-functioning structure that will allow the work to get done. To develop a comprehensive literacy plan, many different players within each state need to be involved, including (at the very least) education policymakers, advocates, researchers, and teacher educators. Furthermore, these participants need to make the work a shared priority, hold themselves and each other responsible for its advocacy, and develop a consistent way of talking about it so that the message is heard. The literacy institutes attracted people from various relevant sectors within each state and created cross-role state teams that had the opportunity to develop common goals and interpersonal trust within the context of the institutes.

The structure of the institutes was designed to foster development of within- and cross-role state teams that could assume the task of thinking comprehensively about literacy development. For example, state education agency staff with responsibility for early literacy and professional development met in cross-state discussion groups to review research, suggest activities that addressed their program responsibilities, and learn from each other, while at other times, all the different members of each state team came together to work on their action plans. Based on what was learned from the first literacy institute, planning for the second involved a more stringent set of criteria for participation: First, a commitment from the governor's office in each state was required. Second, applicant teams had to have been formed at the state level, with some contact among members even before the institute began. As a result, the institute helped each state team constitute itself as a design team for further state-level efforts.

Prior to arrival at the institute sessions, each state team was asked to prepare a document identifying aspects of literacy instruction its state was doing well, either by virtue of addressing those features in preservice or in-service teacher preparation or by attention to those features in state standards and assessments. At the beginning of the institute, each state team made a presentation summarizing the context for its work, including prior accomplishments and looming challenges. There were recurrent themes across the states in terms of both accomplishments and needs. Some of the accomplishments included the following:

- implementing rigorous curriculum standards for English/language arts;
- increasing reading course requirements for teacher certification;
- establishing regional and statewide professional development structures; and
- collaborating with school districts.

Additionally, many of the states reported similar challenges that needed to be addressed:

- how to incorporate scientifically based reading research in accreditation standards;
- how to develop a common knowledge base in reading instruction for preservice and in-service teachers; and
- how to disseminate material and content representing research-based best practices in literacy education to teacher-education programs and through professional development.

State teams used the content from these presentations as a guide while discussing and developing their individual literacy action plans throughout the weeklong institute.

State Plans for Adolescent Literacy

This section highlights the initiatives led by four of the participating states in the years following the two institutes. Supported by NGA grants, all four of these states went on to develop and promote research-based adolescent literacy policies and best practices that reflected the knowledge they had gained at the institutes. In follow-up interviews, institute participants from these four states told us that they had developed adolescent literacy approaches in response to poor literacy achievement among postprimary students, even in cases where

TABLE 1   *Analysis of the Messages Focused On in the Institute Content*

Topics	*Reading First: Focus on primary reading outcomes*	*Reading First Enhanced: Preparing primary-grade students for postprimary reading tasks*	*Beyond Reading First: Postprimary reading instruction*
Phono-logical Awareness	Systematic instruction in kindergarten and first grade	Systematic instruction for students who need it, limited to no more than 20 hours per lifetime	Not appropriate after first grade
Phonics (Word Study)	Systematically taught in all primary grades	Systematically taught in a way that is integrated with a focus on comprehension	Instruction in attacking long, multisyllabic, multimorphemic, technical words may still be needed
Fluency	Procedures to develop automaticity, e.g., repeated readings with feedback (guided reading)	Motivated repeated readings, e.g., poems, performances, readers' theater, and providing models of fluent reading	Assess and provide repeated reading practice if necessary
Vocabulary	Required (research base from postprimary grades)	Requires systematic, daily instruction linked to spelling, writing, read-alouds, book discussions; provides for active use of newly taught words	Expand to focus on academic and technical vocabulary, polysemy, etymology, morpho-logical analysis
Compre-hension	Strategy instruction (research base from postprimary grades)	Multiple forms of comprehension instruction, including discussion of read-alouds with multiple texts, multiple genres, focus on developing world knowledge	Content-area specific reading; explicit instruction in discourse structures, word use, and grammar needed for math, science, social studies, and English/ language arts
Assessment	Focus on fluency assessments to differentiate instruction	Suite of assessments designed to help in differen-tiating instruction, guiding instruction, selecting texts	Literacy assessments needed to assign struggling students to appropriate interven-tions, monitor progress
English-Language Learners (ELLs)	Not addressed	Analyzing native language literacy skills, fostering transfer, special focus on using primary language (L1) knowledge in developing secondary language (L2) vocabulary and world knowledge	Responding to variability in ELL population, using L1 and L2 assessment to identify appropriate instruction for late arrivals

Topics	Reading First: Focus on primary reading outcomes	Reading First Enhanced: Preparing primary-grade students for postprimary reading tasks	Beyond Reading First: Postprimary reading instruction
Oral Language	Not addressed	Development of oral language skills a goal in its own right; also a mechanism for developing comprehension skills to be applied to literate contexts	Continued development of oral language performance (academic talk, discourse skills) and use of discussion to promote comprehension
Writing	Not addressed	Part of a rich literacy program; reinforces spelling, vocabulary, comprehension, and world knowledge	Using writing to respond to readings, deepen comprehension, and practice academic language

the states were seeing improvements in reading performance among students in kindergarten through grade three.

One way to summarize the four state plans is to revisit Table 1 and examine information from each state about how it dealt with the topics listed there. Every state does not address each topic, and the ways they do address the topics vary widely. In late 2007, we interviewed knowledgeable individuals in the education departments of these four states to determine how they were addressing these topics in their state standards, state assessments, teacher-preparation programs, professional development, or other state initiatives. We present their responses, somewhat condensed, in Table 2. Then we provide a brief descriptive summary of the attention each of these four states has given to adolescent literacy issues, and we describe some cross-cutting themes.

Florida

With funding from the NGA Center's Reading to Achieve grant, literacy efforts begun years ago in Florida for early literacy have expanded to include policies and practices to support effective literacy instruction in secondary schools. Even though Florida realized marked improvements in early literacy performance, state data revealed stagnant or declining literacy performance among students in the middle grades. Upon receiving the NGA grant, Florida conducted an audit of the state's K–12 reading plans to determine what was needed to meet Florida's 2012 student proficiency goal. It also held multiple workgroup sessions to develop legislative and education-practice recommendations. As a result of the audit and workgroup recommendations, Florida has begun to lay out a five-year K–12 literacy plan that incorporates current and planned literacy initiatives and forecasts spending needs for entities supported by reading funding (e.g., universities and centers that provide professional development).

The legislature acted to support Florida's literacy activities by securing in statute the Just Read, Florida! office; establishing reading as an annually recurring categorical fund in the state education finance program; placing literacy coaches in the lowest-performing schools; and strengthening requirements for middle school promotion and high school graduation. With state reading funds, Florida has revised guidelines for districts' K–12 Comprehensive Research-Based Reading Plan and provided literacy-related professional development to teachers, principals, and reading coaches. Research is under way to identify the best practices in — and examine the effectiveness of — professional development training and reading coaches. The state is also conducting a study to determine the cost required to provide effective education supports for the lowest-performing students.

Louisiana

Established in 2006, Louisiana's literacy plan is designed to address the learning needs and improve the literacy rates of all students in the state, in various programs ranging from prekindergarten through adult education. The research-based plan was developed as one component of the NGA-funded state high school redesign effort. The instructional model, research-based programs and strategies, and professional development components of the plan are all closely aligned with the model used in Louisiana's Reading First program, but are grade level specific in order to meet the needs of learners at various stages of their education. Louisiana's plan requires a schoolwide model with substantial district and state support and integrates a powerful instructional design from prekindergarten through the twelfth grade. Key components of the state's plan include the following:

- a three-tiered instructional model;
- scientifically based research programs and strategies;
- extended time for reading and learning in grade-level-appropriate amounts;
- ongoing formative and summative assessments to monitor progress, indicate interventions, and assess the model's effectiveness; and
- support for high-quality literacy instruction through preservice training and professional development.

With the support of the NGA High School Honor States grant, Louisiana is also piloting catch-up programs in schools across the state. These pilot schools are providing "double-dose" instruction in reading and math using accelerated curricula selected through an extensive external-review process. Treatment and control groups of students in each school will enable the collection of effectiveness data. At the local level, preliminary results from the 2006–2007 catch-up pilot programs in reading and math are promising. In addition, the state recently received a grant to support collaboration among elementary, middle, and high schools to strengthen literacy across the curriculum. This project includes online professional development for teachers, summer training for literacy facilitators, and the development of adolescent literacy guides for teachers, principals, and local education agency staff.

Maine

As part of the state's NGA High School Honor States grant activities, Maine established an Adolescent Literacy Framework, which includes a self-assessment tool for determining resource capacity and an action-planning guide to develop schoolwide literacy plans. The Adolescent Literacy Framework, tools, and materials — collectively known as the Universal Literacy Elements for Deeper and More Powerful Content Learning and the Literacy Plan Tool Kit — will be disseminated and serve as the guiding documents for literacy professional development training for secondary school teachers, principals, literacy specialists, career and technical education literacy teachers, and academic support teachers.

New Jersey

In response to growing diversity in the state of New Jersey and the urgent need to improve student performance in the middle grades, the state's education department developed a model called Literacy is Essential for Adolescent Development and Success (LEADS) and modified the supporting research matrix (which reflects research highlighted at the institutes) to address and accommodate the special needs of the ELL student populations. LEADS is the New Jersey state model for literacy in the middle grades. With funding from the NGA Center's Reading to Achieve grant, New Jersey has piloted the refined model in fourteen school districts (with more than 600 district staff trained), which entailed six training modules and on-site coaching and technical assistance for participating teachers. As a result of the training, the New Jersey Department of Education produced a comprehensive training manual and a DVD with scenes from classes in action, along with interviews of teachers and students. Next, the state plans to extend the LEADS model to those schools and districts that have been identified as "in need of improvement," encouraging them to adopt LEADS as their restructure design.

Cross-State Themes

These four states have taken similar approaches to improving literacy from kindergarten through twelfth grade. In all cases, professional development is a central focus, although both the mechanism for delivering it and the target audiences differ somewhat. Three of the four states have instituted literacy coaching as a strategy for providing professional development, and all have used some form of intensive literacy academy for various subsets of teachers. Online professional development has been used by Florida for principals and by Louisiana to introduce some of the literacy components to teachers.

TABLE 2 *State K–12 Literacy Plans' Incorporation of the Institute Messages*

State (State Literacy Plan Information)	Florida (http://www.justreadflorida.com/)	Louisiana (http://www.doe.state.la.us/lde/uploads/8629.pdf)	Maine (http://www.maine.gov/education/literacy/)	New Jersey (http://www.nj.gov/education/abbotts/; http://www.nj.gov/education/code/current/title6a/chap10a.pdf)
Topics				
Phonological Awareness	• K–3 and 4/5 summer reading academies • Reading endorsement • Quarterly professional development for coaches • 90-minute required reading block • Annual leadership conference • Florida Center for Reading Research (FCRR) reports, articles, student center activities, and PowerPoint presentations • Delta (online professional development for principals) • Literacy Essentials and Reading Network (LEaRN), an online professional development program for teachers, coaches, and principals • Required in teacher-preparation programs, effective 2008	• Content in coaches' meetings • Language Essentials for Teachers of Reading and Spelling (LETRS) professional development • Extensive study on phonological awareness continuum • Benchmark screening assessment	• Addressed in state standards for grades preK–2	• Literacy coach (including Special Education Literacy Resource Coach) training • Assessed using screening instruments • Addressed in state standards in K–3 • 90- to 120-minute language arts block
Phonics (Word Study)	• K–3 and 4/5 summer reading academies • Reading endorsement • Quarterly professional development for coaches • 90-minute required reading block • Annual leadership conference • FCRR reports, articles, student center activities, and PowerPoint presentations • Delta (online professional development for principals) • LEaRN (online professional development for teachers, coaches, and principals) • Required in teacher-preparation programs, effective 2008	• Content in coaches' meetings • LETRS professional development • Benchmark screening assessment • Preservice teacher standards	• State standards and assessments in grades 3–5 only	• Literacy coach (including Special Education Literacy Resource Coach) training • Systematically taught in primary grades • Word study (e.g., cognates, multisyllabic words, polysemic words) • Assessed using screening instrument • Addressed in state standards K–8 (later as decoding and word recognition) • 90- to 120-minute language arts block

Fluency	• K–3 and 4/5 summer reading academies • Reading endorsement • Quarterly professional development for coaches • 90-minute required reading block • Annual leadership conference • FCRR reports, articles, student center activities and PowerPoint presentations • Delta (online professional development for principals) • LEaRN (online professional development for teachers, coaches, and principals) • Required in teacher-preparation programs, effective 2008	• State literacy conference sessions (2006 & 2007) • Benchmark screening assessment for grades K–3 (all schools) and K–5 (in select districts)	• Assessed at classroom level	• Literacy coach (including Special Education Literacy Resource Coach) training • Assessed using screening instruments and ongoing assessments (benchmarks) • Addressed in state standards beginning in kindergarten • 90- to 120-minute language arts block (80 to 120 minutes in middle grades)
Vocabulary	• K–3 and 4/5 summer reading academies • Reading endorsement • Quarterly professional development for coaches • 90-minute required reading block • Annual leadership conference • FCRR reports, articles, student center activities and PowerPoint presentations • Delta (online professional development for principals) • LEaRN (online professional development for teachers, coaches, and principals) • Content-area reading professional development • Required in teacher-preparation programs, effective 2008	• Content in coaches' meetings • Book studies • Online professional development workshops	• State standards and assessment • Addressed in teacher academies • Addressed in literacy framework	• Literacy coach (including Special Education Literacy Resource Coach) training • Attention to academic vocabulary • Instruction in cognates to support acquisition of second language (Spanish) • Read-alouds in all grade levels preK–12 (daily preK–8), using above-grade-level text • Addressed in state standards beginning in kindergarten • 90- to 120-minute language arts block (80 to 120 minutes in middle grades)

TABLE 2   *State K–12 Literacy Plans' Incorporation of the Institute Messages (continued)*

State (State Literacy Plan Information)	Florida (http://www.justreadflorida.com/)	Louisiana (http://www.doe.state.la.us/lde/uploads/8629.pdf)	Maine (http://www.maine.gov/education/literacy/)	New Jersey (http://www.nj.gov/education/abbotts/; http://www.nj.gov/education/code/current/title6a/chap10a.pdf)
Comprehension	• K–3 and 4/5 summer reading academies • Reading endorsement • Quarterly professional development for coaches • 90-minute required reading block • Annual leadership conference • FCRR reports, articles, student center activities and PowerPoint presentations • Delta (online professional development for principals) • LEaRN (online professional development for teachers, coaches, and principals) • Content-area reading professional development • Required in teacher-preparation programs, effective 2008	• State literacy conference sessions (2006 & 2007) • Content in coaches' meetings • Benchmark screening assessment in grades K–12 • Online professional development workshops	• State standards • Addressed extensively in teacher academies • Addressed in literacy framework	• Literacy coach (including Special Education Literacy Resource Coach) training • Small group/guided reading K–8 • Read-alouds in all grade levels preK–12 (daily preK–8), using above-grade-level text • Addressed in state standards beginning in kindergarten • 90- to 120-minute language arts block with small group instruction (80 to 120 minutes in middle grades) • Guided reading K–8
Assessment	• Progress Monitoring Reporting Network (PMRN) through FCRR • State-provided assessments (DAR, ERDA, Fox in a Box) • Dynamic Indicators of Basic Early Literacy Skills (DIBELS) training and administration • K–12 Comprehensive Reading Plan Decision Tree • Consistent assessments in Reading First schools • Content-area professional development	• DIBELS professional development and administration • System to Enhance Educational Performance (STEEP) (grades 4–12) professional development and administration in literacy pilot sites • Reading First and K–3 literacy pilot sites • Data Summits providing extensive study of DIBELS site data and formulation of action plans	• Addressed in teacher academies • Addressed in literacy framework	• Literacy coach (including Special Education Literacy Resource Coach) training on analysis and use of formative and summative assessments to inform instruction and monitor implementation and effectiveness of curricula • State-level training on collection and analysis of data • Mini assessment conference sponsored by New Jersey Reading First Office • Recommendations/mandates for four levels of assessment: screening, ongoing, summative, and diagnostic

English Language Learners (ELLs)	• K–3 summer reading academies • Reading endorsement • Annual leadership conference • FCRR reports and articles • English for Speakers of Other Languages (ESOL) endorsement crosswalk to reading endorsement	• Contracted with an English as a Second Language (ESL) specialist to provide statewide professional development		• Bilingual law that supports native language instruction • Literacy coach (including Special Education Literacy Resource Coach) training • Matrix of recommended strategies and research • Instruction to ensure Cognitively Academic Language Proficiency (CALP) at all grade levels • Cognate instruction • ESL instruction
Oral Language	• Consistent oral language assessment in Reading First schools (Peabody Picture Vocabulary Test)	• Included in the English/Language Arts (ELA) Standards, Benchmarks, and Grade Level Expectations at all grade levels • Integrated into the instructional practices and content of the Louisiana Comprehensive Curriculum	• State standards • Addressed in literacy framework	• Recommended instructional practice • Increased emphasis at all grade levels
Writing	• K–3 and 4/5 summer reading academies • 90-minute elementary reading block • Annual leadership conference	• Provided statewide professional development	• Addressed in teacher academies • State standards and assessments • Addressed in literacy framework	• State-level training for literacy coaches and district personnel • Integral component of state's middle-grades literacy model (LEADS: Literacy is Essential for Adolescent Development and Success) • Assessed at state level beginning at grade 3

TABLE 2 *State K–12 Literacy Plans' Incorporation of the Institute Messages (continued)*

State (State Literacy Plan Information)	Florida (http://www.justreadflorida.com/)	Louisiana (http://www.doe.state. la.us/lde/uploads/8629. pdf)	Maine (http://www.maine. gov/education/ literacy/)	New Jersey (http://www.nj.gov/education/abbotts/; http://www.nj.gov/education/code/ current/title6a/chap10a.pdf)
Additional Steps	• Permanent funding source for reading through a categorical allocation to each school district	• Literacy observation tools (e.g., Literacy Observation Tool, Adolescent-Literacy Observation Tool) • Intervention observation tools • Extensive professional development for literacy coaches and content-area teachers on content-area literacy strategies (grades 4–12) in literacy pilot sites • Louisiana Literacy Plan for K–12 students	• Development of a comprehensive preK–adult education literacy plan	• Special Education Literacy Resource coaches in more than 40 districts to support special educators and general education teachers • Integration of content areas (science, social studies, etc.) into literacy instruction at all grade levels, particularly through the middle-grade LEADS model • Project-based learning a critical component of LEADS model (connected to community)

Another recurrent response is to modify state standards for student performance and/or teacher preparation; all four states have initiated new or expanded standards specifications. Assessments addressing the various literacy domains are suggested or required in all four states. Florida and New Jersey have required 90-minute literacy blocks explicitly designed to provide time to focus on the many facets of literacy skill.

It is notable that Florida has formulated an extensive set of policy guidelines with considerable specification of how the state is responding to each domain (see Table 2), whereas Maine has a much less differentiated set of responses. Nonetheless, explicit attention to oral language, writing, and content-area reading is visible in all four state plans, and clear consideration is given to ELLs in all plans but Maine's.

Conclusion and Implications

This account of the adolescent literacy plans developed by the four states suggests an understanding among the states that literacy development extends well beyond the primary grades, that instructional resources focused on literacy development in grades four through twelve are crucial, and that while interventions for the most severely struggling readers should be delivered by teachers who specialize in reading, all content-area teachers need to promote literacy skills.

This understanding, which has replaced the "inoculation model" of literacy development (i.e., teach students to read at a third-grade level by the end of third grade and they will do fine thereafter), is a powerful impetus for revising state standards and assessments, developing identification and intervention strategies, revising standards for the certification of secondary content-area teachers, and providing professional development focused on literacy support to all teachers.

In the years since the institutes were held, some states that did not participate (e.g., Massachusetts) have gone on to produce well-formulated adolescent literacy plans, and some states that did participate (e.g., Georgia) have not. Still, it is noteworthy that the four states we focus on here produced plans that showed an awareness of key content taught in the institutes, and participants with whom we spoke reported that they had taken leadership roles in developing these plans after their participation in the institute. Clearly, offering state literacy institutes does not guarantee that all participants will be able to implement strong literacy policies in their states. Resources at the state level are typically scarce, and education policy decisions are often politically fraught. Nevertheless, if researchers want their understanding of best practices to inform large-scale policy decisions, it is incumbent upon them to reach out to policymakers and open the lines of communication. Therefore, we encourage other schools of education that have academic resources related to literacy research and instruction to support states in promoting adolescent literacy. For example, they might do this by hosting literacy institutes to convey the most current research on best practices and by providing teams with access to policymaking guidance. It is through the many resources at colleges and universities that states may find the knowledge they need to create effective adolescent literacy plans, and it is colleges and universities that have the freedom to make research-based recommendations that go beyond current government policy.

As states noted in their self-assessments prior to attending the institutes, their greatest challenges lay in ensuring that reading research drove policies and in providing high-quality teacher professional development. States and schools of education might benefit from institute-like experiences that give teams of key stakeholders the chance to learn about the most recent research and to determine together how they will apply these lessons to practice and policy in their own states. Additionally, the next cohort of states interested in improving the literacy achievement of their postprimary students may learn from the experiences of these and other states that have taken the lead in applying research about effective adolescent literacy instruction and in instituting the policies necessary to promote such instruction. Ongoing evaluations of the literacy coach model, for example, may offer lessons about how best to implement such a model as part of a state's literacy plan. Moreover, because additional information is needed about the kinds of state-level policies that raise adolescents' literacy achievement most effectively, those who wish to support states in developing strong literacy plans may also wish to help them design plans to evaluate the success of their policies.

As NCLB is being considered for reauthorization, there is also discussion at the federal level about extending the funding for interventions, professional development, and literacy curricula beyond the primary grades through a funding initiative called Striving Readers, which expands on the current initiative of the same name. Though proposed federal supports for adolescent literacy may not be included in the final version of the legislation, the attention the proposal has received and the appropriation of federal funding for research on this topic suggests that the message about the importance of adolescent literacy instruction has been heard in Washington and in several state capitals. Authorized in 2005 and funding eight grants totaling $30 million in 2006–2007, the current federal Striving Readers program supports the implementation and evaluation of research-based reading interventions for struggling secondary school readers in high-risk schools.

The several states that have developed adolescent literacy plans provide a preview of the types of proposals that might be submitted for extended federal funding if it becomes available. Understanding how they differ, as well as what they have in common, may contribute to the development of guidelines for effective adolescent literacy planning. Thus far, no cross-state analysis has been undertaken to examine how states obtained the necessary expertise and person power to develop their applications for Reading First funding, or how they have planned to address specific issues of adolescent literacy. We hope that the descriptive analysis presented here represents a first step toward a more systematic and comprehensive cross-state analysis. Such an examination could provide guidance for states not yet fully aware of how much they need effective policies to attack the problem of struggling adolescent readers.

Notes

1. States that were awarded funding through the NGA Center's High School Honor States program were Arkansas, Delaware, Indiana, Louisiana, Maine, Massachusetts, Michigan, Minnesota, Rhode Island, and Virginia. This program funded the development and implementation of comprehensive plans to improve high school graduation and college-readiness rates. States that were awarded funding through the NGA Center's Reading to Achieve: State Policies to Support Adolescent Literacy project were Alabama, Arizona, Delaware, Florida, Idaho, Massachusetts, New Jersey, and North Carolina. Reading to Achieve assists state policymakers in developing strategies and taking action to raise adolescent literacy achievement.
2. To learn more about the Carnegie Corporation of New York's efforts to focus attention on adolescent literacy, see www.carnegie.org/literacy. More information on the Alliance for Excellent Education can be found at www.all4ed.org, and additional information on the Strategic Education Research Partnership is available at www.serpinstitute.org. The International Reading Association's materials on adolescent literacy can be retrieved from www.reading.org/resources/issues/focus_adolescent.html.

References

Berman, I., & Biancarosa, G. (2005). *Reading to achieve: A governor's guide to adolescent literacy.* Washington, DC: National Governors Association Center for Best Practices. Retrieved November 15, 2007, from http://www.nga.org/Files/pdf/0510GOVGUIDE LITERACY.PDF

Center on Education Policy. (2007). *Answering the question that matters most: Has student achievement increased since No Child Left Behind?* Washington, DC: Center on Education Policy. Retrieved December 12, 2007, from http://www.cep-dc.org/index. cfm?fuseaction=document.showDocumentByID&nodeID=1&DocumentID=200

Fuhrman, S. (2001, July 17). The policy influence of education research and R&D centers. Testimony to the U.S. House of Representatives Committee on Education and the Workforce, Washington, DC.

Kirst, M. W. (2000). Bridging educational research and educational policymaking. *Oxford Review of Education, 26,* 379–391.

Lagemann, E. C. (1997). Contested terrain: A history of education research in the United States, 1890–1990. *Educational Researcher, 26,* 5–17.

Lee, J., Grigg, W., & Donahue, P. (2007). *The nation's report card: Reading 2007.* Washington, DC: U.S. Department of Education, National Center for Education Statistics. Retrieved December 15, 2007, from http://nces.ed.gov/pubsearch/

Lindblom, C. E., & Cohen, D. K. (1979). *Usable knowledge: Social science and social problem solving.* New Haven, CT: Yale University Press.

McDonnell, L. M. (1988). Can education research speak to state policy? *Theory Into Practice, 27,* 91–97.

Perie, M., Grigg, W., & Donahue, P. (2005). *The nation's report card: Reading 2005.* Washington, DC: U.S. Department of Education, National Center for Education Statistics. Retrieved December 15, 2007, from http://nces.ed.gov/pubsearch/

Phillips, M. (2005). *Creating a culture of literacy: A guide for middle and high school principals.* Reston, VA: National Association of Secondary School Principals. Retrieved November 12, 2007, from http://www.principals.org

Rein, M. (1976). *Social science and public policy.* Middlesex, England: Penguin Education.

Scott, C. (2006). *Keeping watch on Reading First.* Washington, DC: Center on Education Policy. Retrieved November 15, 2007, from http://www.cep-dc.org

Shonkoff, J. P. (2000). Science, policy, and practice: Three cultures in search of a shared mission. *Child Development, 71,* 181–187.

UNESCO Institute for Statistics. (2003). *Literacy skills for the world of tomorrow — Further results from PISA.* Paris, France: Organisation for Economic Cooperation and Development.

UNESCO Institute for Statistics. (2007). *PISA 2006: Science competencies for tomorrow's world.* Paris, France: Organisation for Economic Cooperation and Development.

Wagner, R., Muse, A., & Tannenbaum, K. (Eds.). (2006). *Vocabulary acquisition: Implications for reading comprehension.* New York: Guilford Press.

Weiss, C. H. (1978). Improving the linkage between social research and public policy. In L. E. Lynn (Ed.), *Knowledge and policy: The uncertain connection.* Washington, DC: National Academy of Sciences.

Weiss, C. H. (1980). Knowledge creep and decision accretion. *Science Communication, 1,* 381–404.

Weiss, C. H., & Bucuvalas, M. J. (1980). *Social science research and decision-making.* New York: Columbia University Press.

Beyond Writing Next: *A Discussion of Writing Research and Instructional Uncertainty*

DAVID COKER
WILLIAM E. LEWIS
University of Delaware

Drawing on their experiences as high school writing instructors, researchers, and teacher trainers, David Coker and William Lewis examine an often overlooked dimension of adolescent literacy: writing proficiency. The authors explore recent research on the skills and strategies students need in order to write with competence and describe analyses of interventions that help students attain writing mastery. They also address divisions and gaps in the field of writing research and instruction and offer suggestions for overcoming these rifts in order to advance understanding of adolescent writing development and effective writing instruction.

> I had not a dispute but a disquisition with Dilke, on various subjects; several things dovetailed in my mind, & at once it struck me, what quality went to form a Man of Achievement especially in literature & which Shakespeare possessed so enormously — I mean Negative Capability, that is when man is capable of being in uncertainties, Mysteries, doubts without any irritable reaching after fact & reason.
>
> —John Keats, in a letter to his brothers, George and Thomas

Although the specific "disquisition" that Keats (1975) describes in his famous letter to his brothers has long been forgotten, Keats's expression of his theory of "negative capability" has not. In this short passage to George and Thomas, Keats gave voice to the aesthetic of a generation of Romantic thinkers and writers who celebrated human intuition, embraced the uncertainty of the universe, and lauded the writers and the writing process that could probe its subtle mysteries. While Keats was describing what he believed to be an essential trait of the successful poet — a type of aesthetic and spiritual flexibility — he

Harvard Educational Review   Vol. 78   No. 1   Spring 2008

could just as easily have been describing the role that today's educators often must adopt when considering how to communicate the mysteries of effective writing to adolescent student writers, who so desperately need help. However, unlike the liberating conception of negative capability that Keats advances, the "uncertainties, Mysteries and doubts" as to what constitutes effective writing instruction are not at all liberating to teachers who are looking for concrete solutions to these problems. Teachers are frustrated and confused as they search for reasoned approaches to teaching writing effectively and for research that can help them make crucial instructional decisions to help their students.

The purpose of this article is to address the important role that writing plays in adolescent literacy and to suggest ways of giving classroom teachers the tools to help students develop the writing skills they need for future success. As former high school writing teachers who are currently researchers of writing and instructors of writing courses for elementary and middle school teachers and teacher candidates, we understand how important this knowledge is to those who are going into these classrooms. Moreover, our experience informs our understanding of how unprepared and anxious many teachers feel when it comes to teaching and assessing student writing. However, we also understand the complexity and tensions in the field of writing research and how they impact the ways research is translated into practice.

To provide a context for understanding both the importance and complexity of the topic, we begin by situating writing within a broader discussion of adolescent literacy. We examine recent research that details the current crisis in the writing proficiency of American students and the relatively stagnant literacy development of students in middle and high schools (Graham & Perin, 2007a). We then explore the difficulty of mastering the cognitive processes behind writing well and discuss analyses of writing interventions that have proven effective in helping students master these processes. We begin with a discussion of three recent publications by Steve Graham and Dolores Perin (2007a, 2007b, 2007c) in which they review the latest research on writing instruction in secondary schools. The first of these publications, *Writing Next* (Graham & Perin, 2007a), can be seen as a companion to a widely distributed report on adolescent reading called *Reading Next* (Biancarosa & Snow, 2004); both were commissioned by the Carnegie Corporation of New York. However, because it offers a meta-analysis of recent empirical research rather than a survey of the literature, *Writing Next* differs considerably from *Reading Next* in its scope and methods. The second paper (Graham & Perin, 2007c) provides a detailed technical discussion of the meta-analysis of the learning-to-write studies described in *Writing Next*. The third paper (Graham & Perin, 2007b) extends the authors' instructional recommendations by synthesizing single-subject and qualitative studies of adolescent writing that were excluded from the *Writing Next* meta-analysis.

Together, these papers provide a useful "state-of-the-field" report and offer teachers a reasonable approach to choosing strategies that can meet the needs of their students. Nevertheless, there is still a lot to be learned about effective writing instruction. There are a number of divisions within the field that impede the development and application of effective approaches to teaching writing. One of these impediments is the significant bifurcation in the literature about what constitutes effective research on writing. This bifurcation is characterized as the divide between the quantitative writing research conducted in educational psychology and the more qualitative and descriptive research primarily conducted in composition studies. Other divisions that we address include the gap between writing researchers and the instructors of pre- and in-service teachers, the divide between school and workplace writing, and the great divide between high- and low-performing adolescent writers that can emerge from these previous divisions. We argue that these divides can lead to more confusion among educators and to the need for more "negative capability" on their part. We conclude this article with some suggestions for bridging these gaps in order to create "positive capability" that can change the direction of adolescent literacy development by creating instructional knowledge and giving students the skills they need to become efficient writers in a variety of contexts.

Reading, Writing, and Postsecondary Literacy

Although a great deal of attention has been focused on adolescent literacy in the last decade, most of that attention has been directed toward reading rather than writing (Graham & Perin, 2007a). Although writing and reading are related processes, as Graham and Perin point out in *Writing Next*, there are considerable differences between these two literacy activities. When reading a text, individuals form mental representations of words produced by others, usually outside of the immediate reading context. In contrast, writers not only have to formulate their own thoughts but also organize and transcribe those mental representations into words that can transcend time and place, a process that few people would describe as undemanding.

In order to communicate skillfully, writers must balance a variety of considerations when they compose, including grammar, spelling, form, and organization, as well as the needs of their audience and their reasons for writing for that audience (Harris, Schmidt, & Graham, 1997; Harris & Graham, 1999). Research into the cognitive processes of expert writers has clearly demonstrated that effective and skilled writing is neither a natural consequence of language development (Graham & Harris, 1988) nor an organic unfolding of natural developmental processes. Writing is a complicated activity that is dependent on a rich assortment of cognitive processes and on the social context of the writer (Bereiter & Scardamalia, 1987; Hayes, 1996).

The difficulty inherent in achieving a mature writing level is reflected in research showing that American students have significant difficulty with narrative and informative writing (Harris & Graham, 1999), and that the argumentative writing of most American students is "poorly reasoned and unpersuasive" (Ferretti, MacArthur, & Dowdy, 2000; Harris & Graham, 1999). This is particularly true when it comes to the writing of learning-disabled students, who often demonstrate inadequate skill in planning and revising (Ferretti et al., 2000; Graham & Harris, 1999) and difficulty with mechanics, choosing topics, and producing and organizing text (De La Paz, 1997; Graham & Harris, 1988; Graham & Harris, 1999). Although many adolescents also struggle with reading, they are not confronted with these particular cognitive challenges during the reading process.

Recent research demonstrates that writing problems are not getting better. According to a recent report from the National Assessment of Educational Progress (NAEP), approximately 70 percent of students in grades four, eight, and twelve were deemed "low-achieving" writers who wrote at or below the basic level (Persky, Daane, & Jin, 2003) and failed to meet the NAEP proficiency goals for writing (Graham & Perin, 2007a). Not surprisingly, a recent report commissioned by the ACT (2005) found that one-third of high school students who plan to attend college do not meet the readiness standards for college composition courses, a finding that Graham and Perin (2007a) predict will make it difficult for these students to learn effectively in college. Students must be able to competently plan, write, evaluate, and revise texts in order to learn the academic material that they will face in higher education and to frame the material that they will be required to present in written compositions (Graham & Perin, 2007a).

Even more problematic is the impact poor writing skills may have on these students as they enter the workplace and the increasing importance writing plays as a "gatekeeping" skill in workplace environments. As was reported by the National Commission on Writing (2004, 2005), the writing skills of employees and job applicants play an important role in promotion and hiring decisions made by businesses and other institutions. Moreover, the importance of good writing to American companies and governmental agencies is certainly demonstrated in the large amounts of money these institutions are willing to spend to improve workers' basic writing skills. According to surveys of human resource directors, U.S. corporations spend an estimated $3.1 billion annually to remediate their employees' writing skills, and state governments spend an estimated $221 million annually for the same purpose (National Commission on Writing, 2005).

It is not surprising that workplace writing is so beleaguered. As Beaufort (2006) suggests, because of the varied and complicated tasks associated with workplace writing and the multiple settings in which it must occur, writing well requires employees to "research" the practices, purposes, and values of their particular workplace discourse communities. Learning to clear these multiple hurdles — including the demands of quickly advancing technology, knowledge of multiple written genres, the communal nature of workplace writing, and writing ownership — can be very difficult indeed. Workplace writing is not only often a shared task, it also carries high stakes (Beaufort, 2006). Client relations, corporate images, and legal decisions may all depend on skillful rendering of the written word. In that sense, workplace writing is very different from writing in school, where papers are written individually and closure comes when a grade has been given; afterward papers are often thrown away. In light of this disjunction between the writing that happens in schools and the writing needed to perform well at work, schools need to better align their writing demands with those of the workplace. As James Moffett, a seminal British writing researcher, remarked:

> Writing has to be learned in school very much the same way that it is practiced out of school. This means that the writer has a reason to write, an intended audience, and control of subject and form. It also means that composing is stated across various phases of rumination, investigation, consultation with others, drafting, feedback, revision and perfecting. (Quoted in Nagin, 2003, pp. 10–11)

Moffet's comments highlight the inauthentic nature of much of the writing students do in school, where they are rarely required to write with a real purpose or for a real audience. Graham and Perin (2007a) explain in *Writing Next* that although flexible writing — writing in different genres and for different purposes and audiences — should be the primary goal of writing instruction in the schools, school writing is often too rigid to accommodate this goal. Writing in schools often focuses on the short essay, including spelling and grammar, rather than on expressing ideas in a variety of written forms. If effective writing requires mastery of a variety of cognitive processes and must be carried out in multiple contexts for multiple audiences, then educators need substantive directives on how to teach the skills and strategies necessary to make this happen.

We believe that several recent analyses of instructional interventions offer educators a useful map. In *Writing Next*, Graham and Perin (2007a) describe a number of instructional approaches that research has shown to be effective. However, they caution readers that these individual approaches do not constitute a writing curriculum and should instead be viewed as possible components of a comprehensive instructional program. It is important, then, for educators to choose from this array of effective strategies and to incorporate their chosen approaches into clearly articulated writing programs. Consulting empirical research to determine what is and is not effective is an important first step in this work.

Writing Next

Writing Next sets the ambitious goal of identifying the most effective, research-based instructional approaches to writing. To accomplish this task, Graham and Perin (2007a) conducted the first systematic review of research on writing instruction since Hillocks's (1986) landmark study more than twenty years ago. Although they note that other reviews have focused on more narrow topics — such as the impact of word processing or the learning of academic content through writing, commonly referred to as "writing-to-learn" (Bangert-Drowns, 1993; Bangert-Drowns, Hurley, & Wilkinson, 2004) — *Writing Next* more broadly describes "specific practices that have demonstrated effectiveness" (Graham & Perin, 2007a, p. 13) for adolescents.

The methods employed in *Writing Next* distinguish it from *Reading Next* and from other reviews of adolescent writing research, such as recent reports by George Hillocks (2006, 2008). While literature reviews, like Hillocks's, rely on their authors' analytical skills and run the risk of reflecting author bias, the procedure of meta-analysis, like that used in *Writing Next*, gives researchers a systematic method for surveying the efficacy of a given intervention. The procedure allows researchers to calculate the impact (the effect size) of the intervention being studied. Then the effect size derived from each study of a particular instructional approach can be averaged to yield a measure of the effectiveness of that approach across many studies.

To appreciate the strengths and limitations of any meta-analysis, one must pay close attention to the criteria used by the researchers when selecting the studies. In the appendix of *Writing Next*, and in their more technical account of the study, Graham and Perin (2007c) recount their methodological decisions in detail. First, to ensure that the estimates were comparable across studies and relatively unbiased, the analysis only included experimental and quasi-experimental studies — in other words, those in which groups of students were assigned to different instructional conditions. Then, to be sure the methods applied to adolescents, Graham and Perin limited the studies to those of students in grades four through twelve. In addition, all of the studies selected needed to provide an overall or holistic measure of writing quality. The holistic measure tapped important features of writing, including organization, ideas, examples, and details. The only studies that did not use a holistic measure were those concerning summarization and writing to learn. The summarization studies depended on measures of accuracy and comprehensiveness as outcomes, and the writing-to-learn studies relied on various measures of content knowledge.

— Selecting and Categorizing the Studies

The authors' initial step in the process was to select the studies to analyze. Graham and Perin (2007a) initially focused on two broad areas — studies on learning to write and those concerned with writing to learn. In an effort to be inclusive, the authors cast a wide net, searching journals, dissertations, books, and conference proceedings, as well as studies indexed in previous meta-analyses.

When the studies were collected, the learning-to-write studies were further categorized into three broad categories: explicit instruction, instructional supports, and mode of instruction. After the categories were established, further organization occurred within each category as studies were grouped by their instructional approaches. Graham and Perin (2007a) used groupings from previous meta-analyses and borrowed terms from the database searches. To handle studies that did not fit into one of the predetermined groups, they developed a procedure for reviewing the articles, creating new groups, and revising the established ones. Once the categories were established and the articles sorted, the techniques of meta-analysis were then applied to each group. When there were four or more studies in each group, the effect size for that group was provided. The authors used Cohen's *d* as an effect-size statistic, which is simply the difference between the post-test mean scores of the comparison and treatment groups divided by the pooled standard deviation of both groups. To account for potential bias from studies with small samples, the authors also calculated weighted effect sizes using inverse variance weighting.[1]

— *Writing Next* Findings

Graham and Perin (2007a) present the results of their inquiry in *Writing Next* as "the 11 key elements of adolescent writing instruction" (p. 15). The instructional approaches are ranked from the most effective (strategy instruction) to the least effective (writing for content learning), although it is important to recognize that sometimes only small differences separate them. They are briefly described below:

1. *Writing Strategies:* Explicit instruction in strategies for planning, revising, and editing (weighted Effect Size = 0.82). Several approaches to strategy instruction exist, but the Self-Regulated Strategy Development (SRSD) intervention (Harris & Graham, 1996) has received the most empirical support. It involves explicit instruction in writing strategies and self-regulation methods, mastery learning, and one-on-one instruction. For example, one approach to teaching students to plan a persuasive essay utilizes the TREE mnemonic, which stands for Topic sentence, Reasons, Examine reasons, and Ending. Students learn why the mnemonic is helpful; they learn to use it; they memorize it; and they have opportunities to practice applying it with support from the teacher before they use it on their own.
2. *Summarization:* Explicit instruction in how to summarize a reading (weighted Effect Size = 0.82).
3. *Collaborative Writing:* Group work focusing on the steps of the writing process (weighted Effect Size = 0.75).
4. *Specific Product Goals:* Specification of concrete, achievable goals for student writing (weighted Effect Size = 0.70).
5. *Word Processing:* Use of word-processing equipment during the writing process (weighted Effect Size = 0.55).
6. *Sentence Combining:* Explicit instruction in combining simple sentences into more sophisticated sentences (weighted Effect Size = 0.50).

7. *Prewriting:* Participation in various planning techniques before composing (weighted Effect Size = 0.32).

8. *Inquiry Activities:* Tasks designed to develop content knowledge applicable to a writing project, such as gathering and analyzing information (weighted Effect Size = 0.32).

9. *Process-Writing Approach:* Multifaceted instruction described by Graham and Perin (2007a) as "creating extended opportunities for writing; emphasizing writing for real audiences; encouraging cycles of planning, translating, and reviewing; stressing personal responsibility and ownership of writing projects; facilitating high levels of student interactions; developing supportive writing environments; encouraging self-reflection and evaluation; and offering personalized individual assistance, brief instructional lessons to meet students' individual needs, and, in some instances, more extended and systematic instruction" (p. 19) (weighted Effect Size = 0.32).

10. *Study of Models:* Exposure to models of good writing (weighted Effect Size = 0.25).

11. *Writing for Content Learning:* Using various writing activities to enhance students' acquisition of content-area knowledge (weighted Effect Size = 0.23).

Writing Next has much to offer researchers and teachers concerned with the current state of adolescent writing instruction. First, the report provides a much-needed update to Hillocks's seminal meta-analysis. Since its publication in 1986, writing research has progressed, necessitating a careful, up-to-date review. On a practical level, the report has considerable value to teachers and teacher educators. As educators work to strengthen instructional techniques, *Writing Next* results offer a set of useful recommendations. Middle and high school teachers can apply the instructional elements in their classes selectively or in varying combinations, depending on students' needs. Furthermore, the strategies can be used by content-area teachers interested in using writing to teach specific content or to strengthen students' content-specific writing skills. The conclusions of this meta-analysis also have great value for teacher educators who work with writing teachers.

Moreover, Graham and Perin's (2007a, 2007c) descriptions of their meta-analysis provide excellent models of how to conduct and write about the analytic process. Graham and Perin take great pains to make their methods clear and transparent. They detail the methodological decisions they made during the study so that readers can decide for themselves whether the conclusions were justified by the analysis.

Another by-product of their transparency is that the limitations of the work are clear; in fact, the authors are forthright about them. One such limitation is the use of a holistic measure of writing quality as the outcome. Since the effectiveness of each intervention was assessed through this outcome, the strength of the conclusions depends on how accurately the outcome measures students' writing performance. This holistic focus may have obscured the impact of the instructional interventions on specific writing skills, such as spelling. Graham and Perin (2007c) also noted that the writing-quality measure differed across studies both in terms of how quality was defined and in terms of the holistic scale that was applied. Because of these differences across studies, the authors caution researchers to interpret the comparisons with care.

Perhaps the most significant limitation of the meta-analysis is that only experimental and quasi-experimental studies can be analyzed in a meta-analysis and, as a result, a large body of writing research could not be included in the *Writing Next* analysis. This constraint will certainly frustrate many teachers and researchers who may view the instructional recommendations in *Writing Next* as limited and unrepresentative of the wider body of writing research. In particular, readers who have studied the work of Nancie Atwell, Lucy Calkins, Peter Elbow, Donald Graves, and other advocates of process writing may be disappointed that these authors' rich descriptions of classroom instruction could not be included. However, Graham and Perin's (2007a) objective was to summarize what is known about the relationship between discrete writing interventions and measurable student outcomes, and it is therefore appropriate that they circumscribed the study as they did.

Readers with a process-writing perspective may also take issue with the list of specific strategies advocated in *Writing Next*. Some practices that are central to many depictions of process writing, particularly the writing workshop framework, do not receive attention in the report. One such practice is the writing conference, in which teachers meet with students individually to learn about their work, listen to their questions and concerns, and provide feedback and encouragement. Many teachers and teacher educators strongly believe in the efficacy of writing conferences. Nancie Atwell (1998), a middle school teacher who has written extensively about writing instruction, has stated emphatically that "writing conferences work" (p. 261). However, the support for Atwell's claim is not built on experimental evidence, and until more experimental and quasi-experimental research on practices such as conferencing occurs, their efficacy cannot be evaluated within the framework of a meta-analysis.

Additionally, readers who are well versed in the process-writing literature may be unfamiliar with some of the direct instructional approaches described in *Writing Next*, including writing strategy instruction such as Self-Regulated Strategy Development (SRSD) and instruction in setting specific writing goals. Both approaches include direct instruction by teachers in either specific writing strategies or goal-setting procedures. Although many early descriptions of process writing did not advocate direct instructional approaches, Pritchard and Honeycutt (2006) have noted that process writing is not incompatible with direct instruction. For example, many teachers use direct instructional methods during mini lessons to address written language conventions or complex processes such as planning and revising. Atwell (1998), too, sees the mini-lesson as a "forum for sharing [the teacher's] authority" (p. 150) and knowledge in a way that provides options for students. As Graham and Perin (2007a) suggest, it may be that process-writing approaches will provide a useful structure for teachers to integrate some of the specific strategies outlined in *Writing Next*.

Despite the omission of much of the instructional literature on process writing, the meta-analysis of experimental studies provides insight into the efficacy of this method. In their examination of the studies on the topic, Graham and Perin (2007a) found that process-writing instruction that included professional development for teachers — usually through the National Writing Project — was more effective than such instruction without teacher training. The finding that students write better when their teachers have more training seems intuitively obvious, but the implications for larger efforts to strengthen student writing through teacher training are substantial. However, before schools throw themselves into large-scale professional development efforts, Graham and Perin recommend that researchers examine the training more closely to determine its specific benefits for teachers.

Writing Next offers additional recommendations for process writing through its analysis of specific practices that are often taught as part of the writing process. For example, prewriting, collaborative writing, and sentence combining are frequently included in process-writing instruction (Nagin, 2003), and each of these was found to have positive effects on student writing. One of the challenges of evaluating the strength of a process approach to instruction is that there is no one, agreed-upon application of process instruction. Instead, it can incorporate a wide variety of practices, as seen in Graham and Perin's (2007a) expansive definition of process instruction. As Pritchard and Honeycutt (2006) note, the process approach has even changed or evolved over time. In order to demonstrate the specific benefits of process writing, researchers need to disentangle the unique effects of each practice (Pritchard & Honeycutt, 2006).

Although *Writing Next* provides a state-of-the-art analysis of the contemporary experimental and quasi-experimental research on adolescent writing instruction, there are limitations in its inclusiveness attributable to the use of a meta-analysis. Graham and Perin recognized the magnitude of these limitations and conducted a follow-up study designed to address them.

After Writing Next

Less than a year after the publication of *Writing Next*, Graham and Perin (2007b) undertook another meta-analysis of single-subject design studies and analyzed selected qualitative studies for common themes. This additional research, which was recently published in *Scientific Studies of Reading*, addressed the central question of *Writing Next:* What does the available research say about effective instruction for teaching adolescents to write?

Single-subject design studies were not included in *Writing Next* because of the small samples used and because effect sizes are calculated differently in such studies. Instead of a control group, single-subject design studies use each participant as his or her own control. This is done by measuring performance on a writing task before, during, and after the introduction of an instructional technique. If writing performance improves after a student participates in a new instructional activity, then the improvement is attributed to the instruction. This body of research is valuable for writing researchers because nearly all the single-subject design studies Graham and Perin (2007b) identified were conducted with struggling writers, some of whom were diagnosed with learning disabilities.

The results of their second meta-analysis both underscore and extend the findings of *Writing Next*. Like previous results, strategy instruction appeared to be the most effective intervention, while use of a word processor demonstrated a moderate effect. Several other approaches also demonstrated small but positive effects on writing proficiency, including teaching students to monitor and track a particular feature of their writing, such as the number of words written. This approach frequently also includes teaching students to graph their performance so that they can easily track their own progress. In addition, direct instruction of specific skills using techniques such as teacher modeling and student practice with teacher supervision had a positive relationship to students' proficiency with the skills being taught. Instruction in grammar was positively related to growth in students' grammar skills but not to overall improvements in writing quality. Finally, behavioral reinforcement, which included "either social praise, tangible reinforcement, or both" (Graham & Perin, 2007b, p. 323), was associated with small improvements in the specific skills being reinforced.

In the same article, Graham and Perin (2007b) also moved beyond the meta-analytic techniques of *Writing Next* by conducting a review and synthesis of qualitative research exploring writing or literacy instruction. Specifically, they selected qualitative studies focusing on exceptional teachers and schools serving students in grades four through twelve. The relevant research was identified during their original searches for *Writing Next*, which yielded five publications authored by literacy researcher Michael Pressley and his colleagues. In their analysis of the studies, Graham and Perin identified ten themes that were common across the descriptions of writing activity. These themes provided additional support for the recommendations made in *Writing Next* and the single-subject design meta-analysis. Most themes reflect the necessity of approaching writing as a process, teaching students strategies for the steps of the writing process (e.g., steps for planning a story or editing a persuasive essay), providing appropriate scaffolding, and creating a motivating, engaging, and supportive writing environment.

Overall, then, Graham and Perin's (2007b) follow-up to *Writing Next* supports their original findings and also identifies other effective teaching strategies, including practices such as self-monitoring. In addition, it offers a thoughtful discussion about the topics and problems that writing researchers need to investigate to push the field forward. The authors note that more research is sorely needed to test new instructional approaches and to validate current approaches in different contexts. They also call for writing research to enrich our understanding of "what dose of each treatment is optimal, how these treatments are best combined, and what combination of treatments work [sic] best for which adolescents" (Graham & Perin, 2007b, p. 328).

By conducting these analyses, Graham and Perin acknowledge (2007b) the limits of their initial meta-analysis and offer a response to critics who might believe that *Writing Next* focuses too narrowly on experimental research. However, their analysis of a small number of qualitative studies is clearly too narrow to accurately represent studies in this area. Furthermore, it is unclear why additional research that does examine effective schools and teachers was not included (e.g., Langer, 2000, 2001). A broader synthesis of qualitative studies certainly seems warranted, considering the small number included in this synthesis. Although several recent reviews of writing research have focused exclusively or predominantly on qualitative research, a broader synthesis is still needed because not all recent reviews target adolescent writing (Schultz, 2006), and others devote relatively little attention to recent qualitative work (Hillocks, 2006, 2008). In particular, we would like to see a synthesis of studies that position writing as collaborative and constructive — much like the writing that goes on in the workplace — as well as a synthesis of studies examining direct-instruction models. Such syntheses might include qualitative research on adolescent writing (with attention to teacher behavior and student attitudes toward writing) and might also include qualitative studies that examine how cognitive strategy instruction becomes integrated into whole-class instruction. However, we recognize that before it is possible to do many of these syntheses, much more qualitative research needs to focus specifically on these issues.

The Great Divide: Instruction, Teacher Preparation, and Assessment

The Graham and Perin (2007a, 2007b) studies examining writing instruction for adolescents offer a powerful synthesis of experimental and single-subject design research, as well as a partial survey of relevant qualitative research. However, any attempts to position these conclusions as being representative of the broad field of writing research and practice will certainly meet resistance due to a number of stark divisions in the field.

A major rift divides researchers into opposing groups with different theoretical orientations, methods, professional organizations, and standards. As Graham and Perin (2007b) note, the groups can be broadly characterized as associated either with educational psychology or with composition studies. The educational psychologists, like Graham and Perin, favor quantitative methods and cognitive developmental theories. Much of their research examines writing in elementary or secondary settings and they frequently work in education or psychology departments. Scholars from a composition studies tradition, such as Hillocks, privilege qualitative methods and sociocultural theories. The majority of their work explores writing in college or high school settings, and these scholars are often affiliated with English departments. The bright line separating these groups is obvious — only 4 percent of the citations in *Writing Next* also appear in Hillocks's (2008) most recent review of secondary writing, even though both reviews target adolescent writing.

Despite the theoretical and methodological divisions between composition researchers and educational psychology researchers, many of the *Writing Next* recommendations should be familiar to members of both groups. For example, much of the research on strategy instruction and setting specific writing goals has been published in journals frequently read by educational psychologists. Similarly, research on collaborative writing and inquiry activities can be found in journals read by researchers associated with composition studies. It may be that the *Writing Next* recommendations serve a dual function for many writing researchers, affirming their support for familiar instructional practices while simultaneously challenging researchers to expand their notions of effective writing instruction.

Although the divide among researchers is wide, it is certainly not the only one in the field. The academic discussions within, and occasionally across, the communities of writing researchers may not inform the preparation and professional development of middle and high school teachers. Much of the research on writing is produced by scholars in research-intensive colleges and universities, and little of it is conducted by scholars in teacher-preparation programs. As a result, students preparing to be teachers may not be reading and discussing the most current literature on writing instruction. When teachers complete their training and enter the classroom, they may begin teaching without the breadth and depth of understanding needed to carry out effective writing instruction.

This gap in teacher knowledge is particularly problematic because there are troubling inequities in writing skill among adolescent writers, and teachers without deep training in writing instruction cannot respond to the needs of these students. Hillocks's (2008) review of recent NAEP writing assessments revealed wide performance gaps attributed to socioeconomic status, ethnic group, and gender. He issued an ominous warning: This is "a problem that we ignore at our peril" (p. 327). Despite this performance disparity, researchers have only begun to explore instructional approaches designed to address the needs of struggling writers. Research on strategy instruction has shown that it can be effective with writers who struggle (Graham & Harris, 2003). However, there are many unanswered questions about how the writing context, the instructional approach, and the factors unique to each student may contribute to writing performance (Graham & Perin, 2007c). Ultimately, writing researchers must design instructional interventions responsive to the needs of all writers, including those who struggle, and they must effectively disseminate this information to classroom teachers and instructional leaders.

Another substantial divide exists when we compare the kinds of writing required of adolescents in school with those required of adults in the workplace. As we noted in the introduction, the hallmark of effective writers in the workplace is their ability to adapt to the demands of various writing tasks. This skill is necessary because much of the writing produced in the workplace has a practical communicative function, involves collaborative construction, and addresses a specific audience (Beaufort, 2006). Since these conditions are rarely static, writers must adapt their processes and products to the task. This requirement stands in contrast to the unique rhetorical characteristics of many school writing assignments, where the development of writing with a real purpose and for real audiences often does not exist. In his seminal discussion of the role of audience in writing, literacy theorist Walter Ong (1975) addressed one such inauthentic assignment, "How I Spent My Summer Vacation," and the problem that this traditional narrative task creates for a writer:

> If the student knew what he was up against . . . he might ask "Who wants to know?" The answer is not easy. Grandmother? He never tells grandmother. His father or mother? There's a lot that he would not want to tell them, that's sure. . . . The teacher? There is no conceivable setting in which he could imagine telling his teacher how he spent his summer vacation other than in writing this paper. (p. 11)

Ong's question — "To whom does this student address such a writing assignment?" — has a clear answer. The student addresses a fictionalized audience constructed in his mind because there is no conceivable audience for such writing in reality. Although the "summer vacation" assignment may no longer reflect the majority of school writing tasks, it is important to understand that workplace writing is essentially social in nature and that the needs of real audiences must be taken into account (Beaufort, 2006). The decontextualized type of writing that is too often practiced in schools can leave students unprepared for the actual demands of the workplace.

Although there are many wide divisions in the field, writing researchers and teachers share the desire to deepen our understanding of adolescent writing and to make instruction stronger and more relevant. To that end, we would like to make some recommendations about how research and practice can address the divisions in adolescent writing, help teachers and researchers reduce their tolerance for "negative capability," and provide some clarity about the mysteries and uncertainties surrounding effective writing instruction. Some suggestions echo those offered by Graham and Perin (2007a, 2007b, 2007c), while others point in new directions. Our recommendations follow the structure outlined by the RAND Reading Study Group (2002) in its report on reading comprehension. Although there are substantial differences between reading comprehension and writing, the two have similar needs, which include attention to instruction, teacher preparation, and assessment.

Instruction

To strengthen writing instruction for adolescents, researchers need to address a broad range of questions. Some of the most pressing questions speak to what might be called the "writing divide" that separates strong writers from those who struggle. As Graham and Perin (2007b) point out, research on cognitive strategy instruction, in particular the Self-Regulated Strategy Development model (Harris & Graham, 1996), has shown considerable promise when used with struggling writers. However, more research is needed to explore the efficacy of strategy instruction with students in varying instructional contexts, such as whole-class instruction versus small-group or individualized instruction. Also, research on strategy instruction needs to be expanded to include students at all grade levels because it has almost exclusively taken place in the elementary grades. Finally, researchers need to explore which of the many components of strategy instruction provide the greatest benefit for students (Graham & Perin, 2007b). It may be that the most beneficial components can be integrated into other instructional approaches in productive ways.

Graham and Perin (2007b) also note that "effective writing instruction for adolescents is not just a 4th- through 12th-grade issue" (p. 328). Struggling adolescent writers might have avoided their difficulties if they had received better writing instruction in earlier grades. By focusing resources on developing high-quality writing instruction for young children, teachers and researchers may help children build strong writing skills so that future difficulties can be averted, or at least reduced.

In addition, considering that struggling writers may include learning disabled students, ethnic minorities, students from low-socioeconomic-status households, and English-language learners (Hillocks, 2008), it seems highly unlikely that only a single instructional approach — or even several — may be sufficient to meet their varying needs. Researchers must be committed to investigating how teachers can address the diverse needs of students who have unique sets of skills, different social worlds, and different patterns of language use. Until we can know better how varying instructional methods support diverse students, inequities in writing instruction are likely to persist.

Another barrier to developing effective instructional approaches is our limited theoretical understanding of writing proficiency and how it develops. With more detailed theories of how cognitive, social, and motivational forces interact as writers develop their skills over time, researchers could create instructional methods that are sensitive to writers' needs (Graham & Perin, 2007b).

To help students develop into more flexible writers who can adjust to the demands of the workplace, writing instruction needs to bridge the gap between school and workplace writing. A more specific focus on creating meaningful writing assignments that have real purposes and real audiences outside of the classroom context is needed (Beaufort, 2006; Hillocks, 2002). Teachers may need to change more than the demands of the assignments; they may also need to change the way students work to allow for wider collaboration and the integration of technological writing tools.

Teacher Preparation

Any comprehensive effort to strengthen writing instruction must include attention to the training of preservice teachers and the continuing education of current teachers. During their course work and school placements, preservice teachers need instruction in a wide variety of evidence-based writing practices (Graham & Perin, 2007b). In many teacher-education programs, including our own, literacy courses devote substantially more attention to reading instruction than to writing instruction. One explanation for this disparity is the deeper body of reading research (Graham & Perin, 2007a). However, in the last twenty years, much has been learned about the writing process, predictors of writing success, and effective approaches to writing instruction (Graham, 2006). Before they enter the classroom, preservice teachers should be well versed in the research on writing development and writing instruction. In their school placements they should have opportunities to design writing lessons and receive constructive feedback from instructors and instructional leaders who are familiar with the extant writing literature. Opportunities to read the writing research should not be limited to prospective elementary school or English teachers. Since writing can be a tool for learning, and many content-area teachers have writing assignments in their courses, content-area teachers should also receive training in writing development and instruction.

Of course, teacher educators also need to be familiar with current writing research. Two factors currently prevent this from happening. The first is the relative scarcity of writing researchers. If more researchers pursued writing-related questions, there would be more writing researchers to teach preservice teachers or to work with teacher educators. A second impediment was characterized earlier as the divide between writing researchers and teacher educators. If better communication existed between these groups, perhaps through professional journals or conferences, then one would expect teacher educators to include more current writing research in their courses.

While training preservice teachers is clearly important, a parallel effort needs to be made for current teachers across the content areas. Since many teachers report entering the classroom with little or no preparation to teach writing — and few states require course work in teaching writing for licensure (Nagin, 2003) — many operate in what Keats called "negative capability" as they learn and create methods and material to teach writing (Grossman, 1990). Once teachers build a repertoire for writing instruction, they may be reluctant to abandon it for new practices (RAND Reading Study Group, 2002). To further complicate matters, given the lack of agreement about how to teach writing, it is likely that teachers are employing diverse approaches to instruction. Until there is better data on how writing instruction currently occurs in classrooms — both English language arts and content-area classrooms — designing high-quality professional development will be a struggle. Furthermore, a spate of questions needs to be answered about how to make professional development effective. We leave to others the task of answering those questions; however, we do want to stress that professional development for writing instruction must build on the most successful existing professional development models.

Assessment

A final important area in need of attention from researchers and teachers is writing assessment. Currently, writing assessment plays an integral role in high-stakes tests, both at the state level and on national tests used for college placement, such as the SAT. One persistent challenge for assessment designers is creating a writing test that is authentic and that taps the full complexity of writing. For example, Hillocks (2002) reported that most state writing assessments allow students a limited time to produce an essay or story responding to a prompt.[2] The prompts offer little background information for test-takers to use in constructing their responses, but this lack of background information is intentional because essays are graded for their structure and mechanics more than for their content. Furthermore, Hillocks found that the model essays published by testing agencies contained poor examples of elaboration and weak and even incorrect evidence. The most problematic result of instituting writing assessments that ignore key features of writing, such as the content, is its impact on instruction as teachers align their writing expectations to the state tests.

Assessments that judge writing as separate from content are particularly troubling, because research suggests that writing should not be considered a subject unto itself but should be fully integrated into the content areas, including math and science (Chapman, 1990). Research also shows that writing is an important means to enhance learning in the content areas (Graham & Perin, 2007a). Therefore, writing that is divorced from content — even though this is a feature of many state and national writing assessments (Hillocks, 2008) — is a type of mandated extension of the decontextualized school writing that Ong complained about (1975). However, along with Ong's fictionalized audience, students now find themselves fictionalizing the writing process — because of the "one-shot," time-constrained nature of the tests — and fictionalizing the support they must use to address subjects about which they know very little (Hillocks, 2002, 2008).

Since writing assessment influences instruction and has real consequences for students, researchers need to turn their attention to the design of writing tests or alternate forms of evaluation to align these assessments with the goals of flexible and authentic writing. First, new writing assessments need to overcome the decontextualized and inauthentic format of many current writing prompts. In addition, assessment methods need to be flexible enough to accommodate the varied writing practices used by students, which may involve searching for relevant information, using technological scaffolds, and perhaps even working collaboratively.

Although writing assessment is a thorny problem with which educators continue to struggle, several educators and writing researchers have suggested ways to make writing assessments more authentic. For instance, Chapman (1990) has suggested that writing assessments should include various types of writing at varying levels of difficulty in order to approximate more closely the writing demands of the workplace. These types might include open-ended essays that draw from students' background and experiences, short-answer writings, or alternative compositions that specifically target parts of the writing process, like planning or revising. Assessments that are attuned to this process could help align effective classroom practice with what policymakers seek to measure. Chapman (1990) and Hillocks (2002) both suggest that student writing portfolios, which are compilations of students' writing over long periods of time, can provide a more comprehensive picture of a student's writing ability, give students a more purposeful and authentic writing experience, and allow teachers a useful tool for tracking growth in students' writing skills over time. In addition, Murphy and Yancey (2008) point out that portfolios offer some solutions to several of the limitations of relying on a single writing assessment to evaluate writing proficiency. These disadvantages include factors such as imposing time limits on writers, which may penalize students who write slowly; using a single measure to assess proficiency, which may not provide a robust measure of a student's skill; and specifying the topic of the text, which may differentially impact students depending on their background knowledge.

Although portfolios appear to hold some promise for assessment, researchers have raised questions about whether they can be scored reliably. Evaluative research done on Vermont's portfolio system has revealed relatively low reliability among the raters (Koretz, Stecher, Klein, & McCaffrey, 1994). Low reliability is unacceptable when portfolio scores are used to make high-stakes decisions about a student's future or a school's progress. However, other researchers have achieved higher levels of interrater reliability with portfolios. For example, Underwood and Murphy (1998) report fairly high reliability when portfolios were scored by teachers familiar with the writing curriculum. It may be that research that explores in greater detail how the raters' knowledge of the writing task and of the scoring system impacts their assessment of a portfolio can productively address the reliability problems of portfolio assessment (Murphy & Yancey, 2008).

Research on writing assessment also needs to address diagnostic measures teachers use to identify struggling writers. Currently, teachers have few curriculum-based writing measures or other resources that allow them to assess a student's writing performance quickly and accurately (McMaster & Espin, 2007). A comprehensive research effort needs to be launched to identify measures that are linked to current theoretical models of writing development and are also sensitive to growth over time. Such measures would have immense practical value because they would allow teachers to track student progress and to identify struggling writers who might benefit from more-intensive instruction.

Furthermore, researchers could use such measures to evaluate the impact of new instructional models and practices.

Conclusions

To mitigate writing teachers' need for "negative capability" in confronting the mystery of good writing instruction, a broad and comprehensive initiative in writing research must be undertaken. We have attempted to outline some of the issues that deserve investigation, but as we have tried to convey in this article, writing is a diverse field with many open questions and many potential opportunities for innovative research and teaching. However, as Graham and Perin (2007b) have noted, a necessary prerequisite for such an initiative is funding, which would stimulate research and encourage more attention to the important problems that remain.

The flexibility researchers need to investigate these problems is as important as funding to move this work forward. We need good communication to bridge the divide in writing research between the scientific approaches that identify effective interventions and the more-descriptive and qualitative approaches that demonstrate how these interventions are used in real classrooms by real teachers. And, just as important, we need to be able to think flexibly about how to communicate this knowledge to preservice and in-service teachers. As Keats (1979) once stated, "There is not a fiercer hell than the failure in a great object" (p. 802). In our opinion, there is no greater object than building effective writing programs that will equip young people to succeed in school, to contribute to a vibrant global economy, and to participate in an increasingly pluralistic civic life — all facilitated by the power of the written word.

Notes

1. Graham and Perin also analyzed whether there was a relationship between the total quality of the study (as indicated by a range of measures, such as publication type and whether random assignment was used) and the magnitude of the effect size, but found no relationship.
2. Since Hillocks's (2002) study, some state writing tests have incorporated more authentic assessments. One example is the Massachusetts state test, the MCAS, which includes short-answer, open-response, and stand-alone writing prompts in several subjects.

References

ACT. (2005). *Crisis at the core: Preparing all students for college and work.* Retrieved November 28, 2007, from http://www.act.org/path/policy/pdf/crisis_report.pdf

Atwell, N. (1998). *In the middle: New understandings about writing, reading and learning* (2nd ed.). Portsmouth, NH: Boynton/Cook.

Bangert-Drowns, R. (1993). The word processor as an instructional tool: A meta-analysis of word processing in writing instruction. *Review of Educational Research, 63,* 69–93.

Bangert-Drowns, R. L., Hurley, M. M., & Wilkinson, B. (2004). The effects of school-based writing-to-learn interventions on academic achievement: A meta-analysis. *Review of Educational Research, 74*, 29–58.

Beaufort, A. (2006). Writing in the professions. In P. Smagorinsky (Ed.), *Research on composition: Multiple perspectives on two decades of change* (pp. 217–242). New York: Teachers College Press.

Bereiter, C., & Scardamalia, M. (1987). *The psychology of written composition.* Hillsdale, NJ: Lawrence Erlbaum.

Biancarosa, G., & Snow, C. E. (2004). *Reading next: A vision for action and research in middle and high school literacy* (A report from the Carnegie Corporation of New York). Washington, DC: Alliance for Excellent Education.

Chapman, C. (1990). Authentic writing assessment. *Practical Assessment, Research and Evaluation, 2*(7). Retrieved November 28, 2007, from http://PAREonline.net/getvn.asp?v=2&n=7

De La Paz, S. (1997). Strategy instruction in planning: Teaching students with learning and writing disabilities to compose persuasive and expository essays. *Learning Disability Quarterly, 20*, 227–248.

Ferretti, R. P., MacArthur, C. A., & Dowdy, N. S. (2000). The effects of an elaborated goal on the persuasive writing of students with learning disabilities and their normally achieving peers. *Journal of Educational Psychology, 92*, 694–702.

Graham, S. (2006). Writing. In P. Alexander & P. Winne (Eds.), *Handbook of educational psychology* (pp. 457–478). Mahwah, NJ: Lawrence Erlbaum.

Graham, S., & Harris, K. R. (1988, April). *Improving learning disabled students' skills at generating essays: Self-instructional strategy training.* Paper presented at the annual meeting of the American Educational Research Association, New Orleans, LA.

Graham, S., & Harris, K. R. (1999). Assessment and intervention in overcoming writing difficulties: An illustration from the self-regulated strategy development model. *Language, Speech, and Hearing Services in Schools, 30*, 255–264.

Graham, S., & Harris, K. R. (2003). Students with learning disabilities and the process of writing: A meta-analysis of SRSD studies. In H. L. Swanson, K. R. Harris, & S. Graham (Eds.), *Handbook of research on learning disabilities* (pp. 383–402). New York: Guilford Press.

Graham, S., & Perin, D. (2007a). *Writing next: Effective strategies to improve writing of adolescents in middle and high school.* Washington, DC: Alliance for Excellent Education.

Graham, S., & Perin, D. (2007b). What we know, what we still need to know: Teaching adolescents to write. *Scientific Studies of Reading, 11*, 313–335.

Graham, S., & Perin, D. (2007c). A meta-analysis of writing instruction for adolescent students. *Journal of Educational Psychology, 99*, 445–476.

Grossman, P. (1990). *The making of a teacher: Teacher knowledge and teacher education.* New York: Teachers College Press.

Harris, K. R., & Graham, S. (1996). *Making the writing process work: Strategies for composition and self-regulation* (2nd ed.). Cambridge, MA: Brookline Books.

Harris, K. R., & Graham, S. (1999). Programmatic intervention research: Illustrations from the evolution of self-regulated strategy development. *Learning Disability Quarterly, 22*, 251–262.

Harris, K. R., Schmidt, T., & Graham S. (1997). Every child can write: Strategies for composition and self-regulation in the writing process. In K. R. Harris, S. Graham, D. Deshler, & M. Pressley (Eds.), *Teaching every child every day: Learning in diverse schools and classrooms* (pp. 131–167). Cambridge, MA: Brookline Books.

Hayes, J. R. (1996). A new framework for understanding cognition and affect in writing. In C. M. Levy & S. Ransdell (Eds.), *The science of writing: Theories, methods, individual differences, and applications* (pp. 1–28). Mahwah, NJ: Lawrence Erlbaum.

Hillocks, G. (1986). *Research on written composition: New directions for research.* Urbana, IL: National Conference on Research in English and ERIC Clearinghouse on Reading and Communication Skills.

Hillocks, G. (2002). *The testing trap: How state writing assessments control learning.* New York: Teachers College Press.

Hillocks, G. (2006). Middle and high school composition. In P. Smagorinsky (Ed.), *Research on composition: Multiple perspectives on two decades of change* (pp. 48–77). New York: Teachers College Press.

Hillocks, G. (2008). Writing in secondary schools. In C. Bazerman (Ed.), *Handbook of research on writing: History, society, school, individual, text* (pp. 311–330). New York: Lawrence Erlbaum.

Keats, J. (1975). Four letters. In C. Kaplan (Ed.), *Criticism: The major statements* (pp. 349–350). New York: St. Martin's Press.

Keats, J. (1979). Endymion. In M. H. Abrams (Ed.), *The Norton anthology of English literature,* (Vol. 2, 4th ed., pp. 802–806). New York: W. W. Norton.

Koretz, D., Stecher, B., Klein, S., & McCaffrey, D. (1994). The Vermont portfolio assessment program: Findings and implications. *Educational Measurement: Issues and Practice 13*(3), 5–16.

Langer, J. A. (2000). Excellence in English in middle and high school: How teachers' professional lives support student achievement. *American Educational Research Journal, 37,* 397–439.

Langer, J. A. (2001). Beating the odds: Teaching middle and high school students to read and write well. *American Educational Research Journal, 38,* 837–880.

McMaster, K., & Espin, C. (2007). Technical features of curriculum-based measurement in writing: A literature review. *The Journal of Special Education, 41*(2), 68–84.

Murphy, S., & Yancey, K. B. (2008). Construct and consequence: Validity in writing assessment. In C. Bazerman (Ed.), *Handbook of research on writing: History, society, school, individual, text* (pp. 365–385). New York: Lawrence Erlbaum.

Nagin, C. (2003). *Because writing matters: Improving student writing in our schools.* San Francisco: Jossey-Bass.

National Commission on Writing. (2004). *Writing: A ticket to work . . . or a ticket out: A survey of business leaders.* Retrieved November 5, 2007, from http://www.writingcommission. org/report/html

National Commission on Writing. (2005). *Writing: A powerful message from state government.* Retrieved November 7, 2007, from http://www.writingcommission.org/report/html

Ong, W. J. (1975). The writer's audience is always a fiction. *Publications of the Modern Language Association, 90,* 9–21.

Persky, H. R., Daane, M. C., & Jin, Y. (2003). *The nation's report card: Writing 2002, NCES 2003.* Washington, DC: National Center for Educational Statistics.

Pritchard, R. J., & Honeycutt, R. L. (2006). The process approach to writing instruction: Examining its effectiveness. In C. A. MacArthur, S. Graham, & J. Fitzgerald (Eds.), *Handbook of writing research* (pp. 275–290). New York: Guilford Press.

RAND Reading Study Group. (2002). *Reading for understanding: Toward an R&D program in reading comprehension.* Santa Monica, CA: Science and Technology Policy Institute, RAND Education.

Schultz, K. (2006). Qualitative research on writing. In C. A. MacArthur, S. Graham, & J. Fitzgerald (Eds.), *Handbook of writing research* (pp. 357–373). New York: Guilford Press.

Underwood, T., & Murphy, S. (1998). Interrater reliability in a California middle school English/language arts portfolio assessment program. *Assessing Writing, 5,* 201–230.

Editors' Reviews

DOUBLE THE WORK: CHALLENGES AND SOLUTIONS TO ACQUIRING
LANGUAGE AND ACADEMIC LITERACY FOR ADOLESCENT ENGLISH
LANGUAGE LEARNERS
by Deborah Short and Shannon Fitzsimmons.
Washington, DC: Alliance for Excellent Education, 2007. 97 pp.

THE LANGUAGE DEMANDS OF SCHOOL: PUTTING ACADEMIC ENGLISH
TO THE TEST
edited by Alison L. Bailey.
New Haven, CT: Yale University Press, 2006. 226 pp. $35.00.

According to national statistics on the reading comprehension abilities of students in grades six through twelve, more than six million U.S. adolescents fall below the basic reading levels needed for high school, higher education, or workforce success. This has been referred to as the "adolescent literacy crisis" (Biancarosa & Snow, 2004; Short & Fitzsimmons, 2007). It is noteworthy that these gloomy statistics are reported to be even worse for English-language learners (ELLs; Abedi, 2006; Abedi & Gándara, 2006; August & Hakuta, 1997).[1] Ninety-six percent of U.S. eighth-grade students who are limited English proficient (LEP) scored below the basic level on the reading portion of the National Assessment for Educational Progress (Short & Fitzsimmons, 2007). Furthermore, students who speak a language other than English at home have an increased likelihood of dropping out of high school and of earning lower salaries, on average, than their non–ELL peers after graduating from high school (Short & Fitzsimmons, 2007). Hence, the adolescent literacy crisis can be seen as particularly burdensome for students who speak English as a second language.

Much of the early research on and recommendations for the instruction of ELLs reflects a deficit model approach. This is a lens commonly used to examine "at-risk" populations, an approach in which students' burdens and obstacles to learning are predominately viewed as deficiencies situated within an individual child rather than as inadequacies in the child's environment or life circumstances (Goldenberg, Rueda, & August, 2006; Harry, Klingner, Cramer, & Sturges, 2007; Valenzuela, 1999). Deficit theory as proposed by McDer-

Harvard Educational Review Vol. 78   No. 1   Spring 2008

mott (1993) and as used here assumes that "language and culture are store houses from which children acquire their competencies" (p. 283).[2] In this manner, some children are seen as needing more and others less. The result is a focus on what individual children lack as opposed to limitations in their surroundings (McDermott, 1993). Subsequent discourse for at-risk populations frames this work in terms of support and services, locating learning problems within the child and his or her "neediness" (Rappaport, 1981). This discourse, which is used frequently in the case of ELLs (Harry et al., 2007), is problematic because efforts for change are misdirected at the students rather than at the institutions that influence and guide their educational options and pedagogy. A deficit model also assumes a one-size-fits-all approach that dictates positive or desirable behavior for all students when the field in fact needs to examine more closely the pedagogical and social-cultural contexts in which these children are situated (Goldenberg et al., 2006; McDermott, 1993). The consequence of operating under a deficit model is a cycle of blaming students. The implicit message — as unjust and unfounded as it may be — is that ELL students are to blame for falling behind due to their poor motivation, because they exhibit problematic behavior, or because they altogether lack socially appropriate behavior or academic capacities (Suárez-Orozco & Suárez-Orozco, 2001; Valenzuela, 1991).

However, many ELLs come from families that sacrifice tremendously to provide them with scholastic opportunities, are highly dedicated to learning English, and often are highly motivated to achieve academically (Suárez-Orozco & Suárez-Orozco, 2001). The deficit model may falsely portray ELLs as adversarial or reluctant learners, when in fact many are eager and driven to succeed. However, a contrasting perspective attributes poor educational performance to inadequate social structures and a lack of resources in schools, making it impossible for a student's existing competencies to function or flourish despite their best intentions (Rappaport, 1981). In fact, adolescent ELL students may be better served by policies and programs based on a framework that places more emphasis on the students' holistic context. When institutions provide programs that accommodate learners with different assets and needs, these institutions accept responsibility for students' learning. Ideally, public schools should be dedicated to encouraging proficiency and even mastery of reading and writing by all students instead of labeling students' inadequacies and then accepting these labels as an potential indictment of students' capabilities without regard for possible instructional inadequacies.

Two recent works provide the opportunity to bring increased attention to the need to reexamine deficit models and consider new structural reforms and interventions associated with supporting ELLs. *Double the Work: Challenges and Solutions to Acquiring Language and Academic Literacy for Adolescent English Language Learners* and *The Language Demands of School: Putting Academic English to the Test,* which address unresolved issues in the field of ELL adolescent literacy, are directed at educators, researchers, and policymakers. The two books represent a call to action to make collaborative and systemic changes that can resolve particular obstacles to ELLs' literacy success. *Double the Work* and *The Language Demands of School* recommend ways to deal effectively with ELLs in the domains of pedagogy, policy, and assessments.

The contributors to *Double the Work* included a panel of researchers, policy-makers, and practitioners working in the field of ELL literacy who met to discuss matters relevant to academic literacy. The report was intended to identify the major obstacles to improving academic literacy among ELLs and to positively influence research, policy, and practice. This report identifies the obstacles as (1) a lack of consistent identification, tracking, and assessment of this population over time; (2) inadequate educator capacity and program flexibility; (3) limited use of research-based instructional practices; and (4) lack of a coherent research agenda. The authors address contextual obstacles that can impede adolescent ELLs' scholastic experiences and propose possible solutions. The report concludes with case studies at the high school and district level, which serve as exemplars of how to implement programmatic and structural changes in schools. The report provides possible strategies for policymakers and educators of adolescent ELLs to shape the context in which ELLs learn, as opposed to promoting the status quo in which ELLs are labeled as having "deficient" characteristics.

The contributors to *The Language Demands of School*, an edited volume from the National Center for Research on Evaluation, Standards and Student Testing (CRESST), focus on issues of academic literacy. They review the theoretical underpinnings and empirical research that support the construct of academic English language (AEL), a concept that distinguishes between difficulty reading in specific content areas and limited language proficiency. Put simply, AEL is used to separate the language used in social settings from language used in the classroom and in content areas, although this bifurcation may not be distinct. The authors argue that AEL skills determine the academic success of ELL students and that the assessment of academic language skills will indicate whether students are able to access the content curriculum. This is in contrast to the common practice of using proficiency tests — those that assess language used in social settings — as an inaccurate barometer for determining the mainstream school readiness of ELL students. Ultimately, *The Language Demands of School* calls for research on the AEL abilities of ELL students, leading to the alignment of testing, instruction, and professional development for teachers grounded in this approach. By striving to improve consistency across the structural domains of testing, instruction, and professional development, practitioners in the field ELLs and all students experience greater success in school settings.

In light of the adolescent literacy crisis, both of these works provide important and far-reaching insights into the critical role that institutions play when supporting ELLs and propose concrete programmatic changes that will surely have a positive impact on the education of this group. However, while both works rightly highlight important possibilities for environmental changes, their most significant contributions — underlying paradigmatic shifts in focus from individual to context and from deficit to enrichment — remain surprisingly implicit. By not explicitly drawing attention to this reframing, the authors *of Double the Work* and *The Language Demands of School* fail to challenge a deficit model that prevails among researchers and practitioners. Consequently, these texts do not reach their full potential to inform ELL instruction and instead tacitly reify the existing prejudicial treatment of ELLs. In the following pages I will highlight the ways these texts draw attention to structural approaches to ELL instructional reform and how the implicit underlying framework in these reports could be brought to the fore. In order to best serve ELLs, educators must acknowledge the pivotal role schools play instead of focusing on the shortcomings of students within unpredictable and often inflexible educational institutions.

The Importance of Ecological Frameworks for ELLs

Structural models of reform that challenge the persisting deficit model of ELLs owe a debt to theoretical work that explores the ecology of human development. An ecological framework emphasizes the importance of settings and contexts rather than focusing exclusively on individuals, and it highlights change over time and across settings (Bronfenbrenner, 1977). Seeing students as embedded in multiple settings is central to this perspective, which views schools as existing within communities, which in turn exist within social and political institutions. This ecological orientation calls for the examination of complex systems of interaction among individuals. It examines aspects of the environment beyond the individual child, exploring the "nested arrangement of structures" in which a person lives and develops.[3] From this orientation, children's behaviors are considered within concentric circles of influence — families, schools, communities, institutions, and political and social climates — that shape their learning and development outcomes. The ecological perspective proposes that contextual factors at different levels influence children's lives both directly and indirectly. For instance, schools have a direct influence on children, while state curricular standards might affect the academic performance of children from a more indirect position. An ecological perspective requires us to consider the influence of all of the contextual factors, including the indirect trickle-down effect of societal values and scholastic standards, as well as the interplay of these factors, such as the simultaneous contribution of family and school that have similar proximity to children.

By focusing on the inadequacies of the scholastic context as opposed to weaknesses in the child, true educational reforms are likely to result, rather than theories that overemphasize why students can't learn and which of their characteristics create obstacles to their learning. The deficit model ultimately does not provide answers for reform; rather, it offers only a negative perception of students and their abilities. Shifting the focus from students' shortcomings to the schools' responsibilities could remove the stigma often associated with ELL status — a stigma that often hinders learning and dampens students' sense of self-efficacy (Valenzuela, 1991). Moreover, I and other scholars argue that the diverse linguistic, cultural, and educational backgrounds of adolescent ELLs demand that we reexamine the flexibility (or lack thereof) of educational systems, given that institutions, not children, are responsible for education (Goldenberg et al., 2006; Lesaux, 2006).

One approach to improving literacy outcomes for ELLs within an ecological framework might be the consistent analysis of the educational settings from a longitudinal vantage point. This would mean tracking students across different settings over time and observing how schools help or hinder their progress, thus providing critical information needed to guide school reform and structural change (Lesaux, 2006). Although *Double the Work* and *The Language Demands of School* do not explicitly advocate for this type of ecological model, both texts do argue for consistent analyses of students across settings and over time. Their recommendations are easily linked to what might be seen as "ecologically sound" next steps: viewing literacy assessments and standards as interactions across contexts (i.e., schools, districts, and states), and monitoring the trajectory of ELL students over time. I will explore the first of these steps by looking at the way these works address student academic progress as it develops over time and their academic trajectories; I will consider the latter by examining the role of interactions or interface across levels and contexts (i.e., state, district, and schools) as marked by assessments.

Academic Trajectories

Double the Work criticizes current nationwide inconsistencies in how ELLs are assessed over time and across states and the resultant limited tracking of these students. This is a valid critique: In contrast to the deficit model that looks at students and ignores the resources and structures that may be marshaled to support them, an ecological approach provides a useful alternative. Measuring progress over time facilitates an analysis of the contribution of context and provides a more comprehensive picture of academic benchmarks (i.e., how many years of English immersion are really needed and do students with more time in bilingual programs do better?).

The report argues that what constitutes an ELL varies widely. However, in the context of research or practice, members of the same population may also be labeled ELLs, limited English proficient, or English as second language (ESL) students.[4] To further complicate tracking matters, criteria for reclassifying an LEP student who has mastered English and is classified as fully English proficient (FEP) varies both by state and district (Lesaux, 2006; Mahoney & MacSwan, 2005). Unfortunately, being reclassified from LEP to FEP often results in a student's no longer being tracked as an ELL because he has "mastered" English, implicitly removing the "language learner" part of the ELL label. However, terminating the tracking of these students as ELLs prevents any longitudinal understanding of their language profiles and/or progress in language learning (de Jong, 2004; Wright, 2005). The report clearly points out these shortcomings and proposes longitudinal evaluations of the academic progress of ELL students. I argue that an ecological model provides a useful lens for correcting identification and tracking inconsistencies. Being able to keep track of individual ELLs after reclassification as an FEP would refocus energies on instructional systems and educational progress within and across diverse pedagogical settings. The report contends — without explicit mention of the ecological lens — that tracking the progress of ELLs would provide information about academic norms for ELL student progress within the educational system. Tracking students after reclassification would be in direct contrast to present practices that fail to follow ELLs beyond their being designated FEPs.

The authors of *The Language Demands of School* also question the tendency to lump all ELLs into a single group: "While ELLs are acquiring English as a second language and share the need to improve their academic skills, they vary in English language proficiency levels and in a range of educationally relevant background variables such as length of time in the United States and years of formal schooling."[5] The book also points out that "there are always new ELLs entering the system; consequently, there is never a single point in time when all students will be proficient." I contend that the diversity among ELLs highlights the importance of the instructional recommendations proposed in *Double the Work* with regard to more flexible pathways, as well as the need to use AEL in schools. In contrast to the deficit model's focus on problematic behavior in the individual and the one-size-fits-all approach, the ecological approach pays special attention to student diversity.

I challenge current practices under the deficit model, which measure students' educational experiences before coming to the United States. Many such assessments aimed at discovering children's deficits focus on individual children and ultimately reflect the extensive variety of experience these students have before beginning school in the United States. The academic paths of ELLs who arrive in middle or high school may have varied significantly, ultimately resulting in their having different skills, expectations, and levels of readiness for school in the U.S. (Biancarosa & Snow, 2004). While assessments of reading readiness are common practice during elementary school, literacy and language assessments in the later grades are dedicated to other forms of testing, such as yearly achievement or exit tests, which do not adequately assess what adolescents do and do not know (Lesaux, 2006). According to *Double the Work*, proposed federal policies to assess English language development from grades 3 through 12 do not disentangle issues of language proficiency, years of schooling, or any of the other factors that may affect these students' academic performance. These kinds of assessments ultimately measure the educational experiences of ELLs before arriving in the United States and lend themselves to the deficiency model of evaluation. I maintain that researchers need to focus on students' converging experiences. When ELLs are not tracked over time and across contexts, there is limited information about the classroom pedagogy and its impact. Tracking students longitudinally after they have been reclassified allows one to see growth in achievement and thus provides the opportunity to highlight the success (or failure) of the educational environments that serve ELLs over time. In contrast, deficit models focus only on salient problematic behaviors among individual students and fail to measure progress or to consider a panoramic perspective of student achievement within a particular context. Deficit models ignore vital information about resources and structures that may help students excel. *Double the Work* does not explicitly acknowledge an ecological framework, but it does propose recommendations and solutions to the shortcomings of research that uses a deficit model approach. I will review the proposed research agenda in the next section with an ecological framework in mind.

Longitudinal Solutions

To amend the inconsistency in ELL labels, *Double the Work* wisely recommends that definitions for ELLs be more consistent over time and across states, and that they include clear benchmarks for the language proficiency tests used to categorize these students. From an ecological perspective, having clear benchmarks shifts the problem from the child to the pedagogical goals and progress in the scholastic environment.

As noted above, the literacy experience of ELLs has often been tracked in the research literature by assessing their performance only in relation to specific transition points in order to identify deficiencies rather than to chart progress (August & Hakuta, 1997). As such, the ELL research agendas emphasize the importance of academic achievement at particular transitional points, such as reclassification from LEP to FEP (August & Hakuta, 1997) and from high school to college (reporting of dropout rates) (Gunderson & Clarke, 1998). A focus on transitions ignores the role of learning over time and the cumulative effect of various factors that may cause changes in performance during transitional periods. For example, these transitional phases might include research on literacy development in the early grades in second-language learners (K–4; Verhoeven, 1991), the entrance or exit of this population from special education (Artiles et al., 2002), and the use of high school exit exams or reporting of college dropout rates (Garcia, 2001). However, the diversity of English-language ability mentioned in *Double the Work* and the authors' proposed shift from a focus on transition indicates a need for research that focuses on longitudinal studies.

Beyond its emphasis on using longitudinal observations of ELLs, the report suggests promoting interactions between contexts in order to reflect the students' diverse scholastic and life experiences. These interactions include flexible program models that accommodate the different students that have traditionally been subsumed in the ELL label (e.g., bilinguals, second-generation immigrants, newcomers, etc.). These models include allotting extra instructional time through an extended school year, year-round schooling, longer daily schedules, spending more than four years in high school, flexible school days that might enable them to participate in evening classes, weekend classes, internships, or distance-learning opportunities. Finally, the report proposes that states consider alternatives to high school exit exams. I argue that the underlying premise behind choice in assessment practices is that educational settings should adapt to different students by providing diverse forms of assessment. This report's charge to be more flexible is an indirect attack on the deficit model and places the onus of improving student performance on the flexibility of school programs. The flexibility of these options allows schools to create more responsive learning environments for its diverse student body and their varying environmental contexts (i.e., home, work, etc.).

From an ecological perspective, the authors of *Double the Work* encourage a focus on the school setting and recommend opportunities for restructuring that take into account the interactions of multiple systems. They do so first by proposing that states and districts adopt practices that promote consistent identification of ELLs. Consistency across these contexts (state, district, school) is pivotal if we are to adequately measure the academic progress of these students over time, and to examine the interchange between multiple settings and their impact on academic performance. Second, the interaction between contexts acknowledges that student participation in family contexts may include a part-time job or responsibility for siblings or elders, and that this may influence their school context. Schools' ability to accommodate and work in tandem with other contexts is crucial for the academic progress of ELLs and for future research examining such progress.

An ecological framework that focuses on changes over time is also applicable to *The Language Demands of School,* in which Bailey explores the use of the concept of academic English language in addressing the context of ELLs' diversity. AEL is relevant to ELLs in middle and high school because it accounts for students' varying scholastic trajectories. Collecting data on ELLs' development of AEL over time permits a more comprehensive tracking of these students and their diverse scholastic trajectories through middle and high school.

In fact, national research and federal policies about ELLs have largely focused on interventions in the elementary and prekindergarten years, leaving little room for resources and research agendas dedicated to equally effective methods in later grades (Snow, Burns, & Griffin, 1998). The preference for focusing on the early grades is a result of the assumption that early interventions can prevent later reading difficulties, but this is problematic because it ignores the context of ELLs entering schools at different grade levels, and therefore at different points along a continuum of literacy instruction. However, the theoretical and empirical research on AEL suggests its applicability "across the grade spans and as regards the entire school curriculum," resulting in a system that can accommodate multiple entry points into literacy instruction. The focus on AEL skills will help disentangle the issues that conflate language proficiency and content knowledge — primarily because AEL measures language that is specifically being taught in schools. Similarly, focusing on AEL skills will help create meaningful benchmarks over time, providing teachers, researchers, and policymakers with a better understanding of the instructional and policy gaps that need to be filled.

Double the Work and *The Language Demands of School* do not explicitly reference ecological frameworks, but the call to restructure programs and collect longitudinal data reflects a stronger emphasis on the consideration of student ecologies and contexts, as well as methods to measure school progress as much as student progress. In addition, the two texts specifically call for an accounting of school progress across contexts. The emphasis on the multiple contexts and their interchange — in this case, between the state and district, the district and the school — appears to implicitly engage an ecological framework. Acknowledging the relationship between contexts provides a more comprehensive picture of ELL learning, allowing one to recognize the various ways in which consistency or discrepancies across contexts facilitate or hinder the ability of schools to provide for these students.

Assessment across Time, Contexts, and Texts: Double the Work and the Language Demands of Schools

While Bronfenbrenner's (1977) ecological framework emphasizing the role of varied contexts in child development and learning has been around for thirty years, instructional reform policies for ELLs over the last two decades have focused primarily on elementary school literacy while virtually ignoring the diverse contexts surrounding the education of ELLs in the later grades. To shift the focus to adolescents — and subsequently to the contribution of schools to academic success — both *Double the Work* and *Language Demands of School* assert the ecologically minded importance of cross-state comparisons. Each encourages a nationwide model of consistent assessments and benchmarks called the World-Class Instructional Design Assessment (WIDA), which uses the same English-language proficiency standards, the same levels of proficiency, and the same English-language proficiency assessments for ELLs in kindergarten through grade 12. WIDA emphasizes the importance of testing throughout the upper grades as well as tracking progress over time. It provides a useful model for implementing constant assessments from kindergarten through twelfth grade and with consistency across the states that use it.

The authors of *Language Demands* stress the importance of frequent and consistent summative and formative testing throughout the grades and from the classroom to the nation.[6] The use of both large- and small-scale assessments applies an ecological framework and creates a coherent system for interpreting and addressing ELLs' language proficiency. An ecological model for analyzing student performance also tracks school efforts, avoiding a deficit model approach and centering on the responsiveness of the pedagogy.

Also in keeping with an ecological model, both *Double the Work* and *The Language Demands of School* stress the importance of multiple assessments of ELLs' language abilities, including in their native language. Native-language assessments can better predict English-language development over time, help to identify different linguistic subgroups (i.e., Spanish dominant bilingual, English dominant bilingual, etc.), and subsequently help to determine programmatic changes.

In addition, multiple assessments and native-language assessments resonate with the need to eliminate the use of the deficiency model for this population. Consistent, diagnostic, and responsive assessments can shift the focus to instruction, professional development, and standards that align with the concept of AEL.

Shifting the Paradigm

Both of these works present research, policy, and instructional agendas for amending the environments in which ELL students learn. The authors' recommendations reflect ecological changes — their visions for systemic improvement. However, this agenda is not explicitly acknowledged as being ecologically minded, and as a result it fails to challenge the predominant deficit-based paradigm for serving ELL students. Ultimately, the failure of these authors to explicitly name this shift in understanding may be a disservice to the potential impact of these reports. Educators, policymakers, and researchers may continue to evoke a deficit paradigm, thus encouraging the continued stigmatization of ELLs and escaping institutional responsibility that could be channeled into important reform efforts. The use of an explicit theoretical framework may prevent a possible misinterpretation of these recommendations. For example, consider how the title *Double the Work* seems to emphasize the idea of learning as burdensome. More important, the idea of doubling the work seems to suggest that an ELL student will have twice as much work to do or, alternatively, that they will have twice as many obstacles preventing their success.

Instead of thinking of ELL education as "double the work," perhaps future research would do better to conceptualize learning contexts, literacy agendas, and policy implications for ELLs as convergent pathways. This new research agenda would stress the convergence of all the factors that contribute to the literacy and language education of ELLs onto paths that lead toward a distinct goal — in this case, achieving academic success. These paths, composed of concentric circles representing the distinct environments that affect ELLs, all converge at a fixed point — academic mastery. This proposed model for future research acknowledges that scholastic paths may vary from student to student, but how these environmental factors meet and interact is important to understanding how to improve the educational experience of ELLs.

In *Double the Work* we see the variability in the academic, linguistic, immigration, and cultural experiences of ELL students. Research suggests that a multiplicity of experiences brings with it an assortment of assets, including increased metalinguistic capacities (Bialystok, 1997) and often increased motivation for learning (Suárez-Orozco & Suárez-Orozco, 2001). Given the diversity of linguistic and academic profiles among ELLs, the focus of research assessment must be on different points of entry into the school system, and on different ways of accessing the academic English language needed for literacy acquisition in the upper grades.

Double the Work and *The Language Demands of School* provide valuable perspectives on how structural changes may promote ELLs' English-language acquisition and literacy skills. However, researchers, policymakers, and practitioners should consider ELL students within an ecological framework in order to avoid any devaluation of linguistic differences and to provide a systemic lens for observing and monitoring the experiences of ELL students.

SABINA RAK NEUGEBAUER

Notes

1. I use the term English-language learners (ELLs) to refer to students who speak a language other than English at home or who have a family member in their household who speaks a language other than English. This definition is drawn from the work conducted by August and Hakuta (1997) and is intended to be an expansive definition to account for the variety of different language backgrounds of this group of learners. This definition also lends itself to definitions proposed in both texts analyzed in this review.
2. McDermott (1993) discusses deficit approaches in the context of students labeled as having disabilities. He argues that learning disabilities are largely a social construction. Disability labels reflect environmentally imposed values as opposed to an actual deficit that resides in the child.
3. While Bronfenbrenner also emphasizes the role of individual agency in child development, this review will focus largely on the roles of structures and context.
4. For instance, the federal government labels LEP students as those between the ages of three and twenty-one who are enrolled in elementary or secondary education, born outside the United States, speaking a language other than English, and without sufficient mastery of the English language to meet state standards and excel in an English-language classroom.
5. *Double the Work* also acknowledges that the diversity of these learners is problematic, not only for tracking purposes but also in regard to instruction.
6. Summative testing helps teachers make programmatic changes, and formative testing helps teachers make appropriate and adaptive lesson plans that help students grasp the academic language and content knowledge simultaneously.

References

Abedi, J. (2006). Language issues in item development. In S. M. Downing & T. M. Haladyna (Eds.), *Handbook of test development* (pp. 377–398). Mahwah, NJ: Lawrence Erlbaum.

Abedi, J., & Gándara, P. (2006). Performance of English language learners as a subgroup in large-scale assessment: Interaction of research and policy. *Educational Measurement Issues and Practice, 25*(4), 36–46.

Artiles, A., Rueda, R., Salazar, J., & Higareda, I. (2002). English-language learner representation in special education in California urban school districts. In D. Losen & G. Orfield (Eds.), *Racial inequity in special education* (pp. 117–136). Cambridge, MA: The Civil Rights Project at Harvard University and Harvard Education Press.

August, D. E., & Hakuta, K. E. (1997). *Improving schooling for language-minority children: A research agenda.* Washington, DC: National Academies Press.

Bialystok, E. (1997). Effects of bilingualism and biliteracy on children's emerging concepts of print. *Developmental Psychology, 33,* 429–440.

Biancarosa, G., & Snow, C. E. (2004). *Reading next: A vision for action and research in middle and high school literacy — A report from the Carnegie Corporation of New York.* Washington, DC: Alliance for Excellent Education.

Bronfenbrenner, U. (1977). Towards an experimental ecology of human development. *American Psychologist, 32,* 513–531.

de Jong, E. J. (2004). After exit: Academic achievement patterns of former English language learners. *Educational Policy Analysis Archives, 12*(50). Retrieved on January 21, 2008, from http://epaa.asu.edu/epaa/v12n50/

Garcia, E. E. (2001). *Hispanic education in the United States: Raices y alas.* New York: Rowan & Littlefield.

Goldenberg, C., Rueda, R. S., & August, D. (2006). Social and cultural influences on the literacy attainment of language-minority children and youth. In D. August & T. Shanahan (Eds.), *Developing literacy in second-language learners: Report of the national literacy panel on language minority children and youth* (pp. 269–318). Mahwah, NJ: Lawrence Erlbaum.

Gunderson, L., & Clarke, D. (1998). An exploration of the relationship between ESL students' backgrounds and their English and academic achievement. In T. Shanahan, F. V. Rodriguez-Brown, C. Worthman, J. C. Burnison, & A. Cheung (Eds.), *47th yearbook of the National Reading Conference* (pp. 264–273). Chicago: National Reading Conference.

Harry, B., Klingner, J., Cramer, E. P., & Sturges, K. M. (2007). *Case studies of minority student placement in special education.* New York: Teachers College Press.

Lesaux, N. (2006). Building consensus: Future directions for research on English language learners at risk for learning difficulties. *Teachers College Record, 108,* 2406–2438.

Mahoney, K., & MacSwan, J. (2005). Reexamining identification and reclassification of English language learners: A critical discussion of select state practices. *Bilingual Research Journal, 29,* 1, 31–42.

McDermott, R.P. (1993). The acquisition of a child by a learning disability. In S. Chaiklin & J. Lave (Eds.), *Understanding practice: Perspectives on activity and context* (pp. 269–305). Cambridge, England: Cambridge University Press.

Rappaport, J. (1981). In praise of paradox: A social policy of empowerment over prevention. *American Journal of Community Psychology, 9,* 10–25.

Snow, C. E., Burns, M. S., & Griffin, P. (Eds.). (1998). *Preventing reading difficulties in young children.* Washington, DC: National Academies Press.

Suárez-Orozco, C., & Suárez-Orozco, M. (2001). *Children of immigration: The developing child series.* Cambridge, MA: Harvard University Press.

Valenzuela, A. (1991). *Subtractive schooling: U.S.-Mexican youth and the politics of caring.* Albany: State University of New York Press.

Verhoeven, L. (1991). Acquisition of reading in a second language. *Reading Research Quarterly, 25,* 90–114.

Wright, W. E. (2005). *Evolution of federal policy and implications of No Child Left Behind for language minority students.* Tempe, AZ: Education Policy.

INFORMED CHOICES FOR STRUGGLING ADOLESCENT READERS:
A RESEARCH-BASED GUIDE TO INSTRUCTIONAL PROGRAMS AND PRACTICES
by Donald D. Deshler, Annemarie Sullivan Palincsar, Gina Biancarosa,
& Marnie Nair.
Newark, DE: International Reading Association, 2007. 264 pp. $28.95.

TAKING ACTION ON ADOLESCENT LITERACY: AN IMPLEMENTATION GUIDE
FOR SCHOOL LEADERS
by Judith L. Irvin, Julie Meltzer, & Melinda Dukes.
*Alexandria, VA: Association for Supervision and Curriculum Development, 2007.
268 pp. $30.95.*

Concerns about adolescents' impoverished reading and writing skills have
existed in U.S. classrooms for much of the twentieth century (Moore, Bean,
Birdyshaw, & Rycik, 1999; National Commission on Excellence in Education,
1983; also see Jacobs in this issue). Toward the end of the century, national
and international organizations[1] began calling for policymakers and practitioners to unite in the common goal of developing a better understanding of
teaching reading and writing at secondary levels. The research community
echoed this call, with adolescent literacy topping the International Reading
Association's annual researcher-generated "What's Hot, What's Not" list since
2001 (Cassidy, 2007).

Following the 2004 release of the landmark *Reading Next* report, and its
introduction of the term *adolescent literacy crisis* (Biancarosa & Snow, 2006, p. 7),
a shift occurred in the publishing world. Although texts on topics related to
adolescents' reading and writing skills were certainly published before 2004
(see Jacobs in this issue), the newly named adolescent literacy crisis prompted
the publication of dozens of adolescent literacy books and reports in the span
of only a few years (see Table 1 for a sample of recently published adolescent
literacy books and reports). The rapid proliferation of literature on adolescent
literacy is an encouraging sign that the field of education is now appropriately
concerned with how to improve reading, writing, and thinking in U.S. middle
and high schools; however, new adolescent literacy materials are appearing at
such a swift pace that even literacy-focused middle and high school administrators and teachers may be overwhelmed when choosing resources to guide
instructional improvement efforts.

Despite the emergence of dozens of new books and reports detailing various aspects of adolescent literacy research and practice, including the previously underrepresented topics of adolescent English-language learners (ELLs;
Short & Fitzsimmons, 2007) and writing instruction (Graham & Perin, 2007),
few (if any) resources have been able to answer the call set forth in *Reading
Next* for a "balanced vision" of adolescent literacy work (Biancarosa & Snow,

Harvard Educational Review   Vol. 78   No. 1   Spring 2008

TABLE 1 *A Sample of Recently Published Adolescent Literacy Books and Reports[6]*

2008

Best Practices in Adolescent Literacy Instruction, edited by Alvermann et al.

Meeting the Challenge of Adolescent Literacy: Research We Have, Research We Need, edited by Conley et al.

2007

Academic Literacy Instruction for Adolescents: A Guidance Document from the Center on Instruction, edited by Torgesen et al.

Adolescent Literacy Instruction: Policies and Promising Practices, edited by Lewis & Moorman

Adolescent Literacy Research and Practice, edited Jetton & Dole

Adolescent Literacy: Turning Promise into Practice, edited by Beers et al.

Double the Work: Challenges and Solutions to Acquiring Language and Academic Literacy for Adolescent English Language Learners, by Short & Fitzsimmons

Improving Adolescent Literacy: Content Area Strategies at Work, by Fisher & Frey

Improving Literacy Instruction in Middle and High Schools: A Guide for Principals, edited by Torgesen et al.

Informed Choices for Struggling Adolescent Readers: A Research-Based Guide to Instructional Programs and Practices, by Deshler et al.

Is Literacy Enough?: Pathways to Academic Success for Adolescents, by Snow et al.

Literacy Instruction in The Content Areas: Getting to the Core of Middle and High School Improvement, by Heller & Greenleaf

Shaping Literacy Achievement: Research We Have, Research We Need, edited by Pressley et al.

Writing Next: Effective Strategies to Improve Writing of Adolescents in Middle and High Schools, by Graham & Perin

2006

50 Content-Area Strategies For Adolescent Literacy, by Fisher et al.

Creating Literacy-Rich Schools For Adolescents, by Ivey & Fisher

Meeting Five Critical Challenges of High School Reform: Lessons from Research on Three Reform Models, by Quint

The Next Chapter: A School Board Guide to Improving Adolescent Literacy, by the National School Boards Association

Principled Practices for Adolescent Literacy: A Framework for Instruction and Policy, by Sturtevant et al.

Reading Next: A Vision for Action and Research in Middle and High School Literacy (2nd ed.), by Biancarosa & Snow

Reconceptualizing the Literacies in Adolescents' Lives, by Alvermann et al.

2005

Reading at Risk: How States Can Respond to the Crisis in Adolescent Literacy, by the National Association of State Boards of Education

Note: Full bibliographic information for these texts can be found in the References section of this review.

2006, p. 5). This balanced vision includes "effecting immediate change for current students" while simultaneously "building the literacy field's knowledge base" (p. 5). Few texts have been able to strike such a balance between action and theory, simultaneously capturing the manifold reasons for the adolescent literacy crisis, mining the current literacy and school reform research for solutions, and then delivering jargon-free answers to common instructional questions. This is an understandably tall order for a single text to fill, yet resources that provide a balanced vision are needed by U.S. middle and high school staff who have limited time to study the growing number of adolescent literacy texts appearing on the market.

Although a single-text solution that effectively presents a balanced vision of adolescent literacy may be unavailable, a potential solution does exist in the form of two recently published books — *Informed Choices for Struggling Adolescent Readers: A Research-Based Guide to Instructional Programs and Practices* (2007) and *Taking Action on Adolescent Literacy: An Implementation Guide for School Leaders* (2007). As their titles suggest, these texts, respectively, provide an overview of current adolescent literacy research and interventions, and an implementation guide for school leaders to enact changes that may improve adolescents' literacy achievement. If these two books are consulted as a pair, perhaps as the focus of a school-based literacy team's work, then school leaders may find both the theoretical and practical supports — the balanced vision — needed to begin improving adolescent literacy achievement now.

Informed Choices: Building Background Knowledge

In striking a balance between adolescent literacy theory and practice, school staff should first consider *Informed Choices for Struggling Adolescent Readers* for its excellent review of current adolescent literacy research and interventions. The premise of the book is that middle and high school educators will make better organizational and instructional decisions if they are equipped with comprehensive information about adolescent literacy research and interventions. In Part One, the first three chapters of the book provide an in-depth understanding of the causes behind the adolescent literacy crisis and an understanding of the components of high-quality adolescent literacy instruction. The final two chapters of this section provide detailed information about the costs and processes associated with improving instruction at scale. The research-based suggestions made throughout these chapters are supported by frequent case-study vignettes from middle and high schools first noted in the book's introduction, providing brief glimpses of the successful translation of research into practice. Building on the foundational understanding of adolescent literacy established in Part One, Part Two provides an overview of the array of instructional programs and interventions currently aimed at improving adolescent literacy.

Administrators and teachers may not read *Informed Choices* in a single sitting, as each chapter is filled with numerous big ideas and scores of references to larger research studies; however, *Informed Choices* is exactly the book that administrators and teachers should, and hopefully will, reference repeatedly as they make organizational and instructional decisions. *Informed Choices* collects and clearly explains much of the recent research on adolescent literacy that otherwise can only be gleaned by reading dozens of books and journal articles. The book's first three chapters respectively address the "myths and realities" of adolescent literacy, the components of adolescent literacy,[2] and how those components can be supported by particular instructional characteristics.[3] Together, these chapters help readers understand why adolescent literacy is important, why adolescent literacy in the United States is currently in crisis, and what instructional components are needed to improve achievement now.

Although current research on adolescent literacy is certainly reviewed elsewhere (see Table 1), *Informed Choices* is written with school staff in mind and highlights instructional suggestions whenever describing research. For instance, in the section on vocabulary and background knowledge (chapter 2), the authors point out that an important part of increasing adolescents' vocabularies is "pushing students to become active learners of words by providing them with opportunities and the motivation to talk about, compare, analyze, and use target words and by providing these opportunities on multiple occasions" (p. 41). As with most suggestions found in *Informed Choices*, this suggestion is buoyed by references to research-based resources such as Beck, McKeown, & Kucan's influential book, *Bringing Words to Life* (2002), and articles by August, Carlo, Dressler, & Snow (2005) and Nagy & Scott (2000) that may be of great interest to literacy specialists and coaches.

Where possible, the authors offer further recommendations for how practices can be modified and improved for particular populations, like including cognate instruction[5] for English-language learners (e.g., teaching ELLs to notice and capitalize on similar spellings, meanings, and patterns behind words that share the same root in both their first and second languages). Following this specific instructional suggestion aimed at adolescent ELLs, the authors end by providing vignettes from Boston's Fitzgerald and Hampshire Schools — two of the case-study schools highlighted throughout the book — demonstrating how such instructional suggestions have been successfully enacted with fourth, fifth, and sixth graders in the Boston area. In many respects, the first three chapters of *Informed Choices* efficiently provide an in-depth, research-based extension of the fifteen elements of effective adolescent literacy programs[4] first presented in *Reading Next* (Biancarosa & Snow, 2006, p. 12) and could easily be assigned as background reading for a school's content-area teachers or for preservice teachers in an adolescent literacy course. At the very least, the "myths and realities" chapter should be read by teacher teams in order to discredit myths such as "Adolescents today can't read like adolescents used to read" (p. 14). Such myths need to be replaced with realities such as "Adolescent literacy demands have changed radically" (p. 18), and "Instruction has not kept pace with demands" (p. 19).

In Part Two of *Informed Choices*, the authors introduce and describe forty-eight programs and interventions aimed at improving adolescents' reading, writing, and thinking skills. This section of the book provides nuanced, research-based descriptions of high-quality adolescent literacy instruction so that administrators and teachers can choose interventions that are best suited for their individual schools. Although Part Two of *Informed Choices* first appears to be a static, glorified list of adolescent literacy programs, it may be one of the most valuable contributions the book makes to the field by providing a resource that administrators and teachers can quickly and easily refer to over time.

The authors state that four basic questions guided their selection of the forty-eight interventions included in the book: (1) Was the program aimed at adolescents? (2) Was the program literacy-focused? (3) Were the materials age-appropriate? and (4) Was the program implemented widely? These are reasonable criteria that mirror the questions school staff might ask when considering the adoption of an intervention. Notably absent from the list is the question, Does the intervention significantly improve student achievement? Or, put another way, Does the intervention work? The authors were wise to not provide clear-cut answers on this front, particularly given the dearth of high-quality evaluations available for all the interventions. Furthermore, the authors emphasize that it is not a simple matter of whether an intervention *works* or not, but more a matter of whether an intervention works for a particular school and particular student population. They suggest that teachers and administrators "take care to go the extra step of determining whether that evidence [of programmatic success] is for students similar to their own. . . . Administrators and teachers should at the very least investigate the number and results of studies conducted with students similar to theirs" (p. 120). Such cautions reflect the overall tenor of *Informed Choices*, as the authors provide background information, not prescriptions.

In a series of four helpful matrices (pp. 122–129), the authors sort the forty-eight interventions by the types of students the programs serve, program features, evaluated features, and skills and strategies the programs highlight. Following the matrices is an alphabetized section of program descriptions that detail the instructional approach, professional development mechanism, available program evaluation information, and contact information for each program. The matrices and program descriptions will serve school staff well, as the information about the programs is displayed in a way that can be quickly accessed and analyzed according to student needs. For example, an administrator looking for an intervention that targets ELLs, focuses on vocabulary, and has strong professional development and technology components can easily use the matrices to find a program such as Accelerated Reader, which seems to fit all of the above criteria. By turning to the subsequent program description, an administrator can read more about Accelerated Reader in order to decide whether or not the instructional approach, professional development, and program evaluation components are a good fit for the school. By designing Part Two of *Informed Choices* to be used in this manner, the authors acknowledge that only administrators and teachers know their schools and students well enough to choose which recommendations, instructional practices, and interventions will work best.

One of the greatest strengths of *Informed Choices* — one of the strongest reasons for disseminating the book widely to middle and high school administrators and teachers — is that the authors never shy away from the complexity of the topic nor from the details of the research underlying recommended practices. At the end of nearly every chapter, the authors are careful to note that developing, implementing, and maintaining a high-quality, literacy-oriented instructional program grounded in the content areas is not a simple task. For example, at the end of chapter 2, after discussing the most promising research behind the seven identified components of adolescent literacy instruction, the authors caution that "an effective adolescent literacy program will not simply meld all of the types of content mentioned [in the chapter]" (p. 47). The authors repeatedly remind readers that improving adolescents' reading, writing, and thinking skills is not merely a matter of piling on various instructional techniques; instead, improvement comes from continual analysis of students' needs and careful selection of the research-proven instructional practices to meet those needs. Such caveats throughout the book serve as necessary (if sometimes painful) reminders that the path ahead for secondary administrators and teachers is neither well marked nor easy to tread. By highlighting complexity at every turn, the authors guide readers through a process of how to think about adolescent literacy and the variety of interventions and implementation options available, without offering quick-fix strategies or belittling the reader by oversimplifying the content.

Informed Choices has many strengths, the most prominent being its clear, comprehensive, and nuanced introduction to the field of adolescent literacy. However, the book has one major shortcoming. Because of its focus on building administrators' and teachers' background knowledge, readers may finish the book with an important question: How do we apply this information? Chapters 4 and 5 begin to address this question, tackling the thorny problems of paying for adolescent literacy interventions and implementing the interventions in schools where content-area teachers may be less than enthusiastic about devoting their time and energy to literacy instruction. Nevertheless, these two rich chapters provide only the briefest of road maps for how to enact change.

Echoing larger discussions of school reform (Elmore, 2004; Fullan, 2001, 2007) and effective literacy reform (Goldenberg, 2004; Langer, 2002), chapters 4 and 5 discuss school improvement efforts without providing clear action steps that spur readers to become agents of reform. For example, chapter 5 presents the case study of a Midwestern high school undergoing reform and outlines its five-year process of change, including enhancing content instruction, and embedding strategy instruction. However, while the process may make a great deal of sense in the case study presented, it is not readily apparent to readers how the change process described can be reproduced in other school contexts. The closest *Informed Choices* comes to a clear guide for implementing reform is found in a discussion of overarching principles that "drive successful adolescent literacy initiatives" (p. 98), such as "Organizations and people must be ready to change," and "Key stakeholders must be engaged in making decisions about changes to be made." These are undoubtedly important aspects of undertaking change efforts, but only the savviest administrators and teachers will be able to translate these principles into actionable steps in a particular school.

The major strength and ultimate weakness of *Informed Choices* is that it suggests that the background knowledge it provides may be enough to help readers make "informed choices" regarding the myriad aspects of adolescent literacy introduced in the volume. Even researchers, policymakers, and practitioners who are well versed in adolescent literacy research may have difficulty making informed decisions after a single pass through the book. Perhaps the book's true power lies in its ability to serve as an excellent reference and companion to a more prescriptive text that guides administrators and teachers down the road of literacy-based school reform. *Informed Choices* provides an excellent "what" and "why" with regard to adolescent literacy instruction, but for middle and high school administrators and teachers who need to make decisions today, *Informed Choices* needs a companion text to further outline "how" to quickly enact change.

Taking Action: Outlining the Change Process

Taking Action on Adolescent Literacy may be the best available companion text to *Informed Choices*, because *Taking Action* is designed as an implementation guide for school leaders (e.g., administrators, teacher-leaders, literacy coaches) to immediately begin changing patterns within a school to improve adolescents' literacy achievement. It is a book that, when read together with *Informed Choices*, provides the much-needed balance called for in *Reading Next*. *Taking Action* contains ideas similar to those presented in *Informed Choices* about *what* to do (e.g., connecting literacy instruction and content-area knowledge); however, *Taking Action* focuses much more on *how* school leaders can create change. Based on the authors' own research and extensive experiences in middle and high schools, *Taking Action* offers wise recommendations about how to form a vision, build consensus, and begin doing the actual work of changing literacy instruction at scale. Weaving together vast numbers of suggestions into a manageable action plan, the authors posit a three-stage model that includes developing and communicating a literacy vision; translating the literacy vision into action; and creating and sustaining a supportive, literacy-rich environment (pp. 2–3). This three-stage plan is further explained through a diagram entitled "Leadership Model for Improving Adolescent Literacy" (p. 17). This diagram guides the structure and content of *Taking Action* after the book's introduction, which helps readers locate particular suggestions within the larger context of the authors' change model.

Written in jargon-free prose, and using fewer citations and more case-study vignettes than *Informed Choices*, the book presents research in bite-size, action-oriented sections that administrators and teacher-leaders will appreciate. On nearly every page, the book answers the question: "What do I need to do *now* to begin improving literacy achievement?" Unlike *Informed Choices*, *Taking Action* does not provide as rich (or as nuanced) descriptions of research studies that can build background knowledge and guide administrators and teachers in their decisionmaking. Instead, *Taking Action* errs on the side of providing just enough background knowledge to help school leaders understand how to follow the proposed comprehensive model for change. *Taking Action* certainly should not be the only resource administrators and teachers consult as they undertake adolescent literacy reform efforts, yet it does provide a powerful framework that could easily be supplemented with the rich information from *Informed Choices*.

The real power of *Taking Action* lies in its robust "Leadership Model for Improving Adolescent Literacy." This multifaceted bull's-eye diagram has three main components that reflect the context, work, and core of adolescent literacy reform. The outer rings of this bull's-eye include "Sustaining Literacy Development" and "Integrating Literacy & Learning." The inner ring includes action steps such as "Implement a Literacy Action Plan," "Support Teachers to Improve Instruction," "Use Data to Make Decisions," "Build Leadership Capacity," and "Allocate Resources." The center of the bull's-eye focuses on improving "Student Motivation, Engagement, and Achievement" — a primary goal of adolescent literacy reform.

Taking Action is organized around the various aspects introduced in this diagram, with the first few chapters focusing on the inner rings: it addresses why adolescents' motivation and engagement is important, why it is essential to integrate literacy and learning across content areas, and how literacy development can be sustained with community and district support. These chapters most resemble the resources provided in *Informed Choices*, ranging from discussions of the literacy needs of ELLs and students with learning disabilities, to ways that leaders can support content-area teachers in providing literacy support. Compared to the descriptions of research found in *Informed Choices*, the first chapters of *Taking Action* initially feel a bit sparse; however, these introductory chapters provide clear rationales for why adolescents need literacy support and why it is up to school leaders and content-area teachers to help provide that support. With fewer citations per paragraph, many bulleted lists, and chapter-ends that include summary "Key Messages," the chapters in *Taking Action* can easily be consumed by busy school staff and can provide a starting point for using the more-detailed information in *Informed Choices*.

Administrators, department heads, teacher-leaders, literacy coaches, and other school personnel in charge of leading literacy-based school change will surely find Part Two of *Taking Action* — the "Action Steps" chapters beginning with chapter 5 — to be most helpful. Each chapter tackles one of the sections of the inner ring of the leadership diagram, presenting school leaders with concrete steps for creating schoolwide literacy action plans that address students' weaknesses and support teachers in improving their instruction in light of students' needs. Helpful charts are presented throughout the five chapters in Part Two, connecting improvement goals (e.g., coordinating curriculum and instruction across subject areas) with time lines, action steps, people responsible, resources, and evidence of success. These charts demonstrate how school leaders can connect research-based suggestions, such as using formal and informal assessment instruments with the individual steps needed to implement these suggestions. Furthermore, these final five chapters are filled with realistic advice about a variety of concerns, including how to work with resistant teachers and how to allocate time for the various activities needed to support change efforts. These chapters will appeal to practical, change-oriented school leaders who might periodically grow impatient with the extensive background knowledge and limited action steps provided by *Informed Choices*.

Overall, *Taking Action* is a highly readable book that mirrors and expands upon brief recommendations made in literacy reform-oriented reports such as *Reading Next* and Torgesen, Houston, and Rissman's *Improving Literacy Instruction in Middle and High Schools: A Guide for Principals* (2007). Administrators can consume *Taking Action* in a day or two and then later refer to the dozens of helpful graphics and charts when planning staff development sessions. The book is structured to be useful to busy administrators, with each chapter organized around a different component of the leadership model diagram, text boxes reiterating why each component is essential, and bulleted lists of "Key Messages" at the end of each chapter summarizing main points. The structure and prose of the book make it easy for school leaders to quickly skim and discover salient next steps. Moreover, the book is immediately useful to literacy coaches and reading specialists who may reference the graphics and bulleted lists when organizing literacy team meetings. The authors of this book understand the reality that most school leaders don't have the time or resources to become experts in adolescent literacy. Nevertheless, *Taking Action* appropriately positions administrators and other staff as instructional leaders who must know enough about adolescent literacy to guide necessary changes.

A Balanced Vision: Why Two Texts Are Better Than One

Administrators and teachers should read *Informed Choices* and *Taking Action* as a pair in order to glimpse the balanced vision articulated in *Reading Next*. These books are near-perfect companions because of their distinct but related goals: *Informed Choices* reviews the manifold research-based possibilities for improving adolescents' literacy skills; *Taking Action* provides action steps for leaders to improve adolescent literacy instruction and achievement in schools. The authors of *Informed Choices* make it clear that there is already a great deal of research providing guidance for what kinds of instruction and instructional settings support adolescents' literacy skills. The authors of *Taking Action* make it clear that if school leaders follow specific action steps, positive changes can occur. Both books provide information and options to administrators and teachers looking for concrete answers about adolescent literacy reform. *Taking Action* provides straightforward suggestions that may appear to gloss over larger debates in the research literature, while *Informed Choices* details the complexity of adolescent literacy instructional decisions while at times appearing to gloss over immediate action steps. Taken together, the books build upon each other's strengths and jointly address any individual shortcomings.

An example of how these texts complement each other is illustrated by their respective discussions of literacy coaching as a form of professional development and support for middle and high school teachers. *Reading Next* identifies long-term and ongoing professional development as a key element of adolescent literacy programs. Both *Informed Choices* and *Taking Action* discuss literacy coaching as one of the more promising professional development models currently available. Although coaching is presented as a promising support in both books, differences arise when one compares how the two sets of authors introduce the topic — differences that clearly illustrate the need for readers to consult the books as a pair.

In *Taking Action*, coaches are introduced with the statements, "A school's literacy improvement effort can be more effective if led by a professional literacy coach. A well-trained literacy coach offers invaluable feedback to teachers, providing a clearer picture of their strengths and weaknesses" (p. 149). These statements are straightforward and suggest to administrators that coaches are a worthwhile investment. In *Informed Choices*, literacy coaching is also offered as a viable form of professional development and support, but it is introduced in a far more cautious manner: "Some states and districts have turned to literacy coaches as a form of support for classroom teachers seeking to meet the literacy needs of their students. As this volume goes to press, there is little systematic research on the efficacy of literacy coaches, particularly at the secondary level" (p. 58).

While the authors of *Informed Choices* are clear whenever the research base does not fully support a particular decision, such as hiring coaches, the authors of *Taking Action* are more willing to make recommendations based equally on research and their own experiences in school reform. Whether or not to spend $50,000 to hire a new literacy coach is precisely the kind of decision that *Informed Choices* does not necessarily help administrators make, and yet the scant research behind literacy coaching is not discussed at length in *Taking Action*. The authors of *Taking Action* are willing and able to take the additional step in recommending practices that they believe school leaders may want to consider, even if the research base has not yet fully endorsed those practices. Although recommending practices that are not fully supported by research is a somewhat risky enterprise, the authors of *Taking Action* are appropriately heeding the call from *Reading Next* to attend to the needs of students in schools today. Administrators who are eager to provide high-quality professional development opportunities for their teachers may want to consider literacy coaching as a promising option even before the practice is fully supported by research. Moreover, by consulting both *Taking Action* and *Informed Choices* in concert, school leaders will be able to cross-reference recommendations before moving forward, thereby safeguarding against making hasty decisions. Neither book's approach may be completely satisfying alone, alternately erring on the side of too little or too much caution; however, together the books highlight the tensions between action and research in adolescent literacy and ultimately offer valuable information about how to make informed decisions now.

Informed Choices and *Taking Action* mirror the tensions that secondary administrators, teachers, and other school staff face on a daily basis. On one hand, middle and high school leaders want to institute research-based organizational and instructional practices that improve adolescent literacy achievement. On the other hand, these leaders must make thousands of decisions every week based on constantly shifting student, parent, teacher, and economic factors. There simply may not be enough research, time, or money to support all of the decisions that must be made. By consulting *Informed Choices* and *Taking Action* simultaneously, and specifically, by using *Taking Action* as an overall guide to reform while using *Informed Choices* to add nuance and complexity to the decisionmaking process, middle and high school administrators and staff have a much better chance of creating change. Middle and high school literacy teams nationwide should consult these two texts as they prepare to meet the challenge of improving adolescent literacy achievement.

JACY IPPOLITO

Notes

1. Such organizations include: the Alliance for Excellent Education (http://www.all4ed.org/), the Carnegie Corporation of New York (http://www.carnegie.org/literacy/), the International Reading Association (http://www.ira.org/), and the National Council of Teachers of English (http://www.ncte.org/collections/adolescentliteracy).
2. Components described in the text (pp. 37–47), include decoding, fluency, vocabulary and background knowledge, direct and explicit comprehension instruction, writing, information and communication technologies literacies, and alternative literacies.
3. Instructional characteristics described in the text (pp. 49–55) include teaching for transfer, diverse texts, self-direction and choice in goal setting and reading, text-based collaborative learning, formative and summative assessment, scaffolds for struggling students in content areas, and technology as a tool. Supports (pp. 57–59), include increased time for literacy, high-quality professional development, teacher teams, coordination across content areas, strategic tutoring, and literacy coaches.

4. The fifteen elements listed in *Reading Next* are: (1) direct, explicit comprehension instruction, (2) effective instructional principles embedded in content, (3) motivation and self-directed learning, (4) text-based collaborative learning, (5) strategic tutoring, (6) diverse texts, (7) intensive writing, (8) a technology component, (9) ongoing formative assessment of students, (10) extended time for literacy, (11) professional development, (12) ongoing summative assessment of students and programs, (13) teacher teams, (14) leadership, and (15) a comprehensive and coordinated literacy program (Biancarosa & Snow, 2004, pp. 3–4).
5. Cognate instruction might include, for example, connecting words such as *admiración* in Spanish with *admiration* in English. Asking students to note similarities and differences provides the opportunity to learn how the word-ending "-ción" often becomes "-tion" when shifting from Spanish to English.
6. For a more comprehensive listing of recently published adolescent literacy books and reports, please visit http://www.adlit.org/researchandreports/ and http://www.carnegie.org/literacy/

References

Alvermann, D. E., Hinchman, K. A., Moore, D. W., Phelps, S. F., & Waff, D. R. (Eds.). (2006). *Reconceptualizing the literacies in adolescents' lives*. Mahwah, NJ: Lawrence Erlbaum.

Alvermann, D. E., Hinchman, K. A., & Sheridan-Thomas, H. K. (Eds.). (2008). *Best practices in adolescent literacy instruction*. New York: The Guilford Press.

August, D., Carlo, M., Dressler, C., & Snow, C. (2005). The critical role of vocabulary development for English language learners. *Learning Disabilities Research & Practice, 20,* 50–57.

Beck, I. L., & McKeown, M. G., & Kucan, L. (2002). *Bringing words to life*. New York: The Guilford Press.

Beers, K., Probst, R. E., & Rief, L. (Eds.). (2007). *Adolescent literacy: Turning promise into practice*. Portsmouth, NH: Heinemann.

Biancarosa, G., & Snow, C. E. (2004). *Reading next — A vision for action and research in middle and high school literacy: A report from Carnegie Corporation of New York*. Washington, DC: Alliance for Excellent Education. Retrieved December 17, 2007, from http://www.carnegie.org/literacy/pdf/ReadingNext.pdf

Biancarosa, G., & Snow, C. E. (2006). *Reading next: A vision for action and research in middle and high school literacy — A report from Carnegie Corporation of New York* (2nd ed.). Washington, DC: Alliance for Excellent Education. Retrieved December 17, 2007, from http://www.carnegie.org/literacy/pdf/ReadingNext.pdf

Cassidy, J. (2007, February). What's hot, what's not for 2007. *Reading Today, 24*(4), 1.

Conley, M. W., Freidhoff, J. R., Sherry, M. B., & Tuckey, S. F. (Eds.). (2008). *Meeting the challenge of adolescent literacy: Research we have, research we need*. New York: Guilford Press.

Elmore, R. F. (2004). *School reform from the inside out: Policy, practice, and performance*. Cambridge, MA: Harvard Education Press.

Fisher, D. B., Brozo, W. G., Frey, N., & Ivey G. (2006). *50 content area strategies for adolescent literacy*. New York: Prentice Hall.

Fisher, D. B., & Frey, N. (2007). *Improving adolescent literacy: Content area strategies at work* (2nd ed.). New York: Prentice Hall.

Fullan, M. (2001). *Leading in a culture of change: Being effective in complex times*. San Francisco: Jossey-Bass.

Fullan, M. (2007). *The new meaning of educational change* (4th ed.). New York: Teachers College Press.

Goldenberg, C. (2004). *Successful school change: Creating settings to improve teaching and learning.* New York: Teachers College Press.

Graham, S., & Perin, D. (2007). *Writing next: Effective strategies to improve writing of adolescents in middle and high schools.* Washington, DC: Alliance for Excellent Education.

Heller, R., & Greenleaf, C. (2007). *Literacy instruction in the content areas: Getting to the core of middle and high school improvement.* Washington, DC: Alliance for Excellent Education.

Ivey, G., & Fisher, D. (2006). *Creating literacy-rich schools for adolescents.* Alexandria, VA: Association for Supervision and Curriculum Development.

Jetton, T. L., & Dole, J. A. (Eds.). (2007). *Adolescent literacy research and practice.* New York: The Guilford Press.

Langer, J. A. (2002). Effective literacy instruction: Building successful reading and writing programs. Urbana, IL: National Council of Teachers of English.

Lewis, J., & Moorman, G. (Eds.). (2007). *Adolescent literacy instruction: Policies and promising practices.* Newark, DE: International Reading Association.

Moore, D. W., Bean, T. W., Birdyshaw, D., & Rycik, J. A. (1999). *Adolescent literacy: A position statement for the Commission of Adolescent Literacy of the International Reading Association.* Newark, DE: International Reading Association.

Nagy, W. E., & Scott, J. A. (2000). Vocabulary processes. In M. L. Kamil, P. B. Mosenthal, P. D. Pearson, & R. Barr (Eds.), *Handbook of reading research* (Vol. III, pp. 269–284). Mahwah, NJ: Lawrence Erlbaum.

National Association of State Boards of Education. (2005, October). *Reading at risk: How states can respond to the crisis in adolescent literacy.* Alexandria, VA: Author.

National Commission on Excellence in Education. (1983). *A nation at risk: The imperative for educational reform.* Washington, DC: U.S. Government Printing Office.

National School Boards Association. (2006). *The next chapter: A school board guide to improving adolescent literacy.* Alexandria, VA: Author.

Quint, J. (2006). *Meeting five critical challenges of high school reform: Lessons from research on three reform models.* New York: MDRC.

Pressley, M., Billman, A. K., Perry, K. H., Reffitt, K. E., & Reynolds, J. M. (Eds.). (2007). *Shaping literacy achievement: Research we have, research we need.* New York: The Guilford Press.

Short, D., & Fitzsimmons, S. (2007). *Double the work: Challenges and solutions to acquiring language and academic literacy for adolescent English language learners — A report to Carnegie Corporation of New York.* Washington, DC: Alliance for Excellent Education. Retrieved December 17, 2007, from http://www.all4ed.org/files/DoubleWork.pdf

Snow, C. E., Porche, M. V., Tabors, P. O., & Harris, S. R. (2007). *Is literacy enough?: Pathways to academic success for Adolescents.* Baltimore: Brookes.

Sturtevant, E. G., Boyd, F. B., Brozo, W. G., Hinchman, K. A., Moore, D. W., & Alvermann, D. E. (2006). *Principled practices for adolescent literacy: A framework for instruction and policy.* Mahwah, NJ: Lawrence Erlbaum.

Torgesen, J., Houston, D., & Rissman, L. (2007). *Improving literacy instruction in middle and high schools: A guide for principals.* Portsmouth, NH: RMC Research Corporation, Center on Instruction.

Torgesen, J. K., Houston, D. D., Rissman, L. M., Decker, S. M., Roberts, G., Vaughn, S., et al. (2007). *Academic literacy instruction for adolescents: A guidance document from the Center on Instruction.* Portsmouth, NH: RMC Research Corporation, Center on Instruction.

Notes on Contributors

ILENE BERMAN is a program director in the Education Division at the National Governors Association Center for Best Practices, which provides policy advice, research, and technical assistance to governors and their advisors. Her areas of expertise include literacy, high school redesign, turning around low-performing schools, and school choice. Berman has coauthored two governors' guides, *Reading to Achieve: A Governor's Guide to Adolescent Literacy* (2005) and *Reaching New Heights: Turning Around Low-Performing Schools* (2003), and a report titled *Providing Quality Options in Education* (2005). Berman also has served as the director of policy, standards, and instruction at the Council for Basic Education, and as the director of research and content for the National Clearinghouse for Comprehensive School Reform. She began her career in education as a high school English teacher in Washington, D.C.

DAVID COKER is an assistant professor in the School of Education at the University of Delaware. He teaches undergraduate and graduate courses in writing, reading, and language development. Coker's research focuses on several topics, including writing development, writing assessment, writing instruction, and the connection between reading and writing. His interest in literacy development grew out of his experiences teaching English in an alternative high school in Atlanta and his work with elementary and middle school students in Cambridge, Massachusetts.

MARK W. CONLEY is an associate professor in teacher education at Michigan State University's College of Education. Conley has worked in teacher education for nearly thirty years and is interested in the connections between curriculum standards and assessment, the role of literacy in content-area classrooms, adolescent literacy and accountability systems, and adolescent literacy in urban settings. He received the International Reading Association's Elva-Knight Research Award in 1991 and was named Reading Researcher of the Year by the Michigan Reading Association in 1990. Conley's recent publications include *Content Area Literacy: Learners in Context* (2008), *Connecting Standards and Assessments Through Literacy* (2004), and *Meeting the Challenge of Adolescent Literacy: Research We Have, Research We Need* (coedited with J. R. Freidhoff, M. B. Sherry, and S. F. Tuckey, 2008).

RONI JO DRAPER is an associate professor and graduate coordinator in the Department of Teacher Education at Brigham Young University's David O. McKay School of Education. She researches literacy instruction in mathematics and science classrooms and how to prepare teachers to support student acquisition of both content-area knowledge and literacy skills. Her recent articles include "The Promise of Democratic Educational Research to Nurture Democratic Educators" in *Action in Teacher Education* (with K. Hall and L. Smith, 2006), and "Different Goals, Similar Practices: Making

Sense of the Mathematics and Literacy Instruction in a Standards-based Mathematics Classroom" in the *American Educational Research Journal* (with D. Siebert, 2004).

ROBERT FITZGERALD is a senior research associate with MPR Associates. In addition to his work on the Southwest Educational Development Laboratory project, he was principal data analyst for a study of an afterschool literacy intervention. He has conducted analyses for the California Commission on Teacher Credentialing as part of their effort to revise single- and multiple-subject credentials. Fitzgerald has also contributed to a variety of studies of postsecondary education, including an assessment of the effect of postsecondary institutional quality on student earnings, as well as analyses of longitudinal student data for the National Assessment of Vocational Education.

ARDICE HARTRY is a senior research associate with MPR Associates, a public policy research and evaluation firm specializing in education. Her K–12 educational research work focuses on the evaluation of public policy and educational reform programs, with a particular focus on at-risk populations. Her previous research has included evaluations of comprehensive high school reform programs, district-level reform initiatives, and a civics education curriculum. Before joining MPR Associates, she was the director of research and evaluation for a large urban school district.

VICKI A. JACOBS is the associate director of the Teacher Education Program and a lecturer at the Harvard Graduate School of Education, where she has taught courses on curriculum development, secondary school reading and writing, literacy and learning, and the teaching of English. Her published works focus on secondary literacy development and instruction and on teacher education. She has served as a codirector of the Massachusetts Academy for Teachers and of the Transition to Teaching Math and Science Program, and as an associate for the Bard College Institute for Writing and Thinking. Jacobs is currently president of the Massachusetts Association of College and University Reading Educators.

WILLIAM E. LEWIS is an instructor in the School of Education at the University of Delaware. He teaches undergraduate and graduate courses in reading and writing in the content areas, young adult literature, and instructional models. Lewis's research focuses on persuasive writing and argument, including research into how older students read, respond to, and write critically about literary texts. Lewis previously taught English for twenty years in Pennsylvania public schools, which nurtured his interest in adolescent writing development and instruction.

TWAKIA MARTIN is a doctoral student at the Harvard Graduate School of Education. Her work focuses on achievement and motivation for adolescent readers and students with disabilities, as well as teacher preparation. Her doctoral thesis investigates whether the designation of "special education" has an influence on how Black males judge themselves as readers, and on their overall reading achievement. Martin previously taught second and fourth grades in urban school districts.

ELIZABETH BIRR MOJE is the Arthur F. Thurnau Professor of Literacy, Language, and Culture in Educational Studies at the University of Michigan, Ann Arbor. She is also a faculty associate in the university's Institute for Social Research and a faculty affiliate in Latino/a studies in the College of Literature, Science, and the Arts. Her research interests involve the intersection between the literacies and texts youth are asked to learn in the disciplines and those they engage with outside of school. She also studies how youth construct cultures and enact identities through their literacy practices outside of school. Moje is coeditor of the forthcoming *Handbook of Reading Research, Volume IV* (with P. D. Pearson, M. Kamil, and P. Afflerbach). Her other published volumes include *Reframing Sociocultural Research on Literacy: Identity, Agency, and Power* (coedited with C. J. Lewis and P. Enciso, 2007) and *All the Stories We Have: Adolescents' Insights on Literacy and Learning in Secondary School* (2000).

KAREN MORRIS is a doctoral candidate in the Joint Program in English and Education at the University of Michigan. Karen was a high school English and math teacher for four years before she returned to graduate school. Her academic areas of interest include grammar and writing instruction and standard language ideology.

MELANIE OVERBY is a postdoctoral fellow working on the Social and Cultural Influences on Adolescent Literacy Motivation and Development project at the University of Michigan. Her research interests include adolescent literacy, social identity formation and socialization, and literacy in informal learning environments. Overby's dissertation explored familial racial-ethnic socialization using narratives provided by cultural museums.

KRISTIE PORTER is a graduate student at the University of North Carolina at Chapel Hill, where she studies public health and specializes in survey design and implementation. Porter worked previously as a research associate at MPR Associates, where, among other projects, she analyzed the achievement gap between advantaged and disadvantaged students, evaluated a civics education curriculum, and managed data collection for the Broad Prize in Urban Education. Before joining MPR, she conducted health research and evaluation in middle schools as an education analyst at RTI International.

CYNTHIA SHANAHAN is a professor in the Department of Curriculum and Instruction at the College of Education, University of Illinois at Chicago, and executive director of the college's Council on Teacher Education. Her primary research focus is adolescent literacy, especially within content areas. As the principal investigator in a National Reading Research Center study, Shanahan examined the use of texts in learning science and history, culminating in her book, *Learning from Text across Conceptual Domains* (1998). She has taught literacy to underprepared college students for more than twenty years.

TIMOTHY SHANAHAN is a professor in the Department of Curriculum and Instruction at the College of Education, University of Illinois at Chicago, and director of the university's Center for Literacy. He has also served as the director of reading for the Chicago Public Schools and as the president of the International Reading Association. His research concentrates on reading achievement and assessment, family literacy, and reading-writing relationships. He is the editor of *Developing Reading and Writing in Second-Language Learners* (2008) and the developer of several instructional programs.

CATHERINE E. SNOW is the Henry Lee Shattuck Professor of Education at the Harvard Graduate School of Education. Her work focuses on literacy achievement among students at risk of academic failure, including children growing up in poverty and those who arrive at school not speaking English. She chaired the National Research Council Committee that wrote *Preventing Reading Difficulties in Young Children* (1998), the RAND Reading Study Group that wrote *Reading for Understanding: Toward an R&D Program in Reading Comprehension* (2002), and the National Academy of Education Committee that wrote *Knowledge to Support the Teaching of Reading: Preparing Teachers for a Changing World* (2005). Snow conducted a long-term longitudinal study of the academic outcomes of urban students living in poverty, entitled *Is Literacy Enough? Pathways to Academic Success for Adolescents* (2007), and she is currently directing the Strategic Education Research Partnership's Boston Public Schools field site.

ALFRED W. TATUM is an associate professor at the University of Illinois at Chicago, where he serves as director of the reading clinic. His research focuses on providing effective literacy instruction to African American adolescent males, and he consults with schools across the nation on this topic. Tatum is author of the book *Teaching Reading to Black Adolescent Males: Closing the Achievement Gap* (2005). Other recent publications include "Engaging African American Males in Reading" in *Educational Leadership* (2006), "Creating Sentence Walls to Help English Language Learners Develop Content Literacy" in *The Reading Teacher* (2006), and "Addressing the Literacy Needs of Adolescent Students: Listening to their Voices" in *The New England Reading Association Journal* (2006).

NICOLE TYSVAER is a doctoral student at the University of Michigan's School of Education. Her research focuses on adolescent literacy, out-of-school learning, community service, and school and community partnerships. She has more than a dozen years of experience working nationally and at the local level with educational enrichment programs that serve children and youth. Tysvaer also coordinates the Real Media Leadership Literacy Training program, a youth-led multimedia community mapping program in Detroit.

Guidelines for Authors

The *Harvard Educational Review* accepts contributions from researchers, scholars, policymakers, practitioners, teachers, students, and informed observers in education and related fields. In addition to original reports of research and theory, *HER* welcomes articles that reflect on teaching and practice in educational settings in the United States and abroad.

HER has a two-stage review process. In the first stage, all manuscripts that are submitted to *HER* go through an initial screening process and are read by a minimum of two Editorial Board members. During the second stage, manuscripts that have passed the first stage are considered by the full Editorial Board and receive written feedback based on the Board's discussion. It is the policy of *HER* to consider for publication only manuscripts that are not simultaneously being considered elsewhere. Please follow these guidelines in preparing a manuscript for submission.

Types of Articles

Research Articles

Manuscripts reporting original, empirical research using qualitative and/or quantitative data related to education should include a literature review and/or theoretical/conceptual framework, methods, and analysis sections. The literature should be relevant to the research topic and findings. The methods need to be clearly outlined and should match the research question or stated purpose of the manuscript. Please include a brief description of any methodologies that are less familiar to educators and the educational research community. The analysis should be clear, and the arguments set forth should emerge from the data presented in the manuscript.

Essays

An academic essay should have a well-developed argument that answers a particular question or several related questions. It should begin with a review of previous work on the chosen topic and, subsequently, provide reasoning, evidence, and examples that prove the author's thesis on the question(s) addressed. Essays are nonfiction but often take on a subjective point of view; they are often expository, but they can also be narrative in style.

Features

HER welcomes feature submissions that report on, or present opinions about, topical issues in education; present analyses of debates and controversies in the field; apply research to practice-based settings in education; present new ideas or theories in education, in short essay form; or present reflections on professional practice or educational experiences in the context of current issues. *HER* also welcomes nontraditional features, such as photo essays and artwork. These nontraditional submissions should be accompanied by a brief (750-word) statement of purpose from the author/artist that explains the author's intent and the piece's relevance to education. Feature articles are meant to be different from traditional research manuscripts. Therefore, features need not contain literature reviews or extensive descriptions of methodology. However, feature articles should do much more than just present personal anecdotes and opinions. Features should demonstrate well-informed and factually sound interpretations of educational issues that advance knowledge in the discipline and/or improve practice in the field.

Voices Inside Schools

HER believes that it is critically important to listen to the voices of people who are working, teaching, and learning inside educational settings throughout the world. Voices Inside Schools articles feature the voices of teachers, students, and others committed to education — psychologists, social workers, principals, counselors, librarians, parents, and community leaders, for example — who interact with students and who have important knowledge and expertise about teaching and learning. We are interested in articles focused on what those involved with education have learned through their practice and/or research; we expect that manuscripts will contain detailed and thoughtful reflection and rigorous analysis of ideas, situations, and experiences.

Book and Essay Reviews

A book review examines one book in 2,000–3,000 words. It presents a book's strengths and weaknesses and then illustrates them with examples from the text. An essay review discusses one or more books in a particular field of education in 5,000–6,000 words. The books are analyzed using a conceptual framework, and the implications of future research and practice are addressed in depth. Authors of essay reviews should adequately cover each work introduced in the review. Book reviews and essay reviews should convey the content of the book(s), the author's approach to the subject of the book, and the author's conclusions. Reviews presenting a chapter-by-chapter listing of themes will not be considered.

Criteria

Significance and Impact

Manuscripts should focus on questions relevant to the field of education. These questions should be pointed and should also have implications for broader educational problems, nationally and/or globally. Manuscripts should contribute to the work of stakeholders seeking to address educational challenges and should explicitly state their contributions, whether theoretical or practical, in order to identify the populations that would most benefit from its publication, such as teachers, policymakers, or students.

Advancement of the Field

The manuscript should push existing theory in a new direction, and/or extend, fill a gap in, or bring a new perspective to current literature.

Clarity and Style

Manuscripts must be well written in clear, concise language and be free of technical jargon. As a generalist journal, *HER* strives for all articles to be widely accessible to non-experts. Previously published *HER* articles can serve as examples of the style of writing appropriate for our audience. We understand that the specific organization of a manuscript may differ according to discipline and the author's aesthetic.

Submission Guidelines

Authors should indicate whether they are submitting their manuscript as a research article, an essay, a feature, a Voices Inside Schools, an essay review, or a book review.

Formatting

- *HER* accepts manuscripts of up to 9,000 words, including footnotes and references, and reserves the right to return any manuscript that exceeds that length.
- All text must be double-spaced, type size must be at least 12 point with 1-inch margins on all sides, and paper size should be set to 8.5 x 11, even if printed on A4 paper.
- Authors should refer to *The Chicago Manual of Style* for general questions of style, grammar, punctuation, and form, and for footnotes of theoretical, descriptive, or essay-like material.
- For all nonlegal manuscripts, authors should use the *Publication Manual of the American Psychological Association* for reference and citation formats. **References must be in APA format.** The *Uniform System of Citation*, published by the *Harvard Law Review*, should be used for articles that rely heavily on legal documentation; because this form is not easily adaptable to other sources, it is usually combined with *Chicago* as necessary. Manuscripts with references and/or citations in another form will be returned to the author(s).

Submission Procedure

Authors must submit three copies of the manuscript, including a one-page abstract. Manuscripts will be returned only if a stamped, self-addressed envelope is included at the time of submission. In addition, please include a clearly labeled CD-ROM containing an electronic version of the manuscript in Microsoft Word format. Manuscripts are considered anonymously. The author's name must appear only on the title page; any references that identify the author in the text must be deleted. Please include a word count, inclusive of footnotes and references, on the title page.

To submit a manuscript to the *Harvard Educational Review*, please send to:

Harvard Educational Review
Harvard Education Publishing Group
8 Story Street, First Floor
Cambridge, MA 02138

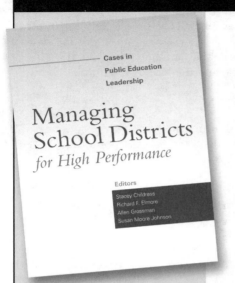

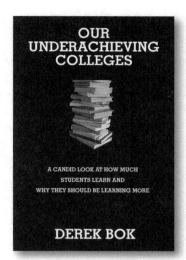

COMMUNITY LITERACY *Journal*

The peer-reviewed *Community Literacy Journal* seeks contributions for upcoming issues. We welcome submissions that address any social, cultural, rhetorical, or institutional aspects of community literacy; we particularly welcome co-authored pieces in collaboration with community partners.

When writing for the Community Literacy Journal, you can assume a wide and diverse audience: scholars in English Studies, Rhetoric and Composition, Education, Linguistics, Technical Communication; you can assume a readership among community workers, literacy advocates, and among federal agencies.

Visit us at http://www.communityliteracy.org/cfp/ for full editorial guidelines.

We are also pleased to offer one-year subscriptions to the *Community Literacy Journal* — two issues per year:

Institutions & libraries: $60.00
Faculty: $35.00
Graduate students & community workers: $20.00

Please send a check or money order — made out to the University of Arizona Foundation to:

Kelly A. Myers
Community Literacy Journal
445 Modern Languages Bldg.
University of Arizona
P.O. Box 210067
Tucson, AZ 85721
Info: kamyers@email.arizona.edu

The subscription fee is not considered a tax-deductible donation.

communityliteracy.org